Farmer First Revi

Praise for the book...

'Farmer First Revisited is a powerful testament to the impact the Farmer First approach to agricultural research and development has had and continues to have in the 20 years since the first volume on this topic was published. From an almost subversive critical movement that challenged the prevailing linear science-driven paradigm, Farmer First has won broad acceptance by rigorously proving its superior efficiency in making science work for the poorest and most marginal farmers. It is indeed a pleasure to see how the established and dedicated practitioners, together with a new generation of committed young scientists, have built upon the original concepts and methods to create this dynamic, exciting and effective corpus of work.'

Joachim Voss, Independent Consultant, formerly Director General, International Centre for Tropical Agriculture (CIAT), Cali, Colombia.

'A brilliant account of why we need to continue questioning conventional assumptions about agriculture, and why multiple knowledges and sources of innovation are more important than ever.'

Judi Wakhungu, Executive Director, African Centre for Technology Studies, Nairobi, Kenya and co-chair International Assessment of Agricultural Science, Knowledge and Technology for Development.

'Farmer First Revisited is a timely publication. I hope that this book will be read and used widely for fostering an evergreen revolution in our farms.'

M.S. Swaminathan, Member of Parliament (Rajya Sabha), Chairman, M.S. Swaminathan Research Foundation, Chennai, India.

'Twenty years on and the concept and practice of Farmer First remain powerful and compelling and even more relevant in today's world.'

Gordon Conway, Chief Scientific Adviser, UK Department for International Development and Professor of International Development, Imperial College, London.

'Farmer First Revisited shows why farmers need the power, organization and knowledge to engage with science, policy and private sector actors to get their priorities addressed. A timely statement of what, why and how.'

Camilla Toulmin, Director, International Institute for Environment and Development, London, UK.

'Farmer First Revisited is an important contribution to our understanding of farmer participation and innovation systems in agriculture research and development. It offers excellent cases and practical experiences of great value to agricultural R&D practitioners, as well as to general on-farm and farmer-oriented research scientists. I strongly recommend it.'

Kwesi Attah-Krah, Deputy Director General, Bioversity International, Rome, Italy.

'First there was Farmer First – followed by a critical assessment in Beyond Farmer First. Since all good things come in threes, Farmer First Revisited is a necessary addition to the series. Seldom have readers had the opportunity to get a clearer view of the development of agrarian development thinking. This book proves the Farmer First movement – and the inspiration behind it – is alive and kicking.'

Louk de la Rive Box, Rector, Institute of Social Studies, The Hague, Netherlands.

Farmer First Revisited
Innovation for Agricultural Research and Development

Edited by Ian Scoones and John Thompson
with a foreword by Robert Chambers

Practical Action Publishing

Practical Action Publishing Ltd
Schumacher Centre for Technology and Development
Bourton on Dunsmore, Rugby,
Warwickshire CV23 9QZ, UK
www.practicalactionpublishing.org

© Institute of Development Studies, 2009

First published 2009

ISBN 978 1 85339 682 3

Since 1974, Practical Action Publishing (formerly Intermediate Technology Publications and ITDG Publishing) has published and disseminated books and information in support of international development work throughout the world. Practical Action Publishing Ltd (Company Reg. No. 1159018) is the wholly owned publishing company of Practical Action Ltd. Practical Action Publishing trades only in support of its parent charity objectives and any profits are covenanted back to Practical Action (Charity Reg. No. 247257, Group VAT Registration No. 880 9924 76).

Indexed by Indexing Specialists (UK) Ltd
Typeset by SJI Services
Printed by Hobbs the Printers Ltd, Totton, Hampshire
www.hobbs.uk.com

Technical Centre for Agricultural and Rural Cooperation (ACP-EU)

The Technical Centre for Agricultural and Rural Cooperation (CTA) was established in 1983 under the Lomé Convention between the ACP (African, Caribbean and Pacific) Group of States and the European Union Member States. Since 2000, it has operated within the framework of the ACP-EU Cotonou Agreement. CTA's tasks are to develop and provide services that improve access to information for agricultural and rural development, and to strengthen the capacity of ACP countries to produce, acquire, exchange and utilise information in this area. CTA's programmes are designed to: provide a wide range of information products and services and enhance awareness of relevant information sources; promote the integrated use of appropriate communication channels and intensify contacts and information exchange (particularly intra-ACP); and develop ACP capacity to generate and manage agricultural information and to formulate ICM strategies, including those relevant to science and technology. CTA's work incorporates new developments in methodologies and cross-cutting issues such as gender and social capital.
CTA, Postbus 380, 6700 AJ Wageningen, The Netherlands, www.cta.int
CTA is financed by the EU

Contents

Part I: Revisiting Farmer First

Part II: Systems of innovation

Part III: The politics of demand and organizational change

Farmers' organizations

Networks and partnerships

Large public R&D organizations

Part IV: New professionalism, learning and change

Figures

Tables

Boxes

Acknowledgements

The 80 participants at the Farmer First Revisited workshop in December 2007 included a number of individuals who attended the Farmer First (1987) and Beyond Farmer First (1992) workshops, all of which were held at the Institute of Development Studies (IDS) at the University of Sussex, UK. Our invitations started with some of these people, recognized as pioneers in the field. But we were also keen to include the next generation of innovative thinkers and practitioners, so we asked early invitees to recommend others who they felt had important new insights and valuable lessons to share. In the end we brought together farmer-leaders, development practitioners, natural and social scientists and private sector representatives from over 40 countries who are involved in a diversity of activities, from research to education, information and communication to extension and facilitation, and from institutional learning and change to agro-enterprise development – and many who cut across these boundaries.

We would like to thank all those authors who prepared papers for the workshop and all participants who contributed to our discussions. The full set of papers can be found on the Farmer First Revisited website at http://www.future-agricultures.org/farmerfirst/. This is immensely rich material, and this book represents only a small selection of the total. Given space limitations, not all papers made it into this collection and many others were edited extensively. We apologize to all contributors for this rather savage editing and hope they will feel we did justice to their incisive ideas and arguments. In addition to the full papers and discussants' presentations, the Farmer First Revisited website also contains a lively blog, podcasts of many presentations and discussions, *YouTube* video clips of participants' views, media coverage and links, further resources and contacts and a wiki-timeline of Farmer First events over the past 20 years. We believe the materials available on the website complement and extend this book, and we invite readers to make use of them.

The workshop relied heavily on a team of able discussants and rapporteurs who summarized papers and presented key points in plenary. We especially would like to thank the session discussants: John Dixon, Maria Fernandez, Susan Kaaria, Melissa Leach, Adrienne Martin, C. Shambu Prasad, Niels Röling, Robert Tripp and Ann Waters-Bayer for their contributions. We should also mention the excellent evening talk by Adewale Adekunle of FARA, the Forum for Agricultural Research in Africa.

The workshop and this book, together with the associated follow-on activities around building an 'Innovation Alliance' focused on Farmer First practice, has been made possible by generous support from the Bill and Melinda Gates Foundation and the UK Department for International Development (DFID), as well as significant contributions from the DFID-supported Future Agricultures Consortium, the ESRC-funded STEPS Centre at the University of Sussex and the Innovation Fund of IDS.

We would like to thank all those involved in the superb workshop preparations and follow-up communications activities, particularly Dominic Glover, Oliver Burch, Julia Day, Jo Glyde, Jan Boyes, Naomi Vernon and Boudy van Schagen. We would also like to acknowledge the inspired work of Susanna Thorp, from WRENmedia and *The New Agriculturalist*, and Gary Edwards, from IDS, who conducted interviews with many workshop contributors and produced the video material found on the Farmer First Revisited website. In addition, we would like to thank Toby Milner and Clare Tawney at Practical Action Publishing for their support throughout this project and for their willingness to promote all three *Farmer First* books across the globe.

Finally, very special thanks must go to two persons without whom this book would not have been conceived or completed. First, we would like to express our sincere gratitude to Kate Schreckenberg who, with a researcher's knowledge of the issues and an editor's eye for detail, assisted us valiantly with the major editing and final wordsmithing that culminated in this book. Second, for his continuing inspiration and encouragement, his deep commitment and belief in the power of ideas to transform the world, and his boundless energy and creative vision, we would like to thank Robert Chambers.

Ian Scoones and John Thompson, Brighton, UK, January 2009

Abbreviations

ARD	Agricultural Research and Development
CAPRi	Systemwide Program on Collective Action and Property Rights
CGIAR	Consultative Group on International Agricultural Research
CIAT	International Center for Tropical Agricultural
CIMMYT	International Center for Maize and Wheat Improvement
CIP	International Potato Centre
F4C	Facilitation for Change
FARA	Forum for Agricultural Research in Africa
FFS	Farmer Field Schools
FO	Farmers' Organizations
FPR	Farmer Participatory Research
GDP	Gross Domestic Product
GFAR	Global Forum on Agricultural Research
IAASTD	International Assessment of Agricultural Science and Technology for Development
IAR4D	Integrated Agricultural Research for Development
ICARDA	International Center for Agricultural Research in the Dry Areas
IFAP	International Federation of Agricultural Producers
IFPRI	International Food Policy Research Institute
IITA	International Institute for Tropical Agriculture
ILAC	Institutional Learning and Change
IPM	Integrated Pest Management
IRRI	International Rice Research Institute
LEISA	Low External Input Sustainable Agriculture
NARS	National Agricultural Research Systems
NGO	Non Governmental Organization
NRM	Natural Resource Management
PAR	Participatory Action Research
PETRRA	Poverty Elimination through Rice Research Assistance
PID	Participatory Innovation Development
PLA	Participatory Learning and Action
PM&E	Participatory Monitoring and Evaluation
PPB	Participatory Plant Breeding
PPP	Public–Private Partnerships
PRA	Participatory Rural Appraisal

PROFEIS	Promoting Farmer Innovation and Experimentation in the Sahel
PROLINNOVA	PROmoting Local INNOVAtion in ecologically-oriented agriculture and natural resource management
PR&D	Participatory Research and Development
R&D	Research and Development
SANREM	Sustainable Agriculture, Natural Resource and Environmental Management Programme
SRI	System of Rice Intensification
SSA	Sub-Saharan Africa
UPWARD	Users' Perspectives with Agricultural Research and Development
USAID	US Agency for International Development
WTO	World Trade Organization

Foreword

Robert Chambers

The road travelled

In the 20 years since the Farmer First workshop, we have come a long way. That workshop, held at the Institute of Development Studies (IDS) in June 1987, followed five years of searching and finding people who were innovating with or writing about participatory approaches in agricultural research. They were marginalized in their organizations. Some felt they had to work in semi-secret, and hide what they were doing from their colleagues. Meeting others similarly placed created a buzz of mutual recognition, reassurance and excitement. We became what now we call a community of practice, with a hope of being part of a wave of the future.

Many of the original Farmer First concerns and insights seem still valid and useful: the three broad categories of types of agriculture (industrial, Green Revolution and the third agriculture that is CDR or complex, diverse and risk-prone); the recognition that the pipeline approaches and methods of transfer of technology (TOT) for the uniform and controlled conditions of industrial and green revolution agriculture did not fit CDR conditions; farmers' practices seen as adaptive performance; the proposition that adoption by farmers is validation of a technology; the comparative advantages of farmers over scientists in innovating for complex systems; and many others. Farmer First was established as paradigmatically different from TOT, and vital for CDR agriculture. It became a movement.

Five years later, in 1992, Ian Scoones and John Thompson convened a second workshop, Beyond Farmer First. This stressed perspectives that broadened and complemented Farmer First: the pluralism of different knowledges; the recognition of knowledge as not a stock but a process; seeing farmers, extensionists, scientists and others as social actors; recognizing political dimensions and the significance of power relations; and elements of a new professionalism in agricultural science.

As a workshop, Farmer First Revisited, held at IDS in December 2007, differed from the original Farmer First. Its organization and efficiency were a dramatic contrast. With Farmer First we had over 40 papers most of which were brought in hard copy by participants as they arrived. All three photocopiers broke down. Much of the conference was a self-organizing system on the edge of chaos, driven and saved by the excitement, energy, stamina and vision of individuals. And we had five days for it. With Farmer First Revisited almost all the papers were submitted and read by synthesizing presenters in advance.

And we managed in only three days. The accomplished organization and facilitation by the IDS Knowledge, Technology and Society team showed how far we have come in learning how to prepare and manage such occasions.

But both were hugely exciting. In Farmer First it was mutual recognition of marginalized innovators, the solidarity of heretics, the sense of being a vanguard, of having a common commitment that could be transformative. In Farmer First Revisited it was seeing how far we had come, how many more domains than just farmer participation were relevant, and how rich the range of innovations had been. In Farmer First the focus was on the complexity and diversity of farming systems and the creativity of farmers. In Farmer First Revisited it was the complexity and diversity of domains of action and intervention and of relationships, and the co-creativity of many different actors.

Revisiting Farmer First, taking stock and looking forward now has been timely. As Ian Scoones and John Thompson summarize in their introduction to this book, much has changed; and agriculture, after a puzzling phase of neglect, is back again high on the development agenda. Food shortages, high food prices, and the focus on poverty reduction, make it ever more a priority. As a sort of Rip Van Winkle who if not totally dormant, has been lurking and listening rather than engaging fully with agriculture during the past 20 years, two changes have struck me with force.

The *first* is the explosive proliferation of participatory methodologies, most of these involving and empowering farmers. These include: as before, farmers' research and participation in research; the many methodologies associated with the Participatory Research and Gender Analysis (PRGA) network of the CGIAR; farmer field schools and integrated pest management; the local agricultural research committees (CIALs) in Latin America; the involvement of farmers in all stages of seed breeding; the multiplicity of participatory approaches and practices in agricultural extension; participatory dimensions of the Institutional Learning and Change (ILAC) initiative in the CGIAR; and farmer participation in collaborative management, in market chains, in impact assessment and in policy processes. And these are not all. Many of these and others are represented in this book.

The *second* is how much realities, practices, vocabulary and concepts have changed and how these have changed in consonance together. Many of the words and expressions used and to be found in this book are either new or were little used in those earlier days. They expand the boundaries of what is seen as relevant. These boundaries have spread and become more inclusive, extending into and intensifying five domains that were earlier ignored or less recognized.

First, *conceptually* in 1987 our concern was to move beyond the reductionism of production and productivity and to privilege the complex, diverse and risk-prone realities of the majority of farmers, focusing on participation on-farm with and by farmers. Now it is the universe of concern itself that is complex and diverse. Many aspects are multiple or multi: we have, again and again, multiple stakeholders, multiple perspectives, multiple realities, multi-functional agriculture, multi-method approaches. Then too there are concepts and domains that are new or new in emphasis like food systems, food sovereignty, green trade, fair trade, market chains, value chains, innovation pathways and most of all innovation systems.

Second, *formal organizations* considered then were primarily those for agricultural research, extension and education. In addition now we have farmers' organizations, farmers' movements, the private sector, marketing organizations, various forms of public–private collaboration and farmer participation in management.

Third, the *relationships, interactions* and *processes* on which we concentrated in Farmer First were between farmers and outsider professionals. Behaviour and attitudes were important. A key insight was Paul Richard's point that farming was an adaptive performance. Participatory approaches and processes were central. Now relationships and interactions are seen more clearly to have dimensions that are political and related to power, trust, transparency and accountability. Relationships are expressed in many forms. We have communities of practice and innovation alliances. Networks and partnerships have proliferated: networks are of many types – social, virtual, grassroots, peer and advice networks, and some sometimes are described as embedded or dense or unsupervised. So too with partnerships: we have public–private partnerships, multi-stakeholder partnerships, messy partnerships, partnerships for action research and others. And for many forms of collaboration we have 'co-' expressions – co-management, co-breeding, co-evolution, co-creation, co-development.

Fourth, pervasively, there is *learning* – action learning, learning alliances, learning laboratories, experiential learning, alternative learning, interactive learning, policy learning, collective learning, discovery learning, shared learning and change, and recognition that many organizations have cultures that can be described as non-learning.

Finally, on the *personal* side, there is now concern not just with capacity building or capacity development, but with mindsets, soft skills, and the language of reflexivity and values.

Language, perceptions, priorities and realities interact. Some language is window-dressing and cosmetic. But these five domains and activities and the language that goes with them represent real change, bringing with them complexity and a higher priority to relationships. All this is manifest, again and again, in this book. And its evidence, analysis and synthesis together provide a foundation, platform and launching pad for future innovation and practice.

Challenges now: to make a difference

Many of the challenges are still those of 20 years ago. The paradigm of pipeline research and transfer of technology, of top-down packages of practices passed on to farmers, of the demand for an Indian-style Green Revolution in Africa, of big and quick fixes, is embedded in mindsets and bureaucratic imperatives. It is resilient and keeps reasserting itself. In prescriptions and programmes for African agriculture that come from outside Africa the transfer of technology model has been not only alive and well but flourishing. In the early years, the mechanistic Training and Visit (T&V) system persisted, at least in Africa, provoking the verse:

> If Asian countries throw it out
> It's only they who have the clout
> In Africa you can insist
> They have no power to resist

Even in Africa, though, T&V was eventually buried, though for a time replaced by the activities of the early Sasakawa Global 2000 programme. The failure to understand the difference between the Green Revolution of northwest India, with its flat and uniform land, reliable irrigation, low rainfall, and good access to inputs and markets and in contrast most of the agriculture of Sub-Saharan Africa, with its undulating, diverse, unirrigated land and often with poor access reflects a failure of agricultural education and of policy makers' perceptions. There has been an inappropriate transfer of mindsets.

The Farmer First Revisited workshop and this book show that we are in another space, more extensive, more complex and more diverse, paradigmatically embracing Farmer First but going far beyond it. If a focus of Farmer First was farmers' potential and performance, and of Beyond Farmer First process and power, the core focus of Farmer First Revisited is people and professionalism. The new demands, emphases and activities point more than ever to the priorities of personal and professional reflexivity, to changing roles and to methodologies.

Reflexivity refers to self-critical self-awareness of one's mindset, mental frames, predispositions, perceptions, and orientations, including values, and what constitutes rigour and valid evidence. At the end of their introduction to this book, the editors point to the need for 'fundamental shifts in thinking in practice', and for innovation systems which normatively engage with issues of 'power, politics, learning and reflexivity'. These have emerged from the Farmer First Revisited process as frontiers now for intense attention.

Roles are now wider, either new or new in emphasis. Farmers, as envisaged in Farmer First, were seen as innovators, as peers who can share experiences, and as experts who could inform scientists; these they remain, but in Farmer First Revisited they also have roles in advocacy, politics, and marketing. Farmers are recognized as social analysts, organizers, activists and politicians. The roles for scientists, extensionists and other non-farming professionals are too being defined more widely and differently: not just as champions or innovators, but as technology intermediaries, translators, brokers, negotiators, and facilitators, all of these demanding orientations and aptitudes beyond their traditional roles.

To support reflexivity and new roles requires new methodologies. These can be high-yielding by extending like other Farmer First Revisited concerns into far more domains than those of Farmer First. The opportunity is to develop methodologies and then enable them to spread, evolving and improving as they go. To illustrate, they might include how to:

- Facilitate collective and individual reflection on mindsets and biases, and move and transform these from transfer of technology and pipeline to people-centred innovation and learning.
- Train in facilitation so that facilitation becomes embedded as a way of interacting and relating with others, as already begun by the Institutional Learning and Change (ILAC) initiative in the CGIAR.
- Brainstorm to identify, explore and move towards centre stage, those domains (high-yielding gaps) whose neglect suggests large unexploited potentials (for example, rooting systems, soil biota and high-yielding principles such as sensitive nurturing of individual plants in conditions that allow the full expression of their potentials, as with the System of Rice Intensification).
- Develop and introduce new curricula, approaches and methods, attitudes, behaviours and relationships of participatory teaching and learning, into agricultural education and training.
- Sustain innovation and synergies of change over years by bringing together scientists, academic teachers, extensionists and farmers for experiential learning, transforming relationships and evolving and establishing new norms of professionalism.

Readers will find more methodologies to add from this book. The challenge is to recognize the importance of methodological innovation and put it more on the map. It is to learn how better to identify points of entry and high leverage, and processes and times and places when small pushes can move whole systems into better pathways. If the Farmer First workshop helped to provoke, inspire and support the explosion of participatory research with and by farmers, can and will Farmer First Revisited help to provoke, inspire and support another rich proliferation of methodologies, but now across a wider range, and their spread and continuing evolution?

So what?

The implications of the many ideas and experiences in this book resonate with, but go beyond, reflexivity, roles and methodologies. For all of these point to the personal dimension, so central and yet so habitually neglected.

What sort of people we are and what we do is fundamental to good practice for all professionals involved with agriculture. And like pro-poor agricultural development, people too are complex and diverse and have multiple dimensions, emotional as well as mental. Participants in the workshop who spoke about this saw no contradiction between head and heart. Heart fuels the fire and commitment that energize head. Anger, passion and enthusiasm were recognized as drivers to be combined with vision and courage; and it is these together that make champions of change.

The test of a workshop and of a book is what difference they make. Ian Scoones and John Thompson have been masterly in ordering, analysing and presenting material that is more complex and diverse, and which covers a far wider range of relevance, than confronted the editors of *Farmer First*. They have managed to make this a resource to bring the reader accessibly up-to-date in a field which has become wider and harder to grasp. The questions now are: Who will read and act on the evidence, insights and conclusions of this book? Who will become the reflexive and committed new professionals? Research scientists and their managers? University faculty and those who design curricula? Fieldworkers in agricultural extension? Front-line staff in NGOs, marketing organizations and the private sector and those who manage them? Government officials, political leaders, staff of funding agencies, policy-makers and influencers who sit on committees? And not least, and increasingly, farmers themselves? It is all of them who can make a difference. It is for all of them that this book is written.

In 20 years' time, if there is another Farmer First workshop, will they say of the latter 2000s: 'By then, they could see the problems and opportunities, and the directions needed for change The elements of the new professionalism were clear: they are there in the book'? And as they look back, will they then ask:

- 'Why was agricultural education not transformed?
- Why did agricultural bureaucracies remain so top-down?
- Why did so much agricultural research remain upstream?
- Why did resource-poor farmers continue to be marginal?
- Why was the cornucopia of promising innovations never taken to scale? and, above all
- Why were behaviour, attitudes and personal reflexivity never put at the core of professionalism?'

Or will they look back and see the latter 2000s as a turning point, with this book playing a part? Will they struggle to imagine themselves trapped in the mindsets, methods, misunderstandings and misprescriptions that had earlier prevailed? Will they see the time of the workshop and of this book as a tipping point, a watershed?

Neither is likely in full. What happens next will depend not least on getting to grips with power, politics, relationships and reflexivity. These have not been traditional concerns of most funders or of those professionally engaged with agriculture. They are outside their normal interests and comfort zones. Yet they are crucial for the transformations needed now. We must find new ways to engage in constructive dialogue around these themes, and to map new directions for agricultural research, education and development.

This book reviews much of the state of the art, is grounded in experience, and provides signposts to the future. The editors and authors are on the frontiers of exploration and innovation. They give a head start for the next stages of the journey. Progress now depends on personal and collective vision and commitment. May many be encouraged by what is presented here, and supported and inspired to become pioneers and champions of transformative change.

PART I

Revisiting Farmer First

Farmer First revisited: innovation for agricultural research and development

Ian Scoones and John Thompson

Looking back to look forward

In July 1987, some 50 social and natural scientists of roughly equal numbers met at the Institute of Development Studies (IDS) at the University of Sussex, UK, for a workshop on *Farmers and Agricultural Research: Complementary Methods*, later more generally known as the Farmer First workshop (Chambers et al., 1989). That event marked a key moment in the development of approaches to farmer participation in agricultural research and extension, drawing together experiences from a diverse range of individuals and organizations from both North and South. Since then, methodological, institutional and policy experiments have unfolded around the world, aimed at 'putting farmers first'.

Twenty years later, in December 2007, some 80 natural and social scientists, farmer leaders and representatives of NGOs, donor agencies and the private sector gathered at IDS to reflect on the achievements, failures and missed opportunities of the past two decades, assess the current state of farmer-centred R&D and consider prospects for the future. This book offers a selection of these deliberations, along with a rich range of case studies. The full proceedings can be found at http://www.future-agricultures.org/farmerfirst/index.html. These include the full-length papers, workshop presentations, discussion summaries, video commentaries, a wiki-timeline and more. The gathering aimed to examine critically how these participatory experiments have panned out, particularly at a time of renewed interest in agriculture for development and the widespread recognition of the need for effective R&D systems. What has worked, what hasn't and why? Moreover, given the radically changed contexts facing poor farmers in the developing world today – including increasingly globalized and vertically integrated agri-food systems, changed configurations of public and private R&D, and new governance arrangements affecting innovation systems – how should the challenges and priorities of farmer participation in agricultural research and extension be seen in the 21st century?

A lot has changed over 20 years. New shocks and stresses are evident – from climate change to HIV/AIDS – with major implications for farming livelihoods (Thompson et al., 2007). New economic relations and connections are apparent, particularly around the market, with increasingly globalized linkages. New patterns of urbanization and industrialization are affecting the roles of agriculture in wider economic and political processes. And new agricultural technologies, including genetically modified (GM) crops, offer both opportunities and risks. Access to technologies is an increasing concern, as patterns of ownership shift towards the private sector and public provision continues to decline. Consequently, complex, uncertain, multi-scaled processes and interactions in agri-food systems are emerging from the intertwining of social, technological and ecological dynamics in different settings (Scoones et al., 2007). These, in turn, are leading to the emergence of and trade-offs between different pathways to more sustainable agri-food systems, and a growing recognition of the importance of surprise and adaptive response in agricultural policy and R&D processes.

Yet much remains the same – particularly in the poorer, marginalized parts of the world: the complex, diverse and risky contexts where Farmer First approaches were first advocated. Poverty remains concentrated in rural areas and most of the rural poor depend, directly or indirectly, on agriculture for their livelihoods. As emphasized in the recent *World Development Report*, agriculture remains the main source of livelihoods for an estimated 86 percent of rural people (2.5 billion people), and for many countries, the main opportunity for sustained, employment-based growth (World Bank, 2007). Furthermore, technology development, adaptation and spread continues to be a key policy concern, with a focus on the potentials for a 'Green Revolution' back on the international agenda, particularly in Africa.

As in the original *Farmer First* workshop and book, here we use the term 'farmer' broadly to include not just sedentary, smallholder farmers, but also farm workers, pastoralists, forest dwellers, fisherfolk and other small-scale producers of food and feedstuffs. Furthermore, we place special emphasis on the needs, priorities and capacities of poorer farmers and on women farmers, who are often neglected by mainstream agricultural R&D programmes and projects, and yet remain vital to food security and rural innovation.

Tracing twenty years of innovative practice

The *Farmer First Revisited* workshop highlighted a vast range of innovative practice and experimentation over the past 20 years in farmer participatory approaches and methods. 'The Farmer First movement' – a loose and diverse coalition of people, networks and organizations committed to developing, promoting and sharing bottom-up, farmer-centred approaches to technology development for agriculture – has made great progress on many fronts. Examples discussed in this book, include:

- Participatory plant breeding involving farmers in trait selection and breeding programmes across a range of crops.
- Participatory extension and learning approaches, including Farmer Field Schools for farmer-based learning about integrated pest management or soil fertility.

- Networks for sharing farmer experimentation and rural innovation as well as new farmer–scientist research partnerships to promote innovation.
- Participatory development of technical innovations and practices, ranging from crop dryers to the System of Rice Intensification.
- The growing involvement of farmer organizations and federations in creating demand and increasing accountability in agricultural R&D systems.
- Efforts to build coalitions and activist social movements to drive policy change at different levels, from the local to the global.
- Novel strategies for empowering communities through agro-enterprise promotion and market-led development, combined with innovative approaches to promoting effective public–private partnerships in agricultural R&D.
- The use of a range of innovative media (video, mobile phones, internet) for farmer-to-farmer sharing of ideas and information.
- Co-management approaches to improve the bargaining power of natural resource users and common property managers.
- Strategies for enhancing institutional learning and organizational change, particularly in large agricultural R&D bureaucracies.
- Pioneering approaches for institutionalizing participation in agricultural education systems.
- Participatory approaches to improve monitoring and evaluation, impact assessment and learning, including approaches for analysing participatory impact pathways and for informing policy from below.

These approaches, and many others, have been documented, tested, adapted and extended across a range of sites and engaging a wide range of organizations – from international research centres, part of the Consultative Group on International Agricultural Research (CGIAR), to national research and extension organizations, to NGOs, and to farmers' and rural people's own organizations, federations and associations. There has been a veritable explosion of activity, some successful, some less so. These experiences and lessons are reported across the diverse papers gathered in this book.

These collected papers raise a number of vital questions. For example, what shifts in approaches to agricultural R&D have occurred over the past two decades? What changes in assumptions have resulted? And what are the new directions emerging? The resulting answers to these questions were debated throughout the workshop, and particularly during a collective exercise looking at the changes in approaches and assumptions. These discussions built on a table produced in 2005 as part of the International Assessment for Agricultural Science and Technology for Development (IAASTD) by a number of participants, including Robert Chambers, Maria Fernandez and Andy Hall. This highlights three common approaches – 1) Transfer of Technology; 2) Farming Systems Research; and 3) Farmer First/Farmer Participatory Research (FPR) – and contrasted them with what was described as 'Interactive Learning

Table 1.1 Changing approaches to agricultural research and development

	Transfer of Technology	Farming Systems Research	Farmer First/ Farmer Participatory Research	People-centred Innovation and Learning
Era	Long history, central since 1960s	Starting in the 1970s and 1980s	From 1990s	2000s
Mental model of activities	Supply through pipeline	Learn through survey	Collaborate in research	Innovation network centred on co-development; involving multi-stakeholder processes and messy partnerships
Farmers as seen by scientists	Progressive adopters, laggards	Objects of study and sources of info	Colleagues	Partners, collaborators, entrepreneurs, innovators, organized group setting the agenda, exerting demand: 'the boss'
Scientists as seen by farmers*	Not seen – only saw extension workers	Used our land; asked us questions	Friendly consumers of our time	One of many sources of ideas and information
Knowledge and disciplines*	Single discipline driven (breeding)	Inter-disciplinary (plus economics)	Inter-disciplinary (more, plus farmer experts)	Extra/trans-disciplinary – holistic, multiple, culturally rooted knowledges
Farmers' roles	Learn, adopt, conform	Provide information for scientists	Diagnose, experiment, test adapt	Empowered co-generators of knowledge and innovation; negotiators
Scope	Productivity	Input output relationships	Farm based	Beyond the farm-gate – multi-functional agriculture, livelihood/food systems and value chains across multiple scales, from local to global; long time frames
Core elements	Technology packages	Modified packages to overcome constraints	Joint production of knowledge	Social networks of innovators; shared learning and change; politics of demand
Drivers	Supply push from research	Scientists' need to learn about farmers' conditions and needs	Demand pull from farmers	Responsiveness to changing contexts – markets, globalization, climate change; Organized farmers, power and politics
Key changes sought	Farmer behaviour	Scientists' knowledge	Scientist–farmer relationships	Institutional, professional and personal change: opening space for innovation
Intended outcome	Technology transfer and uptake	Technology produced with better fit to farming systems	Co-evolved technology with better fit to livelihood systems	Capacities to innovate, learn and change

Institutions and politics*	Technology transfer as independent: assumed away	Ignored, black boxed	Acknowledged, but sometimes naïve populism	Central dimensions of change
Sustainability*	Undefined	Important	Explicit	Championed – and multi-dimensional, normative and political
Innovators	Scientists	Scientists adapt packages	Farmers and scientists together	Multiple actors – learning alliances

for Change'. For the workshop exercise we left the last column, as well as a number of rows, blank and asked participants to suggest ideas against the various criteria. Table 1.1 offers a summary of these deliberations, with the right hand column and all rows marked with an asterisk being a (very condensed) summary of participants' contributions.

Such a table, of course, presents a rather simplistic picture of a very complex reality. It should not be read to imply that 'Transfer of Technology' is all bad and 'People-centred Innovation and Learning' is all good, or that there is a logical, historical, linear progression between them. There are elements of each that are important and appropriate in different circumstances. The aim, though, is to highlight how more recent experiences and thinking challenges certain assumptions and shifts the frame of reference.

Structure of this book

But what does it all add up to? Has the Farmer First movement made a difference? And what are the new challenges, given the new contexts and trends? Drawing on nearly 70 papers and the collective experience of workshop participants from over 40 countries, this book aims to reflect on the achievements and shortcomings of the past but, more importantly, to also look forward – to new opportunities and challenges, new applications and approaches, and new partnerships and alliances.

This book is divided into five main parts, and a series of contributions clustered around different themes. This paper introduces the broad themes of the book, as well as the intensive discussions at the workshop, locating these in wider research and policy debates. It is not, however, a definitive review of the field, nor a systematic summary of everything in the book. Instead it attempts to offer a schematic overview of key issues and questions and, at the end, identifies a number of challenges for the future.

In addition to this overview, the first part includes two introductory papers which set the scene for the rest of the discussion. The first by Andy Hall looks at the challenges of strengthening agricultural innovation systems, and introduces the idea of the innovation system, encompassing more than the farm and farmer, but also wider market chains in the institutional and policy environment. The challenge for a Farmer First approach today, it is argued, is to cast the net wider than the traditional focus on fields, farms and farmers to a wider group of actors and processes. In the next paper Jacqueline Ashby reflects on the wider organizational, governance and political challenges for Farmer First approaches and the need to challenge fundamental power structures in agricultural research and development.

Part II picks up on the debates about innovation systems in two sections. The first looks at the experience of farmer participatory research and technology development with two cases highlighted: Participatory Plant Breeding and the System of Rice Intensification. Adaptive and co-management approaches are discussed in other papers in this section which emphasize the importance of participation in institutional dynamics and policy processes. The next section looks beyond the farm-gate to the challenges of engagement with markets and the private sector. A series of fascinating cases highlight how the participatory approaches pioneered on-farm can be applied to market chain facilitation in favour of poorer producers and consumers.

The politics of demand and organizational change are addressed in Part III, with three sections focusing on farmers' organizations, networks and partnerships and large public R&D organizations. Each suggests how the 'politics of demand' needs to be central to a sustained and effective Farmer First approach, yet building the capacity for this and ensuring accountability mechanisms remains a substantial challenge as the case studies illustrate.

The three sections in Part IV deal with extension, agricultural education and impact assessment. In different ways, each emphasizes the importance of reflexive learning approaches and the importance of networks. Finally, Part V concludes the book by looking to the future of innovation in agricultural research and development. Together, the discussions in this book point to some major achievements over the past 20 years, but some major challenges remaining. The remainder of this paper – and the book as whole – introduces these.

Towards learning approaches to agricultural R&D

Over the past two decades, Farmer First approaches have challenged the standard 'transfer of technology' pipeline model in fundamental ways, arguing that the separation of basic 'upstream' centralized research from applied 'downstream' adaptive, decentralized research was inappropriate and that farmers, as users of technology and research, needed to be involved throughout the research system, as part of a collaborative network, in processes of 'participatory technology development' (PTD). This, it has long been argued and increasingly demonstrated, will produce better products, foster greater uptake and improve impact.

There is a growing body of evidence to support this contention; some of it presented in Part II of the book. For example, the engagement of farmers in

Participatory Plant Breeding (PPB) has been an impressive example with wide impacts in a range of settings, as illustrated by contributions from Jean Claude Rubyogo and Louise Sperling and John Witcombe and colleagues. As Jacqueline Ashby observes, this work has highlighted the importance of interaction with farmers in the early stages of the plant breeding process, when breeding objectives are set, and the advantages of decentralizing breeding programmes to conduct varietal selection with farmers in diverse, local environments.

Farmer engagement through Farmer Field Schools (FFS) has also enhanced the uptake and adoption of new knowledge, skills and techniques in a variety of areas, most notably Integrated Pest Management (IPM) as shown in the contribution from Indonesia by Yunita Winarto. FFS are also used in rootcrop agriculture programmes (e.g. sweet potato integrated crop management), as described by Dindo Campilan and colleagues from the Users' Perspectives with Agricultural Research and Development (UPWARD) programme, an Asia-wide network supporting participatory research and development in agriculture and natural resource management. Some innovative programmes have combined the best of PPB, FFS and IPM, such as the case related by Oscar Ortiz and colleagues on understanding the potato innovation systems in Bolivia, Ethiopia, Peru and Uganda.

As many of the contributors acknowledge, however, despite these successful cases some of these experiences have been relatively limited add-ons, and farmer participation has been bolted on to essentially old-style technology transfer approaches. These have been improved as a consequence – with both better science and better uptake resulting, and should not be knocked. But the more transformative hopes of the Farmer First approach have often not been fully realized, where true reversals of learning, hierarchy and power are central. In these perspectives of course the old categories and boundaries of research and extension break down. These become less meaningful when the metaphors of technology transfer and pipeline are replaced with concepts of co-learning and co-construction. Indeed, some asked why we were asking such questions as 'what is the future of extension?' at all, when such terms themselves are based on outmoded and inappropriate concepts and categories.

Ravi Prabhu and colleagues and Yan Zhao-Li, for example, raise questions about the wider institutional and policy landscape for innovation through case studies of adaptive collaborative management and co-management approaches. Over the past 20 years, these approaches have been increasingly employed in the natural resource management (NRM) field to strengthen institutions for mobilizing effective collective action around common property resource (CPR) use. As these papers reveal, critical lessons have been learned about the challenges of working with highly differentiated 'communities' whose members often compete with others over access and control of common forest, fisheries and rangeland resources. Such approaches have generated some crucial insights for the design of sustainable Farmer First-oriented innovation systems. In these highly differentiated rural settings, which farmers – or, more accurately, which resource managers – come first?

And what institutional mechanisms exist at the local level for defining priorities for innovation? In this same section, Todd Crane uses a political ecology perspective to address these questions of social differentiation and the politics of resources in Mali. He demonstrates how a common failure of most agricultural innovation efforts is to exclude pastoralists from the system. But if the concept of the 'innovation system' is broadened and if accepted notions of 'community', 'resources' and 'farming' are defined differently, then the priorities of pastoralists – and other CPR users – must be given equal weight and attention to those of more sedentary actors in the system.

From farmers and technologies to systems of innovation

As the foregoing shows, a key thread of the contributions in Part II focuses on the need to move beyond a concentration on the interaction between 'farmers' and 'technologies' to a wider systems perspective. The concept of the innovation system is introduced in a number of contributions, and most notably in the Part I paper by Andy Hall. Long used in business studies and assessment of industrial countries, an innovation systems approach is seen to be helpful in extending our understanding of relationships between farmers (in their rich and complex diversity) and other actors through market interactions.

This focus on 'beyond the farm-gate' was an important strand of discussion at the workshop, and one that differed significantly from 20 years ago. There was a general recognition that complex value chains, sometimes stretching to global markets, were a key feature. These offered both opportunities – such as for gaining access to markets for higher value agricultural commodities – and challenges – such as around meeting food safety standards or confronting asymmetries in market power. A number of papers highlight how participatory methods and approaches had been applied to both the diagnosis of market chain challenges and opportunities, as well as the facilitation of change in market systems. Drawing on case studies from Tanzania and Kenya, Clive Lightfoot, Vincent Nyimbo and Michael Kibue reveal how practical, participatory interventions can enhance market access and improve livelihoods through the 'First Mile' and 'Linking Local Learners' approaches. Julieta Roa and Dindo Campilan and others offer overviews of UPWARD's Southeast Asian experience with the 'market chain approach'. Jemimah Njuki and colleagues similarly give examples of how participatory analysis of community agro-enterprises in Uganda and Malawi have identified important entry points for support. Susan Kaaria and others show how the 'enabling rural innovation' approach has empowered different groups, particularly women, to engage with new market opportunities.

Together with an explosion of methodological innovation and a seemingly bewildering range of approaches, methods and frameworks, contributions to Part II show a variety of efforts to create new platforms for interaction between farmers, farmer groups and businesses along the value chain. Applying participatory methods to small, and even large-scale, businesses has been highly productive, as has the wider value chain participatory diagnosis. This blossoming of interest in market linkages and actors beyond the farm-gate has come in response to the particular challenges of structural adjustment and neo-liberal economic reform in many countries, combined with the rapidly evolving dynamics of economic globalization. These processes have had profound effects on farmers. No longer is the small-scale farming world the preserve of benevolent state support and relatively constrained marketing linkages, but, with the collapse or retreat of public support to the farming sector and the growth in private sector activity, farmers are much more exposed to the dynamic challenges of an increasingly globalized market. This brings winners and losers. Many of the experiences discussed in this book are focused on making sure that potential benefits are more widely shared, particularly among women and poorer, more marginalized farming communities.

Markets, businesses and engaging with the private sector

Everyone agrees that engagement with the private sector is critical. This is a new development from 20 years ago. Back then, it was almost exclusively the public sector, and its large, lumbering R&D organizations that were the focus of Farmer First reformers. But today, this is only part of the picture – and a decreasing part in many places. With R&D systems – from seeds, to fertilizers, to chemicals, to information and advice – increasingly owned and controlled by private sector players, often in highly vertically integrated and consolidated large businesses, negotiating relationships with the private sector is key, contributors in Part II argue. Whether this is around gaining access to private sector skills and expertise in high-end technology development, or privately held intellectual property rights over products or processes, a Farmer First approach for the 21st century must address these questions head on.

One of the currently favoured approaches is the plea to develop so-called public–private partnerships (PPPs). As noted at the workshop, rhetoric about PPPs has become a catch-all solution for all sorts of new institutional arrangements, with the category often obscuring more than it reveals. As several papers in this volume show, PPPs encompass very diverse arrangements, including partnerships for resourcing, contracting, commercializing, frontier research and value chain development. These may address different problems from investing in new innovation pathways to ensuring access to proprietary technologies, to leveraging private sector skills and reach in service delivery. And they may involve dealing with large trans-national companies or whole networks of very small private sector operations.

In Part II, David Spielman and colleagues, drawing on an extensive review of 75 different PPPs across the CGIAR, note that, while the partnerships are serving a wide variety of research objectives, the CGIAR's links with the private sector are still at a very nascent stage. Few partnerships are explicitly designed to facilitate joint innovation, an important justification for the use of PPPs.

Still fewer provide for effective management of the risks inherent in PPPs, or provide effective analysis of their poverty-targeting strategies. As a result, they conclude that the deployment of pro-poor knowledge and technology requires different – and often creative – approaches to research and partnership. And creativity itself requires that both public- and the private-sector organizations become more innovative in the ways they conduct business and build strategic relationships with each other.

An important new role has evolved for brokering organizations which manage such partnerships, helping to negotiate between parties, confirming common goals and offsetting risks. The Spielman paper includes a series of boxes which highlight these issues well. Bino Témé and colleagues describe how the Syngenta Foundation's long-term support to the Cinzana Agricultural Research Station in Mali has helped to leverage further donor support and turned the station into a centre of excellence for researchers from around the region. Gospel Omanya and colleagues share the experience of the African Agricultural Technology Foundation (AATF) and Andy Peters presents a brief overview of the Global Alliance for Livestock Veterinary Medicine (GALVmed). Both have brokering functions, but questions were raised at the workshop about who actually benefits from such arrangements. The big question, of course, is how focused are these arrangements on addressing the priorities of poorer, marginalized farmers, and so wider questions of poverty reduction (public goods aims) and social justice? Despite the considerable investment in PPPs, and some substantial public and philanthropic funding being spent on both partnerships and brokering organizations, the answer is not always clear, and the evidence on poverty impact often equivocal, as Dominic Glover's reflections on the Monsanto Smallholder Programme in India reveals.

A deeper scepticism about the abilities of the private sector and more particularly global, corporate agribusiness to meet the challenges of a Farmer First paradigm is held by some. Surely the profit motives of agribusinesses are often antithetical to Farmer First objectives and poverty reduction? The evidence of global capitalism meeting the needs of the 'bottom billion', they argue, are scanty, and instead, as Patrick Mulvany and Maria Arce Moreira suggest, farmers need to maintain and develop their own systems of food sovereignty, based on local economic development and market transactions. How far can participatory interventions go, in the context of a highly unequal economic system, they ask? Even at the micro-scale, a number of the cases discussed in Part II highlight how, when market access was opened up for women, these opportunities were often short-lived as better-off men wanted to capture the benefits. Markets are of course social and cultural, as well as economic, institutions and analyses of gender and power relations, as a number of contributions point out, are crucial.

Debates between the market pragmatists and the radical idealists continued through the workshop and are echoed in contributions to this book. But all agree that, while participatory diagnosis – some of it highly sophisticated and nuanced – is important, the wider challenges must lie in changing the rules of the game – in political, institutional and organizational change, and seeking closer linkages between Farmer First approaches and the political-economic processes of change that are driving new alliances between farmers, businesses and consumers in global food systems. If a Farmer First approach is to make a difference it will emerge through such a focus on the political economy of innovation processes. This is a theme which runs through the contributions to this book, and one which we return to later in this paper.

Governing agricultural R&D

Part III of the book focuses on the questions of the governance of innovation systems: generating effective demand from farmers, ensuring the accountability of R&D organizations and designing organizations responsive to a Farmer First approach. It is perhaps on the tricky issues of organizational change and governance that the Farmer First approaches of the past 20 years have foundered most often. In a powerful contribution in Part I, Jacqueline Ashby argues this case from the perspective of one who has struggled to transform the CGIAR from within, observing that efforts to drive forward the Farmer First paradigm in science bureaucracies were fundamentally flawed by an overinvestment in reforming the supply side of innovation in organizations that lacked then – and still lack – accountability for satisfying demand for innovation from the poor. As a result, the individual actors and champions of change in this process were broadly divorced from other socio-political actors who drive organizational change and lacked a real power base from which to lever changes that were more than cosmetic. The essential challenge for the future is to address the political dimensions of demand for Farmer First innovation in the agricultural sector.

This is an important and sobering lesson, particularly from someone who has pioneered farmer participatory research approaches in the international research system over many years. This emphasis on recapturing the political and normative dimensions was echoed by many other papers, and was central to much of the workshop discussion. For example, Monty Jones and Sidi Sanyang from the Forum for Agricultural Research in Africa (FARA) called for renewed attention to the 'politics of inclusion' and argued for the critical role of farmers' organizations in setting priorities for R&D activities in Africa, if a Farmer First approach is to be realized.

In sum, the challenge centres on how to create an accountable, democratic innovation system which is responsive to the diverse needs of diverse farmers. This is of course no easy task. This requires both building demand and exerting voice from users and ensuring responsiveness and accountability from the agricultural scientists and extensionists. Part III discusses the role of farmers' organizations, the importance of networks and partnerships and the challenges of changing large, public R&D organizations.

Strengthening the capacity of farmers' organizations

A series of contributions from farmers' organizations, from Asia (Beatriz del Rosario), Africa (Nduati Kariuki; Khamarunga Banda) and Latin America (Elizabeth Vargas and William Burgoa; Cecilia Turin) show how, in widely differing political contexts, organizations involving and representing farmers can create demand and improve the bargaining power of their members through cooperation and collective action. But the political clout of farmers' organizations – both in broader national politics or more specifically within R&D systems – is highly variable. The responsiveness of some states where there is an increasing commitment to farmers' demands, such as Bolivia (Maria Arce Moreira and Patrick Mulvany) contrasts sharply with others, such as India (V. Rasheed Sulaiman) and China (Yan Zhao-Li), where farmers are increasingly marginalized from political and bureaucratic processes, with the rise of other economic growth agendas associated with the growing influence of an urban middle class.

A vital challenge identified across these contributions is the need to go beyond the co-option of farmers and their organizations in technology development processes to a more fundamental engagement with institutional and policy issues. Access to research results and information is vital and the role of information 'translators' or 'brokers' is critical, although often no substitute for farmers themselves being engaged in both the conduct and interpretation of research results.

But the experience of full involvement of farmers' organizations in innovation processes is, despite the rhetoric, patchy. Beyond some nominal representation, farmers are often not involved in the overall governance of research organizations, and rarely engaged in budget allocation and priority setting outside often rather orchestrated 'consultations'. The lack of lobbying and advocacy capacity of many farmers' organizations, particularly in Africa, is noted, although this contrasts with some more positive experiences from Latin America, such as Peru (Cecilia Turin). In increasingly globalized agricultural innovation systems, generating influence through organized groups remains an important challenge.

Some critical issues of capacity in farmers' organizations remain to be addressed, relating particularly to fundamental questions of accountability and governance. Areas identified by contributors to this book include issues of representation (who do farmers' organizations actually represent, and which farmers are excluded?), organization (how do global or regional umbrella organizations relate to farmer research groups or other grassroots networks?), diversity (how do farmers' organizations insist on innovation diversity in the face of attempts to narrow and limit options by powerful actors?) and governance (who are farmer 'leaders', how are they chosen and what contact do they have with realities on the ground?).

Examples of ways forward are also discussed, including the testing and development of innovative funding mechanisms for Farmer First approaches, suggestions for more direct engagement with policy advocacy to demand a stake in decision making in public research governance, including in the CGIAR and national agricultural research systems (NARS), and capacity development, platform development and south–south networking for farmers' organizations, particularly around areas of policy engagement and advocacy for appropriate agricultural R&D approaches.

Building alliances and networks of innovation

Alliances to foster farmer-led innovation in agricultural R&D come together for a variety of reasons. These include complementing skills and capabilities, strengthening capacities and leveraging a range of services and resources, including funds and new technologies. This network approach to innovation sees knowledge or understanding as a form of 'distributed cognition', constructed not by the individual 'experimenter' or 'innovator', but by the collective which produced it through debate, dialogue and group interaction. Here the emphasis is on co-construction and co-learning, moving beyond the 'centre of excellence' model, where real partnerships between scientists, extension workers and farmers are created as part of new, dense networks of innovation.

Part III contains some important reflections on recent experiments and experiences of this more fundamental shift. For example, Ann Waters-Bayer and colleagues highlight the efforts of PROLINNOVA (PROmoting Local INNOVAtion in ecologically oriented agriculture and NRM) to build partnerships among major stakeholders in agricultural R&D to enhance processes of Participatory Innovation Development (PID) in a diverse array of contexts. Scott Killough describes World Neighbor's efforts to assist farmers to provide their own advice networks, either through their own organizations or through farmer-to-farmer informal learning linkages. Oliver Oliveros reviews lessons from a competitive grants scheme, the DURAS Project (*Le projet pour le promotion du développement durable dans les systèmes de recherche agricole au Sud*), which aims to encourage the scaling up of innovative practices in southern agricultural research and development organizations and the enhancement of the scientific capacity through multi-stakeholder partnerships. Bernard Triomphe and colleagues analyse findings from a study by CIRAD (*La recherche agronomique au service des pays du Sud*) of 10 multi-stakeholder research partnerships and show how they deal with tensions between partners and generate the adjustments necessary to achieve success in problem-solving and knowledge generation. Edith van Walsum, Awa Faly Ba and Assétou Kanouté stress the importance of global and regional knowledge networks to share practical information and real world experiences with LEISA (Low External Input and Sustainable Agriculture) and PROFEIS (Promoting Farmer Innovation and Experimentation in the Sahel) respectively. Anil Gupta describes how the Honey Bee network combines the virtues of a network and a social movement, so that every member who volunteers to contribute his or her energy to scout grassroots innovators or traditional knowledge holders, document their knowledge, add value, or convert innovations into enterprises and/or protect their intellectual property rights, can expect other members to value their contribution. Finally, Patrick Mulvany and Maria Arce Moreira offer lessons from the growing food sovereignty movement about creating new alliances between farmers, farm workers and local consumers to build locally controlled and socially just food systems.

In all these cases, the focus is on constructing partnerships and networks of innovation, where evolving communities – of farmers, scientists and others – work together towards a common goal. They offer lessons on creating new strategic research alliances to promote innovation, mobilize resources, and document and share lessons at national and even international scales. Most of these cases are, of course, supported and facilitated from outside, usually by NGOs or research organizations, such as CGIAR centres, or fora for 'action research' to promote participatory agricultural R&D. But perhaps the most exciting opportunity for a revitalized Farmer First approach can only be achieved in the context of what Paul Richards calls 'unsupervised networks' of learning and experimentation through which the skills and knowledge of farmers and researchers can be treated on level terms, thus settling a troubling argument that has held back the development of the Farmer First paradigm.

Reforming large R&D organizations and science bureaucracies

Jacqueline Ashby's contribution in Part I sets the scene for a discussion in Part III of organizational change in large agricultural science and R&D bureaucracies. She highlights how farmer participation was captured by a large group of protagonists within the CGIAR whose chief need was to demonstrate adoption of technologies seen to be on-the-shelf and who hoped Farmer Participatory Research would persuade farmers of their desirability. As a result, the notion of conducting research with farmers became steadily diluted over the years. While plenty of examples exist where innovative, participatory approaches have taken root and become central to major programme areas, these are often only on a temporary basis, reliant on the whims of project funding and not seen necessarily as part of core business. And this despite some very positive reviews of such experiences – such as Participatory Plant Breeding – by senior managers, advisory committees and boards.

So what has both promoted and prevented change in different organizational settings? What methodological and institutional innovations have opened up spaces for change? And what has caused closure? Who have been the champions of change, and what has allowed them to be successful? And, overall, what are the core organizational and institutional challenges ahead? There are, of course, no simple answers to these questions. A range of examples are presented in Part III – from within the international research system, such as the CGIAR Systemwide Program on Collective Action and Property Rights (CAPRi) network (Ruth Meinzen-Dick) and the CGIAR Institutional Learning and Change (ILAC) network (Jamie Watts and Douglas Horton), as well as from the national systems of India (V. Rasheed Sulaiman) and China (Li Xiaoyun, Qi Gubo and colleagues). In many respects, all stories were different: highly particular personal and institutional histories conditioned outcomes.

However, the overall assessment was not positive. Many large R&D bureaucracies had run aground, and were performing poorly. Attempts at revitalizing them had foundered on a narrow vision which saw the imperative to move upstream, to engage with the private sector and to work on new advanced (bio)technologies, without a strategy for thinking about how such efforts would be used, and by whom. As V. Rasheed Sulaiman persuasively argues, the case of the Indian national system focus on technology delivery – in the old Green Revolution mode – persists to the exclusion of efforts to deal with institutional and policy issues which are perhaps the key, given the dynamic new challenges faced by farmers. Across the organizations examined, justifications in terms of 'pro-poor development' or '(global) public goods' are often seen to be weak or meaningless, with impact pathways to poverty reduction poorly thought through. Overall, the governance structures of these organizations are hierarchical and unaccountable, at least to the people they are purporting to serve. The involvement of farmers and other key local stakeholders in decisions about funding allocations and priority setting are often tokenistic or non-existent.

The China case study did provide a counterpoint to this general diagnosis. While problems certainly exist, there are some more positive signs. As Li Xiaoyun and colleagues observe, this is a huge system, with more than 1,100 agricultural research agencies from national to regional level across the country in 2001. These are complemented by hundreds of thousands of extension agents at county, township and farm levels. The state's commitment to agriculture, innovation and technology and service delivery is substantial, and those who commit to this national project are given important incentives and awards. The system's incentive system is geared to delivering results, with wide impacts across vast areas. Questions remain around the focus for the poorer smallholder sector, but national policy shifts, generated by dialogue with senior policymakers, are, it seems, in the offing. Could China perhaps be the largest 'Farmer First' effort ever?

A central concern of contributors is how to shift large organizations from ones that are characterized by stasis, conservatism and lack of innovation to learning organizations capable of a nimble, responsive, innovative mode of working, and able to meet the demands of a Farmer First approach? A tall order, some argue. Others are more positive and, across the contributions, some ways forward are suggested:

- Creating institutionalized, open learning spaces within large organizations which encourage sharing of ideas and reflection on research efforts.

- Initiating joint working across institutes by providing learning moments (field visits), events (workshops) and outputs (joint papers). This needs funding and management support.
- Focusing on integrative activities that show the value of farmer participatory approaches to high priority themes, but at the same time changing language and approaches so as to be accommodating and not intimidating, as some social science and policy language can be.
- Maintaining an anger about what is not being done, a commitment to those left behind and a positive vision of what could be done, to motivate and inspire the change-makers.

Building a demand capacity in large R&D bureaucracies is a central and particularly formidable challenge. With the move upstream this is often resisted – the argument being that this should be the responsibility of national governments, applied and adaptive research and so on. But, even if the research is high-end genomic molecular biology in the lab, this still needs a Farmer First approach. Farmer First perspectives urgently need to move from the field to the station to the lab, and back again. This requires greater engagement with users throughout the innovation process, and the creation of innovation platforms involving farmers, as well as governance and financing mechanisms that ensure farmers have the right of veto, and the ability to influence decisions.

New professionalism and organizational learning and change

Given the organizational histories and vested interests of many science and R&D bureaucracies, change, as experiences tell us, does not come easily. China may not be the model everywhere, as the central commitment appears to be absent. So what to do? Part IV concludes the book and emphasizes some positive potentials for encouraging new types of professionalism, reflexive learning and change. For example, what are the opportunities in dissenting networks – outside the formal, mainstream of an organization – which cut across disciplines, sections and departments, and link scientists and extension workers, senior managers and junior staff to farmers and other users? New 'communities of practice' will redefine what we mean by the 'scientific community' – or indeed an innovation system. Insurgency can, it was suggested during workshop discussions, be highly productive, and essential for organizations' energy and innovative capacity, as well as assuring a sustained commitment to progressive approaches, especially when the default mode is so easily resorted to. Yet, as Part IV shows, some major challenges remain. C. Shambu Prasad posed it succinctly during the workshop: 'How do we transform the rich (cacophony of) organizational diversity into (a symphony of) innovation? How do we network dissent, subvert processes and shame institutions towards change?'

Part IV tackles these issues across three themes: how to facilitate responsive and effective extension systems; how to rethink agricultural education; and how to embed impact assessment and learning for change.

Facilitating a responsive and effective extension and delivery system

The field of extension has evolved rapidly in the last 20 years. Gone are the days of large public extension systems with well-resourced extension agents travelling the countryside, training farmers and providing information and demonstrating new techniques. With structural adjustment and public sector 'reform', shrinking public services and the once dominant Training and Visit (T&V) system promoted by the World Bank in dozens of countries coming into disrepute, the standard pipeline public technology transfer and delivery model has all but disappeared. But what has replaced this model, so vilified by Farmer First proponents two decades ago?

The papers in Part IV show how a huge and often confusing variety of alternatives have emerged. Farmers must now contend with multiple sources of information, advice and service support – with, as Rob Tripp argues, some serious concerns about the demands on that scarcest of resources, busy people's time and attention. There are of course the remnants of public extension systems, together with private extension systems run by input supply companies and others, alongside NGO extension efforts which come in all shapes and sizes – from reinventions of the top-down transfer model (as with Sasakawa Global 2000) to model demonstration villages (as with the Millennium Villages project) to demonstration and learning efforts (as with Farmer Field Schools, described by Yunita Winarto) to more bottom-up and community efforts, as discussed for projects by Farm-Africa (Richard Ewbank and colleagues), PICOTEAM (Hlamalani Ngwenya and Jürgen Hagmann) and others in this section. Add to this the increasing access to internet-based information, and other sources and networks supporting farmer information services, and the choice and potential for confusion is bewildering.

Another aspect of innovation in the field of extension over the last 20 years has been in the mode and method of delivery. No longer are extension workers restricted to farmer training sessions and demonstration plots (although these are still important), but joint-learning sessions to understand core principles (as in Farmer Field Schools) or field experimentation in farmer-led trial processes have opened up significant opportunities for more open-ended, non-directed learning (as in Participatory Plant Breeding). And, as Paul Van Mele describes, this is enhanced significantly by the application of new media and information technologies – near ubiquitous cell phones and text messages can become important routes for transferring real-time market information, GIS systems and satellite information can provide site-location support, mobile testing systems can enhance diagnostics of soils, pests and diseases and video technology and rural radio/TV can encourage exchange of ideas and views in ways not possible, or even thought about, 20 years ago.

Choices, opportunities and diversity have thus opened up dramatically. From a Farmer First viewpoint, this *should* be a good thing – there has always been a strong argument for responding to the diversity and complexity of diverse, risk prone settings and wide differences in farming circumstance, for approaches that emphasize a 'basket of choices' or a 'set of principles', rather than fixed recommendations or even domains of recommendation. Farmers of course are good at making choices, and are able to experiment with different options, not taking things at face value. For example, farmers linked to 'organic, sustainable agriculture' networks may well plant GM crops, while those working with transnational companies planting new hybrids or transgenics may use organic, low-input techniques for fertilization or pest management. As ever, the real world is never as simple as the extension messages or the advocacy positions. And with multiple, competing messages and sources of 'extension' (if this is still an appropriate term), this means more circumspection, choice and testing.

However, as we noted above, all this comes at a cost. Farmers' organizations, grassroots research and development groups and other forms of collective organization become critical in helping with sifting information, experimentation and testing of products and assuring quality control. If extension – from whatever source – is like a conversation, then there needs to be a continuous process of interchange – a dialogue – between the different players. But in order to reduce excessive transactions costs and assure quality of information and advice, clearing-house mechanisms are needed, facilitated by alliances and networks which are sufficiently broad and non-partisan, and so going beyond the current models which tend to be allied to a particular vision of what agriculture, farming and farmers should be.

Rethinking educational systems

Over the past 20 years there has been much talk of personal and professional change among Farmer First practitioners. But exactly what this is has often not been clear. A number of contributions to Part IV look at this issue from different angles. Some core attributes come through clearly. These include in particular the need for a normative and political stance in favour of social justice, poverty reduction and equity, combined with the need for openness and an ability to be reflexive (of one's own behaviour, attitudes and actions). But the challenges are also clear. Conventional educational systems and professional hierarchies often do not value such qualities and so do not encourage reflexive learning and change.

Those engaged with the Farmer First movement in the early days talk of how their initiatives often had to be implemented in secret, and how such approaches were seen as subversive and undermining of mainstream approaches. While farmer participation today is seen as very mainstream, when alternative views and practices confront entrenched hierarchies and long institutionalized practices, similar reactions can be seen. The case of the

System of Rice Intensification, introduced in Part II, provides a useful point of reflection. Here is a non-conventional skill and practice-based management approach to increasing rice production, particularly in marginal areas. It has achieved in some places spectacular results and has spread widely. But, despite this, is regarded by some as illegitimate and unproven, and so rejected by some mainstream science organizations. This often out-of-hand rejection has demonstrated an unwillingness to reflect and learn, and an often surprising lack of openness to new ideas and experiments, something usually associated with good science.

How, then, can individual, organizational and professional responses be encouraged which are more open, experimental and reflexive in their approach to learning? Why is it that alternative knowledges and innovative practices and approaches are often excluded, obscured or shunned by mainstream organizations? Much of this comes down to educational systems that set the parameters for professional and organizational behaviour.

While there have been some path-breaking efforts in rethinking agricultural education systems with a Farmer First approach over the last 20 years – for example at Hawkesbury College in Australia or the Department of Communication and Innovation Studies at Wageningen Agricultural University in the Netherlands – these have been scattered and isolated. Mainstream agricultural education, North and South, has been premised on old-style conventional notions, and, where taught, Farmer First approaches have often been seen as an instrumental add-on ('add participation and stir...'). Reforming agricultural education for development is thus seen as a major frontier by contributors to this volume. They highlight a number of key lessons from experiences from a range of recent experiments – from Uganda (Jürgen Hagmann and colleagues), the Horn of Africa (Andy Catley), China (Li Xiaoyun and colleagues) and West Africa (Niels Röling and Janice Jiggins), among others. These include:

- There is a need to build the confidence to think and do things differently which, as Jürgen Hagmann and colleagues argue, means building a sense of collective identity and commitment among learners, whether university lecturers or farmers.
- Shifting mindsets is central. This means encouraging openness and the ability to reflect and learn. This may require substantial shifts in personal and cognitive abilities, and will be conditioned by wider cultural and professional factors which may inhibit such shifts, as Andy Catley shows in his case study of overcoming the resistance of the veterinary establishment to efforts to institutionalize Participatory Epidemiology.
- Styles of pedagogy are needed that enhance such changes. As Jethro Pettit contends, this means embracing diverse sources of knowledge (formal, informal, experiential) and ways of thinking and experiencing the world (to include emotional intelligence and spirituality).

- New forms of curricula are also needed. This may require introduction of a participatory curriculum development methodology guided by insights from modern adult teaching and learning theory and practice, as Li Xiaoyun and colleagues point out in their review of China's efforts to rejuvenate rural development studies.
- Efforts need to be invested in helping faculty to change teaching/ learning methods and styles. This requires incentives and sensitive facilitation. New skills, as Jürgen Hagmann and colleagues point out, may be marketable; for example, faculty at Makerere University in Uganda invested heavily in the change process as they realized that it not only improved their teaching performance but also opened up consulting opportunities.
- Professional rewards and hierarchies need reform to encourage and validate Farmer First ways of doing things. This is linked to incentives, awards and other forms of recognition, as well as support mechanisms and mentoring to encourage younger professionals.
- Organizational and policy change is required within educational systems as a whole, as there is always an easy tendency to return to the default mode, unless alternative ways of doing things are reinforced, as Maria Fernandez and Oscar Ortiz show in their study of institutionalizing a Master's programme on 'Agricultural Innovation for Rural Development' at the National Agrarian University in Lima, Peru.

But in rethinking agricultural education, just as in the wider debate about R&D approaches and innovation systems, there is going to be no one way of doing things. More participatory, learning approaches must go alongside more conventional approaches, and the complementarities, synergies and overlaps must be encouraged and celebrated. However, what has to be avoided is one mode – usually the longer-established, more powerful version – dominating. Thus, a strategic, activist, 'dissenting network' approach may be necessary to get Farmer First perspectives introduced and accepted. This will involve enlisting champions, establishing strong networks of practitioners and encouraging mentoring and support mechanisms, alongside 'Trojan horse' tactics of engaging with the mainstream. Just as a Farmer First innovation system, a new professionalism in agricultural education will not arrive automatically.

Assessing impact, facilitating learning

Such a challenge is perhaps most acute when we come to approaches of assessing impact. Here conventional approaches that assume singular, identifiable and measurable inputs which relate to particular outputs dominate mainstream approaches and often down-play the importance of process and the politics of power relations at play. Yet there has been a massive explosion of activity around participatory monitoring and evaluation and impact assessment in recent years, as shown in the paper in Part IV by Irene Guijt. This work has highlighted:

- A recognition of the political process of framing and defining what is being assessed (what is an 'impact'), and the need to negotiate this among different participants.
- The need for cycles of action, learning and reflection in any research-development process, with monitoring and evaluation about continuous learning and change.
- The requirement to adapt and combine methodologies – quantitative and qualitative, participatory and extractive – in impact assessment and evaluation processes.
- The need to involve all stakeholders in the process in a collective negotiation of objectives/visions, systems framings, methods and results to enhance joint learning and action.
- The need for investment of resources, skills and effort in such processes, not assuming that this can be done after the event.

There is still a significant degree of controversy on how the impact of participatory R&D approaches should be assessed. This is becoming more relevant as agricultural R&D is increasingly located within multi-stakeholder innovation platforms and integrated research-for-development processes. Demonstrating 'impact' has become a core requirement of our audit-driven approach to development. But too often this results in a narrow, mechanical approach where arbitrary measures and indicators and inappropriate counter-factuals are imposed on what ought to have been an embedded, engaged learning approach.

Moreover, in most cases, the emphasis is on 'upward accountability', focusing attention on gathering data and tracking performance to meet the reporting requirements of donor agencies, and in the case of public services, the state. This may meet criteria such as transparency, efficiency and cost-effectiveness, but with little emphasis on 'downward accountability', where the performance of public or private service providers is monitored and evaluated by or for local populations and end users of agricultural services, through, for example, establishing contractual or collaborative linkages between farmers' organizations and service providers.

Accountability to service users implies accountability for results, where their voice is influential in defining and measuring success. Why is this organization choosing this course of action rather than another one? How (with whom) has it defined its 'theory of change' and its strategy? Why select these indicators of success rather than others? Understanding accountability as an *ex post* 'accounting' of what an organization has already done presupposes that organizations possess a unique and fixed understanding of what needs to be done in the first place. This is different from an '*ex ante* engagement', understanding what needs to be done, and the best way to do it and assess it. This requires a means for continuous learning about what worked well, what went wrong, and why.

But convincing others that a more process and systems-oriented approach, centred on participation and continuous learning, is needed is often difficult. And confusions, misunderstandings and parallel initiatives are too often the result. As Adrienne Martin observes: 'There has been important progress in demonstrating the difference made by participatory approaches to outcomes and impacts, but there remain variations in how the contribution of participatory research [and development] is judged, what evidence is considered valid and by whom.'

The contributions in Part IV of the book conclude that there is a need to work on and extend rigorous evaluation and impact assessment approaches, such as those shared by Boru Douthwaite and Dawit Abebe, among others, and make these central to any farmer participatory research and development initiative. Other contributors, including Irene Guijt, Pascal Sanginga and colleagues and Jamie Watts and Douglas Horton, also emphasize the importance of using impact assessments to link action research and action learning to facilitate effective communication and knowledge sharing among practitioners and leaders of pro-poor agricultural innovation processes.

Future challenges, ways forward

What then are the major challenges and ways forward identified by the revisiting of the Farmer First discussions 20 years on? The book offers a rich collection of diverse experiences, all of them highly contextual and particular. But a number of themes stand out, ones that were repeatedly discussed during the workshop and that recur through the contributions to this book. Here we identify three. First, the challenges of scaling up and the dangers of a fragmented, incoherent approach to institutionalizing Farmer First approaches. Second, institutional and organizational change and, in particular, the politics of knowledge involved in negotiating between diverse alternatives. Third, the focus on innovation systems, and the importance of assessing innovation direction, and the distributional implications of technology choices.

The challenges of scaling up

The last 20 years have seen a massive proliferation of agricultural R&D initiatives with the 'participatory' label. Acronyms abound, each labelling a different method, technique, framework or approach. Is this the result of multiple flowers blooming, of a sense of excitement and experimentation across the world? Or has this caused confusion and overlap, competition and unhelpful turf battles? The answer has to be yes to both questions. Farmer First approaches have indeed blossomed over the past 20 years, resulting in a surge of creativity and innovation, as the papers in this book show. But the downside of all this is that a supply-led focus on methods and approaches, often as awkward participatory add-ons to projects and programmes, has meant that a coherence and consistency has not emerged. While some referred to the 'Farmer First movement', giving a sense of common purpose and organization, a more disparate, disconnected networked version is probably more appropriate.

A supply-led approach, driven by a donor-generated enthusiasm for participation, has often meant that efforts have become de-linked from a genuine bottom-up demand. In such a supply-led mode participation can easily become a shallow ritual, a label with little content; rather than carrying with it a genuine sense of shifting power relations facilitating a politics of demand. In Part I, Jacqueline Ashby argues that Farmer First approaches have suffered this fate, particularly in the international agricultural research system. Seen as useful add-ons, something to attract donor project funds in a period of declining core support, farmer participatory research took on many guises (appropriating acronyms along the way), but failed to realize its transformatory potential.

She contrasts this experience with that of microfinance and argues that farmer participatory research approaches failed to build farmer organizations and therefore a basis for demand to match, and keep accountable, the supply-led approach. Equally, they failed to engage early on with the private sector, and so were beholden to an out-dated model of public service provision and state (or NGO/donor) support. The proliferation of approaches and practices, all sharing a 'participatory' label, meant that a set of coherent and agreed principles and standards of what is accepted practice failed to emerge, and 'role conflicts' between researchers pushing particular technologies under the guise of participation surfaced. All these factors have, Ashby argues, constrained the ability of Farmer First approaches to scale up in a sustained way.

A supply-led approach to scaling up will thus achieve little unless it is matched by both effective demand from users and an institutional and organizational setting that learns about success and failure, and adapts accordingly. Perhaps unlike other areas, the agricultural R&D sector has been defined historically by a supply-push approach to technology diffusion and transfer. The Green Revolution in Asia is often interpreted in this way, and new efforts argue that this is all that is needed today; perhaps sped up and honed by farmer participation along the way. Yet, this pipeline model is, as Farmer First advocates have long argued, inadequate. An embedded network model of innovation is seen as an alternative: supported, but not supervised; low maintenance and flexible; adapted to local contexts and generating diverse innovations not standard, 'blueprint' solutions. The emphasis for scaling up, therefore, should not be on any particular set of technologies or even the methods to encourage participation, but the capacity to stimulate and sustain innovation among a diverse range of actors.

Thus, as part of such networks, technology users – farmers, consumers, labourers – need to be involved in the definition of the directions of technology change, often centred on competing visions about agricultural and rural futures. Thus participation, and scaling up, cannot be seen simply as instrumentally pushing more of what has been defined as a 'good thing', but it must be centrally about contests over knowledge and politics and about what vision of agriculture and rural development is wanted in a particular context. This means engaging more concretely with the politics of agrarian change in different settings and working with farmers' organizations and other people-centred organizations as a route to developing a more effective politics of demand in agricultural innovation systems.

The politics of knowledge: institutional learning and change

Picking up on the themes of the 1992 *Beyond Farmer First* workshop and subsequent book (Scoones and Thompson, 1994), many contributions to this volume highlight the need to go beyond the conventional distinctions between indigenous and scientific, traditional and modern, local and global, practical and theoretical knowledge to a more integrative, hybrid version of contested, located knowledges which are continuously in the making. Such knowledges may be made up of technical elements, but also, critically, cognitive processes. Knowledges too are both discursive ('in the head') and practical ('in the body'), based on experiential, emotional and sensory sources. Equally, such knowledges are gendered and socially distributed across networks, institutions and social movements.

This recognition of multiple knowledges and multiple sources of innovation, particularly those associated with farmers and rural people, has of course been central to the Farmer First approach over 20 years. But how does this recognition articulate with a perspective on innovation systems? Is the challenge to try to incorporate diverse knowledges in an innovation system or to recognize that different knowledges – and combinations of these – create different innovation systems, with different values, politics and directions? If it is the latter, then a political perspective on knowledge and innovation is suggested which goes beyond the instrumental project of combining 'stocks' or 'bodies' of knowledge to a focus on negotiating between competing visions and pathways. This inevitably results in fraught encounters and often challenging negotiations over knowledge, the means of validation and the processes of framing. Sometimes behind 'front-stage' consensus, there is much 'back-stage' conflict, and it is this dissent, debate and dissonance which must be acknowledged and embraced in any effective Farmer First approach.

Contributions to this book highlight a wide range of models of spread of knowledge, ideas, practices and techniques. Some are formal and institutionalized; others highly informal. But all show the limits of the standard technology diffusion and transfer models that have so dominated thinking about research, extension and development linkages over time. Different case studies highlight the importance of knowledge entrepreneurship and marketing, of key moments and events, of champions of change and of networks and alliances. Thus, C. Shambu Prasad talks of: 'the messy and playful encounters of everyday practice where farmers, scientists and civil society are engaging in an uneven but dynamic knowledge market place'. Or as Robert

Rhoades puts it: 'The key to reconciling the needs of scientists and local needs is seeking new forms of equitable collaboration which reach beyond the…now somewhat tired discourse of "participation".'

The social and political dimensions of knowledge generation and spread – whether through formal or informal, visible or hidden processes – were emphasized time and again in the workshop deliberations and are highlighted by many contributors to this volume.

One of the big dilemmas facing Farmer First approaches is how to avoid simple co-option by dominant forms of knowledge and practice, with farmer participation becoming a side-lined add-on in a conventional technology transfer project. In the same way, new approaches, based on different forms of knowledge and experience may be very challenging to mainstream agricultural R&D institutions, such as the System of Rice Intensification discussed in Part II, a technique and practice-based approach not amenable to standard experimental verification designed to test uniform technologies. Farmer First approaches such as these may upset conventional wisdoms and confront standard methodologies. Being prepared for such knowledge encounters, and the politics that these entail, is a critical, but often under-estimated challenge.

Thus contestations over multiple framings – of goals and visions, as well as technologies and plans – and processes of co-construction of meanings, interpretations and solutions must be seen as central to the agricultural innovation process; and Farmer First approaches need to get real about the knowledge politics involved. This is an intensely social and political process, involving creating, extending and sustaining complex, hybrid networks – of people, artefacts, ideas and institutions. It is a far cry from simple diffusion of improved technologies and practices from 'centres of excellence' as is so often portrayed, with or without farmer participation.

How should such approaches be organized? For some, such as Paul Richards, this is best done through unsupervised, self-organizing networks. For others, more structured approaches are seen to help facilitate the same ends. For example, Hlamalani Ngwenya and Jürgen Hagmann highlight the 'facilitation for change (F4C)' approach to triggering emancipation and innovation in rural communities, while Edith van Walsum talks of 'global knowledge networking' for sustainable agriculture. In the same way, Bernard Triomphe and colleagues identify the need for 'multi-stakeholder research partnerships' and Jamie Watts and Doug Horton argue for the creation of a 'learning laboratory' at the heart of the CGIAR. These efforts are engaged in creating the space for knowledge dialogues which build bridges between different actors, extend networks and create new, shared languages for action and change. Creating the organizational incentives for such networked activities must be a critical focus for the future, recognizing the contested knowledges and framings at the centre of any deliberations about alternative options.

Innovation systems, innovative directions

As the contributions to the book show, much effort has been invested in going beyond the farm and the farmer, and beyond a focus on technology to the wider innovation system. Over the last 20 years, this has been a vital analytical step which has highlighted the importance of addressing markets, value chains, supply systems and all the links between producers and consumers. But such a systemic, analytical description of innovation systems is not enough. Describing multiple stakeholders and complex connections is important, but there are judgements to be made, and political and normative processes are involved. For example: who defines the boundary of the system? Who is in and who is out? Which elements are important and which are less so? And, critically, where is the system heading – towards what goals and outcomes?

Not surprisingly, it is these more normative-political questions that are of major concern to contributions across this book. Putting farmers first is not just a technical-analytical exercise, but also a highly political one; and a commitment to social justice, equity, gender equality and poverty reduction is thus central to this agenda. This means that an examination of innovation systems cannot stop at a mechanical assessment of the system and its functioning, but must address the thorny, normative questions about directions and trajectories, trade-offs and competing interests. This requires a focus on processes and the properties that emerge from complex, non-linear systems. This, in turn, means asking about system resilience to 'shocks' and 'stresses', such as the increasingly evident consequences of climate change. Thus, while there was much fruitful discussion around the application of value chain approaches linking a Farmer First approach to concerns with market access and input/output supply chains, at domestic, regional and global levels, these were seen as components of a bigger challenge for Farmer First approaches.

Yet, in moving away from a farmer focus to an innovation systems perspective, a number of tensions are evident. Should a Farmer First approach stick to a practical, instrumental, intervention-oriented stance which ensures that farmers get a better deal from technology development or markets or should a more political stand be taken which emphasizes engagement in complex processes, with a strong normative positioning? Both approaches are important, but the latter is probably the least well developed over the past 20 years – and certainly less compatible with the institutionalization of 'participation' in donor-funded project activities and in large, often highly conventional, R&D organizations and science bureaucracies.

Some of these tensions can be illustrated in a simple diagram (Figure 1.1). Here two axes are identified: first, horizontally, different ways of understanding the world and describing causation – along a continuum from mechanical to process-based reasoning. Second, vertically, there are different ways of acting in the world, along a continuum from an analytical to a normative approach.

	Mechanical	Process-oriented
Analytical	Top down, linear, transfer	Complexity systems, emergence, learning organizations
Normative	Instrumental 'pro-poor' approaches	Power, politics, learning, reflexivity

Figure 1.1 Alternative ways of thinking about innovation systems

While such contrasts and comparisons miss out on much detail and nuance, they do highlight some important issues. For, across these two axes, there are a range of tensions, dilemmas, contrasts and polarities highlighted in the contributions to the book. A shift from a mechanical to a process approach thus means moving from 'hard' to 'soft' systems approaches; from instrumental interventionism to emergent processes; from centres of excellence to distributed networks; from planned, managed development to experimental, reflexive learning styles; from top-down, supervised organizational arrangements to bottom-up, unsupervised networks. Similarly, a shift from an analytical to a normative stance means moving towards approaches which emphasize power relations, political interactions and institutional rules and processes, rather than an apolitical focus on organizational form and structure, instrumental indicators and standard measures of impact.

Different people, different processes and different organizations will find themselves positioned along these axes and across these continua at different times and for different reasons. There is of course no right or wrong way of doing things. And all involve action, intervention and a commitment to innovative, systemic change in different ways. But the way such action is defined, its directions and consequences are deeply implicated by the way problems and solutions are framed, and by whom. Thus, depending on where you start, the things you do – whether research, extension, impact assessment or networking – will look very different. Indeed, as we move towards a more normative and process-oriented stance on innovation systems (following the arrow in Figure 1.1 – or moving towards the fourth column of Table 1.1), then the practice of agricultural R&D looks very different indeed.

Conclusions

In conclusion, if Farmer First approaches are to become the mainstream default, rather than something to be done with soft money as a concession to donors or other special interests; if they are to be recognized as the way to put farmers – and consumers, labourers and other poor and marginalized people – at the centre of innovation systems and if they are to be recognized as the way of doing good science and ensuring effective, sustainable technology development, then some fundamental shifts in thinking and practice will be required in the design and practice of agricultural R&D systems.

We have travelled a long way over the past two decades, but, as the contributions to this book suggest, not far enough. In 1989, the focus of the original *Farmer First* book was very much on improving agricultural research and extension by starting with farmers' own priorities and capacities for innovation. Five years later, in 1994, the *Beyond Farmer First* book shifted attention to fundamental issues of knowledge and power to reveal how agricultural research and extension, far from being discrete, rational acts, are in fact part of a process of coming to terms with conflicting interests and viewpoints, a process in which choices are made, alliances formed, exclusions effected and worldviews imposed. By 2009, the recognition is that we must embrace all of these elements and more. Thus, to re-energize the Farmer First movement and to capitalize on the many successes to date, a focus on the politics of demand, combined with attention to organizational and institutional learning and change in networked innovation systems, now needs to be put centre-stage, alongside the many farmer participatory research methods, models and frameworks. For it is only if Farmer First approaches are combined with and reinforced by these essential normative, political and institutional dimensions that they will finally deliver on the promises highlighted some 20 years ago of really putting farmers first.

Challenges to strengthening agricultural innovation systems: where do we go from here?

Andy Hall

Why are we still here?

If anybody had told me 20 years ago that we would still be having international conferences on the organization of agricultural innovation for development I would not have believed them. So why are we still here?

It seems to me that there is a paradox. The question of how to enable agricultural innovation for development is now discussed and researched more and better understood than ever before. At our disposal is a bewildering array of tools, manuals, case studies, frameworks, approaches, experiences and expertise. Yet, the central challenge remains with us: the need to accelerate policy and institutional change in public (and, increasingly, private philanthropic) investments in agricultural science, technology and innovation for development.

This is not to say that the practices and policies of, for example, the CGIAR, donors and national governments and others have not changed. They have. However, there is still an uncomfortably large gap between what is known about enabling innovation for development and what is evident in mainstream policies and practices. The reason we are 'still here' is precisely because of this gap and the tectonic pace at which it is narrowing.

Yet we have long had a fairly clear idea of how agricultural innovation took place and what was preventing it – and those ideas seem to have broadly stood the test of time:

- innovation requires knowledge from multiple sources, including from users of that knowledge;
- it involves these different sources of knowledge interacting with each other in order to share and combine ideas;
- these interactions and processes are usually very specific to a particular context; and
- each context has its own routines and traditions that reflect historical origins shaped by culture, politics, policies and power.

Over the years we have come up with many ways of emphasizing these different ideas, including farmer first and last, participation, participatory rural appraisal (PRA), participatory learning and action (PLA), public–private sector partnerships, local innovation and so forth. We have also been successful in packaging and repackaging these ideas and (re)branding them. Agricultural innovation systems, a repackaging of ideas borrowed from our industrial development friends, is one such brand.

What I want to argue is that instead of seeing 'innovation systems' as a new, and perhaps, competing approach, we view it as a metaphor for innovation diversity. In order to deal with the shocks and opportunities that the modern world throws at us, we need different approaches to innovation; different ways of bringing together ideas and technology. And we need to more effectively mobilize the innovation diversity that we currently have to cohesively argue for the sorts of policy and institutional change needed to create the space for further diversity to emerge – i.e. a virtuous spiral of innovation practice and policy learning. Strengthening agricultural innovation systems is thus less about specific operational and policy recommendations – although clearly there are principles and generic issues. Rather, it is about ensuring that conditions that nurture eclectic approaches to innovation exist, and that competitors join forces with each other to constantly adapt institutional and policy framework conditions for innovation.

Agricultural innovation – second time around

Since the earliest days of development assistance, investments in agriculture through research and technology transfer have been central to rural development strategies. After falling from grace in the 1990s, a rush of new initiatives and the publication of the *2008 World Development Report* on agriculture suggest that agriculture and agricultural science and technology are once again riding high in the development assistance world.

New this time around is the focus on innovation and the idea of innovation systems. The shift in viewpoint that this signals is simple, but fundamental. If we are interested in development, and if we agree that development is about change, let us worry less about the supply of new knowledge and technology from research and concentrate instead on the conditions needed to demand and use knowledge to bring about that change.

If one steps back from this renewed interest in agricultural innovation, it is possible to see this as part of a much longer story of arguments about how agricultural knowledge should be used for development. Some of our recent research on the evolution of the International Agricultural Research Centres found that this has been hotly debated by scientists since the 1960s.

These arguments include: Should plant breeding be conducted in on-station trials or in farmers' fields? Should research be organized around commodities or around eco-regions? Should it take the form of traditional research, farming systems research or farmer participatory research? Is farmer knowledge superior to scientific knowledge? Should technology be modern or intermediate? What types of research lie in the public domain and what in the private? What constitutes international public good research and what is locally relevant applied research and development? For every convincing narrative of one position, there is an equally convincing counter-narrative: high yielding cereal revolutionized food production in Asia, but failed in Africa; privatization of seed supply systems improves client orientation in India, but not in Bangladesh; participatory plant breeding is more client-oriented, but genetic mark-assisted selection is cheaper.

Over time there has been an additive evolution of approaches to developing agricultural innovation capacities in agricultural systems (Table 1.2). But where have we ended up? What can an agricultural innovation systems approach offer – as framework, practice and metaphor?

There are, however, many different and often competing versions of an appropriate way forward. These have proliferated massively in the last 20 years. But which coalition of ideas and interests wins out? Our research on international agricultural research organizations indicates that, perhaps not surprisingly, time and time again it is the more conservative coalition that carries the day. Positive deviants – groups innovating in different and useful ways – have to be lucky, persistent and politically astute to stimulate institutional change.

Table 1.2 The evolution of agricultural innovation capacity development frameworks

Defining features	Classic National Agricultural Research Systems (NARS)	Classic Agricultural Knowledge and Information Systems (AKIS) (as defined by FAO-World Bank 2002)	Agricultural Innovation Systems
What this is?	Organizing framework for planning capacity for agricultural research, technology development and transfer	Organizing framework for strengthening communication and knowledge delivery services to people in the rural sector	Organizing framework to strengthen the capacity to innovate and create novelty throughout the agricultural production and marketing system
Who is this?	1. National Agricultural Research Organizations 2. Agricultural Universities or Faculties 3. Extension services 4. Farmers	1. National Agricultural Research Organizations 2. Agricultural Universities or Faculties 3. Extension services 4. Farmers 5. NGOs and entrepreneurs in rural areas	Potentially all actors in the public and private sectors involved in the creation, diffusion, adaptation and use of all types of knowledge relevant to agricultural production and marketing
Outcome	Technological invention and technology transfer	Technology adoption and innovation in agricultural production and marketing in rural areas	Combinations of technical and institutional innovations throughout the production, marketing, policy research and enterprise domains
Organizing principle	• using science to create knowledge*** • invention driven**	• accessing agricultural knowledge*** • invention driven*	• creating change for social and economic change*** • innovation driven**
Theory of innovation	Transfer of technology	Interactive learning	Interactive learning
Degree of market integration	Nil	Low	High
Role of policy	Resource allocation, priority setting	Enabling framework	Integrated component and enabling framework
Nature of capacity strengthening	Infrastructure and human resource development	Strengthening communication between actors in rural areas	Same as NARS and AKIS and in addition, combination of: strengthening linkages and interaction; institutional developments to support interaction, learning and innovation; the creating of an enabling policy environment

Source: World Bank, 2006
Note: Degree of emphasis: * = low; ** = medium; *** = high

This has unfortunate consequences for agricultural science and innovation policy-making. It means that the diversity of agricultural innovation experiences – precisely because of their very diversity and context-specificity – rarely forms a sufficiently coherent or powerful coalition of interest to influence policy and institutional change. Farmer First/participatory research was one of those rare examples of a successful coalition, but even today there are major institutional roadblocks to such an approach, as Ashby (this book) discusses. More usually one sees many small groups of practitioners and researchers rallying around different innovation experiences, behaving competitively and often waging bitter turf wars instead of expending their energies collectively for policy change. With limited policy and institutional change, diversity is also stifled because routine ways of organizing science and innovation become entrenched and incontestable.

Responding to rapid change

The idea of an innovation system emerged in parallel with economic studies of industrializing countries (particularly in East Asia). Its central ideas resonated with the institutional innovations taking place around agricultural research approaches in the 1990s and the increasingly globalized economic conditions that developing countries were facing. Of course, social equity and the need to improve the livelihoods of poor rural households in developing countries was an additional and unique concern for agricultural development policy. Innovation systems ideas, nevertheless, brought fresh thinking and impetus to the discussion of agricultural science technology and innovation in development that had, in many senses, got stuck in polarized debates, particularly about farmer knowledge and invention without tackling how this could be integrated with scientific knowledge (Bell, 2006).

While there really does seem to be some consensus on the need to nurture networks of dense interaction for innovation across society, it does not mean opposing views have disappeared. However, those who continue to advocate for the 'isolated islands of scientific excellence' mode of agricultural innovation capacity building seem increasingly out of step with agricultural futures, which are, in many senses, already with us. In parallel there is a different understanding of what is needed to build innovation systems. This involves a shift from technology delivery to capacity strengthening and, specifically, the capacity to innovate. Underlying this is the idea that to be effective in an ever-changing world a continuous process of innovation is required to adapt economic processes to presenting situations.

The agricultural sector is moving into an era of rapidly changing market, technological, social and environmental circumstances that are evolving in often unpredictable ways. This is an era where collective intelligences will replace centres of excellence and where the ability to use knowledge effectively in response to changing circumstances will define countries' resilience to global shocks. Coping and prospering in this new era will require scientists, policymakers, consumers and entrepreneurs to seamlessly organize their interactions in order to mobilize knowledge and continuously innovate in the face of change. A dream? Currently, yes. A necessity? No doubt about it.

Features of the future include:

- *Multi-functionality.* The broad range of goals and interest groups the sector must serve: livelihoods for poor people, environmental sustainability, agro-industrial development, sector and technological convergence such as bio-fuels, food safety and eco-tourism.
- *Collective intelligence.* There is no longer a single source of information and technology, and bringing about innovation and change requires a collective intelligence involving collaboration between different knowledge sources.
- *Rapidly advancing technological frontier.* The results of public and private R&D present new social and economic opportunities, but also raise new questions about societies' relationship with science and its governance.
- *Interconnectedness of scales.* Local production and livelihoods are increasingly connected to global preferences and trade standards through international value chains and to global phenomena like climate change and animal disease outbreaks.
- *Knowledge use-related capacities as a new source of comparative advantage.* The ability to use knowledge to innovate is emerging as a new source of comparative advantage, replacing the traditional importance of natural resource endowments as a source of competitiveness for developing countries.
- *Increasing rate and non-linearity of change.* This increasingly interconnected scenario with its multiple interest groups is contributing to the increasing pace of change and its non-linearity, due to the faster transmission of ideas and the wider set of interactions that now exist between markets, policies and technologies.

Not surprisingly, then, the idea of agricultural innovation systems has all of a sudden started to look very attractive, if not essential.

Agricultural innovation systems – a personal state-of-the-art

For every agricultural innovation systems specialist there is an interpretation of what this idea means. One definition is that an innovation system is the organizations, enterprises and individuals that demand and supply knowledge and technologies, and the policies, rules and mechanisms which affect the way different agents interact to share, access, exchange and use knowledge (World Bank, 2006).

There is now a very rapidly growing literature on agricultural innovation systems. My own work has had two major thrusts. First was a series of case studies where we used the framework to explore and explain different approaches to agricultural innovation. This, in turn, helped us firm up the idea of an innovation system as an analytical framework. The second thrust has been on operationalizing the concept in the sense of using it diagnostically to help design interventions to strengthen innovation capacity (for history see Hall, 2007). These two thrusts were brought together in a study we conducted for the Agriculture and Rural Development (ARD) division of the World Bank, where we developed an analytical framework, tested it on case studies and then developed an intervention framework (World Bank, 2006).

The findings included:

- Innovation is rarely triggered by agricultural research and instead is most often a response of entrepreneurs to new and changing market opportunities.
- Promising sectors begin to fail because with ever-changing market demands, patterns of interaction between entrepreneurs, farmers and other sources of technology and information are insufficient to support a knowledge-intensive process of innovation on a continuous basis.
- Lack of interaction weakens innovation capacity and is a reflection of deep-rooted habits and practices in both public and private sector organizations.
- The market is not sufficient to promote interaction; the public sector has a central role to play.
- Social and environmental sustainability are integral to economic success and need to be reflected in patterns of participation and interaction that are considered when strengthening innovation capacity.
- Mechanisms at the sector level that are critical for coordinating the interaction needed for innovation are either overlooked or missing.

The study made two now very familiar recommendations. First, we need a major shift in interventions away from supporting agricultural research and with a new focus on strengthening patterns of interaction across the whole range of actors involved in innovation. Second, within this new focus a priority is to find ways of developing and adapting habits and practices that foster a capacity to innovate that integrates pro-poor and pro-market agendas.

Will this put farmers first? No, but it won't put them last either. Instead, it will help promote the idea of approaches that give equal weighting to different sources of knowledge, including that of farmers, but also others; and that recognizes that there are multiple legitimate agendas in society, including those of the poor, but also those of industry and commerce, and that pursuing both can contribute to development in different ways.

What still needs to be done? My sense is that the big challenges are operational. In particular, the idea of creating innovation capacities that are both pro-poor and pro-market. What is required are coordinated networks of actors relevant to specific challenges or opportunities and locations – accompanied by supporting policies and ways of working specific to those challenges, opportunities and locations. Recent work on the nature of innovation capacity suggests that a range of different types of innovation systems already exist and predicts that this diversity will increase in the future (Hall, 2005). These systems range from public sector, science-driven systems working on food crop productivity, through private sector-coordinated networks innovating around value chains, to participatory partnerships between science and local communities focusing on natural resource management. They rely on scientific and other sources of knowledge to differing extents, and have different governance mechanisms. Some will be largely self-organizing while others will need public intervention to organize interaction.

My argument is that 'agricultural innovation systems' is not another competing innovation narrative in the vein of past polarized debates. Instead, it is a metaphor to explain the principles behind the existence of a diversity of collective intelligence mechanisms for organizing interaction for innovation – some more collective, some less so; some more participatory, some less so; some more pro-poor, some less so. In the fast approaching future the agricultural sector will require this diversity in collective intelligence mechanisms to meet its multiple agendas. It will also need a pattern of diversity that continues to evolve in order to cope with an ever-changing set of demands and opportunities that the sector will inevitably face.

Creating space for diversity and sharing innovation experiences

Ultimately, the question of organizing interactions for innovation is a question of what policies and institutional regimes are going to be needed to make this happen, and happen in ways that best balance the trade-offs among societies' multiple goals. It appears there are two priorities here if we want to help stimulate institutional and policy change.

The first is to create the space for the diversity of different ways of organizing interactions to emerge. The greater the diversity we create, the more innovation experiences there are to help us understand how best to organize for innovation. This, in turn, helps us develop policies and institutions that support the collective intelligence approach across the agricultural sector and the wider society it is located in. This is the virtual spiral of innovation practice and policy learning I mentioned in my introduction.

The problem here is that to bring about policy and institutional changes one needs sufficient diversity of innovation experiences to build our repertoire, draw generalities from and make the case for change. Often, however, policy and institutional settings stifle the diversity of approaches. Anybody working in large agricultural research organizations will know all too well the restrictions placed on doing things differently. I experienced this myself working with participatory research methods in East Africa in the early 1990s. We experienced it again in 2007 with the CGIAR's reluctance to accept the proposal of the Sub-Saharan Africa Challenge Programme of the Forum for

Agricultural Research in Africa (FARA) to experiment with the development of what it terms an 'Integrated Agricultural Research for Development' (IAR4D) approach (see Jones and Sanyang, this book).

This is why policy and institutional change are important. Similarly, this is also why special projects and groups working at the margins of research organizations' mandates are so critical in making space for doing things differently. One can imagine a ratchet effect where new innovation experiences bring about small policy changes that, in turn, open up new space. However, the history of agricultural research and innovation suggests that this process is very slow.

Special projects, NGOs and the private sector have been steadily generating different innovation experiences. Similarly the innovation studies community – while relatively small – has also built on a large body of different experiences and come up with a range of often overlapping policy perspectives on how to promote agricultural and rural innovation.

The second priority for helping with institutional and policy change is to mobilize the existing diversity of innovation experiences. At first glance it might seem that there is little common ground in these experiences. What is common, however, is the experience of how to successfully organize interaction for innovation. In practical terms, what this means is establishing mechanisms and structures to facilitate the sharing of these experiences across the global agricultural and rural development community – including practitioners, policymakers, donors, entrepreneurs and scientists. This sort of approach is usually referred to as a Community of Practice approach.

Do we need it? Well, it seems quite clear that currently the 'space' and process to effectively share different innovation experiences and ideas are absent. In the same vein, the disconnected efforts of different innovation groups have not been sufficient to kick-start the institutional and policy change process at a sufficient scale or speed. To answer my introductory question, this is why we are still here today and it is something all of us have a responsibility to address.

If we are really serious about agricultural innovation systems as a way of achieving our development goals, we must reflect on the sorts of alliances and activities needed to consolidate and share what is known about innovation – in all its diverse forms – and to stimulate the virtuous spiral of innovation practice and policy learning.

Fostering Farmer First methodological innovation: organizational learning and change in international agricultural research

Jacqueline A. Ashby

Addressing the political dimensions of Farmer First innovation

The purpose in this paper is to analyse the effort to institutionalize Farmer First approaches in plant breeding programmes at some of the international and national agricultural research institutes over the past 20 years and to draw lessons for the future. In themselves, these programmes constitute only a small segment of the international and national agricultural innovation systems that have experienced this global change of paradigm. Nonetheless, these organizations, as science bureaucracies responsible for the bulk of public sector provision of agricultural R&D services to the rural poor in developing countries, provide a context for developing insights on some of the most pertinent past difficulties as well as new opportunities for the future.

In this paper I draw on both institutional and personal experience to argue that past efforts to drive forward the Farmer First paradigm in science bureaucracies were fundamentally flawed by an overinvestment in reforming the supply-side of innovation in organizations that lacked then – and still lack – accountability for satisfying demand for innovation from the poor. As a result, the individual actors and champions of change in this process were broadly divorced from other socio-political actors who drive organizational change and lacked a real power base from which to lever changes that were more than cosmetic. The essential challenge for the future is to address the political dimensions of demand for Farmer First innovation in the agricultural sector.

The birth and early development of FPR

The effort to introduce, validate and institutionalize Farmer Participatory Research (FPR) in international and national agricultural research institutes has passed through several stages akin to a life cycle: birth, adolescence and currently, middle-age. (Whether FPR in the international centres is heading into senility or setting the stage for the emergence of a new paradigm, is up for discussion.)

The first Farmer First workshop in 1987 christened a new-born conviction among the minority of professional pioneers working on the margins of these organizations, that conventional, top-down science, basking in the glow of the Green Revolution, was fundamentally bypassing farmers' own priorities and farmers' indigenous capacity for innovation. If you were a participant in that workshop, re-reading the landmark book *Farmer First: Farmer Innovation and Agricultural Research* (Chambers et al., 1989) brings back the excitement of those early days when the social scientists pioneering this work in the international research centres believed that our essential task was to persuade the biological scientists of the importance of including farmers in research teams.

As scientists, we believed that change could be achieved by showing scientifically, how research findings varied depending on the way in which farmers participated in the research process. Early work showed technologies could be developed that met the preferences of poor people when scientists gave credence to farmers' knowledge and advice. In essence, our strategy was based on faith in the power of scientific evidence to open the doors of science bureaucracies and admit farmers into a new role, as researchers.

In several respects, this strategy was highly successful. Early applications of participatory research to the field of plant breeding were driven by social scientists who showed convincingly that the inclusion of farmers as 'barefoot' researchers in sophisticated scientific research teams could contribute essential knowledge that changed breeding objectives and accelerated the breeding process, in some cases saving years of costly experiment station research.

These experiences showed how Farmer First approaches could improve the relevance of breeding products to poor farmers and a small but dedicated group of plant breeders began to build on and scale out those initial efforts. In the early 1990s, evidence from maize, barley, millet, potato, field bean and forage breeding programmes accumulated and individual plant breeders began to incorporate FPR into their programmes' breeding methodology. Most of these programmes demonstrated how setting plant breeding objectives and sharing or delegating certain research responsibilities with farmers contributed to the development of new varieties and cropping systems and accelerated the innovation process leading to significant impact on adoption. Above all, they highlighted:

- the key importance of interaction with farmers in the early stages of the plant breeding process, when breeding objectives are set; and
- the advantages of decentralizing breeding programmes to conduct varietal selection with farmers in diverse, local environments.

In 2000, the CGIAR's Technical Advisory Committee (TAC – now known as the Science Council) commissioned a review of plant breeding in the CGIAR system that concluded farmer participatory plant breeding should be accepted as a useful tool for all plant breeding programmes (TAC, 2000).

Brash adolescence and the 'dark side' of FPR

At this time donor funding for programmes calling themselves 'participatory' began to rise steeply and in response, farmer participation became increasingly a 'must-have' feature for a successful grant proposal. As its popularity grew, the FPR process reached a stage of brash adolescence. Good judgment is not a feature of adolescence, and in this phase, FPR in the international and national institutes became a catch-all for activities that involved little or no research but included pure technology transfer, seed dissemination or on-farm validation using discovery learning, as in farmer field schools.

Paralleling the boom in Participatory Rural Appraisal (PRA) in the development community, FPR in the agricultural research institutes reached a growing population of converts. By the mid-1990s most FPR practitioners were not social scientists and in many cases, social scientists using Farmer First approaches had converted themselves into pseudo-agronomists to enhance their credibility in the dominant culture of the institutes. Many of them spawned numerous methodological variants of FPR that de-linked participation from the original social concern to promote equity or empowerment for the poor. As in PRA, the FPR boom showed the 'dark side' of participation: the dangers of elite capture in processes where farmer participants were self-selecting; and the distortion of agendas away from the priorities of the poor in science-driven consultations with farmers, where priorities were shaped *a priori* by supply-driven, commodity-focused research.

Increasingly, FPR became perceived as a way to convince farmers (and donors) that the existing supply of agricultural R&D was on track to benefit the poor. The proliferation of FPR occurred in tandem with a shift away from unrestricted to project-based funding for agricultural R&D, on which research programmes came increasingly to depend. Programme directors used the 'farmer participatory' label as a sales pitch to compete successfully for development (i.e. non-research) project funding. This provoked a deep-seated resentment of FPR among many scientists who perceived that conventional research programmes were being drained of resources that were being reallocated to participatory (so-called) 'research' that in many instances involved no research and was of dubious value to the poor. In practice, the term 'farmer participation' was captured by a large group of protagonists whose chief need was to demonstrate adoption of technologies seen to be 'on-the-shelf' and who hoped FPR would persuade farmers of their desirability.

As a result, the notion of conducting research with farmers became steadily diluted. A hybrid approach to FPR was popularized especially at senior management levels in Boards of Trustees and among Directors-General where fund-raising was of paramount concern. This involved farmers in validating the supply of technology coming out of the established, pipeline-style of research. This had the bonus of enabling farmers, on occasion, to provide feedback to research, but avoided altering the established balance of power in which science bureaucracies set research objectives and define how research processes are conducted.

A mid-life crisis?

Now in its middle-age, FPR in agricultural research institutes has been moulded into a style of technology transfer that uses participatory learning and many of the PRA tools to reassert the top-down, pipeline model of innovation. Nowhere is this more apparent than in the large-scale Harvest Plus and Generation 'Challenge Programs' established by the CGIAR at the end of the 1990s, to tackle ambitious plant breeding objectives on a system-wide basis. Driven by what scientists perceived to be their comparative advantage in supplying biotechnology-supported plant breeding solutions to researcher-prioritized problems such as micro-nutrient deficiencies and drought, these 'mother' programmes define 'baby' farmers as 'customers' and, at a strategic level, have relegated interaction with farmers to the late stages of delivery of near-finished research products.

The idea of doing research with farmers has gradually dwindled to a few, marginalized activities nursed by individuals committed to the concept, but lacking hard-core, institutional support. The strategy of persuasion by providing evidence of the effectiveness of Farmer First approaches to researchers succeeded in convincing individual plant breeders to use FPR in short-lived projects, but ultimately, the popularity of 'participation' as a sales pitch to development donors undermined the prospect of its institutionalization on any meaningful scale.

Lessons from microfinance

A comparison between what happened to Farmer First approaches in plant breeding and in a different field – that of microfinance – helps to illustrate this central point. By making this comparison, I do not mean to imply that Farmer First approaches in agricultural R&D could – or should – have evolved along the same lines as the microfinance revolution. But an analysis of some key success factors in bringing financial services to the poor does provide some insights into why bringing agricultural research services to the poor has been so much more difficult.

Several elements of the microfinance success story are absent from the experience with Farmer First approaches in agricultural R&D. First, the link with effective demand for innovation from the poor was absent from supply-driven, Farmer First efforts in agricultural innovation. Supply-driven FPR does not require farmers to form and sustain functional group relationships and so there was no inherent necessity for FPR practitioners to build farmer organizations.

A second difference is the absence of early partnerships with the private sector. In contrast to the early engagement with commercial banks in the microfinance sector, protagonists of Farmer First approaches in agricultural research institutes have generally avoided partnerships with private sector service providers. Although getting massive impact out of participatory research relies on some kind of scaling up process to get the products out to large numbers of poor farmers who are typically scattered across a mosaic of highly variable production and marketing environments, FPR did not develop the kinds of large-scale partnerships needed (although some of these are now being developed by agricultural R&D with the private sector and international NGOs to expand technology transfer). This reflects the evolution of a hybrid FPR as a form of technology transfer. In the rare case where the focus of FPR on joint research (also termed co-breeding) with farmers was sustained and the strategy involved other actors in the value chain, participatory plant breeding has engaged private sector partners successfully in early experimentation with delivery (Desclaux and Chiffoleau, 2006).

Third, the cohesion around a basic set of relatively simple and easily replicable microfinance principles that provided the foundation for a franchising approach that fuelled scaling out is missing in FPR. As FPR efforts in agricultural R&D proliferated into a huge diversity of dogmas, most were implemented on a small scale and many reinvented similar wheels in isolation from one another. Minimum standards of what constitute authentic participatory research or genuine Farmer First 'good practice' are still hotly debated and consistent standards are certainly not adhered to by many FPR practitioners (e.g. paying some farmers and expecting others to volunteer for on-farm research).

The fragmentation of methodology that impeded scaling up reflects a fundamental problem of 'role conflict' for FPR practitioners in supply-driven agricultural R&D. In microfinance, bankers do not have an interest in what clients choose to invest in as long as they pay the loan back. FPR researchers, in contrast, need farmers to invest in the technologies they have developed. The performance of FPR is impeded by the friction created when researchers want farmers to choose suboptimal technologies (i.e. technologies that are the researchers' favourites but would not have been the farmer's first choice). Behaviours like these reflect a fundamental structural problem, one that arises when participation from the demand-side is driven exclusively or primarily by the supply-side actors in the innovation system.

The fourth difference between the micro-credit and agricultural R&D experience with Farmer First is the chronic resistance in public sector agricultural science bureaucracies to learning from their own experience and to the use of evaluation and impact assessment as a learning process. A new initiative in the CGIAR, called Institutional Leaning and Change (ILAC) recognizes the impediment to change that this non-learning culture represents (see Watts and Horton, this book). In contrast, impact studies that fuelled debate over inclusion of the very poor in micro-credit have had a vigorous influence on the microfinance sector.

Over a decade of effort to stimulate learning about the impact of Farmer First approaches, especially in plant breeding, has not yet gained much traction in the CGIAR and this probably reflects a fifth, and critical weakness of the Farmer First experience in agricultural R&D: the virtual absence of relationships between policymakers and frontline professionals promoting Farmer First approaches to R&D in agriculture.

The importance of an enabling policy environment for going to scale with Farmer First approaches is widely recognized. With respect to relationships to policy and politicians, it is worth noting that, in Latin America, FPR has taken root vigorously in national innovation systems where political leaders have driven the national political system to be more responsive and even more accountable to the poor (e.g. Cuba, Bolivia).

Re-emergence or senility?

My argument that efforts to introduce the Farmer First paradigm in agricultural science bureaucracies were undermined by an overinvestment in reforming the supply side of innovation refers to these organizations' lack of accountability for satisfying demand for innovation from the poor. The science policy environment structured by development donors created incentives for organizational providers of agricultural R&D to give poor farmers voice without ceding any power to farmers to sanction the performance of R&D providers. FPR has performed differently where this policy environment has included farmers' organizations with the power to sanction R&D providers by withholding funds.

However, a focus on accountability still places the onus on reform of the supply side of innovation systems. Future pay-off to investment in Farmer First approaches in agricultural R&D will depend more on strengthening the demand side of innovation systems. This will involve improving poor farmers' capacity to exert demand over agricultural R&D providers via collective organization and must include an increase in political control by farmers' organizations over a significant portion of the funding for R&D to improve their power to sanction irrelevant R&D. Several initiatives based on this principle are being tried, for example in Mexico and Kenya.

Conclusion

The purpose of looking back on the past is neither to reproach ourselves with what might have been, nor to diminish many very real and significant achievements that have catalysed important change. When I recall that in the early 1980s, the international institute where I then worked had a belief that scientists should not conduct research off the experiment station and that, as a result, our initial forays into participatory plant breeding were conducted in semi-secret, I can affirm that we have come a long way. The point, however, is to draw some insights for how to do better in the future. This analysis has pointed to some potential new ways of thinking about how to approach Farmer First in FPR which stem from the power imbalance between supply and demand-side innovation system actors.

My conclusion from this reflection is that it is timely now to redress the balance towards the demand-side in Farmer First efforts in agricultural R&D. This means FPR must show how it can contribute to investment in strengthening the capacity of the poor to organize collectively and make demands on R&D through improved governance and control over budgetary mechanisms. It also means closer engagement for FPR with political processes of change that are already driving new kinds of alliances between businesses, farmers and consumers in the global food system. Ultimately this requires FPR to demonstrate its relevance to changing how much political power and influence these demand-side interest groups accrue in new kinds of global agricultural innovation systems.

PART II

Systems of innovation

Part II: Opening note

Part II explores systems of innovation – the ways science, technology, markets and institutions interact in agricultural research and development. Contributions build on the paper by Hall in Part I, offering a series of examples of how Farmer First approaches have been applied. The first section on Farmer Participatory Research and adaptive management explores several strands of experience which have been important in the last 20 years. The first is participatory plant breeding, where farmers are involved at all stages of varietal selection and testing. As highlighted in the opening paper by Rubyogo and Sperling, such approaches have been shown to be highly effective in a wide range of settings, including in emergency and post-conflict situations. Co-production of technologies involving farmers and scientists results in particular traits being emphasized and new breeding strategies evolving. The consequence is more rapid uptake and wider spread of new varieties suited to local needs. Witcombe and colleagues share experience from Nepal and India, while Ortiz and colleagues focus on experience in Bolivia, Peru, Ethiopia and Uganda. A point made by all papers is that it is not only the process of participatory field-level experimentation that is important, but the building of a wider seed system, involving seed saving, sharing of germplasm and so on, based on Farmer First principles. This requires investments in institutions and capacity that go beyond standard seed delivery systems, whether public or private.

This focus on the wider system of innovation, based on clear principles and practices, is a theme emphasized in the pair of papers by Uphoff and Shambu Prasad. These document the extraordinary spread of the System of Rice Intensification, from small tentative experiments in Madagascar across the globe. The innovation system is characterized by informal interactions, networks facilitated by the Internet, and a focus on techniques and practices, based on sound biological principles, rather than a particular technology. Shambu Prasad in particular emphasizes how dialogue between scientists, farmers and field practitioners has created a learning alliance, one that challenges conventional innovation systems in many fundamental ways.

An analysis of the wider institutional and policy landscape for innovation is taken up in the discussions of adaptive and co-management approaches by Prahbu and colleagues and Yan Zhao-Li. Such approaches have been highly influential in the natural resource management field with a focus on institutions for mobilizing effective collective action around common property resource use, whether forests, rangelands or fisheries. Important lessons have been learned about processes of participation beyond the farm – and the particular challenges of working with highly differentiated 'communities' making use of resources over which there are major contests. Such approaches have some important insights for the design of effective Farmer First-oriented innovation systems. In highly differentiated rural contexts, which farmers come first (rich, poor, men, women, young, old)? And what institutional mechanisms exist at the local level for defining priorities for innovation? Crane poses these questions with a case study from Mali. Advocating a political ecology perspective which takes social differentiation and the politics of resources seriously, he demonstrates how a common default in thinking about agricultural innovation is to exclude pastoralists from the picture. But if the concept of an agri-food 'system' is broadened and 'resources' and 'communities', together with the accepted notion of 'farming', are defined differently, then pastoralists' priorities must be included.

The second section of Part II moves beyond the farm to the wider market chain, and discusses engagement with markets and the private sector. A key emphasis of innovation system thinking is that it is often in these areas where new ideas and breakthroughs may occur. Certainly the last 20 years have seen a boom of activity around the analysis of commodity or value chains and a greater emphasis on market-based solutions, given the neo-liberal focus of much development policy. Part II highlights a range of Farmer First approaches which aim to develop our understanding of markets and to facilitate market engagement which benefits poorer farmers. Lightfoot and Nyimbo introduce the 'First Mile' project that aims to connect farmers to markets, while Kibue explores market chain development in Kenya. Both contributions suggest practical ways of achieving these aims, often making use of new information technologies to ensure that farmers gain the benefits of markets. A cluster of papers follow – from the Philippines (Campilan and colleagues, and Roa) and from east and southern Africa (Njuki and colleagues and Kaaria and colleagues) – which in different ways offer frameworks for market analysis, and ways of intervening to enable rural innovation. Positive results of such interventions are shown, as well as the challenges, including the capture of community or women's efforts by more powerful individuals and groups.

The final set of contributions in Part II focus on engagements with the private sector, and the challenges of making public–private partnerships (PPPs) ones that put farmers first. A substantial review of PPPs involving the CGIAR system is presented by Spielman and colleagues. This shows it is difficult to demonstrate whether partnerships are pro-poor or not; the emergence of exclusive licensing arrangements, benefiting the private sector players; a potential diversion of international public resources, staff, facilities and funds towards high-value commodities; the focus of most private sector activities, and unclear impacts of market segregation and focused subsidy on wider innovation systems. In addition, some interesting cases of PPPs are discussed in this section, including the long-term commitment by the Syngenta Foundation to supporting a government research station in Mali discussed by Témé and colleagues; new technology brokering organizations of the African Agricultural Technology Foundation (AATF) presented by Omanya and colleagues and the Global Alliance for Livestock Veterinary Medicines (GALVmed) presented by Peters; and the case of Monsanto's smallholder programme in India reviewed by Glover.

In sum, understanding systems of innovation in complex, diverse rural settings is not straightforward. Moving from a field-level experimentation approach, through landscape (co-)management to questions of market chains and wider policy, innovation systems inevitably involve multiple actors, many with competing views. There are multiple sources of innovation – from farmers, scientists, field practitioners and alliances between them – some clear and obvious, but many more hidden. Some innovations are about new technologies (breeds, varieties, machinery etc.), others are about practices (ways of caring for plants and soil), while others are about processes (linking elements of market chains). All are important. Yet, defining an innovation system, and in particular its future trajectory, is as much a political as an analytical act, and one that clearly needs more than just a mechanistic assessment, requiring analyses of social and political differentiation alongside a mapping of market chains and technology options.

Developing seed systems in Africa

Jean Claude Rubyogo and Louise Sperling

Introduction

Seeds are basic agricultural input, and good quality seeds of preferred varieties are critical to farmers' capacity to improve agricultural productivity. Local landraces alone are not the solution to the multiple constraints faced by farmers, and improved and formally bred varieties can contribute to meeting some of those challenges. However, the accessibility and availability of seed is determined by many factors including the crop breeding systems, institutional/organizational arrangements and socio-economic conditions of farmers.

In Africa, the majority of farmers get their seeds from informal channels which include farm-saved seeds, seed exchanges among farmers and/or local grain/seed markets. These channels contribute about 90–100 per cent of seed supply depending on the crop (Maredia et al., 1999). Despite the importance of this system, it rarely receives formal support. But once linked to sources of improved varieties, the informal seed sector can be a reliable and efficient way to access improved varieties of crops, especially those which attract only limited interest from the commercial seed sector.

Using the successful results of enhancing informal seed systems for beans in Africa, this paper shares the experiences of a partnership between farmers, National Agricultural Research Systems (NARS) and the international research system (through the International Center for Tropical Agricultural – CIAT) under the umbrella of the Pan Africa Bean Research Alliance (PABRA).

A brief history of seed production

From the 1970s, African governments and donors recognized the importance of quality seeds and all efforts went to the establishment of a highly subsidized formal seed sector, organized mainly around seed parastatals (Lyon and Afikorah-Danquah, 1998; Zerbe, 2001). However, successes were limited due to issues of financial sustainability and the lack of small-scale farmers' involvement in both variety development and seed supply chains. In the 1980s, there was a policy shift to disbanding the parastatal and encouraging private sector development. However, profit-driven commercial seed companies focused mainly on hybrid maize and high-value vegetables, targeting high potential areas (Zerbe, 2001; Jones et al., 2001; Daniel and Adetumbi, 2004). As a result, seeds of grain legumes, like beans, or other minor crops, such as sorghum and vegetatively propagated crops, were rarely supplied by this sector, unless through relief/bulk purchases by development and relief operations. During the 1990s, NGOs and rural development/relief agencies became interested in the seed sector and supported community-based seed production and supply (Seboka and Deressa, 2000). The aim was to transform local community seed producers into producers of high-quality seeds (Tripp and Rohrbach, 2001). The approach was very successful in improving access to seeds in remote areas and to poorer farmers (Maredia et al., 1999; Seboka and Deressa, 2000).

In the 2000s, there has been a renewed effort to improve seed access, with a focus on supporting the private sector (small and medium agro-dealers), and also on establishing seed business friendly regulations, such as harmonized seed regulations across sub-regional organizations (Rohrbach et al., 2004). Despite these efforts, companies continue to focus on more profitable crops/ varieties, rather than the wide range of crop species which constitute the backbone of resource-poor farmers' food security (Tripp, 2003; Rubyogo et al., 2007). For instance, commercial (certified) bean seed costs two to four times what farmers would pay for seed in local markets – and yield gains do not compensate (Sperling, 1992). Publicly supported commercial seed enterprises have generally not provided options attractive for poor farmers. New avenues are needed, therefore, to provide seeds of improved varieties that respond to the choices and demands of poorer farmers.

Linking farmers to seed systems: assuring seed security

At the household and farm level, seed security is defined as the state in which a farmer has access to sufficient quantities of seeds of their preferred varieties with adequate physical quality, at the right time of planting (Sperling and Cooper, 2003). Most small-scale farmers rely on local seed-saving systems to renew their seed supply. Nevertheless they are always interested in testing and acquiring new crop varieties to respond to ever-changing agroecosystems and increasingly differentiated markets (David and Sperling, 1999; Almekinders et al., 2007; Rubyogo et al., 2007).

Using the case of beans – a low-value crop critical to food security – we outline eight requirements for an efficient seed system for the poor:

1. Set bean research and development priorities with farmers and other stakeholders.
2. Engage farmers and traders in varietal testing.

3. Regularly make foundation seeds of preferred varieties available to both formal and local seed producers.
4. Engage farmers, farmers' organizations, extension services and development organizations in the intervention to gather information and raise awareness about promising genotypes and stimulate demand for effective scaling up.
5. Develop partnerships to share various seed-related activities with other service providers including traders and development partners.
6. Encourage complementarity between the formal and informal seed sector and promote horizontal (farmer-to-farmer) sharing of seed.
7. Ensure production of sufficient quantity to meet demand and increase local stocks of varieties by engaging in yield enhancing technologies as well as non-seed technologies (agronomic practices).
8. In local decentralized seed systems, recognize grain/seed merchants as key stakeholders in seed dissemination and encourage linkages to seed producers.

The following sections outline some of the experiences from east, central and southern Africa.

Engaging farmers in participatory variety selection

As a result of long-term interactions between CIAT and NARS in the region, bean scientists have been developing varieties with end users. Elements of this strategy include: decentralizing selection to target zones (different agroecologies), selecting genotypes under conditions of real farmer input, bringing farmers (men and women, of different wealth levels) into the selection process at an early stage, and giving farmers real choice based on their agroecologies and bean uses. This has resulted in an impressive number of highly appreciated varieties being released and used. Once farmers identify the bean genotypes they prefer, they are named based on their characteristics and/or their uses. In Ethiopia, for example, between 2003 and 2007, 60 varieties were released and used by farmers with names as evocative as *ibbado* (delicious as fresh milk) and *bussuke* (plump and meaty as a well-fed calf), and activities aimed at seed multiplication and dissemination were initiated.

Participatory assessment and testing of different seed systems

Since farmers acquire seeds from different sources, it is very important to develop an inventory of the existing seed systems and assess the efficiency of each, according to different criteria. For instance, the assessment of seed systems carried out by farmers in East Africa is summarized in Table 2.1.

In all the assessment sites, farmers identified decentralized seed systems as the most appropriate way to access improved bean varieties. Such systems

Table 2.1 Comparing decentralized (local) and commercial seed systems in East Africa

Criteria	Local/decentralized systems	Commercial systems
Bean genetic diversity	Supply several genotypes	Fewer, already popular and widespread varieties
Agro-ecological suitability	Adapted to micro-ecology, e.g. intercropping	Wider adaptation
Means of procuring/ accessing seeds	Horizontal diffusion: through seed gifts, seed exchanges, grains for labour, cash	Only cash with prices often higher than local seed price
Access to information about new varieties/techniques	Horizontal information exchanges: neighbouring farmers, demonstration plots, field days, social networks	Very minimal promotion by seed stockists or agents
Types of clients	Farmers based on their interests and needs (varieties, quality and quantity)	Non-government and government organizations (seed aids)
Shaping research agenda	Immediate feedback to scientists, e.g. identification of farmers' selection criteria	Late and interested in already popular varieties
Accessing new genotypes	Interested and possibility to accelerate access to preferred genotypes	More of 'wait and see' attitude
Building partners' (farmers, extension agents) capacity	Strengthening farmers' skills and organizational development, e.g. experimentation/seed systems	Only seed stockists and other formal suppliers
Amount of seed supplied	About 98%	2%

Source: Rubyogo et al. (2007)

entail the production of seeds by local seed producers (mainly women in the case of beans) with a reputation for supplying the local community either directly or through the local market. Dissemination is carried out from farmer-to-farmer or through local traders. In addition to supplying seeds of new varieties, these farmers are also an important source of skills and knowledge about the adaptation and management of varieties. But local, decentralized systems also have shortcomings. These include inadequate linkages to sources of improved bean varieties such as the NARS, inadequate quantity and quality of seeds, and the slow spread of new varieties and information about them to surrounding farmers and beyond.

Integrating formal and informal seed systems

As a few of the varieties promoted through informal networks gained popularity over a period of 5–10 years, a few seed companies became interested in their production and supply for sale through stockists and for relief seed operations.

For instance in Uganda, where three medium-size seed companies operate, their supply is limited to 2 of the 16 varieties released by the national programme. Total seed supply is about 5 per cent of national seed requirement (Nasirumbi et al., 2008), with 20 per cent supplied through village agro-dealers and 80 per cent through relief organizations. Due to the high costs of producing seeds on a large scale, seed companies often contract small-scale seed producers supported by NGOs, government organizations and farmers' organizations. This approach is increasingly taking place in many bean-producing countries such as Ethiopia, Malawi, Kenya and Uganda.

Building local capacity

But such new systems don't just happen. They need investments in training and capacity building in, for example, basic bean agronomy, pest and disease control, seed post-harvest handling, seed/grain marketing and organizational development and technology promotion. For instance, from 2004 the NARS in Ethiopia trained 150 development agents from districts and partner organizations and leaders of farmers' cooperative unions. By the end of 2006, these trainers had trained about 10,500 farmers. This had a tremendous impact on the spread and use of improved technologies especially for white pea beans (Rubyogo et al., 2007).

One of the weaknesses of farmer-to-farmer seed supply systems is the slow movement of varieties. To address this issue, multiple forms of promotion were used. These include very decentralized demonstrations in selected farm sites, organization of field days from national to farmer group level, regular radio and/or TV clips, exchange visits and study tours.

Generating impacts

From 2002–5, an integrated seed system approach led to a dramatic improvement in seed accessibility in Uganda. With each farmer who received seeds passing a certain amount to on average four of his/her neighbours, in less than three years improved varieties had reached about 50,000 farmers in three districts, amounting to a quarter of bean seeds produced (Nasirumbi et al., 2008). In Rwanda, where the seed sector is predominantly farmer based, improved bean varieties have been disseminated through the whole country. For instance, the climbing beans which covered less than 10 per cent of bean growing areas before the early 1980s spread to cover about 40 per cent of the bean areas in the early 2000s (Felicitee Nsanzabera, personal communication). In Ethiopia, where varieties released as early as 1996 were not in the hands of farmers, the introduction of an integrated approach in 2004 accelerated the spread and use of new varieties so that they now constitute about 30 per cent of the beans traded (Rubyogo et al., 2007).

Conclusion

In order to ensure that quality seeds of preferred varieties are accessible to resource poor farmers, a systematic pathway combining a set of activities starting from the identification of preferred genotypes to variety demand stimulation and seed accessibility must be established. Imposing a generic formal seed or private sector seed system may not be the only solution, and a more integrated system, improving on the best of informal, decentralized, farmer-led approaches, is needed.

Client-oriented breeding and seed supply

John Witcombe, Krishna Devkota, Daljit Virk,
Krishna Rawal, Satish Prasad, Vikas Kumar and
Krishna Joshi

Introduction

In three countries in South Asia we have, over more than a decade, derived more participatory and innovative methods called client-oriented breeding (COB) – a term that describes better than participatory plant breeding (PPB) the reason why farmers participate (Witcombe et al., 2005). An integral component of COB is the use of participatory varietal selection (PVS) where farmers test the varieties produced in the COB programme in their own fields. These techniques produce and deliver varieties more rapidly than conventional breeding and better client orientation ensures they have traits that farmers like. Benefits include improved yield, improved quality, reduced costs and earlier harvests. We have done this in regions where conventional breeding has either not delivered varieties that farmers have adopted to any great extent – for example, in the drought-prone rice uplands of India, or where the results of conventional breeding have taken decades to be adopted – for example in more productive areas of Nepal and Bangladesh, where some of the varieties still in use were bred more than fifty years ago.

In this region the commercial supply of seed to farmers – by the private and public sectors – accounts for as little as 2 per cent of the seed that is sown. The rest comes from farm-saved seeds (Tripp, 1997) or from grain purchased in local markets (Frazen et al., 1996). Many development projects have attempted to introduce local seed supply systems that depend on action by local communities – such as seed banks – but these are rarely sustainable or effective (cf. Tripp, 1997). We discuss here two examples of attempting to provide a sustainable seed supply in rice in two contrasting innovation systems: the uplands of India and the more productive regions of Nepal.

Building a drought resilient seed system: the case of India

There have been decades of conventional breeding for upland rice in India, but farmers continue to prefer the local landraces (Virk and Witcombe, 2007). But new varieties bred using participatory, client-oriented methods are liked by farmers and adopted by them. For example, COB-produced varieties, Ashoka 200F and Ashoka 228, have been widely adopted only a few years after their first introduction. In Jharkhand, the local landrace Gora was most quickly replaced, and the only variety grown in 2001 that was still grown to any extent in 2004 was Kalinga III. In Orissa, the diversity of landraces was greater, but the most popular, Asu (also called Tusku), declined from 36 to 5 per cent of the area, and by 2004 the two new COB varieties occupied 80 per cent of the area. These high adoption levels were because many farmers decided to adopt them on all of their rice uplands (Virk and Witcombe, 2007). The Ashoka varieties are qualitatively different to older varieties in their acceptability due to a combination of high yield, drought tolerance and superior grain quality.

Given this superiority, perhaps informal farmer-to-farmer networks would spread the varieties in the farmers' rice innovation system. But there are limits to this. In drought years the area under upland rice can fall dramatically, so farm-saved seed of the Ashoka varieties is simply not planted, and in other cases where it is planted it may fail. The Ashoka varieties are also victims of their own positive attributes as they are the first varieties to be harvested and may be eaten and sold before the later harvest of local landraces. Hence, in the absence of an external seed supply, drought years slow down the rate of adoption and it may take several years before seed supply recovers.

For new varieties to have an impact in a practicable time frame there has therefore to be a substantial input of externally supplied seed, preferably through commercial channels to ensure long-term sustainability. However, where markets are not effective, NGOs have been important sources of seed supply on a subsidized project basis. For example, in eastern India commercial suppliers are few, and those that are active are interested in the production of hybrid seed or seed of transplanted varieties. As a business, the production and sale of upland rice seed cannot compete with that of higher-yielding transplanted varieties. For a profitable business rice seed needs to be multiplied in irrigated fields in the dry season as this minimizes the storage time between harvest and sales for sowing in the rainy season. Unfortunately, no upland variety can yield as much as transplanted varieties under irrigated conditions and the yield gap is substantial.

Why should farmers then produce seed of lower-yielding upland varieties when the market for transplanted rice seed is far from saturated? An alternative to irrigated production is to purchase seed from upland farmers at the end of the rainy season since upland farmers have no option but to grow upland varieties. However, unlike the case for irrigated production there is an inbuilt loss of 7 per cent in moisture when the grain is purchased at the end of the rainy season and stored during the dry season. This loss in moisture results in an equivalent reduction in seed sales since seed is sold by weight and not volume.

Thus external seed supply cannot be relied upon and farmers must be empowered to maintain seed of these critical varieties through drought periods. This can emerge through giving advice on simple techniques for maintaining genetic purity and reducing risk of seed loss by growing small plots specifically for seed in less drought-prone fields (e.g. in medium land with deeper soils). We are attempting to do this in villages where all households are provided with seed to ensure a more secure farmer-to-farmer network for those farmers that fail to produce sufficient seed.

Addressing information gaps: the case of Nepal

In Nepal the varieties that we have produced by COB are for more favourable rainfed conditions (Joshi et al., 2002). There is no inherent lack of profitability in producing seed of these varieties intended for the low-altitude area bordering India (the Terai), but there was a poorly developed commercial sector. We quickly realized that if there was to be seed supply on anything approaching adequate levels we had to encourage groups to produce seed. We did so by working with farmer groups that had already been established by the District Agricultural Development Offices (DADOs) for other purposes such as dairy production. When we started to facilitate seed producer groups there was only one established group in Chitwan (the *Bij Bridhi Krishak Samuha Phituwa* in eastern Chitwan). Since 2000, three new groups *(Unnat, Shree Ram* and *Dev Ujjal)* have been established in Chitwan and the increase in total seed produced and sold is remarkable, rising from 3 tonnes in 2002–3 to 521 tonnes in 2006–7.

However, we had less success in achieving the production of seed of varieties from our PVS and COB programmes. Around 80 per cent of the seed produced by the groups was of very old released varieties, and half the COB varieties produced were purchased by development programmes. By 2007, only 1 per cent of the total production was of COB varieties produced by the groups independently of development agency orders. However, since overall production had increased dramatically the absolute amounts sold were significant: in 2006-7 this amounted to 119 t of seed of which 92 t was seed of PVS varieties and 27 t was seed of COB varieties.

Why this situation had arisen was not difficult to understand. The seed producer groups were responding to demands from local Agrovet-dealers who, in turn, were responding to the demands of their client farmers. Since the farmers were unaware of the new varieties they did not demand them. We were thus in the unfortunate situation that demand would not increase unless farmers could try the seed and seed would not be produced unless there was demand. We have started to turn this vicious circle into a virtuous one.

In any innovation network there can be unmet demand as there is insufficient flow of information between producers and potential purchasers. To overcome this, we have passed demand for seed of new varieties to the seed producer groups even when we knew that they had no seed available. For instance, on receiving a demand by a development organization for 10 t of Barkhe 3004, we asked *Unnat,* one of the producer groups, for seed. Although this could not result in an immediate supply it gave them the confidence to include Barkhe 3004 for seed production in their future plans. We are also holding stakeholder meetings of seed producer groups, Agrovets, farmer groups, DADO extensionists, rice millers, traders and other NGOs – all of the major players in the rice innovation system – to explain the growing characteristics and qualities of the new varieties to stimulate demand and increase knowledge of the new varieties. Whether this will significantly increase the rate of uptake of new varieties is yet to be seen.

There are many factors in the rice innovation system that influence the rates of adoption and adoption decisions. Within a few kilometres of each other, on either side of the border between Nepal and India, farmers get their seed from very different sources (Figure 2.1). In the case of Nepal, little seed is obtained from markets or agencies, so the flow of information will be vital in promoting the uptake of seed from COB programmes.

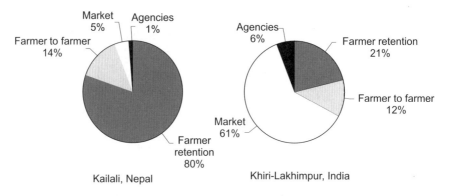

Figure 2.1 A comparison of source of rice seed in study villages in Kailali, Nepal and Lakhimpur Khiri, India (2006)

Conclusions

COB can more rapidly produce new varieties that stand a better chance of being used by farmers as they have desirable traits. Although seed can spread quite rapidly from farmer to farmer, for most varieties unless large-scale seed supply is implemented the adoption process will be slow. The most sustainable way to supply large quantities of seed is by commercial seed production, but in less productive environments this may be difficult to achieve. Attempts in India to initiate commercially based seed production of upland rice varieties from COB have, so far, not been successful. For lower yielding crops, such as upland rice, that have to occupy the same land as seed production plots of higher yielding varieties, perhaps the only long-term solution is some form of subsidy. In more favourable environments, such as the Nepal Terai, it was possible to catalyse seed producer groups to produce substantial quantities of seed. However, invariably information about new varieties is poorly disseminated and this results in a lack of demand. If nascent seed industries are to serve the needs of farmers they should provide seed of recent, not obsolete, varieties. Hence, in this work as much attention has to be paid to information supply as to seed supply. Inevitably, whatever system of large-scale seed production is employed, there are many other social and economic factors that will influence the rate of adoption of new varieties in highly variable innovation systems.

Learning from experience: potato innovation systems and participatory research

Oscar Ortiz, Ricardo Orrego, Willy Pradel, Peter Gildemacher, Renee Castillo, Ronal Otiniano, Julio Gabriel, Juan Vallejo, Omar Torres, Gebremehdin Woldegiorgis, Belew Damene, Rogers Kakuhenzire, Imelda Kashaija and Ignatius Kahiu

Introduction

This paper summarizes the findings of a research project, which aimed to characterize the potato innovation systems in Bolivia, Ethiopia, Peru and Uganda and identify the factors that influence scaling up and out of participatory approaches. It involved case studies including the monitoring and evaluation of 256 participatory trials conducted using farmer field schools, farmer research groups and participatory plant breeding and seed multiplications plots. Monitoring included data collection from trials, focusing on agronomic results, costs and farmer opinions. In addition, between 2004 and 2007, interviews were conducted with farmers, facilitators and institutional representatives in each country combined with participatory workshops, focus groups and participatory observation.

Potato innovation systems: a growing complexity

Table 2.2 shows a comparative analysis of the main characteristics of the potato innovation systems at the pilot sites in the four countries, derived from 10 stakeholder workshops at each site.

Across the country cases, despite variations in the roles of government, private sector and other organizations, farmers remain the central, most important and relatively stable component of the potato-related innovation system. However, the limited interactions between farmers and other stakeholders prevent an efficient development of solutions to potato-related problems. An alternative to enhance these interactions is participatory research (PR). Evidence from focus groups and questionnaires with 125 farmers in Peru and Bolivia gave insight into the factors that farmers take into consideration when making decisions to be involved in PR.

About 63 per cent of farmers highlighted the importance of participatory research for enhancing knowledge and skills for solving the main potato-related problems. However, if accessing information and knowledge is a strong motivation then PR efforts may need to be complemented by other dissemination methods to achieve larger coverage, because the study indicated that most of the information and knowledge farmers manage came from internal sources such as family members and neighbours, with limited participation of extension providers. Therefore, stimulation of linkages between trained farmers and non-trained farmers outside of their own community could improve information flow, knowledge development and technology adoption. Around a quarter of farmers indicated that they were interested in engaging with PR approaches for accessing and evaluating new technologies. Farmers more easily perceived potential benefits of input-based technologies (i.e. new potato varieties or sources of fertilizer) than benefits of

Table 2.2 Potato innovation systems compared

Main features	Ethiopia	Uganda	Bolivia	Peru
Number of components	14	22	31	30
Intensity of interactions	Limited	Limited	Limited	Limited
Role of farmer organizations	Limited	Increasing	Major	Limited
Role of national government	Major	Substantial	Very limited	Limited
Role of local government	Limited	Increasing	Increasing	Increasing
Role of the private sector	Very limited	Very limited	Major	Major
Role of media	Limited	Limited	Limited	Very limited
Main sources of potato-related information	Farmers	Farmers	Farmers	Farmers
Receptiveness of the system to participatory research	Limited	Increasing	Increasing	Limited
Whole innovation system	Less complex and stable	Growing in complexity	Complex and dynamic	Complex and dynamic

knowledge-intensive technologies (integrated pest or disease control). Another attraction of PR for farmers was its contribution to strengthening their own organizations.

Farmers mentioned the time factor as a potential limitation for their involvement in PR. Warnaars and Pradel (2007) showed that time has higher opportunity cost for urban and peri-urban farmers. But rural farmers also have to make decisions about how to allocate time for different on- and off-farm activities with external organizations. This means that there is competition between institutions for farmers' time. PR activities compete with other activities within an innovation system that is growing in complexity of both information and service providers and must generate sufficient benefits to attract attention.

Facilitating and institutionalizing participatory research

There are several factors that limit the institutionalization of PR. Having sufficient logistical support was cited as a critical factor because facilitators need transport, timely access to research and training inputs, and allowances, which need to be provided by their institutions. Local or national government institutions do not usually provide sufficient logistic support to their staff because of limited financial resources. The NGO sector generally has fewer funding constraints and a more flexible administrative system, facilitating the provision of logistic support to their staff.

Participatory methods usually require extension workers, facilitators and researchers to spend additional time on planning and conducting the sessions and experiments. More frequent field visits than necessary for normal extension activities or conventional on-farm research also have greater cost implications. Field staff of the four institutions involved in the project all perceived participatory activities as an additional responsibility.

Instability of staff within institutions is a permanent concern for practitioners. In most cases, staff were working under short-term contracts, which did not ensure sustainability of activities or motivate staff interest in PR as a full-time activity. Research-oriented institutions and NGOs tend to work with projects that last about three years. In government institutions, such as local municipalities, however, changes in administration, policies, procedures and funding tend to occur after each election, which does not ensure continuity of PR activities.

For institutions, one key factor for adopting a PR methodology is the cost involved in its implementation. However, there is little published about costs of PR methods that could be used for institutional decision making. Institutions participating in the project during three years monitored the cost per group of farmers and per individual. This exercise had two objectives namely, providing institutions with the opportunity to monitor and understand real costs so that they could make decisions for future scaling out, and generating evidence that could be used by other institutions for decision making. The monitoring process included the operational costs of implementing the participatory trials, conducting training associated with PR, monitoring and supervision and the personnel costs for facilitation. The total costs of the method were divided into those incurred by the institution and those incurred by the farmer group (i.e. land preparation, labour for managing the crop and some locally available inputs).

The average costs of running one farmer group with 15 to 30 participants varied according to the location and the participatory method. In general, the cost ranged from US$450 to $800 in the different cases, comprising the farmer contribution ($87 to $373 per group) and the institutional contribution ($248 to $667 per group). The average costs of $658 estimated in this study are slightly higher than the average costs of local Agricultural Research Committees ($325 to $486) and Farmer Field Schools ($532 to $586) reported by Braun et al. (2000). An important determinant of the cost is the cost of personnel for running and monitoring the groups (which tends to decrease as staff gain experience), including the level of salaries and per diems paid and the number of PR groups that one staff member can handle. The type of technology also influences the cost: for instance, working on soil fertility using organic sources tends to be more expensive (because of additional input and labour) than evaluating new potato clones or varieties. In terms of cost per farmer, costs in Peru varied from $18 to $90 according to the number of participants per group. These are in the range of FFS costs as reported by Quizon et al. (2001) for the Philippines ($48) and Indonesia ($62).

Institutional representatives highlighted the need to invest in human resources development to ensure that facilitators have sufficient methodological and technical capacities and skill to properly manage the field activities and training sessions involved in PR. In some cases, individuals used the methods instrumentally without enough understanding of PR principles, thus affecting the quality of the method and the results. In all countries, a critical constraint in the scaling up and out of participatory methods, and the technologies derived from them, is the lack of a well-organized training system for interested institutions. In addition, one-off training may not be enough for developing the required capabilities.

Formal research and extension institutions also take into consideration the reliability of information generated by the participatory experience. An analysis of 256 participatory trials conducted in four countries during three years found a relatively high rate of success, with 98 per cent of trials conducted with farmers until harvest and 94 per cent generating results that were useful for the different stakeholders. Farmers analysed the results with the aim of making decisions about using the technologies in their own fields while facilitators and researchers carried out formal statistical analyses.

Analysing a sub-set of participatory trials from Peru (N=48), results indicate that 73 per cent of them were useful for farmers' decision-making, meaning that the results were clear enough for farmers to learn and decide to continue testing or implementing in their own fields. In 58 per cent of the cases farmers' preferences coincided with the optimal treatments according to the statistical analysis. Only in 35 per cent of cases, however, was there a coincidence between farmers' choices and the optimal treatment according to the economic analysis. These results confirm that farmers judge technologies using a diverse set of criteria, which include cultural considerations and perceptions of value beyond productivity and profitability. The fact that farmer and organizational choices may not coincide highlights the need for a combined (participatory, statistical and economic) analysis of the results and negotiation of conclusions, as well as the inclusion of opinions of other stakeholders, to increase the likelihood of providing recommendations that are useful for both local and more general circumstances.

Organizational learning: challenges of scaling up and scaling out

Participatory research experiences are part of a complex and continuously evolving innovation system with multiple stakeholders, which vary across sites and countries. A wide range of institutions (government, NGO and private) are engaged in different types of PR, but often only on short-term time frames and with fragile funding bases. Sharing experiences and results tends to be limited, and efforts are not part of mainstream activities. Among the organizations that participated in the project, inter-institutional interactions are perceived as an important mechanism for accessing information, knowledge, technologies and methodologies. Interactions related to training are limited, however. Lundy et al. (2005) and Ortiz et al. (2008) indicate that it has taken about 12 years for the International Potato Center and CARE-Peru to learn how to extract lessons from their own PR experience and how to share those lessons with other organizations. The need for long-term relationships has also been recognized by Lundy et al. (2005). Learning how to learn is not an easy task for organizations, but PR can become a mechanism for organizations to learn from each other, which supports the innovation process. However, such long-term relationships are not common features in the innovation systems analysed in the project. Embedding PR activities in wider innovation systems across organizations remains a major challenge for the future across the four countries.

Action research with local forest users and managers: lessons from CIFOR's research on adaptive collaborative management

Ravi Prabhu, Carol Colfer, Chimere Diaw, Cynthia McDougall and Robert Fisher

Introduction

In late 1998 the Center for International Forestry Research (CIFOR) began researching a 'learning and collaboration' based approach to forest management that was called, quite appropriately, adaptive collaborative management (ACM). Departing from all previous research approaches at CIFOR, the research team resolved to carry out the research in an action research mode, to ensure that whatever resulted from the research was truly going to be useful to the people who were using and managing the forests.

The ACM research aimed to understand whether it was possible to develop a more flexible, equitable and effective governance based on collaboration (including conflict management), collective action and social learning among various forest actors. The research tried to understand whether such an approach was possible, under what conditions and with what strategies, and what its effects were on people, institutions and forest systems.

We used a variety of methods and approaches to carry out the ACM research. In the main our work was based on the use of participatory action research (PAR). As we use the term, PAR is a process through which members of a group or community identify a problem, collect and analyse information, and act upon the problem in order to find solutions and promote social and political transformation (Selener, 1997). In our case the group of people was a combination of local people and researchers. Action research is usually conceived of in terms of repeated cycles of reflection, action and observation (Kemmis and McTaggart, 1988). In all sites PAR was designed to generate lessons about the process and outcomes of local level decision-making and planning using an adaptive and collaborative management approach.

Lessons and insights

While there were commonalities across the cases, the communities were also very different from one another in terms of histories, subsistence, economic and cultural relationships to the forests. We focus here on three examples to illustrate the influence of devolution context, empowerment status and scale on the impacts of our action research.

Nepal: devolution of decision making

In a context where community forestry had an established institutional framework, with effective devolution to community forest user groups (CFUGs), the PAR focused on aspects of decision making and equity within four CFUGs. In each community, differences in power existed between higher and lower castes, women and men, and according to wealth, and the CFUGs were dominated by 'elites'. The focus of the PAR was to enhance the effectiveness and equity of CFUG planning processes and practices as a means of improving the social, livelihood and environmental outcomes of community forestry. Specifically, we tried to shift away from a central committee based and relatively linear, *ad hoc* management process to a more inclusive approach based on increased reflection and collective deliberation. There was no single model for these innovations – the facilitators simply tried to catalyse and support cycles of planning, action, learning and innovation that were rooted in increased adaptiveness and collaboration, with an emphasis on self-monitoring and joint reflections.

As a result of the PAR the CFUGs ultimately devolved significant amounts of management decision making to *tole* (hamlet) committees. *Toles* became the 'homes' for the first step in the self-monitoring process as well as the platform for generating input into committee and assembly meetings. Self-monitoring became a core of the CFUG planning processes and was very effectively applied to governance issues as well as management outcomes. At two sites, an 'equity assessment process' was developed to track and assess who in the user group was participating in and benefiting from community activities. Critical to its success was the fact that the wealth ranking and on-going assessment was transparent and accessible to all. This process contributed to CFUGs' ability to observe the degree to which decisions and actions, such as benefit distribution, matched their stated objectives regarding equity. Furthermore, in some cases it was used as leverage by marginalized forest users to hold the committee accountable to commitments regarding equity.

Zimbabwe: empowering user groups

The villages around the Mafungautsi State Forest – some of them populated by people forcibly evicted from within the forest – have been organized into 15 Resource Management Committees (RMCs) responsible for licensing the harvesting or management of a range of non-timber forest products. When the ACM research commenced, the relationship between local people and the Forestry Commission (FC) was antagonistic and fraught with suspicion. The RMCs reflected these tensions and were barely functional. At the same time the FC's power had been eroded as a result of economic decline as well as by a deliberate attempt to foster a 'joint forest management' model.

Early attempts at bringing people together within the institutional framework of the RMC failed, due, variously, to their passiveness, a suspicion that the ACM team was working on behalf of the FC, a lack of faith in the RMC as an institution, and gender roles and power deficits among local groups with respect to decision making and collective action.

Training for transformation proved to be a turning point, making it possible to bring groups of people from the villages around the forest together for a series of visioning and action planning meetings. What emerged were natural sub-groupings according to the nature of the resource people were interested in or engaged in harvesting (legally or illegally). Bee-keeping and timber harvesting tended to interest only men, thatch grass harvesting cut across gender lines, whereas broom grass harvesting was of particular interest to women. Through the action research process these natural groupings evolved into informal user groups. Social organization around particular resources emerged as the dominant strategy for re-empowerment. This process of organization was observed and later actively supported by FC staff based in the area, after it became clear that the user groups were willing to play an active role in managing their chosen resources. As a result antagonism and tensions declined and first steps towards genuine partnership were taken, with two-way flows of information and active facilitation of user group initiatives by the FC.

A good example of this is the broom grass user group, which was faced with a resource harvesting dilemma: whether to dig up or uproot the broom grass (considered unsustainable, but more readily marketable) or harvest it with a scythe (sustainable, but poor market prices). They used an action learning approach that involved meetings, visioning, field experiments, collective action and even computer modelling (see Vanclay et al., 2006) to resolve this issue. One outcome was that the group engaged with the RMC and the FC to ensure that by-laws making digging an offence were enforced and requested the FC to liaise with the rural district council to outlaw the sale of 'uprooted' broom grass at the local market. To improve their incomes, the group decided to exert more influence on the process of determining permit prices, by improving the quality of products, through better processing and a grading system and agreeing on a minimum price for their products.

Cameroon: stumbling over power differentials

The Campo Ma'an ACM research site in Cameroon centres on a 770,000 ha national park, established in 1995 with no consultation with the 120 or so multi-ethnic villages in and around the park. The park was managed by the Campo Ma'an Project, which comprised the Ministry of Environment and Forest, responsible for 'conservation' through its forest police (eco-guards), and two Dutch NGOs: *Stichting Nederlandse Vrijwilligers* (SNV), which carried out 'eco-development', and Tropenbos, responsible for park management and bio-physical research. By restricting village territories to 5 km into the forest from their roadside location, and limiting communities' use of the area for hunting, shifting cultivation and forest products exploitation, the project had engendered enormous resentment.

In 2000, the ACM research team began by investigating the means by which to bring all the parties to the negotiation table. Using scenarios, visioning and interactive games as methods for building consensus and for introducing a vision of resource management as a dynamic and learning process, a process of dialogue was initiated. This was a process of bringing to the surface the different mental models and visions of the forest. It was also the entry point for action research with communities, local NGOs and some of the park's staff.

Two years on, it was clear that the more people gained an understanding of their situation and of the evolution of the resources surrounding them, the more they became open to discussions on conservation. During an effort to develop an interactive management plan in collaboration with the park manager and a dozen communities living in and around the park, communities started developing scenarios of community development in the context of a conservation project. They listed their grievances but, for the first time, also identified opportunities related to the presence of the National Park. This was expressed through an 'offer of collaboration' detailing areas where local people felt they had positive conservation contributions to make. Local forest department officials also increasingly saw collaboration as important for the achievement of their own goals.

Despite these positive outcomes, lingering mistrust and mutual rejection, combined with extreme power differences between park managers and local people, provided insufficient incentive for collective action and compromise. The resulting stalemate led to a complete overhaul of the park management, with new institutional actors coming in to replace the Campo Ma'an project.

Outcomes of action research on ACM

The ACM approach tended to increase human capital in all sites, as it emphasized on-going learning and capacity building through a variety of means. This included the development of facilitation skills and leadership, as well as skills in participatory decision-making and planning processes, record keeping, and in some cases, funding-proposal writing. There has been an improvement in skills and knowledge related to communication and negotiation, conflict management and leadership, as well as policies, development of joint action plans, and technical aspects such as developing nurseries. Researchers also noted the increased self-confidence of many forest users, including marginalized ones, in dealing with outside groups.

Ultimately shared – or social – learning by community forestry stakeholders was the engine of the action research in the ACM approach. In most cases, this learning was facilitated with the intention of its being social and transformative, and thus the engine for addressing conflicts and stagnation in governance or management. The second essential element of the approach that all cases focused on was collaboration. In most cases a primary aspect of the collaboration was 'learning together'. The range of actors brought together was different in all cases, but always involved diverse perspectives, and for the most part, on-going tensions. Collaboration was also emphasized in the sense of encouraging communities to more actively explore the potential for collaborative action with other stakeholders (although this did not rule out resisting or challenging other stakeholders as appropriate).

In facilitating learning and collaboration, one lesson taken on early by all teams is that facilitation of action research processes is not neutral. In the Nepal cases, for example, the facilitators were consciously working constantly to create space – and power – for low caste people in a system that traditionally excludes and marginalizes them.

Clearly countries that had formally recognized community forestry and have administrative and extension structures that are designed to support (and regulate) community forestry found it easier to facilitate the emergence of ACM at new sites. This was not without problems however, as the flexibility that ACM demands is often felt to be inconsistent with the nature of government bureaucracies that are charged with supporting community forestry. However, what was more important was whether the communities themselves were in a position to understand the demands of ACM and exert pressure on extension services to support these efforts. Where both conditions were met, progress was good – this was the case at a few sites, such as in Nepal, the Philippines and Bolivia.

It is clear from the ACM research that processes of empowerment, social organization and collective action are key to successful action research. Where power differentials were not too great it was possible to make quicker gains in terms of human, social and institutional capital. This was more pronounced at sites where devolution and governance favoured rights of local people over forest resources. However ACM's action research approach achieved significantly less in the short run in cases where the power differential was too great. On the whole though, the action research seems to have helped to get people to think and act on, and eventually improve, their own circumstances.

Co-management of rangeland resources in the Hindu Kush Himalayan region: involving farmers in the policy process

Yan Zhao-Li

Introduction

Using several examples from the Hindu Kush Himalayan (HKH) region this paper highlights the potential of Participatory Action Research (PAR) to engage all concerned parties, especially the community and government, in equitable negotiation of common goals, and the related responsibilities, entitlements, benefits and actions of each party to achieve co-management of rangeland resources.

Rangeland covers more than 60 per cent of the HKH land area. Sustainable use of these rangelands is essential not only to the livelihoods of local populations but also for the conservation of many rare and endangered flora and fauna species, water capture, carbon sequestration, climate stabilization and preservation of cultural and natural landscapes.

Mountain communities have been managing rangelands for thousands of years in the HKH, accumulating abundant indigenous knowledge of their environment and adaptive production systems. However, contemporary policy-makers and some researchers blame pastoralists for overgrazing and practising 'backward' production and livelihood systems that cause severe rangeland degradation. As the state governments in the HKH generally have ownership rights, rangeland and pasture management decisions are made by people far away from pastoral communities and are often not the best for local people or the environment. Furthermore, the uses of rangeland resources in the HKH, and their consequences, go beyond national boundaries requiring regionally coordinated efforts.

To address these issues, the International Centre for Integrated Mountain Development (ICIMOD) began to promote appropriate rangeland management and regional exchange and sharing on rangelands from the mid 1990s. Researchers used a PAR approach to support communities to gather information, carry out situation analyses, discuss strategies and monitor action processes together with other stakeholders, particularly local government. The three cases below highlight the importance of involving government (at appropriate levels) in PAR in order to ensure that communities achieve their objectives. These include conflict resolution, poverty alleviation and environmental conservation.

Co-management for enhanced livelihoods and conservation

In the Upper Mustang District of Nepal, acute shortage of forage led to a breakdown in traditional winter–spring and summer–autumn pasture systems. The disordered use of seasonal rangelands exacerbated the feedstuff shortage especially during winter and spring, and increased conflicts between households and Village Development Councils (VDCs). The research team supported the formation and function of Pasture Management Sub-Committees (PMSCs) at VDC levels. The PMSCs built participatory three dimensional models and brought villagers together to use these models to jointly define boundaries between VDCs and seasonal pastures. The villagers designated the PMSCs to monitor and enforce their commonly agreed regulations.

In the sparsely populated Chiang Tang Plateau in the northern Tibet Autonomous Region (TAR) of China, local people depend solely or largely on livestock grazing. Shortly after previously communally owned livestock was allocated to individual households, a large number of pastoral families lost their livestock – and thus their means of survival – and became poor due to a lack of livestock management skills, unsuccessful trade or natural disasters. Nima County government first initiated co-management in Jiagu Township by gathering all 39 poor households – the majority of whom survived on begging – from three villages to form one special production group. The government subsidized 16 sheep units per person and rich families also loaned livestock to the poor families – who could return the same number and type of livestock five years later. Each household then pooled their livestock and labour force as shares for co-management. In 2002, after rangeland was privatized, they also contributed their individually contracted rangeland as part of their shares. Agreements were reached on production, benefit sharing, security and some other issues. By 2006, there were no more beggars in the group and households owned an average of 38 sheep units per person, well above the local poverty line of 30 sheep units per person. Similar arrangements are now common in northern TAR.

Nima County lies completely within the Chiang Tang National Reserve. Since the establishment of the national reserve, the population of wild ass (kiang) has increased sharply. Although a welcome development from a conservation perspective, the large herds (which can number hundreds of individuals) forage, trample and destroy the vegetation of the winter pastures when people and livestock move to summer pastures. PAR brought the county government and herders together, leading to joint investment in the building of fences around some vital winter pastures, significantly reducing conflicts between wild ass and local herders.

Conclusion

In the management of commonly shared natural resources such as rangelands, good policy can play a very important role but it is still missing in the HKH. Some Chinese people in remote mountain areas say that the central government policy is like gold when it is formulated but becomes a stone when implemented in remote mountains. This implies the need for flexible and adaptable interpretation and implementation of the policy according to local environmental and cultural settings, which is difficult when the policy implementers do not really understand either the policy intention or the local situation. As shown above, PAR can play an important role in helping to change the mindset of government officials to move towards involving farmers in the policy process – formulation, implementation and revision – to achieve sustainable rural development and management of commonly used natural resources. An important factor in this process is building the capacity of all parties especially building the confidence of farmers to defend their needs and interests and to advocate for policy change.

The System of Rice Intensification (SRI) as a system of agricultural innovation

Norman Uphoff

Introduction

The System of Rice Intensification (SRI), developed in Madagascar some 25 years ago, is gaining increasing acceptance and momentum as over one million farmers in more than 25 countries are now using its methods to raise their rice production while also reducing their use of external inputs. Rather than focus on the innovation itself, this paper will introduce SRI only briefly before considering the transnational system for innovation that has taken shape in response to this agronomic opportunity, which is particularly beneficial for resource-limited households.

SRI differs from most other agricultural innovations in the extent to which farmers have voluntarily invested their own time and resources in taking SRI to their peers in a good example of farmer-to-farmer extension. At the same time, innovative alliances have formed among diverse persons and organizations to disseminate and adjust the methodology, supporting the spread of this innovation in the face of resistance from some established institutions.

An unusual agronomic innovation

SRI is an atypical innovation in several ways. First, its methods can raise, concurrently, the productivity of the land, labour, water and capital invested in irrigated rice production. Such a positive-sum dynamic violates economists' precept of 'no free lunches', assuming that there must always be some tradeoffs. Of course, there are costs involved with SRI adoption, particularly increased labour during farmers' learning phase; and there are some conditions where the methods will be inappropriate or impractical. But with acquired skills and confidence as well as with continuing farmer innovation, SRI can become labour-saving over time, while also saving water and seed, reducing costs, and raising output by at least 25–50 per cent, often by 50–100 per cent, and even sometimes by 100–200 per cent or more. This sounds too good to be true, but SRI's alternative methods have been validated in 30 countries, from China to Cuba, Peru to the Philippines, Gambia to Zambia, even in Iraq, Iran and Afghanistan (see SRI website: http://ciifad.cornell.edu/sri/).

SRI changes the management of the plants, soil, water and nutrients used in paddy rice production. Specifically, it involves transplanting single young seedlings with wider spacing, carefully and quickly into fields that are not kept continuously flooded, and whose soil has more organic matter and is actively aerated. These practices improve the growth and functioning of rice plants' root systems and enhance the numbers and diversity of the soil biota that contribute to plant health and productivity (Stoop et al., 2002; Uphoff, 2003; Randriamiharisoa et al., 2006; Mishra et al., 2006).

The cumulative effect of these methods is to raise not only the yield of paddy – i.e. kilograms of unmilled rice harvested per hectare – without relying on improved varieties or agrochemical inputs, but also the output of milled rice – i.e. kilograms of consumable rice per bushel of paddy – by 10–20 per cent. This bonus on top of higher paddy yields results from having fewer unfilled grains (less chaff) and fewer broken grains (less shattering during milling).

In addition, farmers report – and researchers have verified – that SRI crops are more resistant to most pests and diseases, and better able to tolerate adverse climatic influences such as drought, storms, hot spells or cold snaps. The length of the crop cycle (time to maturity) is also usually reduced with higher yields. Resistance to biotic and abiotic stresses will become more important in the coming decades as farmers around the world have to cope with the effects of climate change and the growing frequency of 'extreme events'. The resistance of SRI plants to lodging caused by wind and/or rain, given their larger root systems and stronger stalks, can also be quite dramatic. In general, we also find that the use of SRI methods can reduce the agronomic and economic risks that farmers face (Uphoff, 2007).

A civil society innovation

SRI differs from most agricultural technologies promoted in recent decades in that it is a civil society innovation, originating not from research stations or laboratories, but from the dedicated work of a Jesuit priest, subsequently amplified and modified through the efforts of farmers, NGOs and other non-state actors. Father Henri de Laulanié spent the last 34 years of his life working with small-scale farmers in Madagascar to devise better ways to raise paddy yields with the aim of reducing the pervasive poverty and hunger in that country (Laulanié, 2003). He sought low-cost methods that did not rely on expensive and environmentally unfriendly external inputs and was able to succeed in his objective by modifying the way that rice plants, soil, water and nutrients are managed (Laulanié, 1993; Uphoff, 2005).

Since World War II, most agricultural innovations have followed a linear sequence in which advances in scientific knowledge are made and then transformed into technological advances, which are disseminated through extension (government) or market (private sector) mechanisms to users. SRI as an innovation follows an earlier pattern where, conversely, technology preceded science, similar to the sequence seen in the emergence of air travel and transport. The science of aerodynamics stemmed from the aspiring and tinkering of two bicycle mechanics.

The spread and improvement of Fr de Laulanié's innovation was initially undertaken by an NGO that he established in 1990 with some of his close Malagasy colleagues, *Association Tefy Saina*. Their effort was expanded through collaboration with a US academic institution that has worldwide networking connections, the Cornell International Institute for Food, Agriculture and Development (CIIFAD).

Styles of science – and the response to SRI

Initial assessments of SRI published in the scientific literature dismissed the innovation as unimportant, or even disparaged it (see Doberman, 2004; Sheehy et al., 2004; Sinclair, 2004; Sinclair and Cassman, 2004; McDonald et al., 2006). Some scientists, however, responded to the SRI challenge/opportunity affirmatively. SRI elicited more interest and acceptance in the NARS (national agricultural research systems) of China, India and Indonesia than in international scientific circles. Scientists taking interest were often ones who were already working closely with farmers and NGOs, not regarding work on research stations or in labs as sufficient. They were willing to visit SRI fields and to talk with SRI farmers, less disposed to rely on *a priori* reasoning and secondary data. They also did not feel it necessary to defend their scientific enterprise against the 'intrusions' of non-scientists who were suggesting reasons for a paradigm shift in rice production. Most of the early work on SRI was taken up by NGOs, farmers, and individuals who were curious to know how it was possible to 'get more from less,' appreciating that this could benefit farmers, consumers and the environment.

Persons who think that farmers' knowledge deserves invariant respect and deference will be surprised by the SRI story, however. Laulanié's empirical work showed that most of the practices that rice farmers have followed for generations – using older rather than younger seedlings, spacing these closely rather than sparsely, and growing them in flooded rather than well-drained fields – are, in fact, demonstrably sub-optimal. It can be shown with solid scientific evidence and reasoning that conventional rice-growing practices constrain yield expression. Several of the practices that Laulanié found to be beneficial – not transplanting seedlings in clumps of many plants, and not keeping paddy fields always inundated – were derived from observing the 'deviant' practices of some Malagasy farmers. But most of the things that rice farmers have done for centuries, some even for millennia, constrain rice productivity. One should therefore not assume that, through years of trials and error, farmers have always worked out the best of all possible practices.

Farmers have not been alone in believing firmly in methods that are demonstrably sub-optimal. Some leading rice scientists have strongly endorsed practices that now are known to be yield-limiting, e.g. asserting that rice plants perform better when submerged in standing water (DeDatta, 1981). For many years, both farmers and scientists have observed, from fields that were not perfectly levelled, that rice plants growing in low-lying areas which were always flooded, struggled and grew poorly compared to those in higher, better-drained areas. Yet neither farmers nor scientists drew the appropriate conclusion from their observations: that rice is not really an aquatic plant and that it grows better in soil that is kept moist but well-drained, even intermittently dried out to some extent.

Keeping paddy soils mostly aerobic, as accomplished with SRI methods, favours better root growth and health while also contributing to more abundant and diverse populations of (mostly aerobic) soil biota. These organisms produce many benefits for a rice crop (Randriamiharisoa et al., 2006). However, the belief that rice grows better under flooded conditions still persists among most farmers and many rice scientists, despite research disproving this, e.g. Ramasamy et al. (1997) and Guerra et al. (1998). Actually, farmers have flooded their paddy fields mostly to reduce the amount of labour required for controlling weeds – not comprehending how big a yield penalty they pay for suffocating the roots of their rice plants and reducing the populations of aerobic organisms that (should) live in the soil for it to be most fertile.

Moreover, for many years agronomists have cautioned against what they call 'the border effect.' Whenever crop-cut samples are taken to estimate the yield of a field, they warn that samples should be taken from randomly selected areas in the *middle* of the field rather than from along the edge. Why? Because it is known that plants growing on the borders of fields – being more exposed to sunlight and air circulation – are healthier and give more yield (Gomez and

DeDatta, 1971). SRI methods achieve 'the border effect' *for the whole field* by introducing optimally wider spacing.

These are just two of the ways in which rice farmers, as well as scientists, have been wrong about what constitute the most productive practices. Past beliefs and derived techniques have suppressed yield potential. As developed by Laulanié and further evolved by farmers, NGOs and researchers around the world over the past decade, SRI is capitalizing on this potential, getting more productive phenotypes from practically all rice genotypes, traditional or modern, local or improved, indigenous or high-yielding.

These insights have come more from field observation and experimentation than from scientifically formulated hypotheses and controlled trials. As a civil society innovation, the main criterion for evaluation of SRI has been farmer satisfaction and demonstrable economic and environmental benefits, rather than peer review and publications in the scientific literature. Both the innovation and the ways in which it has been validated and disseminated are unusual, possibly pointing out directions for other agricultural advances since SRI methods are benefiting other crops as well.

SRI as a system for agricultural innovation

SRI has been explicitly conceived of and presented not as a technology but rather as a *methodology* based on a set of ideas – really, insights – formulated as principles that are to be translated into specific practices. These are employed to create a more favourable growing environment for irrigated rice plants.

To improve rice yields, most agricultural research in recent decades has focused on the G component in what is characterized as the $G \times E$ *interaction*. This formulation emphasizes the fact that all organisms are the result of the way that their initial genetic potential (G) interacts with all of the environmental factors (E) impinging on it. Production efforts are most successful where there is a good fit between G and E. SRI focuses on E rather than G, trying to establish environments that will be most nurturing for any rice genotype. Farmers who can provide the most hospitable growing environment for their rice plants given their resource endowments, soil, climate, etc., will attain the greatest payoff. Part of SRI's innovation is, in practice, to create a system of ongoing innovation, i.e. for experimentation and adaptation, capitalizing on the expression of G rather than regarding this G as giving a predetermined result.

Since SRI is an innovation that encourages further innovation – not a material set of inputs or a packaged set of instructions to be implemented such as constituted Green Revolution technology – it has been dynamic. The core ideas have remained quite stable and robust. However, they have been continuously extended and adapted in various ways, e.g. to unirrigated rice production and to other crops.

SRI was not planned as a civil society innovation; it has just evolved that way. Laulanié and Tefy Saina would gladly have worked with the Madagascar government to refine and spread SRI knowledge, but there was much resistance to the new ideas from national agricultural researchers and, with only a few exceptions, government personnel were hostile. Sadly, this has been true, at least initially, in many other countries where SRI ideas have been introduced. Thus, SRI has been spread, by force of circumstance, through the efforts of a great variety of individuals with NGO, university, farmer organization, private-sector or other affiliations who shared an interest in low-external-input, sustainable or 'alternative' agriculture.

The growth of an innovation network

The spread of SRI through word of mouth, photocopies, unpublished reports and email contacts has been dramatic and fast. Capacities for electronic networking have meant that the 'gate-keeping' role previously played by recognized experts in any field, not just in rice science, has been changed and greatly reduced. This can have some negative consequences, as unvetted and misleading information can now be transmitted freely at the speed of light. On the other hand, valid and productive information can be spread just as fast, and if it proves beneficial, it will gain a growing number of users and supporters.

The first engagement with SRI was by individuals in diverse institutions: a university, a government research agency, an NGO and an extension service, in countries ranging across East, Southeast and South Asia. CIIFAD began facilitating exchanges of experience, information and ideas from 2000 on, and by 2002, with support from a programme officer in the Rockefeller Foundation, it was possible to organize an international conference to assess SRI. This was hosted by the China National Hybrid Rice Research and Development Center and its director, Prof. Yuan Long-ping, world-famous as 'the father of hybrid rice' (see Yuan, 2002).

The outlines of the SRI innovation system were set by this event, which had ripples for years to come. There was agreement on following a two-track strategy for SRI, in which, concurrently, researchers would try to advance the scientific understanding of SRI while extension and NGO personnel working with farmers would attend to the practical adaptation and promotion of the methods. Each track was expected to interact with, contribute to, and learn from the other. Such parallel processing has been a hallmark of SRI, with researchers and practitioners working cooperatively and simultaneously – rather than in sequence – and with farmers interacting with both scientists and extension personnel more as partners than as adopters.

Farmer roles

What went on at conferences, in journals and on list-serves was the visible, trackable part of the SRI innovation system. What has given the innovation 'legs' is much less evident and internationally known: the response and initiative of farmers in many countries to the productivity and resource-saving opportunities which SRI opens up. Already when I visited H.M. Premaratna at his farm at Mellawalana, Sri Lanka, in March 2001, he had trained about 4,000 farmers there in SRI methods, with his own and a neighbour's resources. He had obtained 10–15 t/ha yields with the new methods on his organically managed farm after reading about SRI in *LEISA magazine*. He had become a vocal champion of SRI, teaming up with a Senior Assistant Secretary of Agriculture and the Deputy Minister of Agriculture, both of whom were championing SRI despite opposition from government researchers. Government officials and researchers who dismissed SRI at public meetings were challenged by Premaratna based on his own SRI experience and knowledge of agriculture. When I asked him why he put so much effort into spreading SRI, he replied: 'I want to have rice paddies where my children can play safely'. In Cambodia, the first farmer to try SRI methods, Mey Som, became known, affectionately, by his peers as 'the Professor' because of his tireless efforts to teach other farmers about SRI.

Organizational coalitions

In recent years, an extensive coalition has emerged across an array of different types of organization, including public agencies, research institutes, universities, NGOs, farmer associations and sometimes, though not often, the private sector. In almost all cases the initial interest and effort emanated from one person or a few individuals. However, usually the institutions or organizations became to varying degrees 'infected' by SRI, considering SRI as a benign, even beneficent infection. SRI experience clearly supports Robert Chambers' argument (1983) about the importance of 'the personal factor' in rural development achievements.

SRI has seen the emergence of what Shambu Prasad (this book) calls 'learning alliances'. The SRI innovation system has functioned best where a diverse set of actors with heterogeneous institutional bases have come together to share experience and to learn from and with one another. They have not created a grand coordinated programme, with central direction, but rather a synchronized, mutually reinforcing effort, often with agreements to cooperate and even join together in certain programmes. The structures have been more often informal than formal, although some explicit coordinating bodies have been created, as in Bangladesh and Sri Lanka. More common are the kinds of networks functioning in Nepal and the Philippines. In countries as large and heterogeneous as China and India, such bodies function better at the provincial or state level, either formally or informally. The emerging organizational framework in Orissa state is the first of its kind in India. It may become a model for others as civil society, writ large, seeks to engage more functionally with state institutions and to step up the pace of SRI expansion. Persons working in governmental roles who collaborate with colleagues from other sectors on the basis of their interests, value commitments and expertise, rather than on the basis of state authority, can function as civil-society participants, broadly defined.

Challenges and constraints

Articles reporting SRI results, some with large, multi-year data sets using standard agronomic methodologies, are starting to appear in the peer-reviewed literature (e.g. Ceesay et al., 2006; Kabir and Uphoff, 2007; Namara et al., 2007; Sato and Uphoff, 2007; Satyanarayana et al., 2006; Sinha and Talati, 2007; Mishra and Salokhe, 2008). Probably the most important factor starting to turn opinion is that the three largest rice-producing countries, which grow and consume more than 60 per cent of the world's rice, are now officially supporting the dissemination of SRI while continuing research and evaluation.

- In China, more than 200,000 ha were under SRI management in the provinces of Sichuan and Zhejiang as of 2007, up from 10,000 ha three years earlier (http://ciifad.cornell.edu/sri/countries/china/cnntutrep0807.pdf).
- In India, the central government plans to support extension of SRI to 5 million ha over the next five years under its National Food Security Mission (NFSM). In 2008, under NFSM there were SRI demonstrations in 136 districts across 14 targeted states. The state of Tripura, where SRI was used by 880 farmers in 2005-6, two years later had more than 160,000 farmers practising SRI (see http://ciifad.cornell.edu/sri/countries/india/inntutrep1007.pdf).
- In Indonesia, President S.B. Yudhoyono has called upon the Ministry of Agriculture to promote SRI methods, particularly their organic version, and has described SRI as 'a corrective to the Green Revolution' (video available at: www.srivideo.zoomshare.com with written summary at: http://ciifad.cornell.edu/SRI/countries/indonesia/indopresident073007.pdf).

The International Rice Research Institute (IRRI) and CIIFAD, together with Wageningen University, have agreed to undertake a jointly planned and jointly implemented evaluation of SRI methods, comparing them with what IRRI scientists consider best management practices. This will involve several national agricultural research systems in a collaborative effort to resolve scientific disagreements about SRI's merits and suitability. The most important question for those already satisfied with the evidence confirming SRI is how to support scaling up that is effective, equitable and sustainable.

Because SRI is not dependent on the purchase or distribution of external inputs – involving only the diffusion of knowledge, skill and confidence – its dissemination has unconventional dynamics and conditions, and it probably cannot be a literal model for many other innovation systems. The biggest challenge for scaling up will be how to avoid the kind of top-down pressures and impositions typical of large-scale adoption campaigns.

The main obstacles to SRI adoption remain mental and attitudinal, as farmers who have taken up SRI themselves continually attest. An initial barrier is labour-intensity, while the methods are being learned (Moser and Barrett, 2003). But once farmers acquire skill with and confidence in the methods SRI can be labour-neutral or even labour-saving (Uphoff, 2007). The most objective constraint on SRI adoption is water control, being able to manage irrigation systems sufficiently to provide reduced but reliable amounts of water on an intermittent basis. Where fields are low-lying and continuously submerged or mostly saturated, SRI methods will not produce their best results. Water control can usually but not always be accomplished with appropriate investments in irrigation hardware (control structures) or software (organization). The value of the water that can be saved with SRI can justify considerable financial investment. Farmers in several countries have also adapted SRI concepts to rainfed/unirrigated rice production (Sinha and Talati, 2007; Kabir and Uphoff, 2007).

Pest control can also be a requirement for greatest success. Aerobic soil conditions usually reduce pest and disease problems, but they can encourage some pests such as leaf folder or root-feeding nematodes. Evaluations – and farmer reports – have shown that on balance there is a reduction in pest and disease incidence. Integrated pest management practices are always recommended with SRI.

Conclusion

It is of course premature to try to make any conclusive characterization of SRI as a system of and for innovation, because this system is itself in the process of formulation and reformulation. As such, it offers an opportunity for students of innovation systems to learn from one, albeit a rather unique one, that is in the process of emergence.

Encounters, dialogues and learning alliances: the System of Rice Intensification in India

C. Shambu Prasad

Innovation at the margins

How do scientists respond to ideas that emerge outside the formal agricultural research system? This paper considers answers to this question by reviewing experience with SRI, the System of Rice Intensification, a contemporary grassroots innovation that has emerged from civil society and has been rapidly spreading among tens of thousands of farmers around the globe (see Uphoff, this book). Tracing the evolution of SRI in India, one of the largest rice-producing countries in the world, the paper explores the challenges inherent for researchers when responding to a civil society innovation and to an 'open system' such as SRI. Regarding researchers as part of the growing SRI community or innovation system – comprised of farmers, extensionists, NGOs and administrators – gives a more nuanced understanding of how SRI has and has not spread and helps us see why farmers have been more open to acceptance of SRI than most researchers.

The ability of the research community to adapt to opportunities such as SRI depends on having 'openness to surprise' and an ability to engage in knowledge dialogues. 'Learning alliances' are suggested here as good mechanisms for providing a level playing field for all knowledge actors, building trust, sharing and creating new knowledge, and providing scientists space and opportunity for self-critical awareness. We therefore need to shift our sites of inquiry from larger narratives and perhaps overworked political games of knowledge production to the messy and playful encounters of everyday practice where farmers, scientists and civil society are engaging in an uneven but dynamic knowledge marketplace.

My initial interest in SRI was prompted by a desire to appreciate better the politics of knowledge between formal and informal science, and how this influences research and non-research actors. However, I now feel a greater need to look at how the various SRI actors are adapting, innovating and redefining boundaries through their everyday practice. How can a better understanding enable faster learning within this complex system? As a case SRI can also throw light on questions such as: How does innovation occur at the 'margins'? How is knowledge constructed and understood outside of formal science and technology organizations? What could formal science and scientists learn from these experiments? Can historical studies help ongoing processes? Is an alternate history of agricultural science and technology in India possible as a genealogy of dissent – a series of narratives of creative scientists who did not fight shy of pushing boundaries and learning from diverse sources? How can academics and activists work together without diluting but enriching each other's perspectives? What should be the role of academic institutions in ongoing debates in understanding a system? Alternately how could management professionals/generalists (innovation system analysts) enable knowledge and information flows in a system? I am learning, slowly and sometimes reluctantly, that being 'open to surprise' holds a key not only to understanding SRI but to what SRI and many farmers practising it seem to be telling researchers as well.

SRI and the 'Rice Wars'

Scientists have been reluctant to accept SRI for two reasons (see also Norman Uphoff, this book). The very high yields of SRI reported in Madagascar, where the system was developed, including those that were above what scientists considered to be at or near 'the biological maximum' (15 t/ha) was one reason. The other was the commitment of the scientists to their own methods of increasing rice production which focused in particular on genetic changes that make them more responsive to external inputs, and then increasing such inputs. Because SRI depended on neither kind of change, instead achieving its productivity gains by changing the management of plants, soil, water and nutrients, it challenged the power, interests and mindsets of rice scientists. Scientists at the International Rice Research Institute (IRRI) found it very difficult to accept SRI as it questioned many basic assumptions about rice systems.

Validating the knowledge of SRI presented methodological and epistemological difficulties. How to change not one but six practices – all at the same time? Formal SRI experiments conducted on-station seldom confirmed the results reported from farmers' fields, and scientists naturally assumed that their results were the correct ones. They were reluctant to accept, or investigate, the explanation offered by SRI proponents that on-station soil conditions were less suitable for SRI methods, having had high applications of chemical fertilizer and biocides for many years, which could reduce or inhibit the performance of soil micro-organisms which are credited with a major contribution to 'the SRI effect'.

The conflicting views about SRI reached a peak during the 2004 International Year of Rice and were termed the 'Rice Wars' with opponents wondering if SRI was fantasy or a UFO (unconfirmed field observations). But the framing of the debate was problematic. It treated SRI as a technology (like any improved variety) and not as a system of practices. This circumscribed the debate to scientific disciplines, on the one hand, and economic field assessments, on the other. It ignored other players such as civil society organizations and innovative farmers who often provided multiple meanings to SRI.

The Rice Wars controversy also ignored readings on the history of technology that showed that science does not always precede technology, as in the case of the airplane, developed by bicycle mechanics when there was no science of aerodynamics yet known or even imagined. This reverse sequence is exemplified by SRI and its 'land to lab' yield gap. Scientists were confronted with the question, if they cared to think about it, 'If something works in the field, why is it not replicable in the laboratory' (Shambu Prasad et al., 2005)?

Even as many researchers were constrained by 'normal professionalism', farmers and civil society groups were not only freely experimenting with SRI, but were adding to the body of knowledge through their experiments and insights. In fact, the widespread experience of higher yields obtained by farmers practising SRI has even pushed agricultural science to introduce new axioms for research protocols, one of which is that all trials should be on-farm rather than on-station if they are to have meaning and truly assess SRI.

SRI researchers have also been keen to provide a stronger theoretical basis for their empirical practice by combining field-level empiricism with a dissenting view on the history of rice technology. Conventional rice science could not explain SRI results, but older texts and experiments that described rice plant growth did. Japanese scientists (Horie et al., 2005) found that many of the SRI practices had been used by the most successful Japanese rice farmers in the 1950s.

An interesting fallout of this knowledge encounter between SRI scientists and IRRI scientists was the generation of new knowledge and the finding of newer contexts and applications for older ones. One effect was the increased attention given to soil biology and its relevance to what is now being referred to as 'post-modern' or 'most-modern' agriculture. Research on plants has favoured studies on soil physics and soil chemistry with a neglect of soil biology, and research on the plant organs and environment above the soil has received more support than that addressing the complex processes and mechanisms below the soil (Uphoff et al., 2006).

The counter-intuitive nature of the SRI innovation presents problems not only for scientists but also for farmers. For the first few weeks when the tiny SRI seedlings, widely spaced in a muddy, unflooded field, are not evidently doing very much, innovative farmers trying out SRI methods meet with a lot of ridicule in the community until such time as an acceleration of tillering occurs, and more farmers become satisfied that a hitherto unappreciated growth potential is being tapped. Newer knowledge and understanding often leads to newer practices that also serve as good extension methods. Farmers were encouraged to pull up SRI and non-SRI plants of the same age and to observe the visible difference in root growth, thereby gaining an appreciation of what produces healthier, more robust and productive plants. The visual appeal and difference has prompted some farmers to call SRI 'the root revolution'. Seeing strong, numerous tillers and healthy plants with large, white-coloured root systems convinces farmers more easily than any technical advice or information from extension agents.

Taking root: SRI in India

The story (or stories) of SRI in India indicates a complex evolutionary process of innovation and development. In formal terms, official records indicate that the first SRI trials were started in 2000 at Tamil Nadu Agricultural University (TNAU) as part of an international collaborative project. T.M. Thiyagarajan was the lone Indian representative at the first international conference on SRI convened in China in 2002, presenting modest results. But others soon followed his lead and even initially sceptical scientists soon recognized the potential of SRI once they encountered and tested it for themselves (Box 2.1).

There is, however, a parallel history of SRI with civil-society groups learning about and accessing information and experimenting with SRI since 1999, starting with a publication in *LEISA magazine* (see van Walsum, this book). These organizations and individuals accessed knowledge from diverse sources. In India today, SRI has been introduced in over 18 states, representing not only varied agroecological zones but also varied combinations of civil society organizations (that include farmers' groups and NGOs), and state agricultural universities, research and extension agencies.

Box 2.1 Encounters at the interface and the co-creation of SRI knowledge

The rapid spread of SRI in India started in 2003, and in this scientists like T.M. Thiyagarajan at TNAU and Alapati Satyanarayana at Acharya NG Ranga Agricultural University had important roles in backing the innovation with the governments of their states, which were also experiencing drought and water stress at the time. They were willing to go beyond the bounds of received wisdom and investigate the SRI phenomenon. Openness to new knowledge irrespective of its source is evident from the story of Dr. Satyanarayana and his first brush (literally) with an SRI plant when asked to visit farmers' fields in Sri Lanka in 2003 to learn about SRI's potential first-hand. The sceptical Satyanarayana's accidental brush with the sturdy leaf of an SRI plant (which cut his finger) got him thinking. This had never happened to him before. He could see for himself that SRI methods produced a different phenotype.

Satyanarayana subsequently reworked the principles that led to the healthy growth of rice plants in SRI and later developed an easy-to-understand package of practices for farmers of Andhra Pradesh. The reworking of knowledge that began in Sri Lanka later led to the co-creation of knowledge when he extensively toured farmers' fields in the delta regions of Andhra Pradesh. In one such instance, a farmer named Jagga Raju involved in seed production had started producing rice plants in well-drained flower pots with extensive tillering. Raju had shown empirically that rice is *not* an aquatic plant, and the researcher's interaction with Raju provided the farmer with scientific justification for his practices. At the same time, it enhanced Satyanarayana's knowledge and understanding of the potential of SRI.

The SRI debates in India were no longer on the Rice Wars but on ownership and legitimacy of actors. The questions were not about 'whether SRI?' but 'how to do SRI?' More organizations were involved in research (the Indian Council for Agriculture Research (ICAR) being one of the largest in the world), but few had a good understanding of SRI. Research protocols in many cases were still trying to establish some of the basics of SRI on seedling age, spacing, etc., and invariably all trials compared SRI with scientist-recommended Integrated Crop Management (ICM). But, as chief ministers visited SRI farms, policy support was increasing from the political as well as the research establishment.

Another fascinating feature of SRI has been the interest taken by some extension agencies. There are instances where extension has led research since research agencies have been slow to investigate SRI. The contributions made to SRI by extensionists, farmers and researchers from outside the rice research establishment, notably soil microbiologists and entomologists, to improve SRI practices in India have been considerable and have in fact created conditions for interest from the rice research establishment. However, the institutional capacities of agriculture departments to carry out SRI extension on a large scale remain limited. Not many agencies have appreciated that SRI needs different ways of carrying out extension – an extension that allows for and encourages farmer innovation and participation, not simply transferring technologies and techniques. Government extension systems in India have been geared towards targeting 'progressive' (i.e. big) farmers and have not given priority to the poverty-relevance of an innovation (Ramanjaneyulu et al., 2007; Sulaiman, this book). They are also designed to deliver goods rather than convey integrated ideas or promote learning. This has suggested some new challenges, and new innovations.

Despite the limits of conventional extension services, the number of actors in the SRI innovation system is continually increasing with each cropping season and across newer regions. The last few years have seen a considerable spread of SRI in India. While no data are available on the number of farmers who have tried out SRI, even a very conservative estimate would put this figure well over 150,000. Interestingly most of the recent spread has been among resource-poor farmers in largely rainfed areas, farmers who have not and might never receive the bounties of the Green Revolution package of subsidized irrigation water and agrochemicals.

Knowledge dialogues and learning alliances

The diversity of actors and the systems of innovation in SRI allows for complex interactions involving both cooperation and conflict. In Orissa state, with the cooperation of the Director of Agriculture a state level workshop was organized in June 2007 that had 80 participants, a quarter of whom were departmental research and extension staff. The research agencies in Orissa presented their perspectives on SRI and this was followed by sharing of experiences from farmers of the state. Resource persons from Andhra Pradesh and Tripura were invited to share and answer some of the key technical and institutional issues.

The workshop had some interesting fallouts. The department contributed towards building a database of SRI farmers in the state. The response was overwhelming and we followed up with the farmers, recording their stories and encouraging some to write their own. Most accounts were written for the first time and resulted in the book *Towards a Learning Alliance* (Shambu Prasad et al., 2007). A learning alliance is defined as 'a platform where a range of stakeholders come together that share an interest in innovation and the creation of new knowledge in an area of common interest'.

Learning alliances contribute to healthy innovation systems by building bridges between islands of experience, helping to assess how these results were achieved and what others can learn from this experience (Lundy and Gottret, 2005). These alliances provide a platform for openly sharing knowledge, building trust and creating a shared language thereby increasing the efficiency of learning and dissemination. The concept creates a level playing field for knowledge amongst the participating actors. Learning alliances can enable knowledge dialogues among different and even conflicting knowledge systems.

Our SRI experience with learning alliances enabled us to realize that current institutional arrangements do not have spaces for at least two kinds of activity. Firstly, they lack an open platform for scouting farmer innovations and giving them the legitimacy and respect they deserve. Why is it not possible for instance for farmers to share their SRI experience in a journal of the rice establishment? Why is it assumed that it has to be only in a regional language for farmers? Can scientists not learn anything from a farmer's experiences and experiments (see Gupta, this book)? At another level, scientists too do not have spaces for 'self-critical epistemological awareness' (Chambers, 2002) where they reflect on what it means, for instance, to practise conventional science with increased environmental stress and with a large-scale farming crisis. Where are the learning laboratories and platforms where scientists can learn, reflect and report without always feeling the need to have the answers or seeming to have the answers? How do we build greater openness to 'surprise' amongst researchers – both natural and social?

An interesting debate that has emerged out of discussions about SRI surrounds the question: Where does knowledge reside? Is it in the laboratories or in the fields? The SRI experience in India suggests that critical reflection and constructive debate established through learning alliances open up new possibilities for knowledge to emerge out of *interactions in context*. Questions arise in places where there is a possibility of genuine dialogue and adaptive learning. All of this might not solve the agrarian crisis facing India, but it may at least enable our agricultural research establishment to break its intellectual and institutional shackles, learn from its own innovative and dissenting researchers and reclaim the respect of farmers and citizens.

If farmers are first, do pastoralists come second? Political ecology and participation in central Mali

Todd A. Crane

Introduction

In central Mali, participatory development of technical innovation is complicated by the fact that it is a landscape populated by both farmers and herders of different ethnic backgrounds and different ideas about what rural development should look like. These differences manifest in the micro-politics of participatory projects, as well as in broader-level contestations over land use. Participatory research that is framed and informed by the politics of decentralization risks alienating herders from the process and the fruits of participatory rural development. Herders' views of development involve not just technical innovation, but aspects of institutional organization and land management at the regional level, which often fall outside the scope of local-level projects that are linked to reinforcing decentralization. In central Mali, putting farmers first risks alienating the herders with whom farmers share the landscape. It may even contribute to shifting balances of power between the two groups.

Consequently, participatory research addressing the technical aspects of agricultural and pastoral production must be contextualized in the broader contestations over land and natural resources. Even when farmers and herders are both involved in the development of technical innovation, the process can be significantly affected by the legacies of historic power dynamics, contemporary politics at the local and national levels, and divergent visions for the future of rural development. All of these factors affect degrees of interest in, participation in, valuation of, and adoption of technical innovations.

From 1999–2003, the USAID-funded Sustainable Agriculture, Natural Resource and Environmental Management (SANREM) programme worked with Mali's Institut d'Economie Rurale and the rural Commune of Madiama in central Mali to conduct participatory research on livelihood problems as identified by the community. By integrating participatory experiments on technical innovations with capacity-building workshops, the project sought to enable farmers and herders in the community not only to address their natural resource management problems more effectively, but also to develop the social networks, institutional structures and social problem solving skills that enable them to address the broader sociopolitical aspects of conflict over natural resource management.

Competing visions and political ecologies

In cooperation with the commune's mayoral office, itself a newly elected administrative institution begun in 2000, a Natural Resource Management Advisory Committee (NRMAC) was formed in 1999 with representatives from every village in the commune, including four women. Through a participatory landscape/lifescape appraisal (Earl and Kodio, 2005), local participants identified and ranked the natural resource management problems they faced in their communities. The top three problems were declining soil fertility, declining pasture productivity and farmer-herder conflicts. Research was then undertaken to address these most pressing concerns (Moore, 2005).

Integrating competing visions of development into participatory technological innovation is a little explored topic. In central Mali, agricultural and pastoral production systems are simultaneously in competition with each other (for control of production spaces), mutually interdependent (for exchange of food and labour), and increasingly blurred together (by pressures for everyone to practise mixed agro-pastoralism). Along with rural development policies, several decades of low rainfall, punctuated by severe multi-year droughts, have increasingly pushed many herders into agriculture and pushed farmers into animal husbandry. Madiama, at the southeast edge of the Niger River Inland Delta, is populated by a majority of ethnic Marka and a significant minority of Fulani, all of whom could be broadly described as agro-pastoralists. Relying on exogenous and technical analyses, development professionals would put them into the same subsistence category and expect them to be interested in similar technical innovations.

However, in this region, farming and herding are not just technical production systems, they represent distinct cultural systems. While Marka are strongly associated with farming, cattle herding is strongly linked to the Fulani ethnic group. This historical connection between ethnicity and production systems creates a situation in which the different ethnicities have different bodies of technical knowledge and distinct sets of cultural values in relation to production practices, although both currently use agro-pastoral livelihood strategies. Due to different cultural values, there is significant variation in how innovations in technical knowledge are perceived or adopted, and how they are deployed to political ends. Integrating and anticipating this variation requires an understanding of the connections between technical knowledge, behavioural decision making and broader cultural systems.

The local politics of participation

Despite living in the same commune, Marka and Fulani social networks in Madiama are very weakly integrated. Intermarriage is rare and most villages are ethnically homogenous. The one village with a relatively even distribution of Marka and Fulani is known for substantial intra-village ethnic tension.

From its very inception, the NRMAC exhibited the ethnic politics of technical development in Madiama. Village chiefs were closely involved in the selection of delegates, with the result that close relatives were frequently chosen. Consequently, the only Fulani in the NRMAC is the male representative from the one village that *is* headed by a Fulani. Language was another important axis in the ethnic politics of participation. The majority of the NRMAC representatives speak Bambara as their first language, and few of them speak the Fulani language, Fulfulde. Despite initial training in the value of linguistic egalitarianism, NRMAC meetings were conducted entirely in Bambara.

Linguistic issues, however, represent only a part of the imbalance. From the beginning, SANREM sought to inclusively address issues in both agricultural and pastoral management, but disjunctures between Fulani cultural values and intensive animal husbandry techniques diminished Fulani receptivity and interest in the project. For many Fulani the very focus on management of land *within* the commune defined SANREM as a 'farmers' project' because Madiama does not have any 'real' pastures. The rotational grazing experiments were conducted on plots of land that, by Fulani standards, were too small and marginally productive to be taken seriously as resources for pastoralist livelihoods. Instead, they were seen as only appropriate for small-scale, intensive animal husbandry, such as that practised by Marka farmers.

Thus, though attempting to address management of pastoral resources, the geographic boundedness of the project and focus on intensive techniques precluded Fulani interest in much of the project. Beyond being economically important, herding is the most highly regarded activity in Fulani society, and is central to the Fulani sense of identity (Riesman, 1974). While the Fulani of Madiama are, in practice, mixed agro-pastoralists, their primary interests and aspirations for economic growth lie in *transhumant* pastoralism. Even those Fulani who presently rely on farming for a significant part of their livelihood, still identify transhumant pastoralism as the most important and meaningful activity in their livelihood. Due to the project focus on management of lands inside the commune, the type of pastoralism that Fulani most value was framed outside the scope of the project. While this geographical boundedness can be partly explained by logistical practicality, it also stems directly from broader political processes.

The explicit focus on *communal-level* natural resource management is the result of both national policies and the agenda of the international development community – and specifically approaches to decentralization and the *approche terroir* (Painter et al., 1994; Benjaminsen, 1997). These broad political movements provide a framework within which certain technical innovations are encouraged and others implicitly excluded. This highlights that the ways in which participatory technical developments are framed have implications in the material and discursive constitution of resource contestation at local and regional levels. By focusing on local management of lands, and specifying this 'locale' as the commune, the project from its inception was not framed in such a way as to make it culturally salient to

Fulani, despite its participatory nature. Local politics and language differences acted as barriers to active participation of Fulani as project representatives or workshop attendees, but ethnic ideologies that value transhumant pastoralism also led many Fulani to eschew participation, because it did not address land management and development at a geographic scale that was relevant to their culturally preferred subsistence strategy.

When asked about their ideas for the future of rural development the Marka and Fulani in Madiama provide significantly different visions. Marka respondents insist that farmer-herder conflict is caused by herds entering unharvested fields, while the Fulani blame encroachment of farmers' fields into pastures and trails. In order to reduce conflicts, Marka favour the maintenance of extensive farming practices with intensive herding of cattle and small ruminants in the interstices of an agricultural landscape. According to Marka respondents, this would be accomplished through continuing the devolution of authority over land management to the communal and even village levels. Such a vision of rural development asserts agricultural dominance and implicitly rules out any regional-scale management over pastoral resources, effectively precluding extensive pastoralism and Fulani ways of life and exemplifying Painter et al.'s (1994) prediction that the *approche terroir* would institutionalize pastoralists' disadvantage.

Conclusion

Participatory technical innovation takes place within frameworks of contested land rights, scales of land use and contradictory visions for rural development. While participatory innovation does not explicitly favour one side or another, an agricultural bias is implicit in any local-scale and technical orientation, effectively putting the pastoralists second. This marginalization detracts from herders' sense of ownership of and inclusion in participatory research. In order to make pastoralists' participation fully relevant, technical innovations need to be combined with the development of a secure system of land management, land rights and institutional structures that anticipate the needs of the inherently extensive pastoralism of the Sahel. By defining rights and obligations for both farmers and herders, such an effort would more equally benefit all actors within the regional agro-pastoral landscape.

The First Mile experience: connecting farmers to markets

Clive Lightfoot and Vincon Nyimbo

Introduction

The First Mile experience is about how small farmers, traders, processors and others from poor rural areas learn to build market chains linking producers to consumers. Good communication is vital. First Mile encourages people in isolated rural communities in Tanzania to use mobile phones, email and the internet to share their local experiences and good practices, learning from one another through the Linking Local Learners (LLL) online learning platform.

Starting in mid-2005 the First Mile, an approach developed by the Agricultural Marketing Systems Development Programme (AMSDP) of the Tanzanian government, using the LLL business-to-business platform provided by Rural African Ventures Investments set out to:

- facilitate learning among local groups to improve market linkages;
- generate locally developed good practices in building markets; and
- empower small farmers to get access to information and communication technologies, based on their own needs.

Achieving better market access for small farmers

Many of the best ideas for helping small farmers get better access to markets grew out of the work of small support teams established by the AMSDP in 14 districts. Known as district core groups, the teams include district officials for agriculture or marketing, a representative of the local partner NGO and representatives of local farmers, processors and traders. The groups have played a key role in linking farmers with other participants in market chains by gathering and sharing information and bringing farmers and others together to talk about how to improve the efficiency of market linkages. On occasion the core groups have helped broker agreements that allow farmers to get a better deal when they sell their produce.

One of the most popular and successful best practices to emerge from the work of the core groups is the role of the market spy, or *shu shu shu*. These market investigators are an important link in a communication chain that connects farmers, traders, processors, transporters and others. In addition to information about prices and quantities, the *shu shu shu* collects market intelligence about when, where and to whom farmers' products can be sold. This information is shared with other members of their farmers' association by mobile phone or posted on the village billboard for wider dissemination. The use of mobile phones reduces transaction costs, especially in dealings with people in other towns, and is a way of ensuring a quick response as opportunities arise.

Another important good practice is how to negotiate with a bigger player. Farmers can obtain much better prices if they get organized and talk to processors or wholesalers directly rather than waiting at home for buyers to come to them. This can be achieved through the establishment of a 'business platform', where the different stakeholders in a given market chain can meet and share the challenges they face together as partners. This practice has ensured market transparency and helped eliminate the cheating and mistrust that has hindered fair trade in the past.

Sharing best practices through the internet

Local practices to improve small farmers' access to markets emerged through sharing ideas and experiences through the LLL platform (www.linkinglearners. net). LLL is more than a website: it provides a way of working for local entrepreneurs and farmers that combines face-to-face learning with peer-to-peer learning in which they share ideas and experience over the internet.

It is through the LLL platform that the success stories about *shu shu shus* have spread among the districts. In 2005, members of the Mufindi District core group posted a report on the LLL about how *shu shu shus* could improve market access. The concept of the market spy was not new in Tanzania, but the idea of training them in marketing and bargaining skills was an innovation. After being trained, the Mufindi *shu shu shus* helped members of a farmers' group more than double their profits from crop sales.

Given the limited internet access in many rural areas and farmers' lack of email skills, the district core teams have initially acted as the link between farmers and the internet, documenting emerging good practices in their own districts and sharing them through the LLL website. The website has also helped farmers' groups communicate directly with existing and prospective customers.

Ensuring sustainability through rural service companies

A key challenge remains how to sustain and scale up the First Mile experience. Farmers are willing to pay for information and services as long as they know they will get a profit. In Babati District, for example, mobile phones were provided by the district core team to help the committees get and share information quickly. The cost of running the phones is being covered by the profits made when products are sold at the best possible price and time.

Those district core groups that have succeeded in creating and servicing a critical mass of paying customers want to learn how to set up commercially viable rural service companies that can continue to improve market linkages for small farmers. These would concentrate on preparing business plans, getting loans, setting up business platforms to build and sustain market chains and run effective warehouses and savings societies. In effect, these rural service companies would have to make the transition from public funding to sustained commercial relationships with the people directly benefiting from their services. These could include farmers' associations and others in the market chain, including bigger players such as larger processors, supermarket chains, transport companies and exporters.

Experience indicates that farmers have seen the importance of coordinating the information within their groups and also seeking market information from the outside. It also suggests that not only farmers, but also processors and traders, are benefiting from the improved marketing – increasing the likelihood that they will be prepared to pay to keep these services going.

Conclusion: promoting innovation through information exchange

Linking use of modern ICTs like mobile phones and the internet with 'low-tech' communication channels like face-to-face meetings and village billboards has been one of the keys to the success of Linking Local Learners. Trust and collaboration grow when people can meet, discuss and learn together. However, when these same people use technologies like the internet to exchange ideas and learning with peers who are often far away, they have been able to come up with more innovative ideas. The diversity of situations and the fact that many heads are focused on a common challenge or problem leads to innovative solutions.

Linking learners: livestock marketing chain development in Kenya

Michael Kibue

Two-thirds of Kenya is arid. This massive land surface hosts more than half of the livestock in the country. Pastoralists constitute 25 per cent of the population and are socially and economically dependent on livestock. Since the Livestock Market Division of the Ministry of Agriculture and the Kenya Meat Commission have ceased to operate agricultural commodities marketing, livestock trade and processing are in the hands of private traders and informal microenterprise. This has resulted in a livestock industry with poor operational capacity, low standards and unfair trade practices. Consequently, pastoralists have become poorer due to low prices and consumers have suffered from high prices.

To remove market inefficiencies and improve the returns in the value chain, a small group of stakeholders including pastoralists, livestock farmers, livestock traders, meat processors and butchers set up a non-profit association called the Livestock Stakeholder Self-Help Association (LISSA). The shared vision of LISSA is to upgrade and organize the livestock trade and meat industry in Kenya. It also aims to ensure fair trade practices for all concerned through price discovery and added value in the meat products trade.

Members wanted to follow a process of *learning by doing* to realize their vision of a fair trade market chain from pastoralists to consumers. They set up a LISSA classroom at the abattoir. The inspiration to start our learning came from the 'Linking Local Learners' (see Lightfoot and Nyimbo, this book) workshop in Nyeri, Kenya in 1998. Some members owned and managed a small abattoir in Limuru. Their challenges concerned issues of unfair trade, disorganized livestock marketing systems, poor consumers and low producer incomes. Moreover, low returns rendered investment fragile while lack of knowledge and skill led to resources being wasted. Members wanted to promote fair trade and better business for all members of the marketing chain. They wanted to learn how to make meat affordable to the poor and access their greatest meat market, Nairobi city. Soon after the Nyeri workshop, members organized a multi-stakeholder learning workshop for those in the meat marketing chain, from pastoralists to butchers selling to consumers in the Nairobi slums. This workshop posed three critical learning or empowerment questions:

- *Where are we now?* All stakeholders attending the workshop agreed that they had four main challenges: 1) disorganized livestock marketing; 2) unfair trade practices that marginalized the Maasai; 3) poor meat quality and unhygienic meat production; and 4) environmental issues including pollution from slaughter houses.

- *Where do we want to be?* Stakeholders had a future vision of fair trade among all parties including price discovery and better pricing mechanisms, empowerment of pastoralists to manage change and conserve natural rangelands, hygienic meat processing and higher quality meat and consumer satisfaction and increased trade volume from new market opportunities.
- *How shall we get there?* We proposed to get there through partnership and co-operation between all LISSA stakeholders including pastoralists, traders, the Bahati abattoir, butchers, market centre managers and vendors. LISSA aimed to ensure fair trade practices for all concerned through price discovery.

The first of the ideas we worked on was to better organize our livestock marketing. Here we undertook to organize a market chain starting from the Maasai pastoralists through the livestock traders to the Bahati abattoir and on to the wholesale meat sellers, the retail butchers and finally to the consumers. Our second action was to put in place fair trade practices. The Maasai in Kajiado and Narok have benefited because today they are able to sell their livestock for cash on delivery rather than for promissory notes. A system of price discovery makes the prices within the market chain transparent to all the members. This has realized substantial resources for the pastoral community directly contributing to poverty alleviation. Good meat quality and hygienic meat production was our third action learning point. Here we developed innovations for hygienic processing by building a biogas plant at Bahati abattoir that converts waste from the abattoir into gas which is used for lighting and heating water for cleaning. Classroom training on hygiene, aspects of meat production and environmental issues is conducted regularly. Our fourth learning effort focused on conserving the environment. Bahati abattoir is situated next to a small lake so environmentally acceptable waste disposal methods are essential for legal operations. The waste water used at the plant is treated through a set of ponds to ensure that it does not pollute the lake. Trees have been planted around the area to prevent soil erosion and to encourage birdlife. The sludge from the biogas plant is composted and sold to local farmers.

The last few years have taught us that learning is a continuous process. We have moved from one learning agenda to another. We are now facing the challenge of getting hold of specialized meat processing equipment to reduce wastage and add value to our meat products. Our initial activities have given us capabilities, material assets and social resources that are ripe for further development. How we can augment these resources to access more capital to try out value-adding equipment has become our new learning point. We have also learned what factors have contributed to our success so far. Perhaps the most critical factor was our ability to come up with a shared vision that was agreed by all the key players along the market chain. Another important realization was that learning needs a local champion on the spot to keep the group spirits high – never giving up even in times of hardship.

Beyond the farmer and the farm: users' perspectives and agricultural livelihoods

Dindo Campilan, Julieta R. Roa and Julian Gonsalves

Introduction

This paper presents UPWARD (Users' Perspectives with Agricultural Research and Development) experiences in developing and promoting participatory research and development in Asia. It traces the evolution of UPWARD concepts and methods associated with users' perspectives and participation, and drawn from field experiences in rootcrop agriculture. In particular, the paper highlights experiences and lessons learned as UPWARD combines its core participatory approach with frameworks for sustainable livelihoods and market chains.

UPWARD is an Asia-wide network supporting participatory research and development (PR&D) in agriculture and natural resource management. Launched in 1990 under the sponsorship of the International Potato Center (CIP), it involves over 50 partner organizations including research institutes, universities, NGOs, public-sector development organizations and local governments. Rootcrop agriculture in Asia provides the arena in which UPWARD field-tests PR&D. User participation is a key challenge in rootcrop research and development because of relatively weak support from the formal R&D sector, and of the poor agricultural and environmental conditions associated with these crops.

Users' perspectives

UPWARD's PR&D approach refers to a pool of diverse yet interrelated concepts, practices, norms and attitudes that enable people to enhance their knowledge for sustainable agriculture and natural resource management (Gonsalves et al., 2005). UPWARD traces its roots to earlier client-oriented, participatory and systems-oriented approaches such as:

- *Farmer-back-to-farmer model* (Rhoades and Booth, 1982), which views technology development and application as a process starting and ending with farmers;
- *Food systems framework* (CIP, 1989), which considers technological change as a process covering pre-production, main and post-production phases;

- *Household systems perspectives* (Hardon-Baars, 1997), which takes the household system as a socio-economic unit for decision making, production and consumption;
- *Gender analysis* (ISNAR, 1985), which analyses gender-related aspects of agricultural R&D;
- *Farmer First model* (Chambers et al., 1989), which seeks to develop farmer participatory approaches in agricultural R&D.

While eclectic in its approach, UPWARD was conceived with the following distinct features:

- Unlike most client-oriented approaches influenced by marketing research, UPWARD originated from the household and consumer sciences and therefore views users from an actor orientation.
- It rejects the notion of a farmer stereotype by seeking to explore heterogeneity within the farming population.
- In contrast to farmer-centred participatory approaches, it views farmers alongside other types of key user groups.
- It examines not just farming systems or agricultural production, but the broader food system encompassing the entire food production-utilization cycle.

UPWARD takes 'users' as actors (either as individuals, households, groups, communities or formal organizations) engaged in the creative generation and use of knowledge – in both hardware and software forms – to achieve desired agricultural innovation (Prain, 1995; Campilan, 1995). Users include both end-users who ultimately apply knowledge for their direct benefit, and intermediate users engaged in transforming and sharing knowledge with the former. Meanwhile, 'users' perspectives' represent local people's views and knowledge, their understanding of their biophysical and social world, including the meanings they attach to their experiences, on which their decisions and actions are anchored (Campilan, 1997).

UPWARD field projects focus on needs and opportunities associated with rootcrop agriculture – particularly for sweet potato and potato – in the South-east, North-east and South Asian sub-regions. Examples include:

- *piloting approaches in mobilizing communities* for integrated disease management (potato in Nepal and China) and on-farm conservation of genetic resources (sweet potato in the Philippines);
- *developing and field-testing participatory learning methodologies*, including farmer field schools for integrated crop management (sweet potato in Indonesia) and farmer-to-farmer extension for optimizing use of local animal feed resources (Vietnam and the Philippines);
- *strengthening microenterprises* for agri-food products (Philippines) and linking with markets and the private/commercial sector (potato in Indonesia);

- *facilitating joint experimentation and learning* on local crop-livestock livelihood systems (sweet potato in Lao PDR and Indonesia) through multi-stakeholder partnerships; and
- *enabling support services and markets to serve poor farmers,* such as commercial production of high-quality seed (sweet potato in the Philippines, potato in Nepal).

UPWARD's underlying PR&D capacity development goal is to nurture young and middle-level scientists, especially those from lesser known and non-traditional research and development organizations in the region. It makes use of a mentoring approach that enables junior PR&D professionals to receive individualized and continuous guidance from more senior colleagues. Drawing upon its field project experiences, UPWARD has developed international training curricula covering key capacities for understanding, doing and enabling PR&D. The curriculum and accompanying materials have been adapted by other organizations for use in many regional and national training courses. Several manuals and volumes of papers have been published to promote wider access to and sharing of PR&D knowledge. Foremost of these is a three-volume sourcebook on global experiences in PR&D by over a hundred organizations (Gonsalves et al., 2005).

What have we learned?

In an iterative process of action and reflection, UPWARD's thinking and practice of PR&D has continuously evolved through 16 years of direct experience in implementing field projects, sharing and learning with similar initiatives on participatory research, and strengthening individual and organizational capacities of partners and other interested groups. In this paper, we highlight those that relate to UPWARD efforts in introducing a sustainable livelihoods perspective to its agenda on PR&D for rootcrop agriculture.

From food systems to livelihood systems

UPWARD began with a food systems framework as a means to promote a greater focus on the neglected aspects of agricultural research – beyond field production and into consumption, marketing, post-harvest and nutrition (Rhoades, 1990). This encouraged UPWARD to look beyond on-farm production and the producing farmers, while becoming sensitized to the full range of users in the food chain (Prain, 1995). Using the concept of food systems in undertaking participatory documentation and assessment, UPWARD better understood the role of rootcrops in the diet, nutrition and food survival especially among marginal upland communities and ethnic groups.

For example, research in Indonesia and the Philippines documented the importance of sweet potato as a food staple in remote farming communities, as part of homegarden diversity that contributes to nutrition improvement for household members, and as a buffer crop during crisis situations (Minantyorini et al., 1996; Gayao, 1995). It also uncovered the increasing importance of sweet potato as an indirect food source for households who sold their products to generate cash income (Campilan, 2005), the religious and cultural values attached to the crop (Campilan, 2002), and its role as feed for women-managed animal production (Peters et al., 2001). In taking users' perspectives on the role of sweet potato in food systems, UPWARD began to understand the wider roles of the crop in the livelihood of farming households. As Castillo (1995) pointed out, users have taught researchers that sweet potato is a secondary crop with primary functions – consumption/nutrition, income/employment, natural resource sustainability, and gender/social equity.

From crop production to agricultural livelihoods

Based on a better understanding of users' perspectives, UPWARD organized its research agenda according to three thematic groups: 1) enhancing production systems for soil, seed, pest and disease management, 2) sustaining genetic resources conservation – for documenting, collecting and using local germplasm and associated knowledge, and 3) promoting processing–marketing–consumption to create and optimize value-adding opportunities from rootcrops.

It became clear, however, that field-level problems could not be neatly divided according to these thematic categories. For instance, farmers' interest in participating in season-long field schools on pest management was highly influenced by fluctuations in market prices for sweet potato (Van de Fliert et al., 1997). Similarly, the sustainability of community-managed genebanks hinged on whether the cultivars being conserved, or the crops themselves, have high use-value and market demand (Prain and Bagalanon, 1998). These field experiences suggested the need for an integrated framework for understanding rootcrop-based livelihoods that links production systems, genetic resources conservation, and processing–marketing–consumption.

When the crop-focused framework remained inadequate to understand the dynamics of household decision making and action, UPWARD found livelihoods analysis to be a valuable starting point in PR&D, providing a broader perspective on household needs and opportunities with respect to livelihoods on-farm, off-farm and non-farm. This helped researchers and users to jointly identify: 1) the comparative advantages of rootcrop agriculture vis-à-vis other livelihoods, 2) appropriate innovations for enhancing livelihood benefits from engaging in rootcrop agriculture, and 3) impact contributions of rootcrops to the overall livelihood system of farming households.

From farms to market chains

The adoption of a sustainable livelihoods framework helped UPWARD move beyond the crop and the farmer. Yet its PR&D work still sought participation mainly by farmers/cultivators, and most often on-farm. UPWARD has recently taken on the challenge of undertaking PR&D with actors along market chains – from cultivators to consumers (UPWARD, 2003; Roa, this book).

Among the earlier efforts was the introduction of processing-type potato varieties in Indonesia (Sinung-Basuki et al., 2003). Promising clones were selected, and later approved by the government for official release, based on a series of evaluations involving farmers, traders, snack food factories and consumer groups. The challenge was to combine the often divergent selection criteria used by market chain actors to identify varieties which met everybody's preferences and requirements.

With their strategic role in ensuring timely production of high-quality farm products, formal and informal service providers have become key participants in PR&D for agricultural livelihoods. Seed producer groups in Nepal and the Philippines learned techniques for rapid multiplication and seed selection (Lama and Hidalgo, 2003; Laranang and Basilio, 2003). Together, seed suppliers and farmer-cultivators developed mechanisms to coordinate distribution and marketing with equitable benefits for them.

Conclusion

In sum, as the work of UPWARD has moved beyond the farm and farmers our wider focus on users, firmly rooted in but extending the Farmer First perspective, has resulted in three main achievements: locally adapted socio-technical innovations, field-tested concepts and methods, and enhanced linkages and capacities.

Continuing improvement and innovation in the market chain of rootcrop chips

Julieta R. Roa

Rootcrops and participatory research

Rootcrops in the Philippines are grown on about 0.5 million hectares of ecologically fragile land and are an important source of food and cash for mostly poor farmers. The Philippine Rootcrop Research and Training Center (PhilRootcrops) was created in 1977 to oversee and implement a multi-pronged rootcrop research and development programme. In its early stages, rootcrop technology development was technology-heavy, top-down, fragmented, discipline-oriented and lacked systems thinking. As a result, many reportedly 'mature' technologies (varieties, products, equipments) stayed on researchers' shelves.

The late 1980s marked a turning point. A skeletal social science unit was established and collaboration with the Users' Perspectives with Agricultural Research and Development (UPWARD) network led to the integration of participatory research and development (PR&D) in the national rootcrop programme. UPWARD was instrumental in promoting a paradigm shift by engaging teams of technical and social science researchers in small grant projects to discover local knowledge of sweet potato pests and diseases, investigate indigenous systems of nutrient management, undertake participatory diagnostics of sweet potato livelihood systems, study the people perspectives of technology development, and take part in participatory action projects (see Campilan et al., this book).

In addition to participatory processes, there has been a more recent focus on enterprise and market chain approaches. Here I present the case of *gabi* chips processing in a community in Leyte, Philippines, as an illustration of the Continuing Improvement and Innovation (CI&I) approach to microenterprise development.

The case of *gabi* chips

Gabi chips processing is a classic case of local innovation by rural women. Three household-based food processors in Anilao, a village community in Liloan, Southern Leyte, had been trained by the Department of Trade and Industry (DTI) in banana chips processing, a small livelihood enterprise. Attacked by a disease, the supply of banana became irregular and pushed one innovative processor to try other materials like cassava *(Manihot esculenta)*, sweet potato *(Ipomoea batatas)* and yautia *(Xanthosoma sagittifolium* L. Schott). Of these, yautia or *gabi* chips became well-accepted and popular. Other women processors followed suit, putting Anilao on the native delicacy food map.

Gabi chips, like sweet potato and cassava chips, are crispy snack foods enjoyed by adults and children. They make convenient gift packs and have some nutritional advantages. As orders began to come in, however, conflicts between household processors and farmer-suppliers, and issues relating to input supply price and stability, product quality and unfair competition began to surface. These challenges had to be addressed if the markets were not to be lost.

In mid-2000, therefore, an interdisciplinary research team at PhilRootcrops–Visayas State University (VSU) spearheaded and facilitated the *gabi* chips collaborative project. This project involved different stakeholders, including the women processors, supplier-farmers and support service providers such as the local government unit (LGU) municipal agriculture office, the LGU-based *Techno-gabay* (technology aid), the provincial DTI and Department of Science and Technology (DOST).

Integrating CI&I and participatory action research

The *gabi* chips project was guided by lessons from previous rootcrop integrated development projects and participatory action research (e.g. dried cassava flour-grates, sweet potato-based soy sauce and farmer field schools). It was also intended to provide proof of concept of the CI&I approach pioneered by VSU's ACIAR-funded livestock programme. Using specifically designed tools at each defined stage, the CI&I approach (Figure 2.2) is focused on achieving objectives through a series of incremental, measurable and time-bound improvements. These improvements or innovations are identified by clientele and partners through a participatory process, along with the activities, measurable outputs and timeframe required to achieve them. The timeframe is split into 30-day cycles with a built-in feedback system and the whole process is iterative in nature (Clark, 2002; Timms and Clark, 2004).

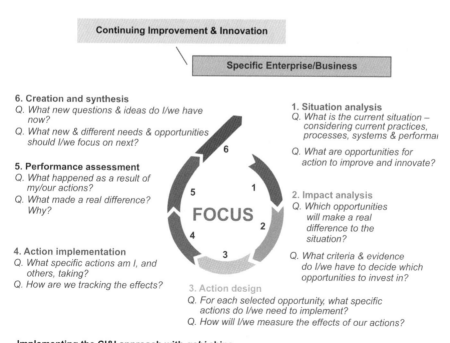

Continuing Improvement & Innovation

Specific Enterprise/Business

6. Creation and synthesis
Q. What new questions & ideas do I/we have now?
Q. What new & different needs & opportunities should I/we focus on next?

5. Performance assessment
Q. What happened as a result of my/our actions?
Q. What made a real difference? Why?

4. Action implementation
Q. What specific actions am I, and others, taking?
Q. How are we tracking the effects?

1. Situation analysis
Q. What is the current situation – considering current practices, processes, systems & performan
Q. What are opportunities for action to improve and innovate?

2. Impact analysis
Q. Which opportunities will make a real difference to the situation?
Q. What criteria & evidence do I/we have to decide which opportunities to invest in?

3. Action design
Q. For each selected opportunity, what specific actions do I/we need to implement?
Q. How will I/we measure the effects of our actions?

FOCUS

Implementing the CI&I approach with *gabi* chips

Figure 2.2 The Continuing Improvement and Innovation (CI&I) approach

The VSU experience showed that the CI&I approach allows for systematic management of PR&D because of its focused, stepwise implementation. It therefore blends well with the community-based participatory action research (CPAR) promoted by the Department of Agriculture by 1) engaging with various relevant partners in the different phases of implementation, from problem and opportunity diagnosis to monitoring and evaluation; 2) being clientele-oriented and sensitive to their needs for opportunities and skills to address these; and 3) being an open, flexible and iterative yet focused process. Integrating CI&I with CPAR tested how the intensive and grounded knowledge generated from the latter could be made more useful when combined with the CI&I analytical and decision tools.

The CI&I approach implies that improving the status of any actor (farmer, processor, consumer) along the chain (wherever the entry point in the development process) involves the improvement of each actor along the production–consumer continuum: the market chain. Thus, farmer benefits or processor profits involve value-adding strategies, improved distribution or reduced costs from the farm to the ultimate consumer. The different components such as production, processing and marketing constitute different levels of focus for all actor(s) involved, and all innovations are understood to contribute ultimately to improvements in a farm or processing enterprise.

Implementing the CI&I approach with gabi chips

The main objective defined during the situation and impact analyses by the processors and other stakeholders was to improve the profitability of the *gabi* chips microenterprise of the Anilao food processors by at least 10% by the end of the project. A focusing framework was used to undertake a step-by-step analysis that highlighted three factors that can improve profitability: product quality (raw material, processing), product presentation (packaging, labelling), and marketing strategies (promotion, market expansion).

The entry point for improvement of product quality was the household processor of *gabi* chips. However, farmers also participated in the process through raw material supply negotiation (price, required cultivar) and *gabi* production experiments to prepare for a stable and increased supply of *gabi* when markets for the chips increase. Other actors included support providers such as the LGU (credit, monitoring, assistance in business licensing), *Techno-gabay* (farmer and market contacts, farmer–scientist experimentation, current good manufacturing practice facility or cGMP), the DTI (packaging, trade fair assistance), the DOST (design of a cGMP facility, canvassing of nutrient analytical laboratory), and PhilRootcrops–VSU (product quality optimization, consumer tests and market promotion, nutrient analysis, bar-coding of product, capacity development, overall coordination and facilitation).

To improve product presentation, a new label and packaging were designed for the *gabi* chips. Their market effectiveness was tested at the 2006 Manila trade fair. A new chip slicer was also developed and tested with the main processor. However, further work is required as it is more expensive and difficult to use than the easily obtained kitchen gadget processors currently use. Consumer testing (for shelf-life of chips) showed a decrease in all parameters (colour, appearance, texture, flavour and general acceptability) after two months, signalling a substantial amount of work still to be done in terms of product quality and product positioning in the market vis-à-vis the hundreds of similarly priced products available.

A preliminary screening experiment identified variety, slice thickness and frying time as particularly important variables affecting product quality. Before the project, *gabi* chips processors in Liloan did not standardize product thickness or frying time, and just bought any variety irrespective of maturity. Two processors were identified as producers of particularly good quality chips because of their higher acceptability ratings.

Resolution of conflicts between processors and farmers was an important activity. At the start, farmers in three yautia-producing villages had marketing arrangements with the processors. Later, this was reduced to one village to control for the required cultivar, maturity of cormels, seasonal rotation of supply, as well as the elevation of production areas. Conflicts related to the business licensing requirement, personality differences, and raw material purchases from other farmers were resolved by meeting both the processor group and the core farmers from Liloan. Resolving price differences and stressing the importance of raw material quality requirements led to an agreement between the processors and the farmers, as well as the addition of technical assistance and monitoring of farms to the project activities.

Project stakeholders were trained in business plan preparation. The business plan included the establishment of a GMP facility for *gabi* chips, and the development of market and supply strategies. Though volumes are still small, *gabi* farmers benefit from the chips market and a guaranteed price for their produce. Consumers benefit from a nutritious local delicacy and the community enjoys the prestige associated with this novelty product.

CI&I: focused, specific, measurable and time-bound

In the *gabi* chips case, the CI&I approach emerged as an effective a way of doing, learning and building skills. The focused incremental improvement(s) designed to lead on to the final goal (defined by stakeholders) improve the likelihood of achieving results by each actor because the progression and targets at each step are clear and doable. All the identified value-adding activities from farm to market in support of the *gabi* enterprise were achieved in about 18 months, providing clear proof of concept for the CI&I approach.

In the context of the market chain, understanding and improving the response to market opportunities, improving access to information and contacts, arranging appropriate and sustainable raw materials supply, and improving markets are critical to ensure greater benefits for farmers and other actors. The market chain context is embedded within the CI&I approach which was able to identify different value-adding activities from farm to market; a holistic strategy necessary in dealing with the complexities of enterprise development, especially among resource-poor housewives and farmers.

The *gabi* chips case shows that the development pathways promoted by the CI&I approach through a participatory process can result in value-adding at various points in the production–consumption chain. Wherever the most appropriate development entry point (farmers, processors, service providers) for a particular problem or opportunity, effective partnerships can deliver the goods. In addition to benefits to household processors and the supplier-farmers, the facilitators and support service providers have greatly learned from the process, with inter-agency collaboration strengthened and spillover technical assistance to microenterprises in other communities already planned.

Community agro-enterprise development: experiences from Uganda and Malawi

Jemimah Njuki, Susan Kaaria, Pascal Sanginga, Elly Kaganzi and Tennyson Magombo

Introduction

Based on an examination of two case studies, from Malawi and Uganda, we highlight the key steps and procedures in building capacity among farmers, farmers' groups, and communities to identify and evaluate market opportunities, develop profitable agro-enterprises and intensify production, while sustaining the resources upon which livelihoods depend. While the approach has been very successful in linking smallholder farmers to domestic markets, these efforts need to be complemented by efforts to develop market institutions that will enable farmers to be competitive and to enter regional and international markets. We also analyse the role of strengthening farmer capacity to understand markets, inclusion of gender and equity in such approaches and the role of farmer organizations in ensuring effective smallholder farmer–market linkages.

In Uganda, the government Plan for Modernization of Agriculture emphasizes strategic interventions on traditional (coffee, tea) and non-traditional (potatoes, bananas, fish) cash crops targeting international markets (Government of Uganda, 2000). In Malawi, the government has introduced the One Village One Product concept for export markets. These approaches have produced mixed results. While many studies have documented impressive results of linking farmers to export markets, smallholder farmers have rarely benefited from these initiatives, as niche markets tend to be highly competitive and specialized, with rigorous quality standards (Diao and Hazell, 2004). There are real risks that such market opportunities may be seized by a few large-scale commercial farmers at the expense of small-scale farmers. Domestic and regional markets, however, still represent a large and growing opportunity for smallholder farmers in Africa to diversify into high-value products.

Applying the rural agro-enterprise approach: two case studies

The Uganda and Malawi cases have both employed the rural agro-enterprise development approach (see Best, 2002; Ostertag, 1999; Lundy et al., 2003). This has a number of steps:

- Building strategic partnerships and selecting pilot sites.
- Participatory diagnosis and community visioning.
- Formation of participatory market research groups.
- Market and enterprise visits.
- Evaluation of enterprise options.
- Farmer experimentation and participatory technology development.
- Design and implementation of agro-enterprise projects.
- Facilitating support services for enterprise development.
- Strengthening local institutions and promoting gender equity.

Case study 1: Nyabyumba United Farmers' Group, Kabale, Uganda

The Nyabyumba United Farmers' Group is located in Kamuganguzi sub-county of Kabale District in south-western Uganda where over 90 per cent of the population is engaged in small-scale agriculture. The farmer group was formed in 1998 as a Farmer Field School with the aim of producing seed potato to improve overall production quality. Group dynamic support was provided by Africare, an international NGO which had previously provided the farmers with other seed materials including beans and hybrid maize seed. In 1999 the group became a member of the Uganda National Seed Potato Producers Association with 20 members and for 3–4 years the association successfully produced seed potato. Most sales were made to NGOs in the area who supplied farmers at no cost. Increased seed potato sales led to the formation of an association of six groups with 120 members, of whom 60 per cent were women. However, by 2004, demand for seed potato had all but ceased as farmers in the area were unable to sell the increased volumes of ware potatoes.

This provided an opportunity for the International Center for Tropical Agricultural (CIAT) to work with the Nyabyumba group and Africare to test an area-based participatory marketing approach. An initial step consisted of the farmers mapping the chain of actors and identifying service providers in the existing system for producing and marketing potatoes. This was followed by participatory market research to identify the various marketing channels for ware potatoes from the production site in Kabale. Farmers identified a number of markets including wholesale markets, retail markets and more formal markets such as the supermarkets, hotels, restaurants and fast food chains. The analysis collated information on basic buying conditions including price, frequency of purchase, quality of produce required, payment conditions and interest in receiving a regular supply from a farmers' group. Based on the market analysis, the Nyabyumba group decided that linkage to Nandos, a multinational fast food restaurant in Kampala, was the most attractive option. Nandos consumes approximately 5–10 t of fresh potatoes every month and this level of purchase fell within the upper limits of possible supply by the farmers' group.

Following the preliminary analysis, a business meeting was held in Kampala, between all players and Nandos to negotiate a deal. Major issues of negotiation were the volume and frequency of supply, quality, price and payment terms. Nandos advised the farmers that if they produced quality potatoes at a competitive price, Nandos would buy more potatoes. Based on these discussions the Nyabyumba group carried out a basic profitability analysis which showed that the farmers could be profitable if they sold to Nandos throughout the year. Terms were agreed by all parties and the farmers moved to detailed enterprise planning, during which they recognized that they would need to change their production system. A participatory technology evaluation process was initiated to test different technologies for potato production with the aim of achieving the market quality requirements. Some of the specific issues of experimentation were new varieties, potato size and moisture content. The farmers also required key services including transportation, access to finance and direct communications in order to support their market linkages, as well as basic marketing and management support from their development partner and the local research centre, which specialized in potatoes.

Although size and moisture content problems led to high rates of rejection for early consignments, time and experimentation reduced rates of rejection from about 80 per cent to less than 10 per cent. Between July 2003 and April 2006, farmers had collectively sold 290,000 kg of potatoes to Nandos with a value of more than US$50,000. With time as farmers gained capacity to engage with the market, their external service providers started moving on to other groups and associations giving only minimal on-demand support to the farmers. To address issues of poor savings and credit service provision the group set up an internal savings and loan mechanism where members could borrow money for input purchases and other needs and pay back with interest.

Case 2: Katundulu Village, Ukwe Planning Area, Malawi

Katundulu village is located in the Ukwe Extension Planning Area about 35 km to the North West of Lilongwe City. Compared to other areas in Malawi, poverty levels are moderate because farmers in the area are engaged in tobacco production and therefore have relatively higher incomes.

Activities in Katundulu began with a visioning process to enable farmers to come up with a common vision for the development of the village. The vision had two broad elements, improving household food security through increased productivity and crop diversification and increasing incomes through better markets for existing products and high-value market options. From this visioning process, the 34 households in the village organized themselves into the Tigwirane Dzanja Club, which means 'Let us hold each other's hand', reflecting the community's belief that individual efforts were insufficient to resolve their food insecurity and market problems.

In partnership with government service providers, the community was taken through the rural agro-enterprise development process. The group was also trained in group dynamics and leadership, gender and HIV/AIDS. The community then established a main committee (which also served as the participatory monitoring and evaluation committee), a participatory market research (PMR) committee, a farmer participatory research committee and a livestock committee.

With very little previous marketing experience, the PMR committee, together with external facilitators carried out market assessments in different markets including open air markets, city markets, hotels, schools and other institutions to identify market options and to understand market requirements. The group analysed the results using profitability analysis and evaluated the options using a set of criteria. From the analysis, two enterprises were selected: beans, a common subsistence crop in the area, and pigs, a new enterprise with which farmers had no prior experience.

Before the start of the pig enterprise, farmers were trained in pig production, pig feed formulation, pen construction and disease and pest management. Being a new enterprise, farmer participatory research was initiated to test different options for pig feeding, and growing of different replacement options for substitute feeding such as pigeon peas, soya beans and potato vines.

While the farmers have been very successful in supplying the local market for piglets (where the main buyers are other farmers and NGO projects), they have been unable to meet the stringent quality requirements of the meat processing factory that is currently importing pork from Brazil. The piglets market is an attractive option as piglets are sold within one month of birth thus avoiding the competition for food between pigs and people that arises during the dry season. By the end of 2007, households had increased their annual income by 173 per cent from the sale of pigs. The farmers are currently unable to meet the piglet demand in the country. Pig production has become a common activity for all households in the village. The farmers also earn additional income from training piglet recipient farmers on pig production and management.

Impacts: has it made a difference?

In both the Uganda and Malawi sites there is strong evidence of a positive impact on income, with average earnings per household being higher in sites where the approach is being implemented than in other sites. For example, the Nyabyumba farmers in Uganda earned an additional US$50,000 (about $400 per household) over two years, an amount well beyond average household incomes in the region. In Malawi, households have increased their incomes by over 170 per cent to an average income several times that of the national average, in addition to having more sources of income than comparable farmers. In Malawi, this additional income has gone into improving food security, the accumulation of household assets, improved living conditions and investments in fertilizer, especially for maize and tobacco production. In Uganda, the emphasis has been on improving living standards and purchase of land due to the readily available land market. An explicit attention to gender issues in the approach has resulted in more equitable sharing of benefits compared to other traditional cash crops such as tobacco.

Whilst forming farmer groups is recognized as essential in making learning more efficient, for receiving external support and achieving economies of scale, simply being in a group does not ensure success in the market place. There is growing evidence that farmer groups which are formed hastily with little reference to building mutual trust, accessing new technologies and linking to markets tend to fail through lack of benefits (Sanginga et al., 2004). Building farmer capacity to understand markets is a vital ingredient if farmers' groups are to access and maintain links to markets, particularly when dealing with higher value and more risky markets. As groups take on more financial risks and increase their physical and financial assets, governance and transparency are essential to success and emphasis must therefore be placed on improving group functioning and accountability processes.

All markets carry risk and prices of agricultural products are particularly volatile. Risks increase as product and market value increase and therefore farmers need to be fully aware of their exposure and ability to deal with financial risk. Contrary to the common view that farmers are risk averse, the Nyabyumba farmers decided to link with a high-value market, taking on debt and investing in high-value capital assets such as purchase of transport trucks. For the less experienced farmers in the Malawi case, taking on a relatively new enterprise was very risky and a step-by-step implementation starting at a very small scale helped to build farmer confidence in managing the enterprise.

Conclusion

It takes a combination of many skills to enable farmer groups to identify and maintain market links. One of the key factors in these case studies is the importance of strong collaboration between research, development and business support service providers that provide technologies, services and capacity building to keep the farmers competitive in the market place.

While this approach has been very effective in reaching small groups of farmers, there are challenges on how to scale this out. Of particular importance is how to link these community micro-level processes to higher macro-level processes where market opportunities and institutional conditions may offer better opportunities for small-scale farmers.

A key strategy is the formation of learning alliances with research and development organizations that already work on linking farmers to markets in order to reach the thousands of farmer groups that they work with. In Malawi, a learning alliance with a consortium of seven NGOs has enabled the approach to spread to seven districts in the country. Another strategy is the institutionalization of the approach in national research and extension systems and this has started in Malawi and will be the next focus in Uganda and other countries. A further approach is the use of networks of farmer groups or second order farmer associations.

Enabling rural innovation in Africa

Susan Kaaria, Pascal Sanginga, Jemimah Njuki, Robert Delve, Colletah Chitsike and Rupert Best

Introduction

Agricultural markets can play significant roles in reducing poverty in poor economies, especially in countries which have not already achieved significant agricultural growth. Dorward et al. (2003) highlight three broad mechanisms through which agricultural growth can drive poverty reduction: 1) through the direct impacts of increased agricultural productivity and incomes; 2) through the benefits of cheaper food for both the urban and rural poor; and 3) through agriculture's contribution to growth and the generation of economic opportunity in the non-farm sector. However, experience has shown that markets can fail the poor, especially the poorest and marginalized groups, particularly women. Johnson (2003) argues that in remote rural areas markets may fail because they maybe too 'thin', or the risks and costs of participating especially for poor people may be too high, and/or there may be social or economic barriers to participation.

Approaches for linking smallholder farmers to markets are often commodity and cash-crop based and use arrangements such as contract farming and out-grower schemes that link smallholder farmers to large growers. Such arrangements, while linking the smallholder farmers to regional and domestic markets, also leave them vulnerable, due to lack of capacity to effectively engage in markets, or to analyse and negotiate with these markets.

How can poorer people, and particularly women, participate more effectively in markets? The International Center for Tropical Agriculture (CIAT) is testing and evaluating one approach – Enabling Rural Innovation (ERI) – with partners and communities in Uganda, Tanzania, Malawi, Zimbabwe, Kenya, Mozambique, Zambia, Rwanda and DR Congo. Here we provide a general overview of the approach, the guiding principles, conceptual framework and steps in the ERI process, and some lessons learned.

Enabling rural innovation

The ERI initiative uses participatory research approaches to strengthen the capacity of R&D partners and rural communities to access and generate technical and market information for improving farmers' decision-making. This initiative has emerged from three main streams of CIAT's expertise and experience: 1) farmer participatory research; 2) rural agro-enterprise development; and 3) natural resource management. Using the most effective elements from these three areas, the ERI initiative aims to build more robust livelihood strategies within the rural community. It promotes an entrepreneurial culture where farmers 'produce what they can market rather than trying to market what they produce' and encourages them to invest in their natural resources rather than depleting them for short-term market gain (Best and Kaganzi, 2003; Ferris et al., 2006). These efforts are geared towards fostering effective public-private partnerships, horizontal and vertical links between networks of farmers' organizations and R&D service providers (Sanginga et al., 2007). Figure 2.3 shows the key steps in implementing the ERI process.

The ERI approach focuses on building the skills and knowledge of communities, local service providers and farmers' organizations to engage effectively in markets. The approach emphasizes a market orientation that enables smallholder farmers to successfully link themselves to potential markets, with support from R&D partners (Ostertag, 1999; Lundy et al., 2003). It recognizes that risk assessment plays an important role in strategy development for smallholder farmers. When selecting products and new business options, therefore, assessment of an appropriate level of risk that a client group can undertake is crucial. Market opportunity analyses of products based on demand and profitability will tend to bias results towards higher risk

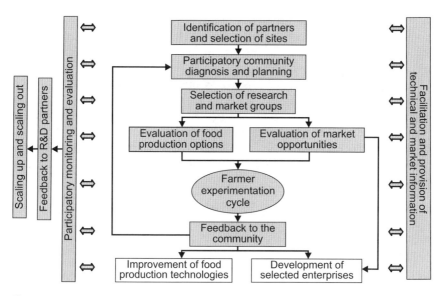

Figure 2.3 Key steps to Enabling Rural Innovation

options. Nevertheless, the greater associated profits may make such high risk options attractive for groups with more marketing experience.

Once the group has selected the most appropriate option, the farmer organization or group then follows a stepwise approach to developing sustainable enterprises. The process begins with a participatory diagnosis that assesses community assets, market opportunities and constraints. An enterprise planning committee is elected to undertake market studies on behalf of the group. Participatory market research builds skills of farmers to analyse markets and permits them to have a better understanding of markets, to consolidate relationships with traders and to negotiate for better prices for their produce. Enterprise selection is based on the analysis of sound technical and economic information, as well as community criteria. Business plans of the best enterprise options are designed and tested for collective marketing (see Best and Kaganzi, 2003; Ferris et al., 2006).

The involvement of farmers as decision-makers in all stages of the innovation process is a hallmark of the ERI approach. Each community or farmer group is supported by a community development facilitator who supports the development of the group. With increasing maturity, communities report dramatic increases in the levels of trust and cooperation, the presence of several committees, regular community meetings and regular interaction with R&D partners. Across sites, horizontal and vertical linkages are created with other farmers' organizations, service providers and governmental departments. Many groups link up with other external organizations and attract additional resources from governmental agencies, NGOs and other rural service providers to support their community action plans. These groups become a vehicle through which farmers can pursue wider development concerns, initiate new activities, organize collective action among members and extend relationships and linkages with external organizations.

Gender equity and empowerment of women are central to the ERI process. Pro-active strategies and gender-sensitive facilitation skills are used to build the capacity of both men and women to identify and evaluate a diverse range of market opportunities, and experiment with a range of crop and soil fertility management technologies. This is achieved using a number of gender-sensitive participatory tools and methods, and constantly focusing attention on three main sets of questions:

- Who has access to, and control over, resources?
- Who does what, when and where?
- Who benefits from what and how?

Our strategy has been to encourage and sustain active participation, and cooperation of both men and women in the project activities, creating gender awareness at the community level through the use of interactive adult learning methods.

With the ERI approach, community-based participatory monitoring and evaluation (PM&E) tools are applied to support self-reflection and a continuous process of learning at both community and project levels. At the local level, community-driven PM&E systems support and enhance group functioning processes, improve local decision making and enhance participation. These systems also enable communities to develop indicators to measure change, collect and analyse their data, and adjust their strategies accordingly. PM&E results also have a wider impact by giving farmers the capacity to make more effective demands of service providers, including holding R&D institutions to account.

Successful innovations result from strong interactions and flow of knowledge within networks of stakeholders. Effective local partnerships between researchers, extension workers, NGOs and farmer communities are key to the success of ERI. Partners are selected not only for their interest in incorporating the approach into their ongoing work, but also on the basis of institutional assessment, including their working relationships with local communities, their objectives and potential to scale up impact.

Lessons from the ERI initiative

A series of case studies were conducted to assess the impacts of the ERI initiative on rural livelihoods, giving rise to several lessons.

Performance of farmers' organizations. A critical success factor in expanding market access is the presence of mature farmers' organizations. Farmer organizations are at the same time becoming an important stakeholder group in agricultural R&D. However, benefits are not equally distributed – with men, educated people or group leaders (men and women) benefiting significantly more than women and the less educated. These disparities are likely to be more pronounced when working with large farmer organizations, thereby creating a need for systematic research into the dynamics, composition, performance and effectiveness of second-order or higher level farmers' associations.

Market linkages benefit women. Participatory approaches for linking farmers to markets do increase the bargaining power of women. This translates into tangible household benefits in the form of increased household income and social capital, more shared intra-household decision making and greater skills in analysing and understanding markets, in conducting experimentation and in taking on leadership positions in projects. The choice of enterprise selected and the farmer-to-market approach are important factors in influencing how much control women have. However, what remains unanswered is how different farmer-to-market approaches shape nutrition and food security outcomes.

Many barriers to market access remain. A majority of small-scale poor farmers continue to face numerous barriers to market participation, including a poor asset base, lack of market information, weak institutions, the inability to capture benefits from value-added processes, and low involvement of the private sector and commercial relationships. Although some farmers make income gains from farmer-to-market linkages, significant income disparities remain between the women and men members. There is still a need, therefore, to identify alternative ways to link women and other hard-to-reach farmers with emerging market opportunities.

Research linkages. An important aspect of farmer-to-market linkages is a strong linkage to research in order to sustain the increases in productivity necessary. Payoffs are higher when agro-enterprise development is linked to research to address bottlenecks along the value chain. Research that removes bottlenecks in production and ensures sustainable supply of quality produce is particularly critical.

The need for policy options. A final key lesson is that policy-related research is a critical missing element and that any approach that aims to link small-scale poor farmers to markets must conduct rigorous assessments of economic and policy-related factors that influence the functioning of input and output for markets. There is a particularly urgent need for comparative research to identify policy options for promoting the engagement of the poor in markets.

Public–private partnerships and developing-country agriculture

David J. Spielman, Frank Hartwich and Klaus von Grebmer

Introduction

Public–private partnerships (PPPs) in agricultural R&D are increasingly viewed as an effective means of conducting advanced research, developing new technologies, and deploying new products for the benefit of small-scale, resource-poor farmers and other marginalized social groups in developing countries. There are, however, few studies that empirically establish whether PPPs fulfil this role effectively.

Here we attempt to fill this knowledge gap by examining how PPPs in agricultural research stimulate greater investment in pro-poor innovation in developing-country agriculture. This paper is meant to provide policy makers, researchers, and business decision-makers with a better understanding of how such partnerships operate, what types of challenges they face, and how their operation can be improved to contribute more to food security and poverty reduction.

We define PPPs as any research collaboration between public- and private-sector entities in which partners jointly plan and execute activities with a view to accomplishing agreed-upon objectives while sharing the costs, risks and benefits incurred in the process. We examine three specific issues with respect to PPPs: 1) whether they contribute to reducing the costs of research; 2) whether they promote innovative research; and 3) whether they enhance the impact of research on smallholders and other marginalized groups.

To do so, the study examines 75 projects undertaken by the research centres and programmes of the CGIAR in partnership with various types of private firms.

What are PPPs?

Conceptually, PPPs represent a means of organizing the production of some output – in this case, agricultural knowledge and technology. Thus the production process is subject to the usual constraints imposed by the costs of physical and human capital. The production process is also subject to constraints associated with imperfections in the market for knowledge. In other words, certain barriers impede the otherwise smooth process of exchanging and using knowledge necessary to the innovation process.

Since their emergence, PPPs have been the focus of extensive study in a variety of disciplines, including economics, public administration and management science. The literature on research partnerships can be divided into at least four analytical categories (Hagedoorn et al., 2000; Hall, 2006; Hall et al., 2003, 2002):

- industrial organization approaches that focus on analysing the economics of inherent failures in the market for scientific and technological knowledge;
- transaction-cost theory approaches that address the implicit costs of producing and exchanging knowledge under different institutional regimes and organizational structures;
- strategic management approaches that examine how firms compete, network or collude in an effort to accumulate and deploy resources and capabilities to strengthen their market positions; and
- innovation systems approaches that examine how collaborations between public and private agents in the generation, exchange and use of knowledge are conditioned by internal behaviours, practices and routines and by the external social and economic context within which they operate.

In general, these studies conventionally define PPPs in terms of joint planning, joint execution and the sharing of costs, risks and benefits. However, this definition is occasionally too narrow to capture the richness of experience gained from other types of public–private interactions in the international agricultural research system. Hence, we expand the definition of PPPs to include any type of formal or informal arrangement between public- and private-sector entities, such as knowledge-sharing networks, technology financing or subcontracted research.

Thus, for the purposes of this study, we can classify PPPs into five functional categories, each with a unique assignment of roles, allocation of risk and potential impact on cost, innovation and poverty (Table 2.3):

1. *Resourcing partnerships.* Public research centres receive funding from philanthropic foundations associated with private firms, or they receive scientific expertise from private firms (see, for example, Box 2.2).
2. *Contracting partnerships.* Public research centres contract their facilities or expertise to private firms or contract private firms to conduct portions of their research.
3. *Commercializing partnerships.* Public research centres transfer research findings and materials to private firms for commercialization, marketing and distribution.
4. *Frontier research partnerships.* Public research centres and private firms jointly undertake research activities characterized by some unknown probability of success.

Table 2.3 A typology of public–private partnerships

Type of partnership	Role			Main risk bearer	Hypothetical impact of different public–private partnership goals[1]		
	Private sector	Public sector	Civil society		Cost reduction	Agricultural innovation	Poverty reduction
Resourcing	Financing	R&D		Public	+++	+	+
Contracting	R&D	Facilities, expertise, funding		Private	+++	+	+
Commercialization	Product deployment	R&D	Product	Private deployment, monitoring, evaluation	+++	+	++
Frontier research	R&D, financing	R&D, financing		Private, public	++	+++	+
Sectoral/value-chain development	R&D, planning, financing, product deployment	R&D, planning, financing	Planning, financing, product deployment, monitoring, evaluation	Public, private, civil society	+	+++	+++

Source: Authors.
[1] *Note:* + indicates the hypothetical degree of positive impact that the PPP may generate in relation to the three goals identified in this study.

Box 2.2 Committing for the long term

Bino Témé, Oumar Niangado, Samba Traoré and Salif Kanté

The Cinzana Agricultural Research Station (SRAC) was established in 1983 with the aim of benefiting small-scale farmers in the drought-stricken Sahel. The product of collaboration between Mali's Institute of Rural Economy, part of the National Agricultural Research System, the private CIBA GEIGY Foundation and the bilateral USAID, SRAC initially focused on improving millet-based production systems. Almost 25 years later, SRAC continues to be supported by CIBA GEIGY's successor, the Syngenta Foundation. Over this period, SRAC's changing research approach has mirrored global agricultural research trends, shifting from a top-down technology transfer approach to a systems approach and then to a participatory approach. A review of the station's impacts in 2004 highlighted achievements in terms of adoption of improved varieties and technologies but also recognized that these activities had not succeeded in alleviating poverty in the region. This has led to a further shift towards improving livelihoods by strengthening organizational and technical capacity of producer groups, promoting new products and facilitating access to inputs and service provision.

In a country with few resources, the long-term contribution of Syngenta to SRAC's operational costs has been very important. It has helped to leverage further donor support and turned the station into a centre of excellence for researchers from the around the region.

5. *Sector/value chain development partnerships.* Public research centres collaborate with networks of public, private and civil society partners to develop a commodity subsector or its associated value chain.

This typology helps to address the research questions posed by this study and sheds light on the policy, institutional and organizational environment underlying PPPs in the CGIAR.

Contributions of PPPs

PPPs in the CGIAR are serving a wide variety of research objectives, ranging from the system's traditional emphasis on increasing food security by increasing yield and output, to new pathways through which to reduce poverty such as value chain development. This trend further suggests that centres are widening their focus from research for technological innovation, to innovation at both a systemic/societal level and an internal/organizational level. Implicit in this shift is also greater awareness of the demand for research derived from markets for both food staple and high-value agricultural commodities – a change from the historic tendency towards a more supply side technology push approach.

Over half the partnerships are collaborations that include *foreign* entities, a category that includes foreign (industrialized country) firms, multinational firms or international/regional industry associations and charitable foundations (see Box 2.3, for example). An equal proportion of partnerships are collaborations that include *domestic* entities, that is, developing-country firms, private research organizations, producer associations, local industry associations and charitable foundations.

When viewed together, these findings suggest that PPPs in the CGIAR are relatively concentrated in three main areas: pro-poor product development via private domestic entities based on technologies relating to crop production and value addition; knowledge acquisitions from private foreign entities to further centre research; and private funding from private entities to support public research.

Reducing costs through partnership

The study goes on to ask whether PPPs reduce the costs of research. Conceptually, PPPs are often thought to improve the management of scarce resources by capitalizing on economies of scale and scope in research, exploiting complementary resources and capacities across the public and private sectors and reducing transaction costs in the exchange of knowledge and technology. Findings from this study suggest that centres leverage PPPs to pursue several types of cost-reduction strategies including outsourcing of research, securing alternative financing and allowing access to markets or business expertise.

Box 2.3 African Agricultural Technology Foundation

Gospel O. Omanya, Francis Nang'ayo, Richard Boadi, Nancy Muchiri, Hodeba Mignouna and Mpoko Bokanga

The African Agricultural Technology Foundation (AATF) is a private, not-for-profit foundation established to help resource-poor farmers in Sub-Saharan Africa (SSA) gain access to proprietary technology. To realize the full potential of new technologies in Africa, where the bulk of agricultural production is in the hands of smallholder farmers, AATF addresses critical components of the technology transfer continuum that bring together all key players in the agricultural development field: the management of Intellectual Property Rights, regulatory compliance, technology acceptance, strategic public–private partnerships, the facilitation of market access for farmers' surpluses, and the domestication of new technologies for Africa. The model for technology transfer involves: 1) managing public–private partnerships that are organized into agricultural innovation platforms; 2) facilitating access to agricultural technologies and freedom to operate; 3) adapting agricultural technology to fit farmers' needs; and 4) stewardship and deployment of proven agricultural technologies in target areas. Partnerships formed by AATF around this type of focus include projects on cowpea, maize, sorghum, bananas and plantains.

The initiative to develop transgenic cowpea is a direct response to addressing one of the major constraints, namely, the pod-boring insect, *Maruca vitrata*, a serious field pest of cowpea which is estimated to cause significant grain yield losses, in extreme cases, exceeding 70 per cent. The cowpea gene pool offers few useful sources of durable resistance to major insects such as *Maruca*. While some sources of insect resistance have been reported in wild cowpea relatives (*Vigna* spp.) as well as in other non-*Vigna* legumes such as African yam bean (*Sphenostylis stenocarpa*), none of these can inter-cross with cowpea through conventional breeding approaches. This has limited progress in the development of insect-resistant cowpea hence the need to use new tools including genetic engineering.

Following successful negotiations with the Monsanto Company that resulted in the signing of a royalty-free licence agreement in May 2005, AATF obtained the right to use Monsanto's *cry1Ab* gene for the development and commercialization in all the SSA cowpea varieties resistant to insect pests (*Bt* cowpea). The licence permits African farmers to export *Bt* cowpea outside Africa for feed and food uses. On the basis of a sub-licence granted by AATF, the Australian Commonwealth Scientific and Industrial Research Organisation (CSIRO) has successfully transformed cowpea using the *Bt* gene. Also, under licence from AATF, the International Institute for Tropical Agriculture (IITA) is doing genetic transformation work on cowpea in Nigeria. To facilitate the transfer of *Bt* gene into elite African cowpea, a plant breeder from Nigeria has been sent to CSIRO for training in transformation, *Bt* gene tracking in offspring lines and introgression of the *Bt* gene into advanced breeding lines. When successfully developed and deployed in *Maruca* infested areas of Africa, adoption of *Bt* cowpea is expected to bring about a range of benefits including reduced production costs arising from fewer field spray applications, reduced incidence of pesticide poisoning among farm workers and increased grain yields.

Firms – particularly small, domestic firms in developing countries – leverage PPPs to secure an edge over their competitors, or to carve out their own niche in an emerging market. This is particularly the case with local seed firms, where PPPs provide access to centres' improved breeding materials that can expand a firm's product line and generate profits over a relatively short time horizon.

But while these cost reductions make partnerships an attractive strategy for both the public and private sectors, findings also suggest that the hidden costs of PPPs are significant. Though difficult to quantify, the transactions costs incurred in searching for appropriate partners, maintaining partner commitment and resolving conflicts among partners are often non-trivial.

Promoting innovation through partnership

Apart from reducing research costs, PPPs are also designed to promote innovation – to transform knowledge and technology into an application of social or economic relevance. However, PPPs in the CGIAR are generally not being leveraged to promote innovation. Some centres do use PPPs to move research from proof of concept to product deployment – an important goal in itself. However, few centres use PPPs as a vehicle for joint processes of technological innovation – as opportunities to interact repeatedly with the private sector and leverage their expertise and assets as a means of enhancing the value of the centre's work. Notable exceptions include apomixes research by the International Center for Maize and Wheat Improvement (CIMMYT) and the East Coast Fever Vaccine research project headed by the International Livestock Research Institute (ILRI) (see also Box 2.4).

Box 2.4 The Global Alliance for Livestock Veterinary Medicines (GALVmed)

Andy Peters

GALVmed is a not-for-profit organization that is uniquely positioned to leverage the assets and expertise of the animal health industry and build partnerships with international and regional donors, NGOs and implementing organizations to develop, register and ensure sustained delivery of animal health products that meet the unique needs of the world's poorest livestock keepers.

Consultations with the private sector (developed and developing world companies) confirm that they have scientific expertise, intellectual property (IP) and resources that could be made available to help tackle the diseases faced by poor livestock keepers. However the private sector will not develop the relevant products on their own because the markets are not large enough to justify the investment. But where the costs and relevant risks can be shared, the private sector is willing to engage on a humanitarian and in some cases semi-commercial basis.

GALVmed ensures that for all projects funded by GALVmed, the benefit will be primarily public and any IP accruing from the funding will be managed for a public good. GALVmed contracts protect against the development and subsequent storage of IP to ensure that IP leads to products.

Four diseases – Newcastle disease, Rift Valley fever, East Coast fever and Porcine Cysticercosis – have been chosen, with the aim of coming up with low cost, appropriate vaccine solutions in partnership with the pharmaceutical industry.

Reducing poverty through partnership?

Ultimately, PPPs in developing-country agriculture are about reducing poverty by providing smallholders and other vulnerable social groups with new technological options. Two immediate issues arise. First, are PPPs identifying the right interventions – the right crops, traits and technologies – that specifically target the poor? Second, are PPPs convening the right partners – public, private and civil society – to generate impacts on poverty? Several examples of less desirable practice emerge, including:

- exclusive licensing of technologies for improved seed that may affect market structure and the availability of seed to smallholders without sufficient *ex ante* assessment of the poverty impacts generated by the research;
- allocation of centre facilities and expertise to conduct research on high-value cash crops (for example, cotton, flowers and oil palm) for which alternative suppliers of research may exist, or from which cross-subsidies for more poverty-oriented research are not forthcoming; and
- *ad hoc* proposals to sell potential technologies in segregated markets (subsidized rates for poor clients, market rates for others) without sufficient evaluation of market size, structure, infrastructure and the effects that segregation will have on the product's price and market performance.

Managing the risks of partnership

PPPs are beset by the same risks found in most research projects, including the possibility that: 1) the research investment will not yield a successful product that is acceptable to its end-users; 2) the product cannot be developed within a time period that attracts sufficient investment; 3) the product cannot pass through the legal and regulatory hurdles needed to move from proof of concept to commercial deployment; or 4) the investment will fail due to changes in the wider social, political or economic environment in which the research is conducted.

But PPPs also differ from other research investments in that they carry some very unique risks. They include the risks associated with coordinating diverse partners and interests; protecting the distinct mandates, missions and reputations of centres and firms; and exchanging proprietary knowledge assets between the public and private sectors. These risks are particularly relevant with respect to agricultural biotechnology research undertaken by centres in partnership with leading multinational firms in the cropscience industry (Table 2.4; Box 2.5).

Few PPP-based projects have adequate risk management or mitigation strategies in place to address the possibility of a worst-case scenario emerging

Table 2.4 Public–private partnerships with multinationals in the crop-science and agri-food sectors, c. 2004

Sector/firm/country of headquarters[1]	Sales (million US$)	Number of partnerships with CGIAR centre[2]	Centre[3]
Crop-science sector			
Syngenta, Switzerland	7,270	7	CIMMYT, ICRISAT, Bioversity International, IRRI
Pioneer Hi-Bred International, United States	4,830	5	CIMMYT, ICRISAT, Bioversity International
Bayer Crop-Science, Germany	7,390	4	ICARDA, IFPRI, IRRI and ICRISAT
Monsanto, United States	5,220	2	IRRI
BASF, Germany	4,170	2	CIMMYT
Grupo Limagrain, France	965	1	CIMMYT
Agrifood sector			
Unilever, United Kingdom/ Netherlands	25,670	3	World Agroforestry Centre, IWMI
Mars, United States	17,000	1	IITA
Coca Cola, United States	19,564	1	ICRISAT

Sources: Corporate and industry publications, personal communications, authors.
Notes:
[1] Includes local subsidiaries and affiliates.
[2] Excludes partnerships with a charitable foundation directly associated with the firm.
[3] CIMMYT is the International Maize and Wheat Improvement Center; ICARDA, the International Center for Agricultural Research in the Dry Areas; ICRISAT, the International Crops Research Institute for the Semi-Arid Tropics; IFPRI, the International Food Policy Research Institute; IITA, the International Institute of Tropical Agriculture; IRRI, the International Rice Research Institute; and IWMI, the International Water Management Institute.

from the project. Few centres and firms have invested adequately in platforms on which to assemble partners, assign roles and responsibilities and resolve internal conflicts as they emerge. Fewer still have adequate legal, financial and communication strategies in place to manage external threats.

Conclusions

While PPPs are serving a wide variety of research objectives, the CGIAR's partnerships with the private sector are still at a very nascent stage. Few partnerships are explicitly designed to facilitate joint innovation, an important justification for the use of PPPs. Still fewer provide for effective management of the risks inherent in PPPs or provide effective analysis of their poverty-targeting strategies. Thus, the international agricultural research system and its private partners could do more in the future to:

Box 2.5 The Monsanto Smallholder Programme

Dominic Glover

The Monsanto Smallholder Programme (SHP) was an initiative undertaken by the transnational biotechnology, chemicals and seeds company Monsanto between 1999 and 2002. The SHP had the stated purpose of providing resource-poor smallholder farmers with a package of agricultural extension services, including technical advice, chemicals, improved seeds and genetically modified traits, as well as other forms of support.

The SHP was conceptualized by Monsanto executives as part of an 'intermediate' or 'transitional' strand of the company's operations that fell between the core business of the firm on the one hand and the company's philanthropic activities (represented by the Monsanto Fund) on the other. The concept of the transitional strand carried with it consciously articulated expectations about helping farmers to make the leap from one realm to the other – as one senior SHP executive put it, 'from the subsistence to the commercial world'. In this conception poor farmers assumed a dual identity as both potential beneficiaries and potential customers of Monsanto's technology.

What involvement did smallholder farmers have in the SHP projects? In fact, there were no opportunities for the farmers to influence Monsanto's upstream research and development priorities. Indeed, one senior executive attested that he didn't see much opportunity for small farmers to help shape the corporate research and development programme because the strategic decision to pursue a particular crop or trait technology was a 'high-level' one, early in the innovation process, after which there was 'not much fine tuning' to which farmer feedback might contribute. The model of agricultural extension embodied in the SHP was essentially a commercial one, informed by assumptions based on a consumerist, market-based model of technology diffusion. Indeed, the focus on market development was entrenched in the organization of the SHP. Over time, the influence of sales and market development imperatives had a strong influence on the content and implementation of the programme. SHP staff found that they continually had to explain and 'sell' the programme to operational colleagues, who were sometimes sceptical or even hostile. They increasingly did so by justifying the programme as a means of developing experimental 'models' for future marketing efforts to the smallholder sector. This undoubtedly shaped perceptions of what the programme was for and business imperatives came to dominate over the more philanthropic goals of the programme. The emphasis on commercial goals ultimately undermined the perceived rationale for a special programme targeted towards smallholders and contributed to the premature termination of the programme.

- combine explicit knowledge exchanges (for example, straightforward technology transfers) with experiential learning approaches in which knowledge is transferred via learning-by-doing, learning through face-to-face interaction, hands-on collaboration and scientific exchange programmes;
- commit resources to building platforms on which to assemble relevant partners, identify incentive compatibility, agree on mutual objectives and assign roles and responsibilities appropriately;
- devise comprehensive strategies to manage and mitigate risks associated with projects that include recognition of the complex legal, financial and political elements that underlie a successful PPP; and
- improve the quality of analysis of the impact pathways through which PPPs improve the well-being and livelihoods of the marginalized social groups they target.

PART III

The politics of demand and organizational change

Part III: Opening note

Part III explores how 'bottom-up' demand can be assured in complex R&D systems so as to ensure a Farmer First approach to agricultural innovation. Beyond the discussions of participatory technology development and linking farmers to markets discussed in Part II, this requires some more focused thinking on appropriate organizational arrangements to facilitate what Monty Jones and Sidi Sanyang describe as a 'politics of demand'.

Farmers' own organizations of course need to be at the centre of such efforts. The first section offers some experiences from Africa (Kariuki, Banda) and Latin America (Turin, Arce Moreira and Mulvany, and Vargas and Burgoa), as well as the international experience of the International Federation of Agricultural Producers (IFAP) introduced by Del Rosario. All of these cases point to some fundamental challenges. First, what is a farmers' organization and what does it do? There are many answers to this: some focus on service delivery or marketing, while others have a more active role in policy lobbying and advocacy. Second, is the thorny issue of representation and accountability: which farmers do different farmers' organizations put first? What accountability mechanisms exist between the leadership and ordinary members? Third, is the political context and the ability of farmers' organizations to have an influence. Again this varies hugely, but often the influence of agrarian politics on mainstream policy is fragmented and selective. Finally, is the linkage between different farmers' organizations and wider federations and movements operating at the regional or global level. How do local concerns and perspectives get relayed to the international stage, mediated by such groupings as IFAP and Via Campesina? All of these issues present some fundamental challenges to the Farmer First approach. For, if farmers are really to be put first, effective, accountable, representative organizations are critical that can operate both at the local level responding to day-to-day concerns, but also at national, regional and international levels providing alternative voices in policy debates, helping to reshape innovation systems in ways that respond to marginalized farmers' needs. This is a tall order, and one that the experiences shared in this book go only some way to achieving. However, these can be built upon, and a major priority for Farmer First approaches into the future will be to work with farmers' organizations – from the very local to the international – improving capacity and effectiveness in order to meet these important challenges.

One route to doing this is discussed in the second section of Part III focusing on networks and partnerships. Here a range of intermediary organizations and networks are discussed that link farmers (and traders, labourers and other rural people involved in agricultural innovation systems) with researchers and technicians, entrepreneurs and business people, new information and advice, as well as sources of credit and finance in ways that enhance the capacity for Farmer First innovation. Partnership and network have become the buzzwords of contemporary development practice, but what does this mean in practice? The experiences of PROLINNOVA (PROmoting Local INNOVAtion in ecologically oriented agriculture and natural resource management) described by Waters-Bayer and others, together with the case study from Ethiopia by Assefa, and the World Neighbors experience introduced by Killough are all instructive. They show how intermediary organizations, often NGOs, can assist in making links to promote local innovation processes. A similar argument applies to the organization of research engagements. Many papers critique, explicitly or implicitly, the 'centre of excellence' model where research results emanate from on high and are transferred in a pipe-line model of innovation.

Facilitating a process where multiple sources of innovation and expertise come to bear on complex problems requires partnerships – across disciplines, across organizations, and across geographies. Contributions by Oliveros and colleagues, as well as by Triomphe and colleagues, highlight the potentials of a networked, partnership model for the organization of research. Similar principles apply to information sharing and communication. The highly successful story of the Low-External Input Sustainable Agriculture (LEISA) information network is discussed by van Walsum, along with the particular West African experiences shared by Ba. A strong commitment to decentralized information sharing in a variety of formats has made a huge difference to the communication of ideas about Farmer First approaches, from very grassroots applications to wider policy change.

But, despite all the warm words about partnerships and networks, there are pitfalls too. As with the discussion of farmers' organizations, such networks and partnerships are fraught with issues of representation, accountability and the politics of control. Tensions highlighted include ones over defining objectives, values and goals (pragmatic results orientation versus big ideas and radical change); over a focused, technical approach versus one that emphasizes broader, community development; over moving beyond traditional comfort zones (such as engaging with the private sector and transnational companies in particular); over funds, issues of transparency and accountability, and over approaches to leadership, codes of conduct and standards of practice. Careful facilitation and a sensitivity to partnership politics is essential if an effective arrangement is to emerge. But when they do, some real potentials for reconfiguring innovation systems in new ways, based on Farmer First principles, are realized.

Networks and partnerships cannot exist in isolation, however, forever dependent on external funding or the facilitation of a particular NGO or committed group. Gupta argues that the Honey Bee network exists in relation to both movements committed to local knowledge and technology, which operate in the wider political sphere at national and international levels, and particular institutions, such as the National Innovation Foundation, with particular functions. The network operates between the movements and the task-focused institutions in order to facilitate activity and share experience. But for this to happen a wider, shared commitment and set of values is required to bind movements, networks and institutions together. It is this broader political commitment to agrarian change – and particularly the principles of food sovereignty – that is highlighted by Mulvany and Arce Moreira in their contribution on Via Campesina and the food sovereignty movement. For, they argue, if the partnerships and networks formed around Farmer First ideals are to have any longer-term purchase, they must articulate with a strong political commitment to change, lest they end up co-opted by mainstream institutions and ideas and merely operate as instrumental providers of services without challenging the structures and policies that put farmers last, not first.

The final section of Part III focuses on the sometimes uphill struggle of getting Farmer First approaches institutionalized in large public R&D organizations – such as the National Agricultural Research Systems (NARS) of India and China discussed by Sulaiman and Li Xiaoyun and colleagues or the CGIAR system discussed by Meinzen-Dick and Watts and Horton. In different ways, all contributions look at ways of shifting large, hierarchical organizations focused on centres of excellence and technology transfer modes to ones where the capacity to innovate in diverse ways across embedded networks is enhanced. This requires research that integrates, networks and is based on partnerships, the ability to respond adaptively to complexity and a focus on learning lessons and reflecting on successes and failures across 'communities of practice'. But many of these experiences remain marginal, poorly funded and with limited core recognition. The incentives to change remain weak, as more and more investment gets pushed towards technical fixes and upstream R&D.

Yet the mismatches between existing organizations and emerging needs are becoming more and more apparent. CGIAR organizations and NARS designed for another era, and a pipeline model of technology transfer, are often not meeting the needs of farmers today. The solution, as Sulaiman argues for India, is not more upstream R&D or 'improved research and extension linkages', but a more fundamental realignment of the priorities and organizational arrangements. Li Xiaoyun argues that the political pressure to respond to the needs of the rural masses of China with appropriate technologies and development initiatives is beginning to have an impact on the way public R&D is conducted, with incentive and reward systems being re-geared towards Farmer First approaches. However, beyond some efforts on the margins, many mainstream national and international research systems and science bureaucracies remain very out of touch, and in need of some urgent reform. The ideas and experiences shared in this section point to some important ways forward.

The final paper by Douthwaite and Gummert offers a salutary lesson about the longer term impacts of international research efforts. Documenting the experience of research on agricultural machinery in South-east Asia, they show that sustained success resulted only in situations where engagement persisted over 25 years, adapting, revising and up-dating the technologies to new circumstances. Their conclusions emphasize the dangers of a projectized, globally focused research agenda which separates researchers from local contexts and prevents sustained engagement with research and technology problems.

Fostering farmer–scientist research collaboration: the role of the International Federation of Agricultural Producers

Beatriz P. del Rosario

The International Federation of Agricultural Producers (IFAP) is the world farmers' organization representing over 600 million farm families grouped in 115 national organizations in 85 countries. It is a global network in which farmers from industrialized and developing countries exchange concerns and set common priorities. IFAP believes that improving the involvement of farmers' organizations in setting, designing and implementing agricultural research priorities is vital to reaching the Millennium Development Goal of reducing poverty by half by 2015. The IFAP Committee on Agricultural Research looks at the processes supporting the collaboration of farmers' organizations and research centres for a real integration of farmers' points of view, from the definition of agricultural research priorities to the dissemination of research results (IFAP, 2007a).

IFAP is increasingly involved in the steering of applied research programmes by a number of international research and development networks, and in the feedback of research outcomes to farmers' organizations. IFAP initiatives include the Regoverning Markets Programme (RMP), a global initiative to help producers in developing countries secure more equitable benefits in response to market changes (Digal, 2007). RMP is a collaborative research and policy support programme designed to: 1) understand the keys to inclusion into restructured markets in order to address implications and opportunities for small-scale producers and enterprises; 2) identify best practice in connecting small-scale producers to dynamic markets; and 3) bring these findings into the wider policy arena with facts and recommendations, practical action for public sector policy and private sector strategies.

In Phase 1 of RMP (completed in March 2008) some 40 case studies were undertaken. The case of NORMIN Veggies of Northern Mindanao, Philippines, provides an example of collective action and organizational innovation involving small-scale producers tapping opportunities in the modern changing markets (Uy, 2007). It adopted a clustering strategy that benefited the growers in terms of their bargaining power (quality, volume and regularity), diversified and more predictable markets (traditional and modern), better income (higher price, 15–25 per cent increase in profits, reduced losses) and better relations among growers (open communication lines and sharing technologies).

There are important implications from the RMP findings with respect to the roles of various stakeholders. For instance, farmers' organizations should: 1) build capacity to understand and adapt to change; 2) engage in collective action to increase their competitive edge in accessing markets; and 3) be politically active and seek to find a single voice whenever possible. The public sector should create and support a research and information base to accompany the change process including early warning systems to identify unexpected changes. The private sector should engage in multi-stakeholder dialogue and understand the need for a transition period when applying standards for food safety, quality, labour standards, etc. Finally, NGOs should: 1) promote adaptation to change in their approach; 2) provide timely advice, information and promotion; 3) interact with the public sector as part of multi-stakeholder forums; and 4) seek to facilitate learning about the management of change rather than providing direct solutions.

Promoting farmer-centred research in Kenya

Nduati Kariuki

The International Federation of Agricultural Producers (IFAP) formally established a Committee on Agricultural Research (CAR) in 2005 to operate through its national member platforms (Derrien, 2005). The main focus of the CAR is to put research findings into use and develop a strategic dialogue with leading research and policy bodies within each IFAP-member country and with regional agricultural research institutions to address farmers' priority issues. These include market-oriented research; integrated pest management; food safety, standardization and quality control; food processing technologies and post-harvest handling technologies; adapted agricultural tools, equipment and agricultural inputs; natural resources management; trade impact on farmers; appropriate organizational processes; and weather forecast information systems.

The CAR is made up of IFAP resource persons who represent farmers on regional and international research bodies. It is chaired by the IFAP farmers' representative on the Global Forum on Agricultural Research (GFAR) Steering Committee. CAR officers are mandated for a two-year period. Through their participation in international agricultural research bodies, the nominated IFAP farmers' representatives gain valuable knowledge and experience. This expertise is being shared within the CAR and used to the benefit of the entire IFAP network.

The farmer-members of CAR believe that agricultural research should include both technical and socio-economic dimensions and should be treated in a multidisciplinary manner in order to concretely improve farmers' incomes and production processes. Thus, the mission of the CAR is to contribute to the improvement of farmers' livelihoods through the development of an agricultural and food research agenda designed, monitored and implemented by farmers themselves.

Regular working relationships with the existing regional and international research networks are the first step to a better acceptance of farmers' recommendations by researchers. Privileged relations have been established with a number of international research organizations, particularly GFAR and the CGIAR (IFAP, 2006, 2007b). Partnerships in place include participation of farmers in the decision-making bodies of regional agricultural research bodies, such as the Forum for Agricultural Research in Africa (FARA) and involvement in various regional research initiatives, such as the Sub-Saharan African Challenge Programme.

In 2007, the CAR visited several key African agricultural research institutions, including FARA, to discuss closer cooperation and also invited them to attend regional meetings of IFAP members to share information. Impressive achievements have been recorded so far. Some research institutions have incorporated a farmer participation component into their research agenda and others have created permanent farmer-representative positions on their boards. This initiative is aimed at transforming scientific research findings into simple and accessible lessons for immediate farm application.

The Kenya National Federation of Agricultural Producers (KENFAP), which is a member of IFAP, is working in partnership with the CAR to promote farmer-centred agricultural research in Kenya. KENFAP is now working closely with leading national research institutions such as the Kenya Agricultural Research Institute in developing a National Agricultural Research Strategy and a Science Technology and Innovation policy formulation process aimed at ensuring farmers' priority issues are firmly embedded in agricultural science policy processes. In addition, KENFAP has also been lobbying research institutions for active involvement of farmers' networks at all levels of research work and advocating for the development of mechanisms for soliciting farmers' research needs from the grassroots, to categorize what research should be undertaken in which locations. Through these activities, KENFAP is working with the CAR to enlighten farmers on what specific research products are available and how these may be of benefit to them, training farmer-leaders on the importance of agricultural research, and strengthening the capacity of farmers' organizations to demand support for prioritized farmer-led agricultural research in Kenya and elsewhere in Africa.

Advocacy coalitions to build participatory processes in the Altiplano: increasing human capacities to adapt to change

Cecilia Turin

More than 30 years of development interventions have not led to a decline in natural resources degradation or a reduction in poverty for the indigenous Aymara communities residing in the Altiplano of Andean South America. The lack of genuine participation in policy processes and top-down development interventions are major contributors to these poor results. To address some of these challenges the USAID-funded Sustainable Agriculture and Natural Resources Management Collaborative Research Support Program (SANREM CRSP) launched a project in partnership with several regional and national institutions in the Andes in June 2006 entitled 'Adapting to Change in the Andes: Practices and Strategies to Address Climate and Market Risks in Vulnerable Agro-Ecosystems' (Valdivia et al., 2006). Working with Aymara communities in Bolivia and Peru, the project aims to contribute to the reduction of vulnerability, food insecurity and natural resources degradation through participatory action research and advocacy approaches.

In order to achieve this, five specific objectives were identified: 1) develop a shared understanding of the Altiplano ecosystem; 2) understand how livelihood strategies are developed in response to farmer perceptions; 3) link local and new knowledge for natural resources management; 4) increase human capacities across people (farmers, researchers, development agents), communities (rural communities, universities, NGOs), disciplines (biophysical, social sciences) and countries (Peru, Bolivia, US); and 5) assist communities to develop strategies with local institutions that contribute to resilience.

A research methodology was developed based on the 'Community Capital Framework' (CCF) and 'Advocacy Coalitions Framework' (ACF). Both approaches are different from those that have already been tried in the Altiplano. This combined methodology emphasizes cultural, human, social and political capital as key subjects to be considered, recognizing the importance of being in a particular socio-cultural and environmental context. The CCF considers seven forms of capital: natural, cultural, human, social, political, financial and physical. Application of this approach showed that in the past most development interventions were focused on building natural, financial and physical capital rather than cultural, human, social and political capital, which are the main strengths of these ancient Aymara communities.

The ACF was employed to study and to understand the relationships among actors and different levels and sectors around natural resources management issues (Fernandez-Baca, 2004). It is based on stakeholder analysis, which aims to understand the positions of different social actors on a specific issue over time. ACF consists of the formation of 'advocacy coalitions' among key actors and among institutions with the same aim, to encourage them to work together toward common goals. During this process external and internal linkages are strengthened through bonding and bridging, thus increasing the social capital inside and outside the community. At the same time this process increases communication between key actors, establishing a two-way dialogue that allows participants of advocacy coalitions to access diverse resources, mainly information and knowledge. This access to information and knowledge empowers key actors, fostering active participation in the decision-making and policy-making process around issues of concern to the community, and thus increasing political capital. The redistribution of power among actors strengthens advocacy coalitions and changes occur due to favouring of one belief system over another (Fernandez-Baca, 2004; Flora et al., 2006).

ACF has been especially useful in natural resource management policies in many countries. In Ecuador, for example, ACF was used to help rural communities to negotiate with the government and mining enterprises to have more participation in the governance of an important bio-reserve (Flora et al., 2006). The ACF in the Altiplano region is providing new insights to improve the impact of research and development interventions for adaptation to climatic and economic change. We expect the ACF to lead to reduced vulnerability and increased environmental conservation through a process by which livelihood strategies are developed through increased community agency.

Farmers' movements and the struggle for food sovereignty in Latin America

Maria Arce Moreira and Patrick M. Mulvany

Towards food sovereignty

Throughout Latin America there is an active process of discussion and promotion of the principles of food sovereignty often complementary to the agroecological movement and those involved in campaigns against free trade agreements and genetic engineering (Windfuhr and Jonsen, 2005; Via Campesina, 1996). The proposed 'corridor of food sovereignty' stretching from Ecuador through Peru to Bolivia, as well as parts of Central America, is an example of efforts by civil society to generate debate and influence national and local policies over local control of food systems.

Food sovereignty articulates the priorities and strategies that farmers' organizations consider essential to respond to the daily challenges and risks they face in their own context (see Mulvany and Arce, this book). An illustration of this importance comes from the Farmers' Movement of Santiago del Estero (MOCASE) which was formed in 1990 in Argentina to defend local farmers against the increasing aggression from large soybean farmers who were destroying their livelihoods. MOCASE has stated:

> Food sovereignty is the right to produce and eat what we want. Our strategy is to strengthen our own production and consumption models based on self sufficiency, production of our own food that we produce in our gardens, and the cultivation of cotton and maize. We protect our own culture passed on from our ancestors and including our animals, chickens and geese and our different breeds of goats. Santiago del Estero is a region with low potential and the mountains are our only source for food. (GRAIN, 2005)

With current political changes in the region, openings to promote the debate and strengthen processes in which they can voice their demands and lay out their agendas for transformation have been established by civil society and farmers' organizations. In Bolivia, national food production is declining and there is increased dependency on food imports and food aid. However, export crops such as soya are on the rise, including the expansion of plantings of genetically engineered varieties, benefiting from policies and legislation enacted by previous governments on behalf of a few powerful interests. The interests and needs of smallholder farmers who constitute the majority were systematically neglected.

The process leading to the establishment of a new constitution (since 2007) has witnessed farmers' organizations and NGOs working together to promote the recognition of the human right to food. In this context food sovereignty plays a key role. Food sovereignty is not a new topic on the agenda of these organizations and its adoption emerges from an analysis of the current dynamics of access to food, the power dynamics inherent in deciding what and how food is produced, and the impact of these on poverty and hunger in the population. The coordinating body for the integration of farmers' economic organizations of Bolivia (CIOECs) clearly highlights the monetization of the right to food – that only allows access to food for those who can afford it – and the development of policies and strategies that promote the commercial gains of a few actors, neglecting the protection of local producers and consumers.

CIOECs and AIPE (the network of education and capacity-building institutions) were engaged in a process in 280 of the over 300 municipalities in Bolivia to discuss proposed changes in the constitution, which concern food sovereignty and its relevance to the human right to food. The process has also included a series of Latin American workshops at which experiences from the region were shared. Food sovereignty is understood as a process of social empowerment and political will at all levels to ensure the social, economic and political transformation that the country requires. There are already some laws to promote the valorization of local products, a school breakfast programme based on local products and a proposed law on agroecological production that supports the implementation of food sovereignty in practice. Additionally, the multi-sectoral programme on 'zero hunger' (PMD-0) is operating in 166 municipalities engaging all relevant sectors involved in food production and promoting the human right to adequate food.

Across Latin America, struggles for food sovereignty are being led by farmers' organizations and local movements. These are shaped by the following principles: 1) the human right to food; 2) revaluing smallholder and indigenous agriculture; 3) strengthening farmers' organizations and local self management; 4) access, quality and food self-sufficiency; 5) development of agroecological and sustainable production systems; and 6) institutional strengthening. These principles are mainstreamed in a series of programmes promoting land reform and redistribution and the human right to food (SEMBRAR), promotion of local and agroecological production (CRIAR) and food self-sufficiency (RECREAR) (AIPE, 2007).

While it is too early to say where this emerging agenda on food sovereignty might lead, it is clear that farmers' organizations are playing a vital role in shaping important national debates and informing key policy processes on the future of food and agriculture in their countries.

Farmers' participation in policy advocacy processes in Bolivia

Elizabeth Vargas and William Burgoa

Contrasting approaches to policy advocacy

Two cases from Bolivia offer valuable insights into effective strategies for farmers' organizations to initiate policy advocacy processes at local and national level. Both initiatives seek to influence policy making relating to soil conservation and sustainable agriculture and highlight the value of taking a thematic approach to achieving policy change.

The first case relates to the Sacaca Committee for Strengthening Ecological Farming (COFAES), a small farmers' organization founded in 2003, which promotes soil conservation and sustainable agriculture in Sacaca Municipality, Ibañez Province, North-Potosi. COFAES is comprised of 297 farmers from 16 of the 187 local communities. In internal meetings and workshops, COFAES members discussed the need to share their experiences with other people in the Sacaca Municipality in order to better participate in policy advocacy relating to sustainable agriculture. With the NGO K'anchay, COFAES organized the First Local Ecological Congress and three workshops in 2005–7 during which COFAES members shared their experiences on soil management and ecological agriculture with peasant leaders and municipal authorities. During the third workshop COFAES and participants jointly elaborated a proposal for a 'vision for development' to be incorporated into the 2008–10 Sacaca Municipality Development Plan.

The second case concerns the National Soils Platform and its proposal for new legislation relating to soil use and sustainable agriculture. Founded in 1993 to contribute to solving the soil degradation problem in Bolivia, the Platform currently has 45 members, mostly NGO members and small-scale farmers working with them on soil conservation and sustainable agriculture, following an agroecological approach. Convinced that local efforts and technical solutions were having insufficient impact on soil erosion, the Platform began by reviewing existing policies and plans relating to soils. On the basis of this assessment, it called attention to the lack of a legal instrument which could give more responsibility and obligations to the State. Platform members therefore elaborated a proposal for a law on soil conservation and use and are now in the process of soliciting inputs from other stakeholders. Platform members understand policy advocacy as a process by which they, as part of the civil society, can participate and have influence on decision makers, especially policy makers (Iturralde, 2007).

Reflecting on the policy advocacy processes and farmers' participation

In both of the cases reviewed, farmers and technicians wanted to consolidate and disseminate their work on soil conservation and sustainable agriculture by exchanging experiences. They are also interested in influencing policy making at local, departmental and national levels through a process of policy advocacy with farmer involvement.

An important factor in enabling them to carry out this process was their organization and experience. COFAES comprises 16 local soil conservation committees, organizes meetings and workshops, and has more than six years of experience working on soil conservation and agroecological farming. The National Soils Platform also has many years of experience on sustainable agriculture and exchange of experience among its members. It has five regional platforms and a national directorate which supported the organization of workshops at regional and national level in order to elaborate the soil law proposal.

The cases differed in the way they approached policy advocacy. COFAES first used their concrete work on sustainable agriculture – emphasizing soil and water management – to inspire and guide the elaboration of policy proposals. Recognizing the legitimacy and political power of their traditional organizations, they decided to work first on influencing their traditional leaders and rely on them to undertake the policy advocacy. Interestingly, the resulting 'vision for development' integrates not only productive but also educational, social and cultural aspects. Little by little, COFAES hopes to elaborate a more specific proposal related to agriculture and soil management. In contrast, the Soils Platform strategy is to directly influence policy making at national level and its proposal focuses on a single resource – soils (under the sustainable agriculture umbrella). Like COFAES, however, it is trying to influence peasant leaders to take the lead in these advocacy actions and is seeking alliances with indigenous, peasant and farmers' national organizations.

Farmers' participation also differed in the two cases. In Sacaca, farmers were the initiators and catalysts of advocacy action, establishing COFAES because they knew their experiences and proposals would be more influential if they were organized. In the case of the National Soils Platform, the process of elaborating the new law was initiated by Platform members, who are not all farmers. However, they believe that the proposal will have no legitimacy unless farmers take over the leadership and are therefore interested in passing on the stick to the main farmers' organizations.

Conclusions

In the current Bolivian political context, indigenous, peasant and small farmers' organizations have political power. Their leaders, however, do not always focus on productive activities, especially farming, as part of their main demands and proposals. These two cases show that thematically focused groups can help farmers undertake policy advocacy to ensure that their real needs and proposals are included in the policy-making process.

Local organizations such as COFAES can provide enabling conditions for farmers and their traditional leaders to take leading roles in initiating policy advocacy processes. NGO-led organizations/networks like the National Soils Platform can also enable farmers to engage meaningfully in policy processes by creating space for them to debate issues, build proposals and subsequently lead advocacy processes.

Although the character of farmer participation has been different in the two cases, both are seeking to influence their traditional peasant and indigenous organizations to take leading roles. Both approaches are valid and can be complementary in ensuring that farmers take a leading role in promoting policy proposals that affect their livelihoods.

Beyond black and white: the National African Farmers' Union of South Africa

Khamarunga Banda

Until 1991, when the National African Farmers' Union (NAFU SA) was formed, there was no national level organization to represent the interests of emerging black farmers in South Africa. Although such farmers were often involved in garden clubs at the local level, there were no higher-level bodies to represent their interests to outsiders or facilitate an exchange of information. Indeed, the only reasonably effective structures for small farmers that existed prior to the launch of the NAFU SA were those supported by the sugar industry in KwaZulu Natal. Therefore, the NAFU SA has had to compete in an arena where white commercial farmers' unions have had years of state and private-sector support and substantial funding for their organizations and operations.

Since its founding, the NAFU SA has faced many challenges, notably, the lack of financial support, especially in its formative years, and limited capacity to forge ahead to redress past inequalities related to access to land and other productive resources and access to services. Yet despite these challenges, membership has grown exponentially, to over 400,000 members in 2007 throughout the country's nine provinces. With this expanding membership, the organization is now emerging as a central player in the transformation of South Africa's agricultural sector.

From its inception, the organization has worked hard to create a platform to give voice to its members. This has brought about the need to streamline support services and to create stronger local nodes of the organization. Though challenged by inadequate funding to staff its operations and contribute to overall implementation of the black farmer's agenda, the organization has forged ahead to be the mouthpiece of black farmer empowerment and agricultural policy change, particularly land reform. Yet the NAFU SA still has to be accountable to its members and play several distinct roles as pacifier, negotiator and fact-finder in an effort to be responsive and accountable to its constituency.

The NAFU SA understands that agriculture in South Africa is an important part of the economy and therefore requires significant investment in research and development. Though agriculture contributes less than 4 per cent to GDP, it still accounts for 10 per cent of total reported employment (mainly of black farm workers and farmers). Agriculture in South Africa is well diversified with field crops, livestock and horticulture the main sectors. Wine and fruit production have been the most dynamic sectors in the past 10 years, with a large share of total output exported, mainly to Europe. Agriculture is also seen as a means to address past injustices – through entry of black farmers into this sector and promotion of equitable land distribution – this being the avenue to accelerate broad-based, pro-poor, rural development.

The experiences of the NAFU SA as an organization can be characterized into four main phases: 1) institution building; 2) developing strategic alliances; 3) professionalizing the organization; and 4) re-positioning and re-organizing the organization. The phases are not well demarcated in practice and blur into one another. The main point is that the Union has been constantly evolving in response to the considerable demands placed on it by its members and to the rapid structural and policy changes taking place in the agricultural sector in the post-apartheid era.

The future for the NAFU SA is full of challenges. There is a growing feeling of unease among some of the Union's core constituents on a number of socio-political and economic concerns, particularly the slow pace of land reform and the associated political developments which could affect the stability of the nation. Yet the Union also has hope for the future of agriculture in the country. For this reason, it is calling for unity among all black and white farmers' unions so that we can forge one powerful, dynamic body that represents the interests of all farmers in South Africa.

The politics of inclusion in African agricultural research and development

Monty P. Jones and Sidi Sanyang

Research for development

The Farmer First approach argued that much of the problem with conventional agricultural research and extension lies with the processes of generating and transferring technologies, and that much of the solution lies with farmers' own capacities and participation in the research process. In general, technologies needed complementary organizational, policy and other changes to enable them to be put into productive use. There has also been recognition that the organization of agricultural research and extension itself was a major reason why science was failing to improve the livelihoods of poor people.

Since these arguments were first made (e.g. Chambers et al., 1989), the African agricultural landscape has changed rapidly. In addition to the conventional research and development institutions (public research and extension), many new service providers are involved in knowledge and technology generation. Sumberg (2005) indicated that by bringing all stakeholders fully into the research process, the focus will shift from 'research for its own sake' to 'research for development' – and that this will mean a 'new way of doing business' for research establishments. More importantly however, this reflects a basic change of dynamic referred to as the 'politics of inclusion'.

The linear research–extension–farmer linkage and technology transfer approach championed by public extension services in the 1960s and '70s can no longer play an effective role in agricultural service delivery in Africa. Since then there has been a proliferation of NGOs, agri-businesses, farmers' organizations (FOs) and other civil society organizations in agricultural service delivery. Here we focus on the experiences and challenges of African farmers' organizations and their efforts to promote demand-driven agricultural research and development.

African farmers' organizations

In the last 20 years, farmers have become more organized although their capacity to act collectively is often limited. National farmers' organizations are organized around commodity and or sector value chains and these form the foundations of the sub-regional farmers' organizations which engage in policy advocacy and resource rights and use.

Although national FOs have existed for decades in Sub-Saharan Africa, it is only in the 2000s that active sub-regional farmers' organizations emerged and this marks an important turning point. The highly significant but weak sub-regional farmer organizations *Réseau des organisations des paysannes & de producteurs de l'Afrique de l'Ouest* (ROPPA) founded in 2000 and the Eastern Africa Farmers' Federation (EAFF) founded in 2001, as well as the Sub-regional Platform of Peasant Organizations of Central Africa (PROPAC) and the Southern Africa Confederation of Agricultural Unions (SACAU) provide an institutional framework and voice for a plethora of previously uncoordinated national farmer organizations. Although the sub-regional farmers' organizations are themselves functional, albeit with some institutional difficulties, they have no common, Africa-wide, platform to coordinate their actions and activities.

Farmers' institutions however, remain generally weak and farmers continue to be poorly represented in agricultural research for development. Although some degree of farmer participation in research programmes exists, their full participation in the governance, planning, implementation, monitoring and evaluation of research is still very poor. Farmer groups themselves have problems of representation and often have limited capacity to efficiently manage internal and external resources and events. The management of farmer groups and retention of interest by the membership remains a fundamental challenge. Farmers and farmer groups do not have the requisite capacity to effectively engage with and participate in international trade negotiations and defend their interests in a global competitive market.

Worse still, sub-regional FOs do not have a common Africa-wide platform to effectively engage with the Forum for Agricultural Research in Africa (FARA), the sub-regional organizations (SROs), national agricultural research systems (NARS) and the global community.

Challenges ahead

In FARA's work with FOs and civil society organizations (FARA, 2005), a number of challenges have arisen:

- representation of FOs and group members at fora and events – who is representing and speaking in the name of farmers and their organizations?
- difficulty in working on regional and sub-regional issues;
- focus on capacity strengthening but yet weak in identifying their specific capacity needs; emphasis on needs and support – what can be done for them?
- weak direct working relationships with national member organizations; poor membership mobilization and retention;
- poor application of the principle of subsidiarity among member organizations;
- poor internal and external communication and governance; and
- lack of a coherent strategic plan and too much focus on a programmatic approach that mainly responds to funding opportunities. Recognizing this, EAFF developed its strategic plan in 2007.

Although farmers' organizations are fairly well established institutionally at the sub-regional level throughout Africa, their linkage with the SROs remains weak. FARA and the SROs should therefore work with Africa-wide initiatives such as the Africa Alliance of sub-regional Farmer Organizations (AAFO), launched at the Africa Agriculture Science Week and 4th FARA General Assembly in Johannesburg, South Africa, in June 2007. AAFO brings together the four main sub-regional farmer organizations (EAFF, ROPPA, PROPAC and SACAU) in partnership with IFAP, the International Federation of Agricultural Producers, to ensure the integration of FOs at the sub-regional level. At the same time, farmers' organizations need to sort out the thorny problem of representation. Additional effort should be made to mainstream appropriate representation and good governance and that should be led by the sub-regional farmers' organizations themselves. Only when these basic issues of organization, capacity and representation – and the politics of inclusion – are addressed will the possibility of a Farmer First alternative emerge, overturning the out-dated and inappropriate linear research and extension model.

Building partnerships to promote local innovation processes

Ann Waters-Bayer, Chesha Wettasinha and Laurens van Veldhuizen

Introduction

An international partnership programme called PROLINNOVA (PROmoting Local INNOVAtion in ecologically oriented agriculture and natural resource management) seeks to build partnerships among major stakeholders in agricultural research and development to enhance processes of farmer-led participatory innovation. It starts with identifying innovations developed by farmers in order to give recognition to their creativity and to serve as entry points to genuine partnership in local-level research and development. The stakeholders involved in Participatory Innovation Development (PID) reflect on how it differs from the way they conventionally go about their work. They consider whether and how it leads to better results, above all, to strengthening the capacity of farmers and other actors to continue to innovate and adapt to changing conditions. They identify what institutional and policy changes are needed to enhance PID. On the basis of their joint analysis and the on-the-ground PID cases, they engage in policy dialogue to bring about these changes.

Here we describe the PROLINNOVA initiative and the concepts behind it, the structure of partnerships at different levels – field, national and international – to promote local innovation and the experiences made in trying to establish them. Particular attention is given to the role of NGOs in facilitating these multi-stakeholder partnerships (MSPs).

Participatory innovation development

The starting point of PID is recognizing and documenting local people's creativity and ingenuity. Innovations developed by farmers and other users of natural resources include new tools, new techniques or new ways of co-managing resources, communicating or organizing (see Box 3.1, for example). Recognizing local innovation changes the actors' images of others and of themselves. When formally educated professionals discover farmers' own innovations, they begin to see farmers in a different light: not just as people who should receive and adopt technologies but rather as people with something valuable to offer that is complementary to their own scientific knowledge. This changes the way they behave towards farmers.

At the same time, the farmers gain in self-esteem. They start to see themselves as people rich in knowledge, ideas and ingenuity in surviving under difficult conditions – as people to be admired. The farmers are more likely to regard their admirers as potential partners in development. Thus local innovations can become focal points for innovative farmers and their communities

---

Box 3.1 Promoting Farmer Innovation and Experimentation in the Sahel (PROFEIS)

Assétou Kanouté

PROFEIS is an initiative to promote farmer innovation in order to contribute to food security and natural resource conservation in Burkina Faso, Senegal and Mali. Started in late 2006 with support from Misereor, and associated with the PROLINNOVA network, its aim is to: 1) strengthen capacities in agricultural research institutions, extension services, NGOs and community-based organizations to provide effective support for farmer-led experimentation and innovation in natural resource management; and 2) accelerate the dissemination to resource-poor farmers of innovations generating improved yields in an environmentally sustainable manner.

In Mali, PROFEIS has been led by a partnership involving AOPP (*Association des Organisations Professionnelles Paysannes*, a network of farmer organizations), ADAF/Gallè (an NGO) and IER (Institut d'Economie Rurale, a national agricultural research centre), in collaboration with ICRAF (the World Agroforestry Centre). The partners have focused on identifying and supporting farmer innovations related to biodiversity conservation and management in Ségou Region since early 2007. Specifically, the initiative has documented and tested farmer innovations relating to the conservation of sorghum and millet varieties, soil fertility management and agroforestry practices.

Among the 38 farmer innovations identified and assessed in Ségou during both the rainy and dry seasons, six have been selected for joint experimentation by the partners thus far:

1. a beaten clay incubator developed by Nouhoum Traoré of the village of Djela (Gouendo Commune);
2. a method for breeding *pintadeau* (young guinea fowl) developed by Bakary Daou of the village of Kanouala (Kéméni Commune);
3. an organizational innovation developed by Moulaye Coumaré of the village of Kalabougou (Farako Commune);
4. a method to combat striga weed with leaf powder from the baobab tree (*Adansonia digitata*) and the néré tree (*Parkia biglobosa*) developed by Bakary Konitié Dembelé of the village of Saye (Sana Commune);
5. a method to combat striga weed with néré powder developed by Bakary Dembelé of the village of Saro (Saloba Commune);
6. a way to graft *gounan* (*Sclerocarya birrea*) and *pegou* (*Lannea microcarpa*) developed by Sidiki Coulibaly of the village of Zembougou-Mangoni (Niasso Commune).

PROFEIS-Mali is now bringing together farmers, extension workers and researchers to explore these and other farmer innovations across Ségou, working through a network of farmer organizations. It is also supporting learning and dissemination through farmer-to-farmer exchanges.

to examine – together with researchers and/or development agents – the problems and opportunities that local people have already identified and then to plan joint experiments to explore relevant ideas further and to evaluate the results together. The interaction of scientists and technical experts with research-minded farmers also builds farmers' capacities to engage in dialogue with other stakeholders.

Multi-stakeholder partnerships to bring about change

Bringing about the institutional change to create space for change on the ground requires collaboration among key stakeholders at sub-national or national level, as well as at international level, starting with platforms that can grow into partnerships. A 'platform' is a space for negotiation created in situations where diverse actors define and struggle for the same set of resources yet depend on one another to realize their objectives. Within the platform, the actors discuss and clarify their viewpoints and seek common ground for planning joint action (Röling and Jiggins, 1998). A 'partnership' implies an agreement between different stakeholders to analyse, plan, implement, monitor and evaluate activities together, sharing resources, risks, costs and benefits. The term 'stakeholders' encompasses all people who have an interest in the issue at hand, in this case, agricultural research and development (ARD). MSPs are partnerships that involve several different groups of stakeholders such as governmental agencies, NGOs, research institutes, business groups, consumer groups and, of course, farmer groups.

The main emphasis in PROLINNOVA has been on building MSPs at country level. The lead is usually taken by a field-based development-support NGO with skills not only in technical aspects but also in social issues such as organizational development, conflict management and gender sensitivity. Inception activities bring together people from the major institutions of agricultural research, extension and education in the country to analyse jointly their experiences in recognizing local initiatives and engaging in participatory ARD. On this basis, each country programme (CP) has developed action plans to improve and scale up such activities, and set up a platform of key stakeholders to steer and learn from the process.

From the start, the CP partners defined a number of important activities required at the international level. These include capacity building and methodological support, web-based information management, documentation and publishing, and international policy dialogue. Special attention was to be given to facilitating mutual learning through comparative analysis of experiences of the CPs. This is done through jointly developed monitoring and evaluation procedures, looking at the operations of the CPs as well as at how the international partnership functions. The national and international partners in the programme thus learn how to strengthen their training, networking and communication activities; how to improve the structure and functioning of the multi-stakeholder platforms; and how to be more effective in policy dialogue and in bringing about institutional change.

Some initial achievements

Energies generated by recognizing farmer innovation

The existence of local innovations and the relevance of these innovations for improving livelihoods of smallholder families has been recognized and documented through inventories and studies of local innovations and related posters, videos, brochures, leaflets and database entries. Amazing energies have been generated among farmers and scientists simply by undertaking this exercise. Farmers are proud to be able to present their innovations to formally educated 'experts', both in the field and at national and international workshops, while scientists are fascinated that farmers have found solutions to problems with which scientists have been grappling for years, e.g. bacterial wilt in *enset* in southern Ethiopia.

Basis laid for integration into mainstream institutions

The CP platforms have organized the training of several hundred people in institutions of research, development and higher education in PID concepts and practices, in an iterative learning approach that involves application in their day-to-day work. Initial activities are underway in several countries to incorporate the methodology and examples of PID into learning at universities and technical colleges.

Piloting alternative funding mechanisms for farmer-led experimentation

PROLINNOVA is addressing issues of power in ARD by piloting research funding mechanisms that allow farmers to exert real influence on research agendas. PROLINNOVA partners developed the concept of 'Local Innovation Support Funds' (LISFs) that would allow innovative small-scale farmers or farmer groups to access funds directly to finance locally mandated research, to hire external resource persons who would support farmers' efforts, to link up with other innovators and further sources of relevant information, and to share their findings more widely. This is expected to increase the relevance of research for smallholders and to speed up processes of local innovation (Waters-Bayer et al., 2005; van Veldhuizen et al., 2006). In the first full year of operation, LISFs in five countries jointly approved 121 applications of farmers and farmer groups with grants ranging from EUR40 (Cambodia) to EUR700 (South Africa). From the outset, attention has been given to issues of fund sustainability; if the LISFs prove to be effective in enhancing local innovation processes, some public funds for ARD could be channelled through them.

Challenges and attempts to deal with them

For most of the NGOs involved, seeking partnership with government agencies has meant a fundamental shift in their own approach, as they had previously taken either separate (often parallel) or confrontational paths. Now their role has become one of creating space for farmers, NGOs and government agencies to come together and find common ground. Such diverse stakeholders will clearly have different perspectives. The process of building partnerships among them goes through numerous phases of contesting theories and 'truths', deconstructing beliefs (e.g. about the abilities and roles of different actors in innovation systems), mediating disputes and negotiating agreements. This has presented several challenges.

Dealing with diversity of interests. Given that PROLINNOVA seeks to bring about a shift in the relations of power and influence and ultimately in how resources are used, conflict cannot be completely avoided even where the responsibilities and benefits of each partner have been clearly outlined. Political awareness and competences are needed to manage this process. Facilitating NGOs often have only a small number of the very capable and committed people with good connections who are needed for this delicate task. In all cases NGOs have chosen to work with engaged individuals within the targeted ARD organizations and thereby to address issues at the institutional and management level.

Dealing with hierarchies. In a partnership, it is important to establish a culture of equality. In many countries, however, government organizations initially find it difficult to accept an NGO as coordinating organization, particularly in ARD activities (cf. Ejigu and Waters-Bayer, 2005). Perseverance and time is needed to gain their confidence. By recognizing the creativity of farmers and giving their knowledge and innovations the same value as those of formally educated scientists, the PROLINNOVA programme deliberately tries to break down hierarchies and to establish working relationships based on mutual respect.

Creating shared ownership. Partnership implies shared ownership of the agenda and programme of activities, and an overall sense of joint responsibility for outcomes. This may be a challenge for coordinating NGOs who do not always realize that this is not their project but rather a joint endeavour. To achieve shared ownership CPs are encouraged to continue participatory planning with partners, to share and be transparent on tasks and resources and to ask partners at all levels not just to receive but also to commit resources.

Dealing with slow-moving mindsets and institutions. Decades of a top-down approach to ARD mean that many formally educated people are slow to comprehend that farmers have developed new technologies and institutions without external support. Even those who do recognize local innovation still often think in terms of transferring the site-specific local innovations to other places where they may not fit, or trying to convince the innovative and potentially 'model' farmers to demonstrate introduced technologies. More meaningful engagement in farmer-led PID, particularly for research institutes, may be promoted by the increasing pressure being exerted by donors and governments on formal research to show its impact – as PID partnerships at various levels offer researchers in the formal sector an opportunity to do this.

Focusing on process rather than innovations. The initial focus on studying local innovations can prevent partners from comprehending that PROLINNOVA is trying to promote local innovation processes, not just the resulting innovations. Rather than measuring success according to how many farmers have adopted certain local innovations, the focus is on enhancing a continuing process of local innovation and scaling up the approach to involve millions of farmers and the mainstream institutions of ARD. Challenging discussions among partners, both face-to-face and virtually, are used for clarifying concepts and bringing in the wider perspective.

Dealing with farmer 'representation'. Because PROLINNOVA aims to institutionalize participatory approaches to ARD, the main 'target' groups are the institutions involved in ARD. These should also include farmer institutions. At the beginning, however, farmer involvement in governance structures was not strong. Only the CPs in Cambodia and Tanzania included farmer organizations in the national steering committee; in other countries, farmers were sometimes 'represented' through networks working on their behalf (e.g. the Pastoral Development Forum in Ethiopia). Where democratic organizations of smallholder farmers are absent, the emphasis is on bringing the perspectives of (research-minded) farmers into the platforms through, for example, farmers who come from Farmer Research Groups or Farmer Field Schools.

Dealing with Intellectual Property Rights. The issue of property rights when studying local innovations has been high on the PROLINNOVA agenda. Generally, partners found that patenting of local innovations is often not feasible and also not desirable. Vibrant innovation systems thrive from open and frequent sharing among people with different experiences and ideas (cf. Douthwaite, 2002). By documenting information about local innovations and innovators and making this more widely available, the partners – including the innovators themselves – agree to bring the innovations into the public domain. But CPs are aware that in specific cases, where commercial interests are potentially high, formal legal protection may need to be sought and are exploring country-specific regulations to do so.

Looking ahead

Progress in institutionalizing participatory ARD is slow, as is the process of building MSPs to bring this about. Most lessons are being learnt by doing, and sometimes through errors. Keeping track of small achievements – and of the difficulties faced – is essential to social learning and institutional change. A key activity is therefore participatory monitoring and evaluation in each

CP and in the PROLINNOVA programme as a whole, trying to analyse and understand the process of building and managing partnerships and bringing about institutional change.

The commitment of current partners and the interest of other individuals and organizations to promote participatory innovation processes are leading to the development of a genuine community of practice. They are communicating with each other because they believe in what they are doing and value the mutual learning and peer support. Partners at country level are increasingly taking their own initiative in generating resources to be able to pursue their jointly formulated objectives. They are beginning to find ways to link the objectives of the platform to their own institutional mandates and are devoting themselves to the task irrespective of individual projects. This vision beyond projects suggests that the partnerships at various levels – from the ground to the global – have some chance for sustainability.

Participatory Innovation Development in Ethiopia

Amanuel Assefa

Promoting farmer-led innovation

PROLINNOVA-Ethiopia is a national learning and advocacy platform of governmental and non-governmental actors that is primarily engaged in the promotion of local innovation and the integration of the Participatory Innovation Development (PID) approach in the formal research, extension and education systems. It is also part of the international PROLINNOVA network, a global community of practice which makes its central learning agenda the process and products of local innovation-based partnership between farmers and others (see Waters-Bayer, this book, for a description of the PROLINNOVA network).

Starting in 2003, the PROLINNOVA-Ethiopia partners conducted several meetings and workshops to define and develop the concept of PID, as well as clarify the vision and mission of the platform. These efforts attracted a good deal of national and international interest by identifying, documenting and supporting the development of local innovations with farmers across the country.

PID is a farmer-led and expert-supported innovation development process, which mainly takes local innovations as a starting point. It is basically a collaboration of farmers, extension workers and researchers, in which 'farmer innovators' who are already trying out new things take the lead. The process emphasizes not only research but also application of the results, primarily by those involved in the PID activities. Others could learn from the experiences of innovative farmers and may be motivated to try out and see how the new ideas work in their own situation. The goal of PID is not to scale up the farmers' technologies that come out of PID in a transfer-of-technology mode. Rather, it is to develop a new culture of research and development in which local people play a significant role in testing and using new ideas in agriculture and natural resource management. In other words, it aims to scale out the spirit of innovation so that all farmers are encouraged to try new ideas, technologies and practices that work in their own realities.

Regional innovation platforms

By 2006, PROLINNOVA-Ethiopia had defined its working areas by delineating major agroecological zones in the country. It has adopted a strategy of establishing regional (provincial) fora to coordinate the work on the ground. Since then, PROLINNOVA has been implementing its work in four broadly categorized agricultural systems. Some of the key farmer innovations that have attracted the attention of the learning platforms and which are in the pipeline of development through collaborative actions include:

Northern highlands zone – mixed cereal-based crop-livestock farming:

- rotary water up-lifter from hand-dug well
- reducing water-logging problems through digging underground canals
- improving 'modern' beehives by making a queen excluder out of local materials, reducing number of frames, and making queen delivery possible

Coffee-growing zone in the south and south-west:

- farmer-made hydroelectric power
- manually operated dry coffee pulper
- coffee plant rejuvenation techniques

Southern enset and rootcrop growing zone:

- treating *enset* bacterial wilt by extracts of cactus
- improving cassava yield by planting techniques
- self-developed grafting techniques

Pastoralist zone in the north-east, east and south-east:

- mixing camel, goat and cow milk to avoid curdling
- pollen transfer of papaya by hand
- repulsion of retained placenta in cows

In general, the activities being facilitated by PROLINNOVA-Ethiopia fall into three major categories. The first comprises the Netherlands Government-supported activities, which aim at identifying innovative farmers in various agroecosystems and initiating PID in these locations. The second activity is a project on Farmer Access to Innovation Resources (FAIR) supported by DURAS (French government) (see Oliveros, this book). The FAIR project is an action research project which is developing mechanisms of providing micro-finance to farmers and their organizations to support their own innovation development activities. The third set includes the diverse work related to PID being carried out by member institutions in their own domains. These activities are not centrally planned and coordinated by the PROLINNOVA Secretariat, but are part of the overall efforts of PROLINNOVA-Ethiopia to accomplish its mission. These include formation and strengthening of Farmer Field Schools, facilitating farmer participatory research, organizing training on PID-related methodologies, and using various fora to advocate for policy change towards supporting farmer-led research and development processes in institutions of formal research, extension and higher learning.

The way forward

Most of these cases are at an early stage of development in the different regional platforms. Thus, it is premature to report results at this stage. Nevertheless, PROLINNOVA-Ethiopia's efforts have progressed far enough to allow some reflection on remaining challenges and future opportunities. We have observed, for example, that the severe livelihood constraints of many poor farmers have prevented them from taking risks and carrying out experiments on their own innovation priorities. This risk-aversion makes it difficult to refine and scale out innovations that have been identified as having significant potential. In addition, some researchers continue to maintain the belief that farmers cannot do research on agricultural innovations and assert that this type of research is or should be the exclusive domain of formally established scientific organizations. For such researchers, the comfort zone is to do research behind closed doors and on station, rather than to work directly with farmers in real-world settings. Fortunately, there are a growing number of researchers who are keen to work with innovative farmers to help them design and conduct their own experiments to solve problems in complex, diverse, risk-prone environments. However, many of those who are seeking to strengthen the innovation capacity of smallholder farmers find it difficult to balance the requirements of PID and the classical scientific approaches with which they are most familiar. The role of PROLINNOVA-Ethiopia, therefore, is to support these emerging 'innovation facilitators' in the scientific community, as well as the 'farmer innovators', so that both groups may learn from one another and benefit from the participatory innovation development process.

Partnerships for action research

Scott Killough

Introduction

For the past three decades (in some cases, longer), development organizations have worked with individuals and organizations at the grassroots to analyse local problems and identify possible solutions to agricultural and rural development. Much of this experience has been through the use and application of action research methods – which encompass a broad range of processes designed to allow participants to systematically learn from practice. Initially, many of these experiences were supported and promoted by NGOs, building on their long association with rural communities in many countries of the South to achieve broad community development aims (i.e. establish community organizations, offer rural credit, promote health and nutrition programmes, etc.).

In the area of agricultural development, the primary aim of much of this practice – usually led by professionals – was to identify and analyse 'problems' and then work with community members to formulate 'solutions'. Over time, farmer-based, and often farmer-led, approaches emerged (e.g. building on indigenous technical knowledge, the use of participatory rural appraisal (PRA), farmer innovators, etc.) and were recognized as having greater benefits in terms of high community involvement, shared ownership of results, sustainability, etc. (Wettasinha et al., 2006; Gonsalves et al., 2005; Scarborough et al., 1997). More recently, partnerships – particularly multi-stakeholder partnerships – have been increasingly viewed as a pathway to improve both the processes and outcomes of action research among farmers, development actors (especially NGOs) and research actors (Horton et al., 2003).

Below I offer a personal perspective on nearly two decades of practice-based involvement with partnerships around action research for participatory agricultural research and extension. The observations draw from my own partnership experiences with two development NGOs – the International Institute of Rural Reconstruction (IIRR) and World Neighbors (WN) – through their work on rural and agricultural development.

Partnerships for agricultural development

In recent years, a number of reasons have been put forward and highlighted for farmers and agricultural development organizations to consider partnerships as a mechanism to achieve their own aims and objectives, including (among others) to:

- complement own experiences, skills and capacities;
- create synergies which would accomplish outcomes beyond what could be expected from individual efforts;
- build and develop capacity (skills and knowledge) in partners that can be sustained; and
- leverage resources, especially funds.

In addition to these explicit objectives, are there other – possibly 'hidden' – rationales for partnerships? What motivates or drives organizations to seek and cultivate partnerships with others? Are there specific factors that farmers and their organizations consider important when contemplating entering into partnership?

Farmers are overwhelmingly keen to partner with others. They outline a number of reasons (benefits) that motivate them to seek and establish partnerships with 'outsiders' – a desire to gain access to experience, knowledge and resources, to learn about new information or technology, to gain status among their peers, etc. Over time, their attention and commitment to the partnership grows as they perceive the relationships that are built, as well as the benefits which they accrue. Farmers recognize the merits of relationships with outsiders that are based on values that are important to them ('on their own terms'), including trust, honesty, empathy towards their situation, sincere recognition of their contributions to the process and respect for their culture, among others. Most farmers also articulate the added value that they derive from the processes of 'accompaniment' in working with agricultural professionals, rather than only pursuing agricultural experimentation or farmer-to-farmer processes in which farmers/community members seek solutions to their problems on their own (Killough, 2003).

Key elements of partnerships for action research

Below are a number of key elements of partnerships for participatory agricultural research and extension.

Trust

Though not often perceived as important by professionals or organizations, the aspect of building and maintaining trust among partners – especially with farmers – cannot be overemphasized. Possibly this is the most important element of a successful partnership; certainly, to the actors at the grassroots it is paramount. Trust is required not only to initiate activities, but to sustain and build momentum as the action research activities move through different stages of action, learning and 're-action' (O'Hara, 2005). Trust becomes particularly important – though often more difficult to establish – as more partners are included in a partnership, especially if they are not like-minded partners.

Transparency and accountability

One of the power dynamics of any action research partnership is that 's/he with the gold, rules'. Issues around transparency in partnerships often stem from concerns about resource use, and the power dynamics which result from one or few partners having a say in those decisions. Resources within a partnership can also often skew accountabilities toward those partners which manage the funds. To counter this, the PROLINNOVA programme is testing the use of 'local innovation support funds' as a mechanism to put resources directly into the hands of farmers or their organizations to support local innovation activities (see Waters-Bayer et al., this book).

Personal contacts and risk-takers

Personal contacts are often an important impetus to spark partnerships. This factor may be more important than we would prefer to acknowledge and may be one of the obstacles to replicating partnerships more widely, especially between and among heterogeneous organizations. Just as for professionals, this is an important determinant among community members who rely on a combination of personal contacts and trust when becoming involved in, or encouraging others to become engaged in, action research processes. Community members who are willing to 'try something different' are susceptible to potential embarrassment or scorn from their community peers. Sharing that risk seems to be a bit easier with people (often relatives or neighbours) who you personally know and trust (Selener et al., 1996). Many partnerships begin with and are built around 'risk-takers' who are willing to work outside of their own institutional or societal constraints.

Recognition of and appreciation for multiple perspectives and realities

Different partners bring to any partnership their own perceptions, understanding, analyses of the context, issues, opportunities, potential problems, as well as possible solutions. A successful action research partnership – especially one that aims to foster local capacity for endogenous development – needs to be built on the principle that these multiple perspectives are each valid and real (O'Hara, 2005). The bringing together of these 'multiple realities' through dialogue, joint analysis, reflective learning and other processes, and working toward a 'joint reality' crafted by several partners is where true learning and change can happen.

Local leadership to sustain action

Leadership by community members to continue and sustain action research processes is critical to moving beyond initial successes and avoiding dependency on outsider partners. Even in apparently farmer-led processes such as farmer innovators and farmer-to-farmer extension, initial impetus is often given by outsiders to things that farmers are already doing but maybe on a small scale or not systematically. Over time, as community members seek to sharpen multiple skills around action research, the emergence of local leadership to foster the continuation of action research into the future – even if the outsiders are no longer engaged – is extremely important (Killough, 2005).

Implications for organizational change

If partnership arrangements are to spread and become more integrated into operational norms, organizations will be required to consider changes which will allow them to seek and foster partnerships (Lizares-Bodegon et al., 2002). Three core challenges are identified below.

Organizational mandate or 'space'

Most agricultural development organizations have not organized their programmes and activities around partnerships, but rather the opposite – they have pursued their aims and objectives on their own. Efforts to pursue partnerships have therefore had to be based on an explicit mandate to do so or some tacit agreement within the organization of the (possible) benefits of such partnerships. Some organizations have been quick to embrace partnership-based programmes and activities (especially within the NGO sector), though many are still somewhat cautious of centring programme operations around partnerships. Within most agricultural development organizations the debate around whether to partner or not, or under what circumstances to do so, is focused on weighing the balance between the recognized benefits and costs of partnership. However, even when there appear to be no obvious benefits, other factors such as resource capture, donor pressure and potential for learning may convince organizations to enter into partnerships.

Staff skills, knowledge and attitudes

As organizations embrace partnerships, individual staff must then make the partnership arrangements operational and functional. The competences required are typically not taught in educational institutions or universities, and are often not even recognized as valuable within the staff development systems of agricultural development organizations. They include:

- Skills – facilitation, inter-personal and social interaction, consultation, networking, dialogue and communication, conflict management and resolution;

- Knowledge – understanding the dynamics (or politics) of their own and the partner organizations, understanding what motivates partners to be in the partnership;
- Attitude – willingness to make compromises/adjustments, patience to work through the necessary steps of a successful partnership (e.g. define objectives, set the agenda, etc.), and willingness to share the successes and to bear the risks of failure.

Accommodations or adjustments to organizational culture

Differences in organizational culture, practices and norms among different partners, especially related to required protocols, hierarchies, etc., may present major challenges. Though it may be difficult to expect changes to respective organizational cultures as a way to better support partnerships, recognition that there are differences, being sensitive to those differences, and deliberately searching for ways to accommodate those differences is possible and can be very effective. Fostering a common vision for a partnership is often an important first step, though often more difficult in the case of multiple partners. This may require seeking a balance between technocratic approaches (especially in areas such as agriculture and health, for example) versus more generalist, community development approaches – typically characterized as holistic, integrated, or multi-sectoral.

Conclusion

Partnerships for action research among farmers and formal agricultural research institutions have become more prevalent and are receiving much more attention as mechanisms to drive agricultural innovation and learning. However, in most contexts these partnerships are very localized and limited in scope, often in spite of considerable investments of time, effort and resources. To date there are no examples of how partnership approaches can become an integral and systemic approach to 'doing business' by the formal agricultural research and development sector.

Over the past 20 years, we have certainly made tremendous progress to better understand, promote and institutionalize Farmer First approaches into the concepts, practices, and institutional actions of agricultural research and development institutions. We should also be optimistic for the future as we continue to support Farmer First experiences. Much work remains to be done; partnerships, I believe, are a powerful mechanism to realize much of the work that lies ahead.

The DURAS project: funding research partnerships

Oliver Oliveros

Introduction

The concept of the 'agricultural innovation system' implies an opening-up of the sources of agricultural innovation, to include actors beyond the agricultural sector as well as to involve stakeholders who have traditionally not been involved, such as NGOs and farmers' organizations (FOs). The DURAS project, *Le projet pour le promotion du développement durable dans les systèmes de recherche agricole au Sud* (project to promote sustainable development in southern agricultural research systems), was conceived in order to support the opening-up process being promoted by the Global Forum on Agricultural Research (GFAR), and especially to help strengthen the involvement of southern stakeholders in the agricultural research and innovation process by ensuring that their voices are heard at the international level.

The project was launched in April 2004, with funding from the French Ministry of Foreign and European Affairs. One of its components is a competitive grants scheme (CGS), which aims to encourage and promote innovation, the scaling up of innovative practices in southern agricultural research and development (ARD), and the enhancement of the scientific capacity of southern partners. The CGS prioritizes multi-stakeholder partnerships, with particular attention to the involvement of non-traditional players in the research process. Each project therefore involves at least three types of stakeholder groups, one of which is an NGO, Farmers' Organization (FO) or Small and Medium-sized Enterprise (SME), and partners from at least two Southern countries and a European country. The projects are expected to facilitate the opening up of research institutes towards a more systems-oriented approach to national agricultural research. This opening-up process will include ensuring a more functional relationship among the various stakeholders, especially non-traditional actors. It is hoped that the experience of working in partnership with others will help stakeholders to appreciate the value of putting partnership at the core of ARD processes and influence their behaviour in the future.

Following two calls for proposals in 2004, 12 projects are currently being implemented in 19 countries in Africa and three in South-east Asia. Here I outline some lessons from the process of selecting and supporting the projects.

Lessons learned from the CGS

Ensuring a clear, independent and flexible governance structure and process

The clarity and independence of a governance structure is key to any initiative or organization that claims to promote participatory approaches and multi-stakeholder partnership, but ensuring these factors are present is a huge challenge. Where multiple organizations are involved, roles and responsibilities should be clearly defined. At the same time, however, the project structure should be streamlined and kept simple. In the light of these challenges, the following questions arise:

- To what extent can one spell out rules and regulations, without appearing – and being perceived to be – overly prescriptive and 'dictatorial'?
- How can the need for rules and guidelines be balanced against the need not to constrict the creative energies of the actors involved in the project?
- How do you balance the need for stakeholder representation without offending the donor which is financing the project?

Involving partners in developing project proposals

The DURAS project team attempted to ensure that stakeholders were fully involved in the project development stage. This included provision of preliminary grants to groups to enable them to develop their proposals jointly with beneficiaries. DURAS team-members conducted occasional site visits, but this was an insufficient mechanism for evaluating the depth of stakeholders' participation. In practice, DURAS staff depended heavily on the project leaders' three-monthly reports. The need to maintain regular interaction among project participants continues throughout project implementation, monitoring and evaluation. This highlights the need to develop an effective monitoring system to assess the functional involvement of stakeholders at every stage.

On geographic restrictions and biases

The limited geographic focus of the first two calls for proposals to countries prioritized for French aid may well have missed promising innovations from other regions. To reflect its international character and to tap into the wealth of ideas from various corners of the world, the project's geographic coverage should be expanded. This should be done in a way that does not antagonize donors and their geographic focus, and without sacrificing the 'manageability' of the whole project.

Finding common ground on basic principles

Prior to the launch of the projects, the successful applicants were brought together to discuss and agree a minimum set of indicators and a common monitoring and reporting system. Nevertheless, differing interpretations and understandings of agreements and guidelines mean that disagreements have not been avoided. Some funding recipients have failed to comply with reporting and accounting agreements, which has resulted in delays in the release of their own project funds. A great challenge in this respect is how to ensure that administrative procedures are not seen merely as inconvenient requirements but important commitments to be respected. In a multi-stakeholder, multi-country initiative, involving people and organizations from diverse disciplinary and professional backgrounds, it is important to ensure that there are common understandings of project norms and respect for agreements reached.

Further strengthen civil society involvement

The DURAS project experienced relatively weak participation by civil society organizations and SMEs. A special effort needs to be made to reach out to less-vocal stakeholders and build the capacity of applicants to write effective grant applications.

Communicate!

An initiative like the DURAS project must be widely publicized in order to encourage high levels of interest from an array of potential grant-applicants. Likewise, emerging results should be disseminated widely, using various suitable media. Resources need to be allocated for this purpose, including for tasks such as translation. Finally, suitable recognition and acknowledgement needs to be made of all the organizations involved.

Monitoring and evaluation: focus on partnership quality

The DURAS project aims to improve the quality of North–South and South–South collaboration. Suitable methodologies and indicators for assessing quality, such as participation, knowledge management, capacity building and institutionalization need to be further refined and made more practical.

Measure project impacts... but be realistic!

Before the 12 projects were launched, a workshop involving all the project applicants defined a set of indicators for measuring a project's contribution to sustainable development, taking into account the specific nature of each project. However, in the case of a research-oriented grant-giving scheme like the DURAS CGS, it is extremely difficult to evaluate impacts and outcomes within the short time-frame of the recipient projects. Due consideration must be given to the time required for scientific research to produce usable technologies that may be taken up by users. *Ex post* evaluations, three to five years later, are therefore more suitable. Future schemes should consider a financing horizon commensurate with the nature of research projects (about four to five years).

Sustainability: What happens next?

What happens to the projects when funding ends is a critical measure of sustainability. 'Sustainability' in this context refers not only to the long-term development and scaling up of a technology, but also to the mainstreaming or institutionalization of the CGS approach within the organizations involved. The DURAS project is 'forcing' organizations and people to work in partnership. However, transforming established ways of working is not easy. The momentum created needs to be accompanied and followed through in order to sustain this organizational transformation. Sustainability is most likely to be achieved if the research yields some kind of new technology or process which itself generates sufficient funds to cover costs and yield a profit. Linkages with the private sector can be important in this respect.

Research involving multi-stakeholder partnerships

Bernard Triomphe, Henri Hocdé and Guy Faure

Over the 2005–7 period, CIRAD carried out a study (Hocdé et al., 2008) to systematize and compare ten contrasting experiences in which research had been conducted with local actors (such as farmers and farmers' organizations, extension services, governments, private sector, etc.). The analysis confirmed that each experience was the result of a unique encounter among specific individuals, who purposefully broke away from paradigms reigning locally or institutionally for effecting change. The study also showed that research and innovation are not linear processes with discrete, well-planned phases and cycles. Rather, they result from how projects deal with tensions between stakeholders and how they generate the adjustments necessary to achieve success in problem-solving and generating knowledge.

Factors shaping the efficacy and efficiency of multi-stakeholder partnerships

Identification of common values and goals

The desire to innovate is not sufficient by itself to unite stakeholders. Innovation needs to be seen as a means to achieve higher-order goals, such as making family farms viable within the context of agrarian reforms. It is the desire to contribute to these goals which brings partners together. Cementing lasting partnerships depends heavily on creating common ground and trust among heterogeneous actors through recurrent negotiations around goals, values and perceptions. Support for acquiring the corresponding negotiation skills may be necessary for many partners, especially for the weakest ones.

Clarifying operational and governance arrangements

Governance and operational arrangements often remain largely unformalized, or are formalized gradually. But their design and management is crucial for effective partnerships, even though the quality of interpersonal relationships will also play a key role. There needs to be a clear formulation of rules, ethical frameworks, roles and responsibilities, while also allowing sufficient flexibility to adapt to unpredictable, non-linear evolutions over time. There should also be effective mechanisms for communication and mutual learning, robust mechanisms for conflict-resolution, and effective monitoring and evaluation of both results and processes.

Dealing with asymmetries among partners

Asymmetries among partners have a powerful effect on the functioning of partnerships. These asymmetries may involve information and knowledge, economic strength and resources, political power, institutional and organizational cohesion, negotiation skills, or simply motivation and the capacity to take the initiative. Smallholder farmers and their organizations are frequently among the weakest members in a partnership and need special capacity-building to ensure that their concerns and proposals are effectively taken into account. Researchers also have to learn to step back, in order to create a space where farmers can propose their own ideas and suggestions, and act accordingly, with the full support of other stakeholders.

Institutionalizing the partnership approach

Research institutions, as well as individual researchers, face significant challenges when embarking on action research partnerships. They must learn new roles and functions, such as negotiation and facilitation, and pay due attention to qualitative processes. Researchers also need to maintain an uneasy balance between conducting quality, formally publishable research and simultaneously engaging in action-solving and capacity-building activities.

There is an urgent need to evaluate the efficacy and efficiency of partnership approaches through well-documented case studies and cost-benefit analysis, using adequate indicators. But case studies will not be enough to change the existing paradigms and deeply embedded practices and routines of research institutions and individual researchers (Kuhn, 1962). For one, researchers need to get properly educated and trained in innovation systems, action-research in partnership and other relevant concepts, approaches and practices. Institutions also need to change and provide the correct signals and motivation. Finally, donors should increase their funding and adjust their standard terms of reference to accommodate the specificities of action research partnership projects. In particular, this means not predefining how a project will operate or what outputs it will deliver, since these should only be designed and negotiated on the go among the partners, once the project has commenced.

Learning to value LEISA: experiences in global knowledge networking for Low External Input Sustainable Agriculture

Edith van Walsum

This is the story of a growing global knowledge network for the exchange of knowledge and information on Low External Input Sustainable Agriculture (LEISA). In 1984, the Centre for Information on Low External Input Sustainable Agriculture (ILEIA) brought out the first issue of the *LEISA Magazine* (then called *ILEIA Newsletter*). It was distributed to 1,000 development field workers. Today the *LEISA Magazine* appears in six languages, in a global and six regional editions, and is read in Latin America, Africa, Asia and the global North by a quarter of a million readers. Below, I describe and reflect on ILEIA's journey, identifying important lessons for the future.

Crafting a concept (1981–1994)

In the early 1980s, Green Revolution approaches to agricultural development began to be recognized to have made many farmers more vulnerable, revealing the inadequacy of social safety nets and humankind's incomplete grasp of the holistic character of the natural environment. ILEIA was among the first to identify this crisis. ILEIA was established in 1981 by a small group of 'practical visionaries' who were part of the ETC Foundation, an innovative consultancy group based in the Netherlands. ILEIA wanted to better understand the extent and nature of this agricultural crisis, but it was also keen to learn more about alternative practical strategies towards agricultural development.

ETC managed to get funding for this 'out of the box' project from the Dutch official development agency, DGIS – this was clearly a time when there was space for innovation. A 1981 survey to learn about organizations and individuals involved in developing low external input sustainable technologies found that activities were fragmented, and there was little or no systematic guidance from established institutions.

In the course of this search process for a different, more self-reliant type of agriculture, ILEIA crafted the term, LEISA – Low External Input Sustainable Agriculture. The new concept was informed by the conviction that High External Input Agriculture (HEIA) was reaching a phase of increasing problems. It was clearly not appropriate for many small producers worldwide, particularly for those in degraded, ecologically fragile dryland areas. These regions, however, are often characterized by a high cultural and biological diversity. ILEIA's hypothesis was that there must be a wealth of knowledge 'out there', but it would remain local and scattered unless a forum could be created that would encourage people to articulate this tacit knowledge and share it with others working in similar conditions elsewhere.

ILEIA envisaged a need for a new farmer-centred, participatory and knowledge-intensive approach to agricultural development. Since there are no standard solutions, locally specific knowledge about agricultural options would have to be unearthed and, if necessary, blended with 'external' knowledge about suitable technologies and approaches.

Thus, the first issue of the *ILEIA Newsletter* was launched in 1984. Farmers, field level workers (NGOs, government) and researchers were encouraged to share their practical experiences of LEISA approaches in the *Newsletter*. In particular, ILEIA wanted to encourage farmers and field-workers themselves, for the first time, to write down their practically informed experiences and insights. At first, this involved only a small group of people known to ILEIA, but gradually the network grew.

Networking was done both by increasing the readership for the *Newsletter* and by bringing core groups of stakeholders together in workshops. The outcomes of several such workshops convened during the late 1980s and early 90s were published in a series of readers (Haverkort et al., 1991; Hiemstra et al., 1992; Alders et al., 1993). The book *Farming for the Future* (Reijntjes et al., 1992) was a comprehensive effort to systematize the state-of-the-art in knowledge about LEISA, considering the technical, environmental, social and economic aspects.

This was a truly pioneering phase. There was no readily available conceptual framework. Commonly used methodologies were not appropriate. However, this process was helped by a sympathetic reception, a positive political climate, and support from DGIS, the primary donor. ILEIA's reputation and international network of contacts grew.

Nevertheless, in spite of the growing interest in LEISA, there was also perceived to be widespread doubt about the wider relevance of LEISA and its suitability in the light of the need to increase agricultural production and feed an expanding, urbanized population. The development sector was splitting into two camps, a slowly growing number of 'LEISA believers' on the one hand and 'LEISA critics' on the other. The main criticism of ILEIA was that it was ideological and should become more scientific.

Elusive evidence (1994–1999)

After 13 years of funding, DGIS, ILEIA's financial lifeline, wanted to see more tangible results. Although ILEIA could show several impressive communication products, mainstream institutions were not yet convinced about the validity of the message. They wanted to see evidence that LEISA was relevant to both farmers and policy.

Comparative assessment studies were initiated with the aim of comparing LEISA with conventional agricultural methods in different agroecological contexts. Taking up the challenge, ILEIA wanted to ensure that the research would be participatory and inclusive. Unfortunately this collaborative research programme collapsed in 1996, resulting in the near-collapse of ILEIA itself. Looking back at this crisis, it appears to have been at least partly due to an over-ambitious effort to bridge the gap between a participatory, constructivist research paradigm and the conventional R&D paradigm. There was no shared Theory of Change, neither explicit nor implicit, and ILEIA and ETC found it hard to manage the situation.

The research programme re-started in 1997 with a modified set-up; yet it became a difficult compromise between two different needs. First, there was the 'external' need to generate evidence on the validity of LEISA, as demanded by DGIS and others. Second, there was the 'internal' need of ILEIA itself to engage in participatory research, rather than merely reporting the experiences of others.

In September 1999, a special issue of the *ILEIA Newsletter, Finding Common Ground,* concluded that the research programme had been more successful in creating learning on the dynamics of multi-stakeholder processes than in providing quantitative data, facts and figures. Articles in the issue were apologetic about the failure to accomplish a robust, quantitative validation of LEISA methods. They attributed the inadequacy of the research to adverse weather conditions and other problems. While ILEIA's disappointment is understandable, attributing this 'failure' to adverse and unpredictable weather conditions and other variable factors appears excessively defensive. These examples could and should have been used to illustrate the point that unpredictability and variability are themselves an essential feature of LEISA farming, and that therefore the research design itself may have been part of the problem. ILEIA should have learned the lesson that LEISA research requires an approach that takes these uncontrollable factors as a starting point, rather than as disruptive factors.

The more quantitative the research became, the greater the tension with the participatory spirit ILEIA sought to maintain. Efforts to combine farmers' assessments with scientific validation, using separate sets of tools that were useful and relevant by themselves, proved unsuccessful and frustrating. Field staff and farmers were not used to collecting quantifiable scientific data, and supervision was lacking, resulting in poor quality data. The participatory dimension was also damaged. Farmers in India commented 'Why do we have to produce so much data? ... We are convinced about the technologies long before we can convince the researchers'.

Good learning emerged, however, about collaborative processes between farmers, NGOs and researchers and Ministries of Agriculture. For instance, an account from Ghana described how:

> Mutual respect developed between farmers, NGOs and scientists. A sense of collective responsibility was generated and the confidence of both scientists and farmers in farmer-led research increased... The informal character [of the project working group] had created space for experimentation without jeopardising institutional relationships. In a relatively short time the working group had succeeded in raising the interest of other stakeholders as well as district directors of agriculture, universities and research institutes. (ILEIA, 1999)

These mixed experiences showed that research can serve to *prove a point* or to *improve a learning process*, but mixing these different functions without clearly articulating them is bound to lead to messy processes and endangered partnerships.

After four difficult years, ILEIA closed its research programme. A review recommended that the organization should return to what it was really good at – producing a good newsletter. It also recommended that ILEIA should decentralize and regionalize.

Building bridges and beyond (1999–2006)

From 1997 onwards, ILEIA successfully supported the establishment of six regional editions of the *Newsletter* (which was relaunched as *LEISA Magazine* in 2000): the Spanish-language, Latin American edition *LEISA Revista de Agroecologia*, set up by ETC–Andes in Peru in 1997; *LEISA India* (in English), by AME Foundation in Bangalore (1999); the francophone edition *AGRIDAPE*, by IED Afrique (then IIED Sahel) (2003); the Bahasa edition *SALAM* by VECO-Indonesia (2003); *Agriculturas*, the Brazilian edition, by AS-PTA (2003); and 可持续生态农业 (*LEISA China*), implemented by CBIK, a Kunming-based support

NGO (2006). By December 2007, the regional editions collectively had almost twice as many subscribers as the global edition of the *Magazine*. All editions together now reach at least a quarter of a million readers. Surveys indicate that readers of the magazine use the information in a variety of ways, for instance it finds direct application in the field, it is used in teaching and training, and one out of four subscribers translates articles into regional languages, making it more accessible to others in their environment. As a complement to the *Magazine*, the website www.leisa.info is attracting growing numbers of visitors (presently 41,000 per month); it has been rated as one of the top five websites on agriculture and development (Hurst and Brown, 2006).

What is it that makes *LEISA Magazine* unique? What holds it together? These questions are emerging as ILEIA is about to reach its 25th anniversary. Internal reflection as well as various external assessments carried out over the years point to some crucial factors:

- LEISA is an inclusive concept that provides direction rather than clear boundaries, inspiration rather than prescription. This practical, non-dogmatic approach has set ILEIA apart since its conception.
- *LEISA Magazine* is a powerful, unique vehicle for knowledge- and information-sharing in support of sustainable agricultural development and poverty alleviation in the South. The magazine reaches many readers with no or very limited access to the internet or other sources of agricultural information. This is especially the case in Africa where 50 per cent of subscribers still have no access to the internet – though this is changing fast.
- An important, undervalued aspect of the work to produce *LEISA Magazine* is in the discovery and documentation of practical experiences. This is a learning process in its own right, in which local stakeholders, experts and academics engage in practical enquiry to understand and assess the value of local practices and new technologies (see Ba, this book). At least a thousand authors, mostly practical experts, share their LEISA experiences through the magazine each year. This illustrates the strength of the global LEISA network in mobilizing and sharing local knowledge.

Relevant and resilient (2007–)

Moving into the future, ILEIA and its six regional partners face some important challenges. Agriculture, conspicuously absent in the development policy debate for several years, is back on global and national policy agendas. What role can ILEIA and its partners – small actors with large networks – play in informing the renewed policy debate on agriculture? How can a convincing case be made that LEISA has much to offer, not just as a micro approach to addressing small farmers' problems in an increasingly complex and unpredictable environment, but also as a relevant alternative approach to address agriculture, food and environment issues at macro level?

One thing is clear. With the renewed interest in agricultural development, advocacy for the LEISA approach is urgently required. LEISA experience world wide needs to be systematized, as a first prerequisite to reduce the gap between practice and policy. Current development policy thinking emphasizes, on the one hand, commercial agricultural production and, on the other, the creation of social safety nets for the most needy. Many small-scale producers fall in-between these two categories. For some 600 million small-scale family farmers, farming continues to be a way of life, a crucial source of livelihood and food security, which is safeguarding the resilience of agroecological systems, nurturing biodiversity and holding communities together. There is a wealth of relevant knowledge and experience about this type of agriculture in its hugely diverse expressions; the challenge is to make strategic use of this 'capital' to argue the case that small farmers ought to be seen as (potential) assets rather than liabilities.

Communicating farmers' knowledge: AGRIDAPE and PROFEIS experiences

Awa Faly Ba

AGRIDAPE – the francophone edition of *LEISA Magazine* (see van Walsum, this book) – offers a space for all stakeholders to express their views. A key objective is to enable producers to share their knowledge with other producers, development agents, researchers and political decision makers.

Part of the PROLINNOVA initiative (see Waters-Bayer et al., this book), PROFEIS (Promoting farmer experimentation and innovation in the Sahel) is a programme designed to strengthen the capacities of research institutes, agricultural councils, NGOs and local communities to support farmer experimentation and innovation, and to promote political and institutional arrangements that take farmers' capacities in these areas into account. PROFEIS activities have brought together multi-disciplinary teams with farmer organizations and research institutions to identify and document agricultural innovations.

Within one year 25 innovations were identified in Mali and 20 in Senegal. However, describing and analysing these innovation experiences in a way that was accessible to other actors proved a challenge. The need for a methodology to capitalize and build on farmers' research experiences has contributed to a degree of convergence between the AGRIDAPE and PROFEIS programmes. To facilitate the process of acquiring, collecting, organizing and analysing information relating to a given experiment, a 'capitalization' framework was developed that systematized description of certain elements of the experience, including simple analysis criteria.

The same analytical framework can be applied both to experiments carried out by small producers and those resulting from conventional research. This may appear to be a trivial benefit, but in fact it helps to facilitate an exchange between the two sides. The process of applying the framework also stimulates dialogue between actors, because the evaluation of an experiment and analysis of its results requires both scientific and practical insights. More than merely supporting exchanges between actors, the joint examination of the key features of a farmer's innovation and discussion about the conditions necessary for replicating it, lead to joint experimentation.

A few key lessons have been learned from the implementation of these programmes. One is that there has been a greater recognition of the capacity of farmers to contribute to generating agricultural knowledge. Another is that collaborative modes of working, based on a levelling of the relationship between researchers and producers, is possible and can even become a key criterion for evaluating the relevance and success of research projects. The long-term impact of such processes, however, will depend on whether they can be institutionalized and integrated into agricultural policies.

Network, institution and movement: the case of the Honey Bee network

Anil Gupta

Introduction

Many grassroots social movements have spawned institutions to support various day-to-day activities. The birth of institutions in some cases may be mediated by the creation of networks. For the long-term growth of social movements and for the achievement of their objectives, their relationships with institutions and networks have to be synergistic. Institutions mobilize resources, provide logistical and infrastructural support and look after the implementation of the decisions taken by the networks, as well as their own structures of governance. A network mobilizes the participation of people with different ideas, resources, innovations and backgrounds in different knowledge systems, but with more defined responsibility to carry the social movement forward.

Here I discuss the challenges the Honey Bee network faces in sustaining the social movement to make India innovative. In the process, the role of the institutions it has spawned will also be discussed. My major contention is that the success of the advocacy and policy reform functions pursued by a network hinges on the efficiency with which the institutions operationalize their mandate and support the network.

The Honey Bee network

In 1986–7, after I spent a year in Bangladesh, I began to question the roles of intellectuals in dealing with people's knowledge in a fair and just manner. It became obvious that the behaviour of academics like myself was not different from other exploiters in society. They exploited land, labour and capital markets, whereas I exploited the ideas market. What was the difference? For me, the dilemma had to be resolved constructively. Thus evolved the philosophy of the Honey Bee network. Knowledge of people should not be taken without their acknowledgement, proper attribution, reciprocity and feedback. Knowledge providers should not remain anonymous. People-to-people communication should be encouraged through local language exchange. And any surplus arising out of people's knowledge used with or without value addition should be shared with them in a reasonable and fair manner.

Once such a framework developed, a lot of action followed. Since its foundation, Honey Bee has documented more than 70,000 innovations and traditional knowledge practices in a database of ideas. While we do not have the resources that would let us fully evaluate the effectiveness of all of the knowledge we have documented, much of it is currently being assessed or has survived more detailed scrutiny. A handful of inventions have resulted in patents and spawned joint ventures. The *Honey Bee Newsletter*, which includes information on these inventions and discoveries, now reaches people in over 75 countries. My parent institution, the Indian Institute of Management in Ahmedabad (IIMA), provides editorial and logistical support while the Society for Research and Initiatives for Sustainable Technologies and Institutions (SRISTI), which was set up in 1993 to provide backup support to the network (www.sristi.org), helps print the newsletter in several Indian languages.

Slowly a network has evolved (Box 3.2). In 1997, as a follow-up of the International Conference on Creativity and Innovation at Grassroots held at the IIMA, the first Grassroots Innovation Augmentation Network (GIAN) was established as an incubator to convert innovations into enterprises. In February 2000, the National Innovation Foundation (NIF) was set up by the Indian Department of Science and Technology. In 2003, the first Micro Venture Innovation Fund (MVIF) was founded to provide risk capital for supporting grassroots innovations. In May 2007, the Tianjin Declaration was issued to create a global GIAN to provide an online and offline incubation platform for grassroots innovations.

Box 3.2 An evolving grassroots innovation network

Local knowledge diffuses throughout the Honey Bee community in several ways. SRISTI, the institutional extension of Honey Bee, has a helpline that people can call to get answers to questions. It also publishes local language newspapers. Collaborators have organized training programmes to educate youth and others about animal treatments and ways to make herbal pesticides. New plant varieties developed by farmers have diffused mainly through the farmer-to-farmer network, and sometimes through locally branded seeds sold by commercial dealers. Over time, these activities evolved and Honey Bee now focuses on developing the herbal formulations derived from grassroots practices into viable, user-friendly and marketable products through conventional research and development. We have gathered information on approximately 30,000 herbal and biologically based innovations and traditional practices for aiding plant, human and animal health.

Now Honey Bee has formed a partnership between scientists and the traditional knowledge base with the dual goals of adding value to traditional practices and helping pool the best ideas. That partnership has matured beyond our initial debates in the *Honey Bee Newsletter* and has been formalized into the National Innovation Foundation of India, established in 2000 with a budget of US$5 million. In 2004, the NIF signed an agreement with the Council of Scientific and Industrial Research to support four areas of research: herbal, mechanical, food processing and nutraceuticals (engineered foods with added health benefits) and energy. NIF formed a similar partnership with the Indian Council of Medical Research in 2006 to add value to non-codified, folkloric traditional herbal knowledge through medical research.

One example of how science has added value to local traditional practices comes from recent research into the tradition of using milk to manage diseases in crops. Farmers and scientists alike have described milk as a natural inhibitor of plant viruses; it also sticks well and spreads well. It has proven effective against viruses and fungi in various plants, including winter wheat, tomatoes, peppers, tobacco, potatoes and sugar cane. In 1992, the *Honey Bee Newsletter* published an editorial about a farmer's practice of dipping his hands in milk before sowing tobacco seeds. In 2005, researchers in Jodhpur examined two other specific applications of milk and shared their results in the newsletter. In one study, they compared the effectiveness of two treatments to prevent downy mildew in pearl millet plants: soil treatment with *Gliocladium virens*, a biological pesticide, versus seed treatment using raw cow's milk. They found both treatments to be equally effective (Gupta 2006).

Building a network: some lessons learned

When the Honey Bee network began to evolve, the norms of accountability and transparency were inherent in the way new members joined. People could choose to be inside or outside the network, but this should not injure basic trust and mutual respect. The leadership of the network and the social movement ought to be polycentric, as I learnt long ago when I visited a settlement of the Chenchu tribe in the Sri Salem forest in Andhra Pradesh. This tribe was one of the few remaining food gathering and hunting tribes which had evolved very interesting rules to govern their social and ecological functions. After studying the pattern of allocation of resources and responsibilities, I found that three general principles guided their activities: 1) leadership was iterative: the person who was leader in a honey collection group could be a follower in a hunting or food gathering group; 2) leadership was linked to skills and not to social or cultural status: the traditional leader did not necessarily have a say in every matter; and 3) pooling was independent of redistribution: those who went on a particular hunting or food gathering expedition, did not share their finds or game only with the members of the expedition. All the members of the band or larger social group got their share of the food or game. The implication is that we should realize the need to evolve norms in networks or movements, which respect individual specialization and generate responsibility among sub-group members for the larger group at the same time. How we create a similar iteration and differentiation in responsibilities without losing the cohesion of the larger group is a challenge. It is imperative therefore that those who mobilize financial or physical resources for the network do not acquire any more power than those who mobilize social or knowledge resources.

In the context of the Honey Bee network, every member who volunteers to contribute his or her energy to scout grassroots innovators or traditional knowledge holders, document their knowledge, add value, or convert innovations into enterprises and/or protect their intellectual property rights, expects other members to value the contribution. We convey this by frequent consultations, periodic reporting of outcomes and recognizing that failures are not intentional and successes could be collective and take time. The network grows when different members value the benefits of affiliation, collective achievements and social relations more than the individual contributions they make.

Fostering synergies

The institutions spawned by Honey Bee, such as SRISTI, NIF, GIAN and others, have an important role in fulfilling the expectation of the network and advancing the social movement. There is no doubt that what the network could do with its limited resources in the first 12 years, an institution like NIF, by building upon its legacy and lessons could surpass several times in the last eight years (of course with the help of the Honey Bee Network). Resources played only a small role. A larger role was played by the synergy between the network and the institution. This synergy can come under strain if mutual roles, responsibilities and respect are not calibrated from time to time.

The institution has to perform several functions. In particular, it should:

- provide support to the networks, bring in new members and encourage collegiality;
- be transparent in the allocation of resources within and outside so that the trust of different stakeholders increases;
- balance the interests of those who are less articulate, assertive and aggressive in making demands;

- generate new opportunities for the members to learn from each other; it should ensure that resources spent on establishment and actual support to people are balanced; and
- regularly reassess, rejuvenate and realign its own goals and missions with that of the social movement and the network.

The social movement to make India innovative needs a whole range of stakeholders. Having scouted innovators or traditional knowledge holders, it needs the support of professional scientists, technologists, designers, entrepreneurs, investors, marketers and communicators and many others. Each of these stakeholders belongs to different professional cultures and organizations. One cannot always expect voluntary help from all of them (though some will), even if the network collaborators have voluntarily scouted the innovations to which these stakeholders have to add value.

Some tensions are bound to emerge in making a transition from the knowledge chain to the value chain. The former is still possible through voluntary help. The latter requires dealing with markets with well-established norms and processes. Exceptions exist, however. For instance, almost all the patents for grassroots innovators or traditional knowledge holders have been filed in India or abroad through the *pro bono* help of attorneys. Yet this is a very small activity compared to the other major goals of value addition and diffusion through commercial or non-commercial channels sharing benefits at the same time. In that respect, the network has to reach major milestones in the years to come. Formal collaboration with the Council of Scientific and Industrial Research, the Indian Council of Medical Research, the National Botanical Research Institute, the Botanical Survey of India etc., has heralded in a process of blending formal and informal science.

People-to-people learning: from farmers to labourers first

The work of the Honey Bee network on scouting and documentation of innovations has revealed the tremendous potential of promoting grassroots innovations by farmers, artisans, pastoralists and others. Mehtar Hussain, a small farmer-cum-labourer in Assam developed a windmill made of bamboo to pump water for US$100, while another farmer in Vietnam, Pham Ma Nhi, developed a windmill for under $25 (Nguyen Thanh Tung, 2007, personal communication). This is a new revolution in the making. Distributed knowledge management by creative people throughout the world could herald a new way of sustainable development. People-to-people learning across the world is becoming possible. This windmill has now been adapted through GIAN for pumping briny water for small-scale salt farmers in Gujarat.

Should we, however, restrict our learning to farmers? The role of labourers in improving productivity and performing most of the drudgery-filled tasks has remained less recognized. Those labourers who contribute new insights about efficient agriculture or non-farm activities deserve to be respected as co-researchers. They notice the need for slow and fast irrigation at different stages of the crop so that the roots of the plants are not affected or exposed (Wala, personal communication to Riya Sinha, 2007). They develop sickles with a sandwich blade on two sides. As labourers visit more farms than farmers, they observe much greater diversity. Their knowledge, insights and innovations also deserve a chance. Should we not move from farmers first to labourers first and ensure that mediating institutions place less emphasis on method, and more on ethics and still more on authenticity in engagement? I have no doubt that a Gandhian belief in building upon local best practices could once again provide a way of revitalizing the science and technological knowledge systems in formal and informal sectors.

There are many unresolved goals of the last two decades of farmers first. The next two decades will hopefully help to meet those goals and engage with the mission of labourers first.

Food sovereignty: a farmer-led policy framework

Patrick Mulvany and Maria Arce Moreira

Changing contexts in the global food system: challenges for the Farmer First approach

The Farmer First approach was born out of a growing frustration of development workers that (western) technology-driven, top-down approaches to agricultural development were not reaching poorer farmers nor were they helping them to analyse their situation. These development workers, initially NGOs and researchers, recognized the expressed demands of farmers to be more involved with designing and carrying out research building on their own existing experimentation and knowledge. These models of extension were also promoted in areas that were complex, risk-prone and diverse, untouched by the industrial agricultural technologies of the Green Revolution. In such areas the Farmer First approach was successful, as in the food security project initiated by ITDG (now known as Practical Action) in Chivi District, Masvingo Province, Zimbabwe, started in the late 1980s. This project worked with communities to find practical ways of responding to the political challenge of reducing food insecurity and food aid disbursements through improving the resilience of agricultural production (Murwira et al., 2001).

But in the past 20 years, the technologies and processes developed by or for the corporate private sector and protected legally by Intellectual Property

Rights (IPRs), commercial contracts and use restriction technologies have facilitated the concentration of power in ever fewer hands for the benefit of a privileged and often unaccountable minority. This increasing imbalance of power has challenged and undermined the Farmer First approach as financial resources are moved from research and development to support the production of diverse foods by local farmers to focusing on genes needed by industry.

Agricultural development policies have changed through the recognition of IPRs on naturally and artificially developed living organisms, which has driven the development of science and technology, and related industries, for genetic engineering, nanotechnology and synthetic biology. These may decisively impact food production, human health and the environment and will facilitate the transfer of power from smallholders to corporate agribusinesses. The conclusion of the GATT Uruguay round of negotiations, which ended with the formation of the World Trade Organization (WTO) but without agreement on international agricultural trade, has had profound impacts. Subsequently the development of bilateral and regional free trade agreements containing restrictive clauses requiring countries, among other issues, to recognize IPRs and allow imports of goods produced by protected novel technologies, are a more recent threat to smallholder agriculture (Tansey and Rajotte, 2008).

The changing rules that govern food and agriculture at all levels – local, national and international – are designed *a priori* to facilitate not local, but international, trade. This reduces diversity and concentrates the wealth of the world's food economies in the hands of ever fewer multinational corporations, while the majority of the world's small-scale food providers, transformers, local traders and consumers including, crucially, the poor and malnourished, are marginalized.

The unrestricted availability of seeds, livestock breeds and so on to local food providers is increasingly under threat from, among other things, their privatization, as required for crop plants by the WTO Agreement on Trade-Related Aspects of Intellectual Property Rights (TRIPs), specifically Article 27.3(b). This much-disputed article requires all members of the WTO to provide plant variety protection through patents or *sui generis* forms of monopoly privileges. It imposes a system that weakens informal sector knowledge systems and thereby facilitates the concentration of knowledge and power (Mulvany, 2005).

This has led to increased concentration of ownership of genetic resources for food and agriculture. For example many thousands of plant breeding companies provided farmers' seeds in the 1980s before the patenting of genes was permitted and in the early stages of plant variety protection laws. In 2002 only ten companies controlled a third of all sales. By 2005, ten companies controlled nearly half of global seed sales and in 2006 nearly 60 per cent of global seed sales were in the hands of the top ten seed corporations, many of which also dominate the market in genetically modified seeds (ETC Group, 2007). In livestock production a similar concentration of ownership is also occurring. Only four companies own the genetics of commercial poultry production worldwide (Gura, 2007).

This continuing trend of commodification, privatization and concentration of knowledge and the ownership of genetic resources results in the loss of control by, and benefits for, the farmers, gardeners, livestock keepers and their communities in the informal sector that developed agricultural biodiversity.

From corporate-dominated to farmer-led: turning the world's food system upside down

Building on, but going beyond the original Farmer First formulation, there are now new ways of challenging corporate dominance and the marginalization of poorer farmers based on the food sovereignty policy framework, a new approach to food and farming. Food sovereignty is a policy framework designed to put food providers and consumers, rather than corporate agribusiness, at the heart of decision making in what should become localized rather than global food systems.

The concept of food sovereignty was agreed at the International Conference of Via Campesina, the global farmers' movement, in Tlaxcala, Mexico, in April 1996.

> We, the Via Campesina, a growing movement of farm workers, peasant, farm and indigenous peoples' organizations from all the regions of the world, know that food security cannot be achieved without taking full account of those who produce food. Any discussion that ignores our contribution will fail to eradicate poverty and hunger. Food is a basic human right. This right can only be realized in a system where Food Sovereignty is guaranteed. (Via Campesina, 1996)

Since its launch at the World Food Summit in 1996, where the objective was to encourage NGOs and civil society organizations to discuss alternatives to the neo-liberal proposals for achieving food security, the development of food sovereignty ideas and principles has gathered pace. There have been important meetings in 2001 – World Forum on Food Sovereignty, Havana, Cuba; 2002 – Forum for Food Sovereignty, Rome, Italy; and 2007 – Nyéléni 2007: forum for food sovereignty, Sélingué, Mali. It is important to note that the term, originally translated from Spanish, is not a 'brand' but a set of principles in a policy framework. Similar sets of principles are also espoused by those who call for food democracy, as well as by many in the agroecology, organic and consumer movements.

Food sovereignty was also developed as a reaction to the impact of 'food security' policies. The definition of food security agreed by governments focuses on all peoples having enough food to eat each day, increasingly supplied by imports, but it is silent about where the food comes from, who produces it, and how and under what conditions it has been grown. The result of this limited policy focus has been that smallholder farmers are increasingly forced off their lands as they cannot compete with increases in (often subsidized) imports of food. Food security policies may, thus, contribute to more poverty, marginalization and hunger. Food sovereignty not only deals with power relations, trade issues, the right to food and knowledge systems, it also supports agricultural systems that have been developed based on principles of cooperation with nature. This has led to highly complex agro-ecological systems which provide multiple functions in support of food provision.

The lessons of citizens' juries in India (Pimbert and Wakeford, 2002) and Zimbabwe (Coupe and Lewins, 2007) show that when provided with full information, farmers can select the most appropriate technologies that they need to defend their production systems and the food sovereignty of their communities. These and many other examples show how food providers are resisting the imposition of the dominant agricultural science and technology (Pretty, 2005; ILEIA et al., 2007; Development Fund, 2007) but few are recorded as being able to survive, for any significant length of time, a distorted market and skewed funding of agricultural science and technology. Exceptions include the rapid growth of organic and agroecological markets in many parts of the world; the solidarity of local consumers who promote Community Supported Agriculture systems; and the smallholders who survive economic shocks through barter markets (Marti and Pimbert, 2006).

Democratizing science and innovation

In agricultural science and technology a new paradigm for research is urgently needed.

> Conventional agricultural research must be reorganised for greater democratic oversight and priority setting to combine the strengths of farmers and scientists in the search for fair, sustainable and locally adapted food systems. Transforming agricultural research is also increasingly necessary to ensure that the food we eat keeps us healthy... local people and citizens should be the ones who decide which new policies and technologies are needed when, where and under what conditions... There is a need to transform knowledge – using ecology as the basis for sustainable agriculture and de-colonialising economics from narrow definitions of wealth... This will require more direct citizen participation in decisions about new technologies, research priorities and policies for food and farming. (Pimbert, 2007)

This will require a fundamental democratizing of science and technological R&D, with some major institutional and methodological innovations. Deliberative processes of inclusion and their results are now being used in several African countries. For example, the outcomes of a Mali citizens' jury are being used in negotiations with national governments by the key national and regional farmers' organizations (CNOP in Mali and ROPPA in West Africa) and the regional civil society network COPAGEN (IIED, 2006), and similar processes have been used in Zimbabwe (Coupe and Lewins, 2007).

In the twenty-first century, for the effective implementation of Farmer First approaches, the decisive inclusion of farmers and other food providers in the institutional and political fora that define agricultural and trade policy needs to be enhanced.

The struggle for food sovereignty

Food sovereignty is being developed and discussed as a counter-proposal to the mainstream development paradigm built on liberalized international agricultural trade, trade-based food security, and industrial agriculture and food production by well-resourced producers. Food sovereignty has become the new policy framework, championed by social movements, for challenging current trends in rural development and food and agricultural policies that do not respect or support the interests and needs of food providers, local consumers and the environment (Windfuhr and Jonsén, 2005). Food sovereignty covers all dimensions of a food system that will provide food in the long-term rather than short-term profits. It focuses on food for people rather than internationally tradable commodities. It values food providers rather than eliminating them. It localizes food systems rather than dependence on inequitable global trade. It puts control locally instead of by unaccountable corporations. It builds knowledge and skills that conserve and develop local food production and rejects alien technologies such as GMOs. It works with nature in diverse agroecological systems rather than energy-intensive production methods which damage the environment and contribute to global warming.

The original propositions of Farmer First fit clearly into this framework but their interpretation over the past two decades has resulted in a shift further away from the possibilities of farmer-led policies and actions. As Biggs (2008) argues, the mainstream advocates of participatory technology development have become 'apolitical' and concerned with management tools and frameworks that would be 'scaled out and scaled up'. In another context, this type of activity has been called 'paradigm maintenance' – not questioning the power relations and impacts of the dominant discourse. However, Biggs notes, there are others undertaking academic studies who seek to understand how change actually takes place in science and technology, and to make suggestions for research and development intervention based on this knowledge.

Power relations and dominant discourses are being challenge by food sovereignty and right-to-food movements across the world. In at least 22 national constitutions, the human right to food is recognized and specific processes have been promoted by various governments to discuss and internalize the fundamentals of food sovereignty in their existing legal frameworks. This is a clear sign of political will that recognizes the political nature of the food, agriculture and poverty debate and intends to address the inequities of its development in recent years. Examples of this type of process can be found in Mali and Bolivia where, after many decades of groundwork, mainly by civil society organizations and social movements, the political space for this discussion has been opened recently and opportunities for new legislation and strategies led and informed by poor farmers and their organizations have finally been realized. Farmer First approaches could support this farmer-led movement to realize the more equitable food sovereignty policy framework but they will need to be embedded in and accepting of the new agenda for a change of paradigm, methodology, power relations and politics.

Farmer first or still last? Uneven institutional development in the Indian agricultural innovation system

V. Rasheed Sulaiman

Introduction

Over the last two decades, the agricultural innovation system (AIS) in India has become increasingly diverse, complex and chaotic. With the liberalization of the economy in the 1990s, there has been increased private sector participation in research and extension, an expansion of interventions by civil society organizations (CSOs) in agriculture and considerable weakening of public sector research and extension. At the same time Indian agriculture is facing greater challenges from the unsustainable use of natural resources and significant threats (as well as opportunities) from the opening up of agricultural markets. The country's agricultural research and extension community has failed to respond effectively to these changes and this has contributed to the current crisis in Indian agriculture.

There is considerable scope to increase rural incomes through increased productivity, enhanced competitiveness and the creation of an efficient marketing system. But this would only be possible with the development of an improved agricultural and rural innovation system that can respond quickly to current and future challenges, supported by adequate investments in rural infrastructure. Below I analyse why the AIS in India has not been able to use its rich organizational diversity to enable the necessary innovation and suggest ways of strengthening its capacity to do so.

The Indian agricultural innovation system

A national AIS has been defined as 'a network of organizations, enterprises, and individuals focused on bringing new products, new processes, and new forms of organization into economic use, together with the institutions and policies that affect the way different agents interact, share, access, exchange and use knowledge' (World Bank, 2006). One of the major attractions of the innovation systems framework has been its explicit recognition that innovation is not a research-driven process simply relying on technology transfer. Instead it is a process of generating, accessing and putting knowledge into use (Hall et al., 2001, 2004; World Bank, 2006). Central to the process are the *interactions* of different people and their ideas; the *institutions* (the attitudes, habits, practices and ways of working) that shape how individuals and organizations interact; and *learning* as a means of evolving new arrangements specific to local contexts.

Actors and institutions

India has an extensive National Agricultural Research System (NARS) comprising a network of 189 centres and co-ordinated projects funded and managed by the Indian Council of Agricultural Research (ICAR), including one Central University and 31 State Agricultural Universities, about 100 private and voluntary research and development organizations, and several rural and women's universities. Each State Agricultural University has several research centres dealing with specific crops and agroecological zones. Although these research centres have developed several technologies and some have been extensively adopted, a significant number have remained either on the shelf or in compendiums. While many blame a resource crunch for the disintegration of public systems of research and development (R&D), there are others who strongly believe that the unwillingness to reform institutions (rules, norms and working practices) within the agricultural R&D community is mainly responsible for the current crisis.

Private sector participation in agricultural R&D has been on the increase. Recent estimates reveal that business funding for agricultural R&D constituted about 11 per cent of the total R&D funding (Pal and Jha, 2007). The largest private investment occurred in chemicals (pesticides and fertilizers) and food processing, followed by seed and machinery. More recently, growth has been in plant breeding and biotechnology, animal health and poultry (ibid). While this has added to an improved flow of new technologies, there are concerns about the higher costs of these technologies and the resulting restricted access.

The last two decades have witnessed the increasing involvement of civil society – including research foundations, NGOs and producer associations – in agricultural research and extension. Many have been working with the poor and have a broader approach to innovation, thereby enabling the poor to access, adapt and apply new information, knowledge and technology. In the public sector, the extension machinery of the state Department of Agriculture (DoA) reaches down to the block and village level. The DoA's village extension workers continue to be important sources of information for farmers in India, even though information is clearly targeted at grain production, visits are irregular and the service is pre-occupied with the implementation of government schemes linked to subsidies and subsidized inputs. With external support drying up as the Training & Visit system of extension ended in the early 1990s, states have been left to fund their extension machinery and this has led to considerable weakening of public sector extension. The number of Krishi Vigyan Kendras (farm science centres mainly involved with farmer training) funded by the ICAR has increased during this period, but their effective reach is marginal.

Considering the changing nature of agriculture, producers currently need a wider range of support, including organizational, marketing, technological, financial and entrepreneurial support. Unfortunately farmers are not able to get this kind of integrated support from either the public or private sector. According to the Planning Commission (2006),

> Low farm incomes due to inadequate productivity growth have often combined with low prices of output and lack of credit at reasonable rates to push several farmers into crippling debt. Even otherwise, uncertainties seem to have increased (regarding prices, quality of inputs and also weather and pests) which, coupled with unavailability of proper extension work and risk insurance have led farmers to despair.

The failure of reform

Although research and extension systems have been subject to numerous reforms during the last two decades, these have been more organizational and have not addressed key institutional issues. Our analysis of partnerships and institutions in agricultural research and extension has revealed some of the critical institutions that continue to determine the way public sector research and extension functions in India (Hall et al., 2002, 2004; Sulaiman and Hall, 2002, 2004; Raina et al., 2006).

Norms of linear R&D

The development and diffusion of technologies in a linear fashion – from the science that generates it to the extension effort that disseminates it and the farmer who uses it – continues to be the major institution defining the functional boundaries for research and extension. Despite being discredited this linear model survives as it ensures enhanced funding and legitimization through econometric estimation of returns to investment. Steps taken to promote research–extension linkages have not yielded any success and farmer participation in research and extension remains restricted to token representations in planning meetings. This also leaves several other actors critical for innovation outside the knowledge generation and application process.

Narrow evaluation norms

While research is assessed mainly in terms of technologies developed and papers published, extension performance is assessed in terms of technologies adopted, trainings conducted or farmers contacted. This tradition of assessing performance has effectively stifled attempts at sharing expertise, adapting technologies to suit specific situations and collaborative activities for promoting innovation. This has further strengthened the linear mode of functioning, ensured compartmentalized accountabilities and prevented research and extension from interacting with and learning from others. While research blames extension for poor results in the field, extension blames research for developing irrelevant technologies, and both research and extension blame policies for not creating the right conditions for technology uptake.

Mistrust of other actors

This tradition of working independently – together with a mistrust of other agencies such as the private sector, NGOs and also other public agencies existing in different domains – has led to the effective isolation of public sector agencies. Complementary knowledge and expertise necessary for innovation has thus remained blocked in many of these different agencies. Although some measures to promote public–private partnerships were initiated, these have not received continuous attention. Co-ordinating the activities of different agencies and promoting joint efforts to develop sector competitiveness therefore remains a major challenge.

Rewarding only successes and reluctance to report and analyse failures

This has led to a situation where people are not willing to take any risk by experimenting with different approaches to technology development or promotion. Opportunities for learning and trying better ways of functioning therefore do not exist and this has resulted in the search and promotion of 'models' for replication. Moreover, the research and extension community also does not learn from the experiences of others.

The challenge of institutional change

Institutional reform became a catchword in the literature on agricultural research and extension organizations in India in the 1990s (Raina et al., 2006). While organizations are relatively easy to establish or change, however, this is not true of the institutions that govern them.

The usual policy recommendations include: increased investments for R&D (1–2 per cent of agricultural GDP) and extension; better research priority setting, strengthening research–extension linkages, increased use of Information and Communication Technologies; contracting extension services to NGOs and private sector; delegation of powers to decentralized units, etc. However, all these recommendations do not, unfortunately, change the way knowledge is produced or applied and utilized in society. Despite endless conferences, workshops, research papers, policy briefs and policy consultations, little institutional reform has occurred in public sector agricultural research or extension that allows it to cater effectively to changing demands for agricultural innovation. This relative unwillingness to reform the institutions is a feature that marks Indian agricultural research and extension (Lele and Goldsmith, 1989; Raina, 2003).

Where do we go from here?

While there has not been any significant institutional reform of public sector research and extension, CSOs and the private sector have evolved better institutions for promoting innovation. There is a lot to learn from the experiences of CSOs on ways of promoting pro-poor innovation. Their success was found to depend on:

- facilitating a culture of experimentation and learning;
- partnering with a wide range of actors;
- ability to contextualize and continuously adapt technologies to suit varied user demands;
- encouraging efforts at influencing the institutions and policies among other actors to promote innovation; and
- participating in wide sector related networks (Sulaiman, 2006).

However, both CSOs and the private sector have not been able to develop productive interactions with the public sector. Increasingly, the trend is to give up on the public sector and its role in agricultural development, although public sector research and extension can and should play an important role in ensuring equitable development and enhancing sector competitiveness.

Conclusions

Institutional development in the Indian agricultural innovation system is uneven. Although characterized by many diverse actors with complementary expertise, weak patterns of interaction among these actors constrain knowledge flows, and thereby, innovation. Moreover, there is no effective mechanism for sector co-ordination. However, even under these difficult situations, the CSOs in India have been relatively successful in providing broad-based support to farmers and promoting pro-poor innovation. Yet, the public sector, which still dominates research and extension, does not seem to be either learning from these experiences or responding effectively to these new challenges. While the lack of institutional changes plagues the performance of agricultural research and extension and its contribution to agricultural innovation, reform strategies continue to be structured around calls for more resources (for R&D), improved priority setting and better research–extension linkages.

Performance of the Indian agricultural innovation system depends crucially on two aspects: its ability to foster institutional change and the creation of effective mechanisms to co-ordinate its diverse actors. Institutional changes are necessary not only in research and extension organizations but also in others involved in agricultural and rural development. Though growing in number, policy researchers and policy-makers who recognize these issues and are willing to initiate changes are still few and far between. There is a need to create mechanisms to consolidate and support their efforts so that they can facilitate the institutional change process. Any further delay in addressing institutional bottlenecks would further marginalize public sector research and extension. This will have serious implications for India's ability to tackle agriculture and rural development challenges and its strategy for an inclusive growth.

Emergence of farmer-centred agricultural science and technology policy in China

Li Xiaoyun, Qi Gubo, Xu Xiuli and Mao Miankui

Introduction

China's agricultural science and technology system has benefited the economy more than it has benefited its smallholder farmers. In fact, the country's agricultural science and technology policy, together with a centrally planned management system and official incentive system, hindered the emergence of a viable smallholder sector, despite the fact that the system has actively embraced a livelihoods focus. Recently, however, institutional and policy reforms have brought about the emergence of a more farmer-centred agricultural research and extension system which appears capable of meeting diverse technological needs.

A focus on production and food security

For 30 years after the foundation of the People's Republic of China, national food security dominated the thinking of those responsible for guiding the development of China's agricultural science and technology policy. Increasing agricultural output and productivity as rapidly as possible were the over-riding goals. Macro-economic and social policies were fashioned to serve and protect national food security (National Committee on Science and Technology, 1997). An associated priority was the development of China's chemical industry as agriculture increased its dependence on chemical fertilizers and other agricultural inputs. Agricultural research concentrated on applied areas expected to result in increased total grain production and unit yields. Management of the system was organized in a parallel fashion, with research units responsible for research and the people's work units on communes and state farms responsible for production. Universities played an educational role using pedagogy largely divorced from the realities of farmers' fields while government departments issued scientific research and production targets. The system was highly centralized and controlled, driven by administrative edicts reflecting China's centralized planning structure and goal-setting processes.

Market opportunities

In the years immediately after China's radical 'open-door' reforms of 1978 and thereafter, the importance of market signals as factors in resource allocation decisions at the farm level increased. Over subsequent decades, the sleeping giant of China's agriculture shook off its torpor as farmers across the country responded to the new opportunity to produce for the private market. In the most favoured regions, well resourced farmers prospered, leaving their poorer and less favoured cousins behind. The impact on productivity and national food security was remarkable. By the end of the 1990s, the problem of food security had slipped from centre stage. China was not only producing enough to feed its population, but its consumers also had the where-with-all to buy the food brought to the market. At the same time, the income gap between poor and non-poor farmers and between urban and rural households widened dramatically. The conflict between the desire of smallholders for higher farm-gate returns, and national objectives that emphasized cheap food as a means of containing inflation and upward pressures on wages, gradually emerged as an important issue in rural poverty reduction.

Agricultural science policy quickly found itself between a rock and a hard place, escape from which had to combine increasing smallholders' incomes while at the same time containing any inflationary pressures that would come from increasing farm-gate prices. Consequently, the core objective of agricultural science and technology policy shifted to (i) improving the quality of the agricultural products farmers delivered to the market; and (ii) promoting the diversification of smallholders' incomes. While these policies have benefited consumers and farmers in general, they have provided little benefit to smallholders at the bottom of the poverty pyramid.

A new impetus for science and technology

The new millennium saw yet another sizeable shift in China's approach to agriculture and the role of science and technology. China began its entry into 21st century agriculture by promulgating a 'Program for the Development of Agricultural Science and Technology 2001-10' (Deng and Wan, 2001). This new policy sought to integrate objectives that had previously been dealt with as separate and almost isolated areas of public policy. On the one hand the pursuit of food security remained of high importance, as did the protection of farmers' incomes to prevent newly prosperous farmers from sliding back into poverty. On the other hand, government now added goals concerning the environment and resource sustainability, plus improvement in international competitiveness in keeping with the freer trade that followed China's entry into the World Trade Organization (WTO).

The supporting role of agricultural science and technology policy changed in tandem. Science and technology would continue to help farmers upgrade their skills and access 'scientific approaches' to rural production, but science and technology would also acknowledge the importance of environmental concerns, the unique differences between renewable and non-renewable resources, as well as the technology transfers needed to ensure that China's farmers could compete with the rest of the world. Polices such as the 'Project of Technology Entering Into Farmers' Households', the 'Spark Plan', the 'Project of Agricultural Experts in Village Yards', the 'Science and Technology Correspondence System', and the 'Agricultural Technical Services 110' promoted research on farmers' livelihoods and sustainable development but did little to tackle the plight of the poorest (Xu, 2004).

Systems of agricultural science and technology innovation in China

In 2001, China had more than 1,100 agricultural research agencies at state, provincial and regional level, of which 636 focused on planting, 125 on stockbreeding, 125 on fisheries, 171 on mechanization of farming and 43 on other issues (National Bureau of Statistics of China, 2006; Ministry of Agriculture of China, 2007). At national level, the Ministry of Science and Technology formulates the science and technology development plan based on plans drawn up by its specialized research ministries or bureaus. The State Council is the lead department while the State Committee of Development and Transformation facilitates the process of overall agricultural science and technology development planning and the Ministry of Finance is responsible for budget planning. This structure is replicated at provincial and regional levels with different agricultural research agencies managed by government departments at the same level.

In parallel to the research system, and managed in a similarly hierarchical manner, a vast extension system exists. In 2006, China had more than 20,000 agricultural extension agencies at county level and more than 150,000 at township level (Ministry of Agriculture of China, 2007).

Alongside the public agricultural research and extension system there has emerged a non-public system that is profit and client driven, which includes enterprises, professional associations, individuals and some other organizations or agencies that support not only new technologies but also extension services to farmers. In 2001, there were more than 100,000 professional agriculture associations in the country and more than 400,000 village technology service organizations, as well as uncountable agriculture enterprises and other types of organizations or agencies (China Agricultural Technology Extension System Reform Research Taskforce, 2004). This system has flourished because the public system, for all its reforms, remains constrained by tradition and bureaucratic inertia. Non-public sector providers have found a niche where flexibility and responsiveness to farmer's needs can generate profits.

Increasingly there is an overlap between public and non-public systems of agricultural research, at least at the technology adaptation and extension end of the spectrum. With the rapid development of civil society – and influenced by participatory development projects introduced by international donors since the late 1980s – more and more grassroots NGOs, associations, research agencies and some government officials are practising and promoting farmer-centred agricultural research to meet the needs of farmers, especially poor farmers. An informal academic group called the Farmer-Centred Research Network (FCRN) consisting of around 16 provincial Agricultural Academies in China has been implementing a farmer-centred research approach since 2000 (see Box 3.3). At the same time other similar organizations have been emerging. An exciting result is that farmers who participated in the process not only had higher income but also higher capacity compared with non-participants. Instead of government agents or researchers, farmers themselves took on the key role in decision-making about what technologies or services they wanted.

Incentives and awards: impacts on farmers

An important driver of the existing innovation system – and particularly that part within the public sector – is the system of incentives and rewards for researchers and extensionists. The official reward system provides awards at national, provincial and local level. In 2003, there were five major awards under the theme of science and technology, including the State Supreme Science and Technology Award, the State Natural Science Award, the State Technological Invention Award, the State Scientific and Technological Progress Award and the International Science and Technology Cooperation Award. Similar awards are established at provincial and ministerial level and by key research projects to promote achievement of long-term science and technology planning goals.

Box 3.3 The Farmer-Centred Research Network, China

Qi Gubo, Li Xiaoyun, Xu Xiuli, Dindo Campilan, Ronnie Vernooy

The Farmer-Centred Research Network (FCRN), an informal research group in China, has been working with governmental and non-governmental research institutes to institutionalize a farmer-centred research (FCR) approach in the present agricultural research system. Over the past seven years, partner institutions have tested and refined the approach in an array of research projects across China and introduced FCR concepts, principles and methods to their affiliated organizations and the communities they serve. The main activities of the FCRN consist of providing small grants to fund participatory research, facilitating exchange visits between partners, organizing workshops and trainings on FCR, and managing communications, networking and outreach activities.

Over time, the FCR teams have become increasingly diversified and multi-disciplinary, typically involving a rural sociologist, entomologist, regional planner, agronomist, economist, engineer, breeder and local farmer-scientist. The research areas are also diverse, with participatory research activities covering a wide range of topics in response to farmers' requirements in different provinces. These include rangeland management experiments for improved sheep production in Ningxia, sweet potato planting and packaging technology development in dryland areas of Shaanxi, a study of the linkages between scientific and local fertilization technologies in Inner Mongolia, participatory cassava and maize breeding and selection in Guangxi, a participatory water-saving rice production technology experiment in Jilin, an integrated livelihood improvement project in Yunnan, a participatory integrated crop management system in Guizhou, a participatory integrated cropping and animal husbandry system development in Hainan, and the application of participatory technology development in initiating farmers' associations in Shanxi.

According to a recent survey of 215 researchers who have contributed to the Network, we found that there have been significant changes in individual scientist's FCR research capabilities induced by their involvement in FCRN activities. Their increased ability to employ participatory research methods to diagnose problems and identify solutions with farmers was seen as the most significant change. Another review on the contribution of farmers and scientists to decision-making in the agricultural innovation process, showed that the choice of innovations to test and apply is no longer controlled by the state and scientists and farmers are actively participating in identifying which issues to investigate and which technologies to experiment with (Li et al., 2006).

Networking has proved to be an effective way for sharing innovations among the FCRN partners. Though there are still many obstacles to be overcome, the joint learning process has enhanced the network's capacity to institutionalize the FCR approach in a number of leading agricultural institutes across China.

From an early focus on basic research, the official incentive and award system is increasingly shifting towards rewarding more applied research focused on improving farmers' lives through the large-scale application of agricultural science and technology achievements. The social reward system, as an important component of China's agricultural science and technology reward system, has made up for the system defects of the official incentive system through its preference for practical application of technology and basic pioneering innovation. The benefits of awards include improved reputation, social status, income, subsidies, more projects and some other organizational privileges. These less visible benefits are important in motivating researchers to do research and submit applications for awards.

A planned reform of the evaluation and reward system, with an increased focus on practical achievements and extension activities, has the potential of developing a more demand-driven innovation system, with smallholder farmers at the centre.

Conclusions

The institutionalization of China's agricultural science and technology policy has played a significant role in promoting agricultural development and improving farmers' living standards. Policy reforms, better linkages between agricultural research and extension, and improvements in the official reward system are leading to more attention being paid to farmers' actual needs for applied technology development. The state agricultural research system still suffers from a fragmentary structure. However, reforms are promoting more decentralized management and the involvement of non-governmental scientific research institutes. These changes are leading to the emergence of a more varied, demand-oriented agricultural science and technology policy system capable of meeting diverse technological needs, including those of smallholders.

Reflections on the CGIAR Systemwide Program on Collective Action and Property Rights (CAPRi)

Ruth Meinzen-Dick

Introducing CAPRi

The Systemwide Program on Collective Action and Property Rights (CAPRi) of the CGIAR is not, *per se*, a farmer participatory research programme, but it helps to explain why participation may or may not take place, and why innovations may or may not be adopted. Bringing the analysis of institutions into agricultural research systems has been challenging, but we have seen considerable progress in demonstrating the value of these approaches. Here I review the history of the programme and describe how CAPRi has worked to develop a more nuanced understanding of collective action and property rights, and action research methods to study them appropriately, and to promote this understanding with practitioners and policymakers.

In 1994, the CGIAR began inter-centre initiatives designed to get the international agricultural centres to cooperate on common themes, such as livestock, water, genetic resources or participatory research. Around that time, several CGIAR centres had approached the International Food Policy Research Institute (IFPRI) to collaborate on the study of land tenure in rangelands and trees. Rather than just collaborating bilaterally with each centre, IFPRI proposed to start an inter-centre initiative on Property Rights and Collective Action (later renamed CAPRi). The initiative was launched in 1995 with five centres attending the inception meeting. Although there was initial scepticism about why agricultural research systems should deal with seemingly abstract institutions like property rights and collective action, within two years, the programme had expanded to include all 16 CGIAR centres. Today, it includes people from over 500 institutions worldwide, from local NGOs to national research institutions and international organizations.

At the first meeting, we developed criteria for selecting priority research themes, including: 1) addressing important problems in natural resource management (NRM); 2) generating strong international public goods; 3) applying across resources and sectors; 4) generating synergies and positive externalities between centres; 5) relating directly to the CGIAR mandate and to other eco-regional and system-wide initiatives and programmes; and 6) having a strong policy focus.

From these agreed criteria, the following themes were selected: 1) technology adoption; 2) accommodating multiple uses and users of a resource; 3) structuring devolution; 4) role of environmental risk; and 5) demographic change, especially feminization of agriculture. Later, two additional priority themes were added: 6) changing market relationships; and 7) genetic resources. This initial list of seven priority themes highlighted to all 16 CG centres – both those 'commodity centres' primarily involved in crop breeding and the 'NRM' centres – that there were topics that they deal with that relate directly to collective action and property rights.

Showing the relevance of institutions for agriculture and NRM

The first major workshop in 1997, on the role of property rights and collective action in technology adoption, brought together CGIAR researchers at the International Center for Agricultural Research in the Dry Areas (ICARDA) in Alleppo, Syria. The first day was a field trip onto the steppe, where we talked with farmers about the collective action that had maintained a cistern since the Roman era. Then, under a Bedouin tent, we heard government officials and pastoralists debate the contentious issues of property rights over shrubbery plantations that the government was developing to restore the range: who had the right to set limitations on access, the government or the tribe? This interaction reminded us that the issues we are dealing with are not abstractions, but real forces that affect people's lives. Every subsequent workshop has had a field trip as an integral part of the workshop to see the work of the hosting centre and local communities.

While the field trip was very grounded, at the other extreme was a conceptual framework developed to show the relevance of collective action and property rights for the adoption of innovations – both technologies and NRM practices. This 'CAPRi Box' framework (Figure 3.1) has been our most effective tool for enabling non-social scientists to understand the importance of these institutions (Meinzen-Dick and Di Gregorio, 2004; Knox et al., 2002).

When presented with this framework, many biophysical scientists recognize that at least some of the issues that they have been dealing with in developing agricultural technologies relate to one or another of these issues. For example, watershed management practices may be introduced that call for farmers to work together and make long-term investments in their land. But if there is low social capital or tenure insecurity, this is not likely to work. Efforts can then go into building collective action or providing stronger property rights, or the technologies may be adapted, e.g. by using natural vegetative strips instead of terracing to have shorter repayment periods so that tenants can also benefit. Institutions are not immutable, but they also cannot be changed overnight or 'engineered' into existence.

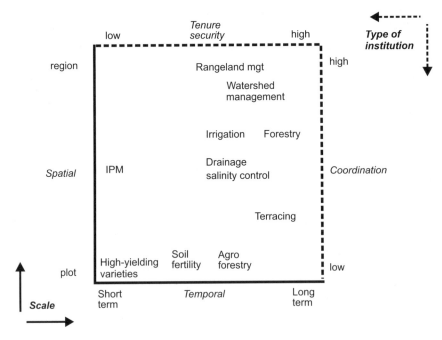

Figure 3.1 'CAPRi Box' showing relevance of collective action and property rights for innovation in agriculture and NRM

Deepening understanding of collective action and property rights

Once people understand the relevance of these institutions, the next step is to look at them in more depth. Thus, CAPRi has worked on developing and sharing appropriate methods for understanding these institutions. The study of property rights, for example, includes looking at tenure at the appropriate scale (plot, household or community), the elements of tenure security, and going beyond simple 'ownership' to look at bundles of rights, including access, withdrawal, management, exclusion and alienation rights as separable and often overlapping rights that could be held by different individuals and institutions (Place and Swallow, 2000).

Though the CAPRi concepts and methods may sound quite abstract, they have very real implications for communities and agricultural research centres to engage with them. The conceptual framework helps to make visible the institutions such as collective action and property rights and to highlight the importance of dealing with them. Methods such as participatory action research provide a systematic way for communities and researchers that are working together to strengthen collective action, to critically reflect on the lessons from each round of action. This can provide important lessons for those that seek to expand or scale up the collective action in other communities. Experimental games are not only a way of measuring a community's likelihood of cooperating, but there are also indications that playing collective action games and then reflecting on them within a community may be a useful entry point for discussing and strengthening collective action. Comparative studies across a large number of sites help to identify the 'fertile ground' – the conditions under which collective approaches are more likely to succeed, especially when programmes are expanded beyond a few pilot sites. An especially important aspect of this has been to learn to identify existing bases of cooperation and people's own innovations in developing arrangements to manage resources.

Coordination and governance issues

Getting communities to work together is one thing. Getting research institutes to work together is another, and often even more complicated. Although collaboration between 'sister centres' can generate sibling rivalry, CAPRi has been relatively successful in minimizing this by applying principles derived from studying collective action.

A key principle is the importance of establishing clear and transparent rules (operational rules) as well as mechanisms for setting those rules (collective choice and constitutional rules). Another lesson from farmers working on NRM is that it is often easier to get cooperation to enlarge the pool of resources' than to divide up a fixed amount. Because we did not have much money to begin with, we spent it on public goods – things that would benefit all members. This also gave us time to develop a track record of performance and rules for allocating resources when they did come in, so that we could have competitive calls for proposals for research grants to CGIAR centres with their national partners, and for PhD students to work with centres. (It probably also helped that many of the people who work with communities to understand collective action are themselves more cooperative.)

These governance arrangements demonstrate another important principle of CAPRi: the 'ripple effect', like when a pebble is thrown into a pool of water and the ripples spread out beyond the initial point of impact. With limited financial and human resources, we could not address all the needs for work on collective action and property rights in NRM. We therefore tried to act as a catalyst by working with interested researchers in the CGIAR centres and, through them, reaching their networks of collaborators.

As much as possible, we have also made our materials available to others in a variety of forms including training materials, working papers, a list-server and a website. This has contributed to a community of practice, in which people involved in CAPRi pass on information to other networks that they are involved in, including several other CGIAR initiatives (e.g. ILAC (see Watts and Horton, this book), UrbanHarvest, etc.) and other professional networks, e.g. the International Association for the Study of the Commons (IASC).

Conclusions

Far from being academic abstractions that are removed from people's lives, the institutions of collective action and property rights play a fundamental role in shaping how people interact with each other and with their physical environment. The CAPRi programme has worked to create a space and legitimacy for serious attention to these institutions within agricultural research organizations. Much of the value added from CAPRi lies in helping people to step back from the work they are doing with individual communities, to reflect on broader patterns. We also strive for output that is sound, but also understandable (not caught up in the jargon of a particular discipline) in order to facilitate learning across disciplines, regions and resources.

For me personally, as a sociologist working on water resources mostly in South Asia, some of the most exciting moments have come from bridging between what I had learned and what an economist working on rangelands or forestry in Africa, for example, had learned. What things did we find in common? What were important differences? Did these relate to characteristics of the user groups, the resources or the approaches we were using? Seeing people pick up ideas from each other, put them into practice in their own work, and pass them on to others to ignite the next round of learning is a process of innovation within the research community that parallels the innovation processes in farmers' communities. And the ultimate aim of this is to feed back into community processes to make them more effective for the development and adoption of innovations that will help to make agriculture more productive, equitable and sustainable.

Institutional learning and change in the CGIAR system

Jamie Watts and Douglas Horton

Introduction

When the CGIAR system was formed in the early 1970s, its main goal was relatively simple: to assure food supplies in the developing world using agricultural science to increase the productivity of major food crops. The institutional model underpinning this goal involved the creation of international centres of scientific excellence to develop technologies to be transferred to national programmes and onwards to farmers. Implicit in this design was the assumption that scientists could identify research priorities and act as the central source of innovation.

However, as development goals and processes have become more complex and better understood, the research agenda of the centres has expanded to include the triple goals of agricultural productivity, environmental sustainability and a more explicit focus on poverty reduction (Hall et al., 2000). The centres are challenged by the need to address this expanded agenda with an approach and a culture that were intended for a narrower and simpler task, in a context where the intensity and pace of change and context for development was very different. To be relevant and effective today, CGIAR programmes must have a more responsive mode of operation in which partnership and client orientation are core principles. To achieve this, major institutional changes will be needed. Although the institutional arrangements of the CGIAR have evolved substantially over time, much remains to be done to complete the transition from a 'centre-of-excellence' model to one of effective participation in innovation systems.

Here we describe the experience of the Institutional Learning and Change (ILAC) initiative in supporting this process. ILAC consists of an evolving community of individuals committed to increasing the contributions of agricultural research to sustainable poverty reduction around the world. ILAC promotes research, methodology development and capacity development to increase understanding of agricultural change processes and increase the effectiveness of interventions to stimulate pro-poor innovation.

Origin and evolution

ILAC emerged from a debate about impact assessment that began in earnest at a conference entitled 'Why has impact assessment research not made more of a difference?' This conference was convened by the CGIAR Science Council and the Economics Programme of the International Center for Maize and Wheat Improvement (CIMMYT) in Costa Rica in 2003. It responded to concerns expressed by evaluators, researchers and donors about the way that impact assessment was being organized within the CGIAR. This was largely based upon three major assumptions: first, that there is a direct causal link between research and impact; second, that this link dominates other variables; and, third, that inputs and impacts can be accurately measured or predicted using economic and statistical methods (Ekboir, 2003).

A project to assess CGIAR impacts on poverty alleviation questioned these assumptions and broke new ground by examining poverty impacts using both qualitative and quantitative methods and by exploring the wider livelihood context of the poor. It showed that impact is influenced not only by technology, but also by the way the research is carried out and by the institutions that guide research and technology development (Adato and Meinzen-Dick, 2007). CGIAR impact assessment methodologies were found wanting. Problems included too much focus on success cases, inconsistent use of counterfactuals and over-attribution of benefits to centres (Matlon, 2003).

During its first phase, ILAC's work showed that institutional learning and change for poverty alleviation involves three inter-related elements:

- *Institutions.* Agricultural innovation takes place within systems of multiple players at different levels, and norms and rules that govern their interactions.
- *Experiential Learning.* This involves analysing and understanding the work we do and seeing learning as a social process of reflection and analysis.
- *Change.* Applying lessons learned in order to improve on-going and future programmes.

However, there remained a tension between the learning and change objectives promoted by ILAC and the evaluation and impact assessment procedures promoted by the CGIAR Science Council, which focused on performance measurement and impact assessment for advocacy purposes, rather than learning and continuous improvement.

Since 2007, the focus of the ILAC initiative has shifted from impact assessment and evaluation within the CGIAR towards the more inclusive and strategic goal of increasing the contributions of international agricultural research to sustainable poverty reduction, by:

- generating new knowledge on innovation processes of practical use to agricultural R&D managers;

- strengthening the capacity of collaborative programmes to foster pro-poor innovation;
- fostering leadership for pro-poor innovation in the agricultural R&D community; and
- facilitating effective communication and knowledge sharing among practitioners and leaders of pro-poor agricultural innovation processes.

Fostering learning

The ILAC initiative combines action research and action learning in a 'Learning Laboratory' to foster knowledge production, capacity development and behavioural change. Members of a number of collaborative R&D programmes come together to share their experiences (positive and negative); identify common barriers to pro-poor innovation; plan applied research activities to address these barriers; test new approaches for planning, managing and evaluating collaborative programmes; and reflect on the results of the research and experimentation carried out.

ILAC has already begun to build capacity in the CGIAR through its training courses in facilitating participatory decision making. By the end of 2007, over 150 people from all CGIAR centres and many partner organizations had participated in these courses. Most participants have been at middle or senior management level. Organizational culture, incentive systems and other such factors linked to the internal environment are also being addressed.

From its beginnings, ILAC has been oriented towards collaborative and participatory research within an innovation systems context (including such things as partnerships, alliances, consortia, networks and eco-regional initiatives). ILAC's focus will be on how to assess the impacts of collaborative and participatory research, and how best to organize, manage and institutionalize such approaches to achieve sustainable poverty reduction.

Conclusions

ILAC remains a work in progress, itself an experiment in social learning and innovation, and in this spirit invites collaboration, feedback and ideas about how to support learning and change within individuals, the organizations they work for and the institutions that govern them, so that they can better address the dynamic and complex challenges facing poor farmers.

Learning selection revisited

Boru Douthwaite and Martin Gummert

Introduction

Ten years ago we developed the learning selection model to describe the development and early adoption of agricultural equipment in South-east Asia. Here we update the innovation histories of the three main technologies upon which the model was based. In the case of the most successful technology, we find that success was largely because the R&D team was able to work with the same networks of partners, in the same innovation trajectory, for 25 years. This finding is contrary to a view that researchers in the CGIAR system should avoid adaptive location-specific research because of its high opportunity cost.

Enabling innovation

In the late 1990s, we worked together on a Postharvest Technologies project funded by the German government which developed and promoted rice harvesting and drying technology in South-east Asia. Martin led the project which was based at the International Rice Research Institute (IRRI), the Philippines. Boru subsequently based his PhD thesis on the work, the main output of which was a model – called the 'learning selection model' – that describes how successful grassroots innovation processes begin. One of the main findings was that the most successful rice harvesters and dryers were the ones that had been most modified by local manufacturers and users. This ran contrary to the then dominant view that agricultural engineers, given their professional training, could and should design machines that worked without subsequent tinkering. The learning selection model described an evolutionary-like process in which scientists and engineers (R&D) work with interested manufacturers and farmers (the key stakeholders) to modify a technology, select what works and spread the results.

Boru subsequently wrote a book called *Enabling Innovation* in which he found that the model helped explain other grassroots innovation processes such as the development of Linux and the Danish wind turbine industry (Douthwaite, 2002). Based on the learning selection model and various case studies in South-east Asia, he derived a ten-point guide to fostering a grassroots-based innovation process:

1. *Start with a plausible promise.* Begin an innovation process with a 'plausible promise'; something that convinces potential stakeholders that it can evolve into something that they really want.

2. *Find a product champion.* The next step is to identify the innovation or product champion. He or she needs to be highly motivated and have the knowledge and resources to sort problems out.

3. *Keep it simple.* A plausible promise should be simple, flexible enough to allow revision, and robust enough to work well even when not perfectly optimized.

4. *Work with innovative and motivated partners.* Participants in an incipient innovation process should select themselves through the amount of resources they are prepared to commit, in particular their time.

5. *Work in a pilot site or sites where the need for the innovation is great.* Early adopters will be influenced by their environment. Their motivation levels will be sustained for longer if they live or operate in an environment where the innovation promises to provide great benefit.

6. *Set up open and unbiased selection mechanisms.* During early adoption, the technology should evolve and become 'fitter' through repeated learning selection cycles. This requires setting up efficient and unbiased ways of selecting what works and abandoning what does not.

7. *Don't release the innovation too widely too soon.* When people show enthusiasm for a prototype it is very tempting to release it as widely as possible but this should be resisted. The technology will always be less perfect than one initially thinks.

8. *Don't patent anything unless it is to prevent someone else privatizing the technology.* In learning selection, people co-operate with each other because they believe that all will gain if they do. The process is, therefore, seriously damaged if one person or group tries to gain intellectual property rights over what is emerging. Patents are monopolies that immediately reduce the novelty generation rate and thus slow down future development and the flow of ideas.

9. *Realize that culture makes a difference.* Culture, gender and power can influence the degree to which knowledge is guarded within a particular group, or spread around.

10. *Know when to let go.* Product champions need to become personally involved and emotionally attached to their projects to do their jobs properly. This makes it easy for them to go on flogging dead horses long after it has become clear to everyone else that the technology is not going to succeed. Equally, project champions can continue trying to nurture their babies long after they have grown up and market selection has begun. It is, therefore, a good idea to put a time limit on the product champion's activities.

Does the learning selection model hold up?

Recently, we returned to the field sites in South-east Asia where we undertook our original studies of three technologies – a flatbed dryer, a low-cost dryer and a stripper harvester – some 10 years ago. We wanted to see whether their development over the past decade supported or challenged the understanding of how successful grassroots innovation unfolds provided by the learning selection model in general and the ten-point guide in particular.

Of the three technologies, the flatbed dryer is clearly the most successful. There are about 6,000 units installed in Vietnam and the technology has been exported to five other South-east Asian countries. Its success in Vietnam is in part due to its continuing development in response to changing market requirements. This confirms the basic evolutionary algorithm upon which the learning selection model is based.

The findings all largely confirm and add insight to the ten-point guide to fostering a grass-roots innovation process. The low-cost dryer failed to prove itself a plausible promise in the Philippines, Cambodia and Indonesia for different reasons. As a result co-development of the technology with users did not start.

A product champion proved crucial to the success of the flatbed dryer in Vietnam. The same R&D team championed the flatbed dryer for 25 years in which time they made major improvements to the technology and strove to maintain quality through, amongst other things, developing and providing blower test kits. They also linked to extension services and helped provide credit.

Interested and motivated individuals were vital for the success of the stripper harvester and flatbed dryer in Indonesia, and the flatbed dryer in Myanmar. In all three cases they were motivated by the need for the respective technologies in their areas and the fact they appeared to make a plausible promise of meeting that need. The individual characteristics of the adopters themselves made a big difference. Some were motivated to make major changes before properly testing the original design and improving on that (e.g. flatbed dryer in Laos; stripper harvester in Indonesia). This tendency appeared in engineers and manufacturers who wanted to make the design their own. While this reduced the 'fitness' of the technology and slowed progress in the short-term, it also led to major innovations (e.g. stripper harvester in Indonesia).

Staff from the IRRI Postharvest Technologies project played an important role in helping to select beneficial modifications and spread them. An important example of this was the training course they organized for manufacturers from different countries to learn how to build the Vietnamese design of the flatbed dryer. The technical expertise required to both suggest and evaluate modifications was largely missing in the flatbed dryer development in Indonesia, and was initially lacking in Laos. Perhaps closer contact between dryer researchers and innovating manufacturers and engineers may have helped them avoid early mistakes. The fact that certain types of people are more likely to behave in a certain way showed that at least professional culture makes a difference.

Politically motivated government machinery supply programmes still risk promoting equipment too widely.

A patent battle in Indonesia showed that patents taken out to stop others privatizing a technology must be taken out country by country to be effective. It also showed the serious damage that a struggle over intellectual property rights can do to an innovator's motivation and cash-flow.

The biggest insight from the findings relates to the tenth point – knowing when to let go. According to the learning selection view of early innovation, the R&D team should withdraw after a couple of years of co-development to become 'consultants'. This clearly did not happen in Vietnam, where much of the success of the flatbed dryer can be attributed to the fact that the R&D team have been involved for 25 years. The flatbed dryer innovation history suggests that to really make a difference, the R&D team should seek to generate major novelties within the same innovation trajectory. It implies that researchers should be embedded in networks that include key stakeholders (the people who make, promote and use technology).

Implications for science and technology policy

The idea that more public sector research should be carried out within networks that link researchers to information about need, use and future trends has major implications for the CGIAR system. The previous Science Council Chairman said that CGIAR Centres should not undertake location-specific research because of the high opportunity costs involved (Ryan, 2006). But if CGIAR scientists are not involved in location-specific research then they may not be located within a network of individuals and organizations who are responding to a real need, in a real locality. The flatbed dryer story shows that researchers can generate international public goods (IPGs) while carrying out location-specific research as they respond to needs that are not location-specific (Harwood et al., 2006). It shows that, within an existing innovation trajectory, research can generate IPGs that begin new innovation trajectories (e.g. the low-cost dryer). Hence probably only a small percentage of research should be 'blue sky', i.e., research that attempts to establish new innovation trajectories without being embedded in an existing one.

But projectization of research together with the emphasis on production of IPGs makes it increasingly difficult for CGIAR scientists to embed themselves in this way. More often than not, a coalition of partners comes together to meet the donor's requirement, work together (or not) for three years to develop an IPG and then dissolve. If they are lucky they will get an extension. Project proposals are rarely evaluated on the track history of the network of people proposing them, and whether that network does link the researchers to the key stakeholders. Instead donors want to be associated with something new because history means they might have to share credit with a competing agency. We're setting up a straw man here, we realize, but it rings true to our own experiences.

Conclusions: research for development

These innovation histories of three rice technologies confirm the evolutionary algorithm upon which the model was based. However, in the case of the most successful technology – the flatbed dryer in Vietnam – the R&D team did not withdraw once a critical mass of manufacturers and users were familiar with the technology, as the model says should happen. Rather the team continued to champion the technology. In the process they developed new dryer designs, and major improvements to the original design. They achieved far greater impact than any other team, largely because they were able to work with the same networks of partners, in the same innovation trajectory, for 25 years.

This finding challenges the conventional wisdom in the CGIAR system that researchers should avoid carrying out adaptive location-specific research and rather develop so-called IPGs that have broad applicability. Rather it suggests a 'research-for-development' approach that ensures researchers are solving real needs of real people in real localities, for extended periods of time. IPGs will be generated in the process, almost as a spin-off. Researchers do not need to be physically in each locality working with every farmer or manufacturer. Like the flatbed dryer R&D team, they need to be embedded in networks through which they become aware of need, opportunity, how the technology is being promoted and used and what the market is likely to demand in the future. This structure is similar to that enjoyed by plant breeders in the CGIAR system and by many researchers in the private sector. It is a way of putting the dictate to 'act local, think global' into practice.

PART IV

New professionalism, learning and change

Part IV: Opening note

Part IV concludes the book, and starts by exploring the challenges of shifting extension and education systems to meet the challenges of a Farmer First approach. As discussed in Van Mele's contribution a huge variety of information sharing and learning approaches can come under the label extension. These include: group extension, farmer-to-farmer approaches, Farmer Field Schools (FFS), video and new media-supported learning, links to colleges and schools, and much more. This is all a far cry from the standard diffusion models of the past, epitomized by the Training and Visit system. Van Mele and Salahuddin and colleagues use the case of the PETRRA project (Poverty Elimination through Rice Research Assistance, supported by IRRI) to illustrate the potentials of facilitated farmer participatory learning based on a core set of principles – rather than the pushing of a particular technology or practice. The long-running experience of Farmer Field Schools focused on Integrated Pest Management in Indonesia is explored by Winarto. Her engagement with this programme over many years highlights some of the challenges of institutionalizing learning-focused approaches to agricultural extension at a national level where entrenched practices, based on 'Green Revolution thinking', persist. Ewbank and colleagues and Ngwenya and Hagmann offer experiences from projects in Tanzania and South Africa where farmer participatory research and extension have been combined, with the conventional distinction between 'research' and 'extension' broken down. These projects have attempted to institutionalize participatory research and extension in national systems, but emphasize the real challenges of shifting mindsets and standard bureaucratic routines as part of the process.

Two final papers in this section offer some important cautions regarding the flood of organized participation that has dominated NGO and other projects in the past 20 years. Tripp asks are these sensitive to the scarcity of poor farmers' time? In a provocative paper on the 'economics of attention' he asks whether participatory research and extension approaches might be rethought so as to reduce time requirements and transactions costs, into a priority focus on building robust rural institutions. Richards complements this argument by suggesting that in fact flexible, unsupervised networks of farmer-to-farmer learning might be the most effective route in many settings to enhancing the exchange and spread of information in complex networks characteristic of rural farm settings.

The need for a new Farmer First professional and the rethinking of the agricultural education systems is the focus of the next section. This is important frontier work where shifting curricula and professional incentives and peer support networks are central to facilitating sustained change. A number of experiences are shared. First, Hagmann and colleagues report on their experience of facilitating change in the university sector in Uganda. A similar experience is shared by Fernandez and Ortiz with the initiation of a new Master's programme for professionals working in rural Peru. Catley looks at curriculum change in veterinary schools, and the challenges of institutionalizing participatory approaches to epidemiology. The particular challenges of trans-disciplinary science involving multiple stakeholders are emphasized by Röling and Jiggins, while the political commitments to shifting the power relations in research and education are highlighted by Rhoades. Finally, Pettit emphasizes the need to encourage diverse forms of creative, emotional and embodied knowledge in education, to complement standard, academic and technical training.

Yet, as acknowledged across the papers, it is not just shifts in attitudes and behaviours – focused on individual attributes of learning and humility – but a wider politics of education that is important. Whose knowledge counts – and gets taught and professionally recognized – depends on the power relations at the heart of the educational establishment. Change processes that tackle these, reversing professional biases through new methods, practices and ethical codes, are central to the Farmer First agenda, and, as these contributions attest, have only just begun.

The final section of the book looks at impact assessment. Adrienne Martin's opening paper asks the question: so what difference does it make? For all the talk of the importance of Farmer First approaches – from moral, political and social standpoints – does farmer participatory research really have a positive impact on people's lives and livelihoods? This is a controversial point, and one where intensive methodological debate comes into play. It of course all depends on what you want, and on your definition of positive change. Much discussion in the papers focuses on the limits of conventional approaches to monitoring and evaluation, focused as they are on quantitative targets and narrow framings. Guijt explores how to evaluate impacts in the context of highly complex, dynamic systems, with competing actors with different values, objectives and visions. Douthwaite and colleagues offer Participatory Impact Analysis as one route forward, an approach which engages stakeholders in defining visions of the future and mapping impacts. Sanginga and colleagues use an After Action Review with locally defined indicators to track changes in social relations, while Dawit and colleagues combine qualitative and quantitative approaches to collect data on impact for influencing policy in pastoral settings in Ethiopia. Shifting from a standard, indicator-based assessment approach to one focused on sequential learning and reflexivity is clearly a major leap, one that many agencies and projects find difficult to take. Yet, if farmers – and other users of research – are to shape future directions and priorities, and draw lessons from past experience relevant to their own contexts, then a revolution in monitoring and evaluation based on Farmer First principles is required. The papers in this section provide both conceptual and practical clues to the way forward.

Strengthening rural extension

Paul Van Mele

Introduction

International agricultural research increasingly has to justify its relevance in reducing rural poverty in a sustainable way. Uptake and impacts have become more important than outputs (technologies and methodologies). This contributes to orienting the CGIAR centres towards working more in an innovation systems mode, whereby uptake and partnerships have to be thought through from the beginning of the innovation process rather than at the end (as in the pipeline model of technology transfer).

Here I present the Poverty Elimination through Rice Research Assistance (PETRRA) project in Bangladesh in which the International Rice Research Institute (IRRI) developed and managed a tender mechanism that facilitated the emergence of multiple service providers, each developing locally embedded extension methodologies (see also Salahuddin et al., this book). The results confirm the key insight that farmers need to be presented with underlying scientific principles, rather than ready-made technologies. I go on to explore how CGIAR centres can play a role in developing regionally relevant learning tools that draw on this insight and that can be easily used by multiple service providers.

Managing diversity in extension methodologies: the PETRRA case

The PETRRA project established a values-based research management scheme in Bangladesh from 1999 to 2004. The 45 sub-projects had a focus on three broad areas: pro-poor policy (6), technologies (19) and uptake and extension (20). In what follows I highlight some of the findings related to extension and add new insights on how to improve the effectiveness of development interventions, as reported by Biggs and Smith (2003).

Learning helps to transform information into knowledge. Even if extension workers improve the poor's access to information, questions arise about the extent to which farmers can apply this information. What does it help to listen to a lecture or radio programme if the vocabulary is too pedantic or academic? And what is the best time and method to reach poor women, considering that the majority in rural areas are illiterate? Clearly, the effectiveness of learning depends on the educational approach, the content and the way tools have been developed, and the context. Creativity is needed in developing farmer-education methodologies and tools, but equally in engaging multiple service providers in pro-poor development (Bentley and Van Mele, 2005).

Many of PETRRA's extension methodologies were developed within the organizational culture of each partner, and were created or adapted locally through feedback from farmers. Encouraging local researchers and extension workers to think creatively and competitively about extension may have been as important in the long run as the new techniques they invented for growing rice. PETRRA encouraged a real diversity of extension methodologies (Table 4.1). Some were created fresh for this project, such as picture songs, or the prototypes came from elsewhere and PETRRA helped to shape them, such as Going Public. PETRRA also took some established methods and gave them a new angle, as in making videos with adult education experts and rural women, for women.

Several extension methods combine well. Going Public and farmer field schools (FFS) could interact with the media in interesting ways (see Bentley et al., 2003). FFS could be turned into radio and video studios, where farmers

Table 4.1 Multiple extension methodologies

Methodology	Circumstances under which methodology may be used
Women-led group extension	Requires communities where a certain critical mass of social capital is in place.
Family approach in training	Is applicable for any community, irrespective of the level of social capital.
Farmer-to-farmer extension	Requires solid organizational support for it to be effective at larger scale and will work best if implemented alongside other rural development activities.
Farmer field schools	Requires skilled facilitators and high investment cost. Best used in pilot phases to develop technologies and learning tools that can then be taken up by other methodologies.
Video-supported learning	Requires multi-disciplinary approach in developing scripts. Adds value to any other methodology. Can be effective to educate farmers in remote areas without the need for well-trained facilitators.
Going Public	Can be tried by any service provider with little preparation. Lends itself well to reach people in remote areas where general organizational support may be weak.
Entertainment-education	Has a higher investment cost compared to video and if no use is made of radio or TV, the method is limited to areas where live performers operate. As it is more embedded in local culture, the scaling-up potential may be more limited than educational videos.
Primary school and college education	Requires flexibility of education system and teachers' corps to include processes and tools of farmer field schools, or to organize video or agricultural entertainment shows. Children welcome this as a shift from sterile teaching methods in most rural areas.

Source: modified from Van Mele et al. (2005b)

could speak in their own words to describe their experiences for the millions of farmers who will never be fortunate enough to attend a field school.

From technologies to principles

Despite the frequent citation of one of the first articles on farmer participatory research by Rhoades and Booth (1982), it is striking how little their groundbreaking insights that farmers need fresh ideas and should be presented underlying scientific principles, rather than ready-made technologies, have been applied in research and extension. Discovery learning exercises like those used in participatory learning and action research or FFS form the exception, but experience indicates that only a limited number of people have the capacity to develop such exercises.

During work in Bangladesh supporting farmer-to-farmer extension around seed management we soon realized some of the shortcomings: farmers would promote their own particular technology without elaborating on the principles underlying the technology. The *purdah* (a local custom, used for women's physical veiling and symbolic separation from outsiders, men and elders) restricts women's movements outside their homestead. These conditions limiting scaling up inspired us to develop four learner-centred videos dealing with on-farm seed management (Van Mele and Zakaria, 2005; Van Mele et al., 2005c).

Through multiple partners, the videos rapidly reached large parts of the rural communities. To test the videos' effectiveness, the project surveyed 1,252 resource-poor women across Bangladesh. New technologies such as manual seed sorting and seed flotation were adopted by 24 and 31 per cent respectively. More than 70 per cent improved seed drying. The use of botanicals such as neem, to deter storage insects, increased from 9 to 67 per cent (Van Mele et al., 2008). Most interestingly, the videos had triggered farmers to apply new ideas to their own context. Their experimentation led to a wide range of solutions. Seed quality and crop yields improved and women applied the principles to other crops. Some NGOs even developed professional seed enterprises.

In Bangladesh, the Agricultural Advisory Society (AAS), a small national NGO having strategic alliances with a large number of local NGOs and community-based organizations, distributed videos to village tea stall owners who organized 8,600 shows on their premises at no cost, motivated by increased business. One year later, by the end of 2006, about 157,000 farmers had watched the videos 1–6 times. The Bangladeshi national TV continues to freely broadcast the videos, reaching over 40 million rural people.

Zooming-in, zooming-out

Centres of the CGIAR are required to develop international public goods. Apart from producing regionally relevant rice videos, five years of process evaluation had allowed us to develop a new approach to enhance the efficiency of learning within national innovation systems. As extension systems become decentralized, many service providers develop their own materials and methods, with variable success. Most development actors are hungry for appropriate learning tools. Hence, based on experiences in different contexts the Africa Rice Center (WARDA) developed, tested and documented an approach for effectively communicating agricultural technologies with the rural poor. The Zooming-in Zooming-out (ZIZO) approach (Figure 4.1) provides guiding principles to produce high quality farmer-education tools that are locally appropriate and regionally relevant (Van Mele, 2006).

ZIZO starts with a broad stakeholder consultation to define regional learning needs. Only then are communities approached to get a better feel about their ideas, knowledge, innovations and the words they use in relation to the chosen topic (zooming-in). Educational videos are produced in close consultation with the end-users (and with farmers who have collaborated earlier in participatory research), and building on Rhoades' principle of communicating ideas rather than ready-made technologies. Consequently, when showing the draft videos to further villages (zooming-out), more novelty is identified, and further adjustments made.

If the topic is truly of regional relevance, multiple service providers will be ready to incorporate the videos in their own programmes. Some facilitation to make this happen may be required, such as networking and translating into local languages.

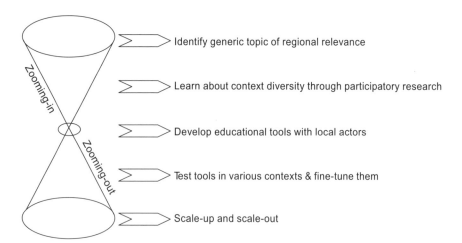

Figure 4.1 Zooming-in zooming-out: scaling up sustainable innovations

Evidence shows that based on a few well-selected local innovations, and merged with appropriate scientific knowledge, video was able to explain underlying biological and physical principles. The more these principles resonated with what farmers already knew and did, the more video became useful as a stand-alone method. Facilitation increased the level of experimentation with sustainable technologies, but was not always a prerequisite (Van Mele et al., 2008). Ideally, FFS graduates or farmers engaged in participatory research should take part in developing videos.

The relevance of the technologies alongside a creative communication approach has resulted in the videos being scaled-up to millions of farmers in Asia and Africa through both facilitated group discussions and non-supervised learning, such as video shows in tea stalls and mass media. Farmers can learn by watching other farmers on video, if the programmes are well planned and simply structured. The ZIZO approach can be applied for any learning tool, whether videos, radio programmes, posters or fact sheets. ZIZO aims to enhance the efficiency and effectiveness of pro-poor rural learning systems.

Policy implications for agricultural R&D

- Experiential learning can be stimulated in many ways, and considering the limited financial resources of national extension systems, more attention needs to be paid to improve ways of unsupervised learning.
- The role of International Agricultural Research Centres (IARCs) can and should extend to building national capacities in developing high quality, learner-centred education tools and strategies. This will require them to open up to a different type of professional.
- IARCs have a role to play in facilitating processes, mechanisms and institutions supporting farmer-centred approaches in both technology development and dissemination.
- IARCs can help in scientifically assessing the efficiency and effectiveness of uptake methods, rather than just focusing on measuring the impact of their home-grown technologies.
- IARCs that have strong links with the national R&D systems ought to play a role in facilitating and documenting processes of innovation.

Stimulating IARCs to expand or modify their roles in national innovation systems requires donors to create more flexible learning environments and move away from logical frameworks with pre-set quantifiable targets. Development returns to donor investment in research will only be boosted if linkages between multiple actors in the innovation system are strengthened, not if the focus remains on strengthening scientific capacities in isolation. In developing countries, 'R&D is mostly about learning, rather than about creating new knowledge' (Arnold and Bell, 2001).

To move beyond the 'islands of success' of participatory research and interventionist reflections on innovation systems, more resources will need to be allocated to a different type of research, including research on pro-poor and gender-sensitive 'extension' tools, mechanisms and alliances. Without this, innovation systems' thinking is unlikely to make a positive contribution to the livelihoods of poor farmers in developing countries. Donors have a part to play in supporting organizations equipped to strengthen the quality and effectiveness of the multiple extension and service providers.

Institutionalizing values-based research: lessons from the PETRRA Project, Bangladesh

Ahmad Salahuddin, Paul Van Mele and Noel P. Magor

A values-based research approach

The Poverty Elimination through Rice Research Assistance (PETRRA) was a research project implemented in Bangladesh from April 1999 to August 2004. It operated with a budget of £9.5 million, funded by the UK Department for International Development (DFID) and managed by the International Rice Research Institute (IRRI) in close partnership with the Bangladesh Rice Research Institute (BRRI). The project aimed to enhance the livelihood security of poor farmers by increasing production and productivity of rice-based farming systems through poverty-focused research. Its objective was clearly reflected in the title of the project, which contained 'poverty' and 'elimination' as key words. Rice was the entry point, and research was to support a strategy for poverty elimination. Rather than target production technologies and large producers, PETRRA started with resource-poor farm households (Orr and Magor, 2002; see also Van Mele, this book).

PETRRA identified a number of cross-cutting issues which formed the value-base of the project and played a crucial role in conceptualizing and materializing PETRRA's agenda:

- working with resource-poor farmers to address *poverty*;
- conducting research as per *demand* and priority of resource-poor farmers;
- conducting, sharing and evaluating research with both *men and women* of resource-poor households;

- conducting research that ensured *participation* of resource-poor men and women in all stages of the project cycle: planning, designing, implementation, monitoring and evaluation;
- conducting research by establishing appropriate and effective *partnership* of agencies that ensured resource-poor farmers' interest: pro-poor technology, dissemination methods and policy;
- ensuring that research outputs were sustained through *linkage and network* development with appropriate agencies that were considerate of the interests of the poor;
- *communicating* effectively with farmers and policy makers to disseminate, scale up and scale out, and to consolidate learning; and
- using a *competitive* process as a way of identifying competent suppliers of agricultural R&D that facilitate influencing desired pro-poor outcomes.

These practices evolved through the process of working with poor households. At the same time PETRRA worked out the definition, scope, concept and practical means to translate these into actions. All these elements together formed PETRRA's values-based research approach. Salahuddin et al. (2008) provide a detailed analysis that captures its systematic unfolding and the link between the values and PETRRA outputs. Here we look at how the values-based research project was institutionalized in Bangladesh.

Institutionalizing values-based research

The scope of the initial PETRRA proposal was rather limited, but did not prevent the project from becoming innovative. Supported by donor and host agencies that were appreciative of novel ideas and innovations, the project management unit was open-minded and strove to be responsive to the needs of resource-poor farmers. It initiated ideas, included new outputs, adjusted project purpose, invited and entertained new ideas from project stakeholders and outsiders, reviewed suggestions and reacted according to the situation. It also exercised the freedom to be neutral, even towards its own organization, IRRI.

Although the project recognized and brought into practice various values, a lot could still be done to establish these within agricultural research institutes like IRRI and BRRI and to identify appropriate ways to institutionalize these in the overall R&D system. Some researchers emerged as champions embracing values, but a question remains as to the extent to which this learning carries over into day-to-day work beyond specific projects. To establish a culture that embraces values within a project is not enough; these need to be embedded in the agencies so that the praxis continues. Through PETRRA, IRRI showed that it can facilitate and establish an effective values-based research culture with continued impact. For instance, the World Bank and the International Fund for Agricultural Development decided to jointly support the National

Agricultural Technology Project, with an estimated grant of US$84.5 million (BARC, 2007). This included many of PETRRA's values such as demand-led research and extension, poverty focus, partnerships and the competitive grant system.

IRRI with its partners acquired two grants from the CGIAR Challenge Program for Water and Food that allowed further follow-up on their successful PETRRA sub-projects. Two projects, implemented in Bangladesh and other countries, provided IRRI with further experiences to consolidate and internalize values-based research.

The 'Focal Area' concept developed during PETRRA is now commonly used by government agencies and NGOs to jointly address poverty in northern Bangladesh. Moreover, under PETRRA, many NGOs discovered the strength of agriculture programmes as a tool for building community trust and providing a shorter path to sustainable poverty elimination. For example, RDRS, a well-respected regional NGO in the north-west of Bangladesh, had no rice programme before participating in PETRRA in 2000. By the time PETRRA ended in mid-2004, RDRS had established community-based rice seed production, processing and marketing enterprises in many of its community-based organizations (Van Mele et al., 2005a). RDRS recognized agriculture as a vital programme for poverty elimination with rice playing the role of pathfinder.

Partners formerly involved in extension research continue to expand their activities in-country (e.g. farmer-oriented seed models) and across South Asia (e.g. women-led video production). BRRI continues to develop the Bangladeshi version of the rice knowledge bank (www.knowledgebank-brri. org) which targets semi-literate farmers and extension workers. These are but a few examples.

Future prospects

At the international level the introduction of the Institutional Learning and Change (ILAC) concept (see Watts and Horton, this book) in the CGIAR very much complements the notion of sustainability within international agricultural research. The Millennium Development Goals helped set the agenda for national governments committed to poverty elimination and, together with the resulting poverty reduction strategy papers (PRSPs), have laid the foundation at national level. Additional policies such as the National Agricultural Extension Policy of Bangladesh provide good examples of government commitments towards pluralism in extension. It is time for international agricultural research institutes such as IRRI, to scale up their few but rich experiences in values-based research and development, through all possible means. Most importantly, these include partnerships and linkages at national and international level with civil society organizations.

PETRRA offered an opportunity to experiment with socio-technical and institutional innovations towards the development of a pro-poor agricultural innovation system. It created a lot of enthusiasm among its partners and wider stakeholders. Although its implementation efficiency was criticized, this was the price it paid for operating in a mode of experiential learning. PETRRA successfully showed pathways as to how such an endeavour can be shaped.

Putting farmers first in Indonesia: the case of Farmer Field Schools

Yunita T. Winarto

Introduction

Agricultural research and development in Indonesia are at a crossroads. On the one hand, an increasingly enabling atmostphere is serious about putting farmers first. On the other hand, farmers' struggles to take control of their own development are being constrained by the heavy hand of the bureaucratic structures still working to out-dated paradigms. An example of this is the state's handling of Farmer Field Schools (FFS) as projects rather than as a means for promoting a process of farmers' long-term learning. Here I provide a personal reflection on the complex challenges of implementing the Farmer First paradigm derived from 17 years of engagement with the Indonesian integrated pest management (IPM) programme.

Moving forward, holding on

Over this period there have been significant changes toward empowering farmers. First, there was a transfer of the national IPM programme from the National Planning and Development Agency into the Ministry of Agriculture in 1993. The bureaucratic system and procedures for handling administrative matters in agricultural development were put to work in implementing a programme aimed at changing farmers' perspectives, knowledge and skills. The same ministry that first implemented the Green Revolution with all its institutions and facilities was now responsible for the paradigm shift to empowering farmers to grow healthy crops.

But how could such a responsibility be taken on by a complex bureaucratic system with such an entrenched history in Green Revolution thinking? Indeed, the challenges soon became apparent. My observations at the grassroot level of implementing the FFS in Central Lampung (southern province of Sumatra island), suggested it was hard to find the 'spirit' of farmers' empowerment and adult learning processes. Government officials in the plant protection and extension services managed the school as a project with a ready designed curriculum without seeking advance consent from farmers and frequently accompanied by late financial disbursement. A group of IPM farmers, with experience gained from facilitation by an international NGO, named this kind of programme a 'fiesta' (*pesta* in Indonesian) or a feast with no follow-up. *Pesta* is also an acronym of *tipis-tipis tapi merata* (shallow but widely spread), a cynical term referring to the emphasis on having a large number of 'schools' with no depth or quality of learning process (Winarto et al., 2000).

Despite the international acclaim for the growth and development of Indonesia's IPM Programme, this did not mean that its paradigm would replace the Green Revolution in agricultural development. Within the bureaucratic system of the Ministry of Agriculture, the IPM approach was the responsibility of a plant protection division for the management of damaging organisms, thus constituting just one dimension of the entire agricultural research and development system. The programme was also project-oriented rather than based on a long-term vision of empowering farmers. Once the intended project was carried out, that was it. The indicator of success was the number of farmers being trained despite the reality that the programme left most of these farmers with no further support.

Empowering farmers

To counter such problems, an international NGO in collaboration with farmers in Central Lampung tried to improve the learning process and sustain the activities following a FFS. As a result, a strong self-governed farmers' organization was formed. Farmers themselves were able to plan and carry out the schools for other non-IPM farmers (see Winarto et al., 2000; Winarto, 2002). This was not the case with the IPM farmers trained in a 'one-off fiesta project'. The lessons learned by the alternative FFS effort were a positive though unintended consequence of the programme. As the 'school' – one 'model' of training and empowering farmers – was spread all over Indonesia through the national programme, the idea of such a training and its advantages was also being dispersed through various kinds of media and collaborative networks. The 'school' gradually became part of the external structures not only of farmers, but also of various non-profit organizations within Indonesia and abroad and hence, became their point of reference in seeking appropriate means of engaging with farmers.

The work by many NGOs in adopting the FFS methods brought financial support from national and international donor institutions. One example is the FFS on participatory plant-breeding designed and developed by the PEDIGREA programme (Participatory Enhancement of Diversity of Genetic Resources in Asia) of Wageningen Agricultural University in collaboration with local NGOs in several South-east Asian countries (The Philippines, Cambodia and Indonesia). Over the last decade, FFS in Indonesia has gradually become established as the 'appropriate method' to change farmers' knowledge and practices in various aspects of crop farming.

While NGO-supported programmes proliferated, the national IPM programme closed towards the end of the 1990s along with the termination of the World Bank's financial support. The lack of a sustained national programme provided an opportunity for the IPM farmers themselves to stand up and move forward. Responding to the programme's termination, representatives of IPM farmers from several provinces in Indonesia agreed to form a farmers' federation or alliance. This alliance was formed with the objectives of strengthening farmer's organization at the group level (grassroot), improving farmers' capacity through education and providing advocacy. The association's vision is to empower farmers and balance the ecosystem and to strive for farmers' rights (Hidayat and Adinata, 2001). At its first national assembly, the Indonesian Integrated Pest Management Farmers' Alliance (*Ikatan Petani Pengendalian Hama Terpadu Indonesia* – IPPHTI) selected a network instead of a hierarchical structure and created a logo representing the spider's web with some Indonesian islands in its centre. At the same time, the significant decentralization programme or 'regional autonomy' underway in Indonesia is opening the way for a changing relationship between state authorities, the bureaucracy and farmers though the ability of the two parties to communicate varies from one place to another (Winarto, 2005).

Recognizing the power of television, farmers in Indramayu IPPHTI, West Java, collaborated with the Anthropology Department at the University of Indonesia to produce a film *Bisa Dèwèk* (We can do it ourselves) to document their experiences of developing participatory plant-breeding, organic farming, and innovative means of managing pests. The farmers developed their own dissemination strategy with the aim of obtaining support and recognition at the regency level. Working their way through a hectic schedule of film-screenings at village and district level they succeeded in first building up a body of support among local authorities and finally reached the regency level. Here their strategy paid off and the farmers were asked to submit a proposal for a Participatory-Plant-Breeding FFS programme that is to be funded by the authority with the full support of the legislative body – the first time in this area that farmers and the authority have collaborated in equal partnership.

Change in the making?

A diverse yet promising climate for farmers to move forward is in the making. The seeds have been planted here and there: farmers' movements are mobilizing and organizing, and a new relationship between the people and the state is emerging. Yet, a major constraint exists: the underlying paradigm of agricultural development in Indonesia on the basis of the Green Revolution still dominates discourses, mindsets and practices. While an alternative has been demonstrated to work, the capacity to scale up within the large state bureaucracies of Indonesia, despite decentralization and an increasingly effective farmers' movement, is still limited. Debates about putting farmers first must thus move beyond demonstrating success of methods and approaches to tackling the core issues of power and control of ideas and practices in the mainstream. If it fails, then it will forever remain on the margins.

Farmer participatory research in northern Tanzania: FARM-Africa's experience

Richard Ewbank, Aloyce Kasindei, Faithrest Kimaro and Salutary Slaa

FARM-Africa Tanzania began Farmer Participatory Research (FPR)-type activities in Babati in 1990 with the implementation of the crop improvement component of the Babati Agricultural Development Project. The first phase of this project (1990–3) operated in five villages in Dareda ward, expanding to cover both Dareda and Madunga wards for the period 1993–6 and all five wards of Bashnet Division from 1996–2000. The component was primarily focused on improving three crops – potatoes, maize and beans. Both crop diseases and low yields were identified by farmers as the priority constraints, to be addressed by on-farm trials of improved varieties.

In 2000, based on the success of the earlier work and demand from farmer groups across the district, FPR was formally incorporated as a component in the Babati Rural Development Project (2000–5) operating district-wide (Ewbank et al., 2007). The two key methodological differences in the FPR approach as compared to the earlier crop improvement work were: 1) farmers themselves identified the problems to be addressed, rather than the project; and 2) Farmer Research Groups (FRGs) were formed through a process of village selection rather than by the project with the local extension officer.

Group formation was based on the identification of typically 12 members (six men and six women, although in practice often more of each), using criteria such as ensuring representation of sub-villages (usually three to four per village), gender balance and the identification of research-minded farmers able to share results with others. FRG members were formally approved at a village assembly, following which a FARM-Africa facilitated planning meeting was convened to identify alternative solutions to priority agricultural problems that could be tested under on-farm conditions. The FRG members elected group leaders and began the work of developing their plan for the season, which included training on improved agricultural practices, testing of improved seeds, soil and water conservation, and preparing demonstration plots on their respective farms.

With implementation expanded to cover the whole of Babati District, FRG formation was guided by a number of geographical criteria, so as to:

- ensure accessibility by the maximum number of farmers;
- be spread over the five agroecological zones found in the District; and,
- focus on areas with relatively lower densities of Village Extension Officers.

Although the target was to establish nine FRGs, by the end of 2002, 11 had been established and supported. A further 13 groups were added in 2004–5, three of these being jointly supported by the Nou Participatory Forest Management Project as they were established in forest-adjacent communities. From 2005–7, FPR work continued as a stand-alone project with these 24 FRGs. The project's approach to FPR essentially involved a six-step process including:

- group formation (two to three farmers per sub-village for a 12 member FRG) by village selection;
- leadership election;
- planning (including selecting technologies for testing and capacity building);
- design of on-farm trials/plots;
- implementation of on-farm trials (including exchange between groups and training for agricultural innovation); and,
- dissemination and information sharing to other farmers (each FRG member trains three to five other farmers, two field days/season, exchange visits).

Innovations tested included both hybrid and composite maize (hybrid maize performing better in the long growing seasons found in cooler agroecological zones at the top of the Rift Valley wall), beans, soya, sunflower and vegetables. In addition, agricultural techniques were tested such as the use of fermented cow's urine to control maize pests, liquid fertilizer (from African marigold leaves) and terracing and contour bunds to control soil erosion.

The FARM-Africa project in Babati District has had a considerable impact in terms of the productivity improvements of the innovations tested through on-farm trials with 24 FRGs. This has led to a substantial degree of uptake by farmers outside the research groups, particularly in relation to maize and bean cultivation. The project has evolved through a number of stages as it addressed the existing and emerging priorities of smallholder farmers in the district. This process has developed a demand-led participatory model of farmer research and extension, the core of which is the FPR approach and the subsequent capacity building of farmer groups in managing microfinance and input retailing. The remaining challenges in developing the model primarily revolve around issues related to extending FPR to priorities not yet addressed, the strengthening of microfinance institutions and the enhancement of smallholder marketing capacity.

Facilitation for change: triggering emancipation and innovation in rural communities in South Africa

Hlamalani Ngwenya and Jürgen Hagmann

Facilitation for change

Successes of participatory approaches have been reported and celebrated over many years. However, little attention has been given to the role of facilitation in triggering the change processes. The deep dimension of the concept 'facilitation' is often underestimated and its articulation has not yet evolved to an extent that it has a common meaning. In our observation, the word is used in different situations ranging from 'bribing', 'paying per diems', 'chairing' meetings to facilitation and as a means for stimulating fundamental change in individuals and organizations. The latter is the kind of facilitation underpinning the implementation of the innovation system approach we have been practising. We call it 'Facilitation for Change' (F4C).

F4C aims to stimulate the 'creative orientation' of people both at individual and organization levels, and is built on the domains of organizational change and/or development through action learning and learning organization theories (Argyris and Schön, 1974; Schein, 1992) and systemic approaches (Senge, 1990). F4C reflects a strong psychological perspective on human development.

Here we look at F4C in the context of a facilitative participatory extension approach that aims to influence change at the different levels of the agricultural innovation service delivery system (demand side, supply side and organizational/policy support side). Our focus here is on the demand side and we highlight the role of facilitation in mobilizing communities to better articulate their demands and strengthen local organizational capacities for better linkages with service providers and enhancing creativity and innovations. A key insight is that the quality of facilitation and the related competence both for training extension agents and for community facilitation is a crucial factor in the process.

The context for F4C: the participatory extension approach (PEA)

PEA was initially developed with some success in Zimbabwe in the 1990s (Hagmann et al., 1999) and, from 1998, was adopted, adapted and further developed as an alternative approach to innovation service delivery in South

Africa. Since 2001, PEA has been implemented successfully in the Dominican Republic, Tanzania and Cambodia.

PEA is an alternative to conventional extension approaches where technical experts give advice to farmers about enhancing production (technical advisory services). Such a commodity-based linear model does not reflect the 'whole system' which influences innovation in terms of social dynamics in a given community. This often results in only a minority of farmers being involved in research and extension activities.

PEA focuses on a combination of 'social extension' and 'technical advisory services', and takes into consideration that agricultural challenges are complex and need to be dealt with in a complex manner. This model deals with the social dynamics and looks at service functions required in a problem-solving based innovation system in smallholder farming. The focus is much more on establishing a common platform for trying out new things and includes the majority of farmers/community members in this process. It aims to enhance people's adaptive capacities and addresses all factors including social (behaviour and practice), economic (markets and resource mobilization), ecological (natural resource conservation) and organizational (leadership) matters. Both technical advisory services and social extension components are required to support communities in their own development. It is therefore not about 'either/or', but about successful integration of technical advice and research into a sound social innovation process.

The PEA learning cycle (see Figure 4.2) is a reflection of the operational steps of the PEA process as implemented at the community level. The learning integrates a variety of extension methodologies in a consistent learning process to deal with different issues in agriculture and rural development. It consists of six component/ phases which are:

1. initiating change;
2. searching for new ways;
3. planning and strengthening local organizational capacity;
4. experimenting while implementing action;
5. sharing of experiments; and
6. reflecting on lessons learnt and re-planning.

Local organizational change is the backbone that cuts across all phases as a continuous process. Each component/ phase is carried out in a series of sub-steps, which build upon each other. The implementation of these components is not in a on-off mode, but follows a cyclical mode, where reflection and feedback to the communities take place at the end of each component.

The intention of F4C in the community

F4C is a strong instrument to operationalize the social development agenda of PEA in terms of inclusion, cohesion and accountability of peoples' institutions.

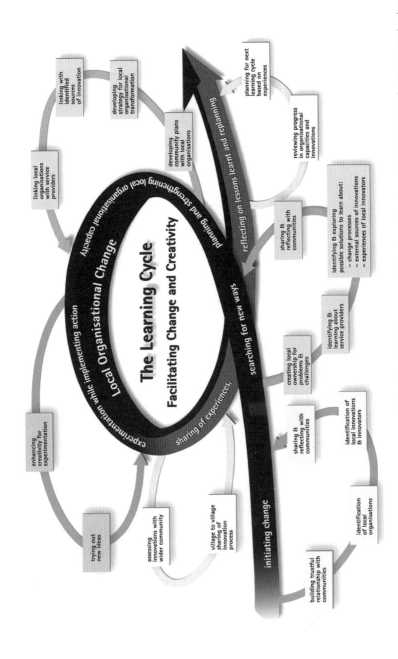

Based on experiences in Zimbabwe, South Africa and Dominican Republic. The approach has been implemented in a range of other countries in Africa, Asia and Latin America. (www.picoteam.org)

Figure 4.2 The PEA learning cycle

It has a high potential to support the development of a renewed social capital and social innovation in the communities and to create social processes in which the technical innovation process can be embedded.

The main objective in facilitating PEA is to:

- develop the individual and organizational capacities of rural people and their communities to be able to deal with the dynamic challenges and changes of development (adaptive capacity);
- facilitate a process of self organization and community emancipation to enable people to better articulate and represent their needs for agricultural and social services *vis-à-vis* service providers and administrative organizations;
- develop and spread technical and social innovations in a process of joint learning, which builds on the life world and local knowledge of rural people who have agriculture as a common foundation and then spread to other fields of rural development and is connected to decentralization and municipal development and service delivery in South Africa; and
- link rural people and organizations to external service providers, input and output markets and sources of innovation in order to create a functional innovation system where the demand side and the service supply are both well developed.

Experience shows that there is a direct link between impact of participatory approaches and the quality of facilitation. What matters most is not the plans and tools underpinning approaches, but how these approaches are implemented. In our cases, F4C played a significant role in triggering the process of community emancipation and innovation.

Some methods and techniques for operationalizing F4C

Questioning techniques are central to F4C. Through provocation and probing people are challenged to think and reflect. The questioning techniques can be learnt rather quickly, but the content of the questions needs to be linked to solid experiences in organizational development and change management – as well as a vision of emancipatory development. In terms of questioning and provocation, we have learnt a lot from Farelli and Brandsma's 'provocative therapy' approach (1974), which is being used as a brief-therapy approach in psychotherapy. Many of the questioning techniques come from the systemic questioning domain – which is also used a lot in psychotherapy and in team and organizational development. Another inspiring source has been Peavey's strategic questioning techniques (1994). F4C also draws its strength from the use of a variety of solution-focused approaches (e.g. Berg, 1994), Freire's social change approaches operationalized as Training for Transformation (cf. Hope and Timmel, 1984) as well as concrete tools, some from the PRA toolbox, and the use of visuals and pictures, models and simulations, demonstrations, proverbs, songs and slogans (very powerful in oral societies) and role-plays.

Space prevents us from going into the details of operationalization, but overall it is clear that this kind of facilitation goes far beyond the notion of a few facilitation techniques and nice tools. It is very demanding and not everyone may have the knowledge, skill or commitment to become an excellent facilitator. Below we discuss some of the resulting challenges for large-scale implementation.

Development of competence in facilitation

F4C is like holding up a mirror – almost a therapeutic action. It triggers a deep psychological confrontation with oneself and challenges deeply entrenched patterns and beliefs. It is this confrontation with all its ups and downs which opens the way for real transformation and going beyond the usual. If the facilitator is able to create a high level of honesty to oneself in the process and a political incorrectness which allows things to be called what they are in a forward looking, constructive way, it can set free a very high level of energy for change – individually and collectively. This energy can make a system become pro-active and enable people to dare to be in charge of their lives and discover their power for change.

F4C aims at developing emancipation from inside to enable people to better use the space they have and develop their – often underutilized – potentials. This dimension is often neglected in the empowerment debate. Empowerment is more linked to 'giving the space' through rights, resources, etc. F4C is about 'utilizing, developing and expanding the space' – transformation. It informs the process through questions and self-reflection. To be able to guide such processes and add value, the facilitator needs to have a full grasp of the vision and the matter of the process. Good facilitation therefore requires a high level of competence and professionalism, well beyond the few 'facilitation techniques' which can be learnt in a short training course. There are several key components of training good facilitators.

Learning versus training

F4C requires complex competences which cannot be dealt with in a conventional mode that puts emphasis on training rather than learning. Ultimately it is about developing the profession of 'change making'. The learning process is based on the co-generation of knowledge grounded in people's experience, rather than receiving it from one who knows better. Getting people to this level requires substantive effort and high quality training, learning processes and trainers. Bringing out the real issues, confronting and provoking requires a deep experience and orientation of the trainers.

The use of short-reflective cycles (integration of learning workshops and field practice) has been crucial in enabling action learning and reflection, in making the process more manageable and to help fuel the energy. The longer the time without contact with the learners the more it slowed down. This process allows for flexibility and adaptive capacity to accommodate emerging issues along the process, while enabling capacities to emerge and a better understanding of the process.

Mentoring and coaching is crucial to provide guidance to Peer Learning Teams (PLTs) during operationalization of PEA. PLTs are comprised of 3 to 4 trainee members who are implementing in 3 to 4 villages. The trainers/mentors, who are well ahead in terms of the process, provide mentoring and coaching to the PLTs. Each mentor is responsible for 3 to 4 PLTs, depending on the geographic area. The purpose of PLTs is to provide support for each other during the field practice in terms of planning together, giving each other feedback and also giving moral support when facilitating community meetings. There is a high correlation between good relationships between mentors and their PLTs – including regular joint planning and feedback meetings – and the high performance of those teams.

While these principles have worked very well, this puts a high demand on the quality of trainers. This has been a major challenge for the scaling up process.

The systemic nature of PEA

It is important to maintain a systemic intervention approach at all levels. The competence development process needs to address issues in a holistic manner. The stimulation of the whole-brain functioning, and the blending of theory (learning workshops) with practice (field practice), allows for simultaneous intervention at different levels of the system. Facilitation of such a holistic process with its interconnected parts is a great challenge and the future trainers have been struggling. One should not expect quick successes through a training-of-trainers approach, but rather see developing trainers as a longer term coaching process to develop both their competence as practitioners and as trainers.

Feedback and sharing of field experiences by trainees

Trainees are encouraged to share their experiential learning. During learning workshops, trainees would challenge each other and demand transparency and evidence of progress made from their fellow trainees. This created a lot of peer pressure for the trainees to be active during their field experience, in order not to lose face. This form of 'encouragement' was considered very important by the learners. The sharing also served as a platform for developing a pool of possible solutions to the challenges faced by trainees.

Peer pressure and the peer support system as motivators

The PLT concept used during the learning cycle was appreciated and commended by the learners in the sense that it exerted pressure for collaboration and joint learning and sharing of experiences. The officers who – beyond the learning cycle – find peer support, perform better than those who work in isolation. Another important aspect that encourages continuity is the institutional support that some of these extension officers get from their local supervisors. The fact that supervisors and the department are interested in what they do is seen as a positive pressure to work harder.

This shows that one of the sustainability factors of PEA is creating a platform that encourages peer support even beyond formal learning and, moreover, institutional support. The PLT concept used during the learning cycle needs to be replaced by some form of peer professional teams across the generations/cohorts. This is in line with the current on-going notion of Community of Practice widely recognized not only as a benefit for the individual involved, but also a means for enhancing organizational performance and as a knowledge management tool (Lesser and Stork, 2001; Seely and Duguid, 1991; Wenger and Lave, 1991).

Besides effective professional networks of facilitators and functioning knowledge sharing mechanisms is the need for a rigorous quality assurance/management system. We see a distinct dilution of quality of competence from generation to generation, both of trainees and trainers. Although the LDA has put in place a process of institutionalizing PEA into its mainstream administrative procedures, it has not managed to continuously nurture the quality of the practitioners and the trainers. Our fear is that the quality will be eroded with time as the most experienced staff also move on after some time and no new ideas and methods come in.

Scaling up the F4C process

As the process expands with more people getting involved at different levels and activities intensifying, the process becomes complex, and needs complex measures to manage it.

Quality

The significant increase in the number of people involved as the process evolves from one generation to another results in a great loss with respect to the quality of PEA. What distinguishes PEA from other methods is its emphasis on personal development, learning through self-reflection and learning by doing. All these were more profound in the first generation and reduced on the way, with the 3rd generation inclined to move more towards information-giving approaches – back to where we came from. There is a need to make space for new learning to take place in order to balance the dilution of 'knowledge transfer' and to contribute to the ongoing theory of PEA.

Technology versus process

The intangibility of processes makes process knowledge travel slower than technology knowledge. People remember what they see, and what they have achieved, but tend to forget how they got there in the first place. Technologies were spreading from one village to another without the learning process. Such spread in technologies is a great achievement. However, developing farmer trainers who conduct farmer-to-farmer training in technical areas has proven not only to help spread PEA in an organized manner, but also to encourage farmers to learn, since they learn better from their fellow farmers.

Scale and inclusiveness

As the process expands in size, geographical scope and complexity, the inclusiveness of the process also suffers. Apart from the trainers who gain recognition by nature, the others who worked exclusively in the communities are less visible. The most vulnerable and least included are those PEA learners who did not manage to complete all the steps of the operational framework during the formal learning cycle. This increases the likelihood of the process collapsing without warning. A coherent follow-up structure would be required to maintain the link and create the learning and sharing. The challenge is how to keep the majority on board while creating champions to take the process further.

Institutionalization of F4C

Both institutional support – the support that PEA learners get from their supervisors and other personnel – and institutionalization – the formal integration of PEA into departmental procedures – affect the effective implementation of PEA and its sustainability. There is a need to get the buy-in of the management from the beginning of the process. A change management team that oversees the institutionalization of the process needs to be put in place as otherwise the initiative gets personalized and creates resistance. The team needs to look at issues of financial support, quality assurance mechanisms and harmonization of the process with existing programmes. This cannot be managed in a conventional manner, but requires process-related competences.

Conclusion: what does all this mean for participatory innovation system development?

Our impression is that the challenge of what participatory development means is notoriously underestimated. This is exemplified by the many 'quick-fix' kinds of trainings which do not reflect the whole system capacities. In terms of innovation systems, we are not dealing with market failure or technology development, but rather system failure.

Due to the daunting conclusions, many spheres of development are still in a state of denial and do not want to see the dimension of the challenge. When dealing with system failure, it is not sufficient to look at linking farmers to markets and bringing some actors together in technology development. System failure has to do with how people interact within the communities (the demand side) and the interface with the supply side (extension, research and other service providers) and the support side (provincial governments and policy makers). It is the deeper systemic capacity which is insufficient to make the system work as a system rather than as disconnected parts.

F4C as described in this paper has a potential to develop this capacity. However, it needs to be recognized that we are in a different dimension with the kind of competence required to facilitate high quality learning and change processes – no matter at which level we operate. When it comes to the local level, the local extension agents and other frontline staff are often at the lowest level in their organizations, the least cared for, the lowest paid and often the least motivated. Using the analogy of a private company, if sales representatives had the same low status and low pay as these public sector 'change agents', most companies would go bankrupt very quickly. Why do we expect that things can and should work this way in development?

We were very fortunate to have had a long-term commitment of projects and departments in a few countries which enabled us to develop our PEA and F4C methodology for facilitation further. South Africa was the longest and most rigorous experience where we had the opportunity to demonstrate what impact a heavy investment in human resources for local-level quality facilitation can generate. Still, while this is generally recognized and admired at the case basis, most departments and projects are shying away from such a long-term investment, trying to find cheaper short cuts which in most cases do not go very far after the end of the projects. The professionalism required is rarely found among the cadre of technocrats we encounter regularly.

We once calculated that the costs for PEA competence development on a large scale would amount to about US$1500 per person in South Africa, which, given the training budgets of many government departments and development programmes, it would be possible to meet. Looking at other dimensions of innovation system development, the principles of F4C do not only apply on the demand side. There is a need to develop capacities at other levels too – service providers, innovation platforms, policy and organizations – and to look at the whole issue of personal transformation to become more creative and entrepreneurial in the way in which one deals with complex challenges in a more systemic manner.

To conclude, there is rarely one meeting (at least in South Africa) where one does not hear that 'attitude and mindset change are pre-requisites for success and impact in development'. When challenging people on how this should be done, there is a normally a big void or hazy explanations. If we are serious, we need to accept that we are still at the beginning of understanding sustainable and scalable change processes and how to create them and that mainstream 'development professionalism', while not quite a contradiction in terms, is still far from becoming commonplace. Our tools for making change are still raw. We hope that F4C can contribute to moving the practice in that direction.

Crop management innovation and the economics of attention

Robert Tripp

Introduction

Both plant breeding and crop management research have profited from the development of farmer participatory approaches over the past quarter century. In some respects crop management is more amenable to participatory approaches because it necessarily involves local-level experimentation and iterative adjustments. Here I focus on one type of crop management project, aimed at promoting low external input technology (LEIT). LEIT is not a perfectly defined category, but includes the use of locally available biological or mechanical inputs for improving soil fertility, soil and water management, crop establishment or pest management. LEIT may be promoted as a way of lowering or eliminating farmers' dependence on input markets, or as part of integrated agricultural technology development. Although there is no strict link between LEIT and participatory methodologies, the majority of LEIT projects utilize farmer-centred approaches and promote the development of local knowledge.

We are often told we live in an information economy, but Simon (1971:40) observed that 'in an information-rich world... a wealth of information creates a poverty of attention'. In knowledge-intensive approaches to agriculture, such as LEIT and participatory research, 'the economics of attention' (Lanham, 2006) is thus a key concern. Van der Veen (2000) suggests that information transmitted to promote natural resource management may be of three types: 'reproductive' (straightforward information on crop management);

'communicative' (guidance on how to develop such information); or 'transformative' (motivation for generating this information, often related to a 'style of farming', cf. van der Ploeg, 1993). The next sections review how these types of information are managed and utilized for LEIT.

The performance of LEIT

An extensive review of the literature and three cases studies (Tripp, 2006) revealed that the patterns of uptake for LEIT are not dissimilar to those of conventional technology. Although there is some variation among cases, it is difficult to find instances where the most resource-poor farmers are the principal beneficiaries of a LEIT project, despite the pro-poor focus of many of these efforts. The same farmers who would be expected to take up seed and fertilizer technology (the better-resourced and those with better links to agricultural markets) are those who are most likely to take an interest in LEIT.

Those households where farming is for subsistence and that have a range of other income sources based on off-farm labour are generally less likely to be attracted to LEIT. This is not a surprising result from the standpoint of the economics of attention; the smaller the proportion of household income derived from farming, the fewer the incentives for pursuing information related to agricultural innovation. If Farmer First was a rallying call for addressing the needs of the rural poor, it may have to be amended to something like, 'Rural households that balance a range of off-farm income sources with farming and only occasionally bring produce to market – First'.

Not only did the study find that poorer, subsistence-oriented farm households were less likely to take up LEIT, but also that they were usually less likely to participate in activities that introduced or generated such technology. A technique such as farmer field schools (FFS) is an important innovation, but it usually requires that farmers devote a half-day each week during the cropping season to meetings and activities. Some observers call for shortening the FFS curriculum, but there are concerns that this would compromise the communicative learning that takes place. Thus the dilemma is how to identify methods that engage farmers in technology generation and yet do not demand so much time that only a minority of the farming community can take advantage of them.

The concern about the time investment required for learning about some types of LEIT is related to a broader question about so-called 'information-intensive' technology. As Lockeretz (1991) has observed, it is important to distinguish between technologies that only require time for initial mastery and those that require a continual investment for activities such as monitoring and adjustment. The likelihood of farmers being able to take advantage of the more demanding examples is conditioned by the efficiency of the modalities that introduce the technology and the ability of farmers to obtain and manage the information needed for the continued performance of the technique.

The time to learn and manage a new technology also needs to be distinguished from the time to actually implement it. Although LEIT has a reputation for being labour-intensive, the study showed that these technologies are sufficiently diverse that such generalizations are not helpful. But the study showed that in nearly all cases the distinction between technologies relying on external inputs and those based on farm labour is of decreasing relevance because farm labour is itself often a purchased input. As rural populations increase, average farm sizes decrease and income sources diversify, hired labour is an increasingly prevalent input on even many of the smallest farms.

Thus the decision to invest in labour-demanding technology may be based on access to cash (and thus often on market links) rather than on the status of household labour supply, and in this sense LEIT is like any other technology. But farmers still need adequate information to encourage them to invest. The introduction of LEIT often depends heavily on farmer participation. We have seen that the time requirements of this may be problematic, but there are other challenges as well, particularly with regard to the skills that farmers bring to the table.

Farmer experimentation

Farmer experimentation is a prominent feature of many participatory techniques, but it is helpful to recognize different types and purposes of experimentation. In many cases the experimentation is designed to build farmers' confidence. In FFS in irrigated rice, farmers often do experiments that illustrate that leaf damage early in the season does not warrant insecticide application. Although the results of the 'experiment' are already well-established, farmers' involvement helps deliver the message, through communicative learning. But given the time involved in such activity, it may be asked if there are not more efficient ways of presenting this information that might reach more farmers.

In other cases the experimentation is more truly exploratory, as farmers are expected to adapt techniques, such as conservation tillage, to their own conditions; or farmers are encouraged to experiment more broadly on their own accord. There are relatively few examples where LEIT projects have led to a significant amount of independent experimentation. While no one would argue against strengthening farmers' experimental capacities, it is not clear if such projects are the best way to go about this.

Even when experimentation is done on behalf of a wider community of farmers, this does not resolve the problem of how to deliver the techniques or principles that emerge. Many LEIT projects put considerable faith in the process of farmer-to-farmer technology transfer, but the study showed that this is not as common as often assumed. Farmers of course observe each others' practices and exchange information; many examples of the rapid diffusion of new crop varieties attest to the fact that seed and information are often transmitted quite rapidly. But there is much less evidence that the information required for LEIT (whether it is the rationale for lowering insecticide use or the techniques of soil conservation) is transmitted very effectively between farmers, due to the lack of learning networks (see Richards, this book). Despite the fact that many LEIT projects not only provide access to specific technologies and methods but also promote a low-external input philosophy (an example of transformative learning), there are few instances in which such projects are responsible for the emergence of consistently 'green' farmers. Farmers who take advantage of the substance of LEIT are less likely to also adopt a style that makes environmental concerns the major determinant of decisions about input use.

The hopes for more effective communication among farmers are also linked to the aspirations of many LEIT projects for building social capital, in particular the assumption that participation in the development of LEIT (often as part of a group) will lead to permanent farmer organizations dedicated to further technology generation. This has rarely been the case, however. Farmer groups formed under one project may be inherited by a succeeding project, but sustainable, independent farmer organizations do not often emerge from the experience of collaborative technology generation.

Farmers' attention – a scarce resource

Although there are a number of examples of adoption and adaptation of these techniques, they are not widely used, particularly by the most resource-poor farmers; learning about them may involve a considerable time investment; they often require additional managerial skills but the actual labour for implementation is increasingly likely to be hired; despite the communicative type of learning associated with much LEIT the experience does not significantly strengthen experimental capacities or social capital; and despite the distinct style of many LEIT efforts, farmers rarely cite environmental awareness as a primary motivation.

Larger issues need to be addressed in order to provide an environment where farmers can efficiently acquire information about options and methods. This does not mean that innovative efforts at technology generation are unimportant, or that all resources should be devoted to long-term institutional development. But it does mean that business as usual, with a continual stream of disconnected projects and no thought to the broader context that governs the efficiency of farmers' access to information, is not acceptable.

Beyond the favoured strategy for communicative learning of 'farmer groups', there are a number of communication technologies that can be enlisted to make better use of scarce attention resources. Computer-assisted learning, expert systems, and similar innovations are often discussed, but their immediate relevance for resource-poor farmers needs to be examined. More mundane possibilities, such as periodicals and FM radio, may deserve investment. A farmer magazine in south India provides not only factual information about innovations but also offers a forum for debating the performance of technologies and alternatives (Padre et al., 2003). Radio programmes can also offer opportunities for this type of discussion. Such media can be used for the development and transmission of information related not only to agriculture but also to a range of economic endeavours and political concerns of relevance to rural residents (see Van Mele, this book).

Donors and governments need to review their priorities. How much focus should be directed to *ad hoc* farmer groups and how much to supporting strong, broad-based rural organizations? How much should be invested in farmer field schools and how much in basic rural education? What should be the balance between civil society technology development projects and developing farmers' capacities to demand better service from public research and extension? How much should be spent on sophisticated information technology projects and how much on developing media that provide opportunities for engaging rural residents? And how much should donors devote to pursuing their own portfolios of short-term projects rather than providing incentives for people to work behind the scenes to ensure that strong local institutions have a chance to emerge?

Knowledge networks and farmer seed systems

Paul Richards

Introduction

Proponents of a Farmer First approach argued that experts had no monopoly on technical knowledge when it came to improving small-scale agriculture for poverty alleviation. Brave attempts have been made to operationalize and scale up this insight, many described in this book. Yet three decades after the initial debates it is still common to hear the objection 'are you trying to say farmers know better than scientists?' In fact, as Ashby (this book) describes, the experts have extensively colonized the new participatory fora for farmer knowledge. Surveying the extensive experience with farmer field schools in Uganda, Isubikalu (2007) was forced to conclude that farmers' own research problems remained low on the list, elbowed aside by researcher priorities.

This paper argues that the Farmer First model of learning urgently needs to be changed. We need to move from an 'in head' model of cognition and knowledge formation of individuals to the idea that cognition is distributed across a network of actors. This rests on the superiority of unsupervised over supervised learning in complex networks for the exchange and utilization of genetic (and other agrarian) information.

Seed systems make a logical starting point, since they seem to lend themselves both to the methods of distributed cognition and neural network modelling. Here I discuss ongoing work looking at the adaptive potential of rice seed systems in coastal Upper West Africa – from The Gambia to Ghana. Such developments identify a new focus and a new lease of life for a pluralized, socialized variant of the Farmer First paradigm.

Knowledge networks

Mainstream approaches to learning and cognition still stress the brain as the cognizing tool, and the individual as the seat of learning. This viewpoint was further entrenched by the success of brain/computer analogies. We live in a (machine) world in which it is widely presumed that computers require 'brains' (central processors) to be able to compute. However, the 1980s saw the development of a new approach, focused on 'experiential learning' (Chaiklin and Lave, 1993). Then, in his path-breaking book, *Cognition in the Wild*, Edwin Hutchins (1995) explicitly sought to revive the social approach to cognition. Focusing on ship navigation systems, knowledge, it became clear, was the product of team work. No single member of the team held a complete picture, and yet so long as the team did its work the ship sailed safely.

Paralleling these developments, computer scientists began to question Turing's brain/computer analogy (Whitby, 1997) and rediscovered the potential of network computational devices (artificial neural networks, ANN). In ANN there is no single 'central processor' with an overview of the task, issuing sequential commands. Memory and knowledge are properties of the system as a whole, not of specialized modules within the system, as in conventional computers (Picton, 2000). ANN typically involves high levels of interconnection and feedback. The passage of traffic (electronic signals and so forth) in ANN depends on the frequency with which different interconnections are activated. Memory and other cognitive functions such as pattern recognition or categorization arise from the way nodes become weighted by use (or lack of use). Some networks can be primed to recognize patterns (i.e. they are taught); others achieve pattern recognition through stochastic processes (Hopfield, 1982).

Seed systems as complex networks

Thus this distinction between supervised and unsupervised learning is conceptually useful in re-addressing our central problem of what it is that 'farmers' and 'researchers' know. How might we apply some of the insights of experiential learning, distributed cognition and neural network computation to issues of Farmer First knowledge in the context of West African seed systems?

Crop farming requires planting material (seeds, etc). In West Africa the earliest seeds of indigenous crops (millet, *Digitaria*, African Rice, cow pea, etc.) were collected from the wild. Over many generations seed types were modified by repeated selection, e.g. types prone to reduced shattering began to dominate (Fuller, 2005). These were true cultivars (i.e. dependent on human management), although seed systems for indigenous cultivars typically involved links with wild gene pools. Existence of cultivars implies conscious human strategies to retain, maintain and distribute seed for planting. Such local seed systems are crop specific (e.g. vegetatively propagated crops such as yam require different systems from grains, such as African Rice).

In some cases markets became important elements in local and regional seed systems, but more generally small-scale West African farmers remain significantly dependent on local informal modalities of seed acquisition. For planting, supply from the previous year's farm remains the dominant source in many areas, supplemented by loans-in-kind from merchants or better-supplied farmers. Local seed systems have a second important aspect – experimentation (Richards, 1986). Experimentation with unfamiliar seed types is common. Farmers typically beg, borrow or are given small amounts of seed they assess for suitability in their own farming conditions. Women are very active in this area, and much material passes through informal kinship or friendship channels. Some is acquired through natural or accidental processes of seed dissemination (e.g. wind or water, or activities of birds and grazing mammals). Other items are 'borrowed' from research sources by labourers who are also local farmers.

A full description of the functioning of, and knowledge states within West African seed systems would require account to be taken, therefore, of a range of seed acquisition strategies and distribution processes, including on-farm selection and retention strategies, seed loans, market acquisition and local and scientific experimentation. Seed systems thus assume complex network forms. Attempts to attain planned outcomes, such as widespread adoption of a few superior seed types, tend to founder on this complexity.

Distributed knowledge in seed systems

Technology studies can be divided into two broad fields – engineering approaches and the study of skill (i.e. technique). The latter is the predominant approach of social scientists interested in technology. In a foundational move, Mauss and Hubert (1902 [Mauss, 1972]) identified the basic significance of experimental technique. They stress that all experimentation involves a social context – an anxious group of stakeholders with a problem to be solved (i.e. a user network). Technique is stabilized as practice through the social endorsement it receives. Modern studies utilizing this approach refer to knowledge or understanding as a product not of the individual experimenter but of group interaction and distributed cognition. The distinctions between supervised and unsupervised learning and between individual and distributed cognition is important here, as these capture quite well some of the basic differences between the kinds of seed system outlined above.

The focus here is on the local seed system as an instance of distributed cognition in an unsupervised artificial neural network. Farmers receive, process and pass on seed materials in a probabilistic manner. Seed can be begged from friends or gifted impulsively. Some is acquired truly randomly (from accidental finds). Farmers test and select unfamiliar materials, and chance (rainfall fluctuations, choice of site, pest damage, etc.) plays a part in sifting material for continued usage. Farmers with unusual material recurrently hand on small amounts through a variety of channels, depending on availability.

Each agent can be considered a 'synapse' in a network, with a specific propensity to hand on or receive material through 'weighted' connections – reflecting strength and density of bonds of kinship, friendship, clientship, etc. Patterns of activation influence the likelihood of future transactions taking place. Frequently activated links are more likely to 'fire' on subsequent occasions. Subsequent knowledge states (i.e. patterns of distribution of adapted seed materials) are distributed across the system as a whole, shaped by feedback activity. In short, the seed exchange network is modelled as a stochastic recursive system with emergent properties, based on an 'unsupervised learning' mode.

By contrast, controlled attempts by governments and development agencies to shift knowledge states among a mass of small-scale farmers towards use of breeder seeds may be seen as a kind of supervised learning. Breeders know what works, and the aim is then to induce the mass of farmers to adopt superior genotypes. This is the classic Green Revolution approach. The Farmer First approach, by contrast, is to place more reliance on the myriad actions of farmers screening and diffusing locally adapted seed materials. But the battle is lost when it is conceived as a contest between the individualized knowledge of breeder and farmer. The argument could be usefully restated in terms of the relative merits of supervised and unsupervised learning. Viewed as unsupervised learning farmer seed exchange can be seen as a 'feedback' driven process through which local seed systems attain genotype–environment equilibrium. When the environment changes the system hunts for a new equilibrium. It is possible too that unsupervised learning may confer greater adaptive flexibility in regard to environmental fluctuation.

Linking knowledge networks

An advantage of the supervised model is that it links seed users with genetic information in a rather direct way (the teachers in the system – i.e. plant breeders – know a great deal about the genetic pedigree of recommended seeds). In the model of local seed systems as unsupervised (farmer-to-farmer) learning the relationship between farmer seed exchange activity and genetic information is less clear.

Unsupervised neural networks sometimes encounter a problem of local equilibria (i.e. they settle into sets of localized stable states rather than assuming a system-wide pattern). In seed system terms, we might anticipate such results where groups of farmers exchange different named varieties across a linguistic boundary that turn out (on closer analysis) to have the same basic genetic composition. System learning has taken place, but it is (in adaptive terms) 'wasted effort'.

When do unsupervised learning approaches reach some kind of limit? For example, if it was known that farmers were 'fishing' in a locally exhausted gene pool systematic base-broadening might then be attempted to 're-boot' the farmer seed system. How can we find some way of heightening the responsiveness of local seed systems to precise genetic information, but without harming the recursive properties that convey adaptive flexibility?

Some important questions emerge for a re-energized Farmer First agenda:

- What are the contexts in which (increasingly readily available) genomic information add value to learning activities in local seed systems?
- In what ways would genomic information 'register' within unsupervised seed systems learning (more specifically, is a genetic component already reflected in existing farmer seed networks, and if not, how could such a component be introduced?)
- What are the practical and organizational opportunities and limitations to providing such information in African countries?

Learning to make change: developing innovation and change competence in African universities

Jürgen Hagmann, Paul Kibwika and Adipala Ekwamu

Introduction

African universities, especially in Sub-Saharan Africa, are being challenged on their relevance to solving the problems of poverty, food insecurity and disease. Below we describe an action research experiment to develop systemic competence and skills among academic staff at Makerere University, Uganda, with the goal of enhancing the university's impact on development change. The action research process was conducted over a two-year period with 26 lecturers from three agriculture-related faculties (Agriculture, Veterinary Medicine, and Forestry and Nature Conservation).

Background

During the 1990s, the Rockefeller Foundation supported a programme to develop the skills of mid-level professionals in agriculture-related disciplines in Kenya, Uganda, Malawi, Mozambique and Zimbabwe. After 10 years, there was no convincing evidence that the programme would achieve its intended impact on poverty and food security. In 2001, the Rockefeller Foundation convened a workshop to discuss curriculum reforms, but the event led participants to focus on more than just the curriculum itself.

Participants recognized that present training in agricultural faculties emphasized only the technical or 'hard' skills of agriculture and was grossly deficient in social or 'soft' skills (Patel et al., 2001). In order for agriculture graduates to influence development change in societies, they would need to be able to integrate across disciplines and use both hard and soft skills. They would have to be critical, creative thinkers with excellent communication, facilitation and management skills (Hagmann, 2002).

It was also recognized that the university lecturers themselves lacked soft skills. Curriculum review would be insufficient, unless the lecturers themselves were able to think and facilitate learning in a different way. Hence, a skills-development programme was needed for the academic staff in order to change mindsets and values, integrate disciplines and knowledge systems, and impart skills for facilitating interactive learning.

Personal Mastery/Soft Skills learning as a response

Based on the lead author's experience in facilitating systemic change in research and extension organizations, an approach centred on 'personal mastery' was deemed essential. Personal mastery is a discipline that aims to enhance growth and personal vision in individuals as a base for improving their performance and their satisfaction in life (Senge, 1990). People with high levels of personal mastery are acutely aware of their ignorance, their incompetence and their growth areas. They are more committed to their work and have a greater sense of responsibility.

Personal mastery is based in part on unquantifiable concepts such as intuition and personal vision. The soft skills required also encompass the cross-cutting management skills necessary for every professional to work effectively within organizations. They are the skills that enhance communicative, interactive and facilitative abilities to influence change in society.

The Personal Mastery/Soft Skills (PM/SS) learning programme was established as a holistic change programme, integrating six thematic areas, namely:

- Personal development – focusing on emotional intelligence as an internal driver for enhanced performance and productivity.
- Team development – developing individual characteristics to enable effective teamwork, understand team dynamics and help manage teams for improved organizational performance.
- Facilitation methods and techniques – building skills for facilitating learning and other collective action processes, using techniques other than the conventional lecture method of teaching.
- Communication – application of communication tools for problem solving, negotiation skills and conflict-resolution.
- Organizational development – understanding organizations as dynamic social systems, requiring flexibility and adaptation.
- Technical issues – building technical skills in facilitating and managing interactive learning processes, action research and consultancies.

'Facilitation for Change' (see Ngwenya and Hagmann, this book) and feedback were critical cross-cutting elements that integrated the six themes.

Lecturers were encouraged to take part in the programme by emphasizing the value of the new skills as ways to improve their marketability for carrying out the kinds of consultancy and funded research projects that most lecturers want to do in order to supplement their meagre salaries. Hence, the participants' motivation to improve their teaching methods came from the motivation to practise the facilitation skills with which a better livelihood could be achieved. This created a win–win situation for the lecturers, the students and the university.

Design of the intervention

The PM/SS programme was modelled on the metaphor of constructing a house – the personal mastery house (Figure 4.3). The foundation is the shared vision, values and commitment of all the stakeholders. In this case, the vision was to enable Makerere University to influence development through training, research and service to community.

The pillars of the house are four complementary learning approaches: learning workshops, practice, peer-learning groups and self-learning. The workshops were for engaging in conceptual issues, skills building, reflection, synthesis of lessons learnt and joint planning for continued learning. Four peer-learning groups were formed to further learning in areas of: enhancing undergraduate training, enhancing graduate training and research, facilitating community learning initiatives and facilitating institutional change processes. For each period of practice, a learning workshop was convened for sharing experiences across peer-learning groups and for nurturing the learning with new concepts, approaches and tools. Self-learning is for individual study and reading. The roof represents anticipated outcomes of the learning process such as better teaching approaches, facilitation and advisory skills and personal development.

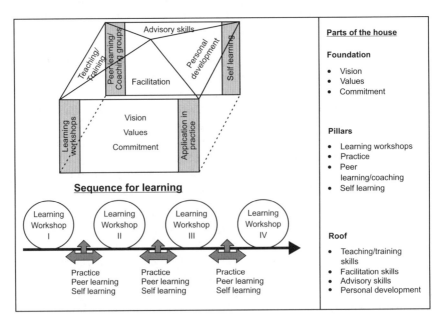

Figure 4.3 The PM/SS innovation competence learning model (Source: Hagmann, 2002)

Setting up an intervention process

Step 1: Consultations with university managers and selection of participants. Consultations were conducted with the Deans, Heads of Departments (HoD) and other key personnel, as well as stakeholders outside the university to enhance local ownership of the programme. The Deans and HoD committed themselves and undertook to select the 26 participants for the programme, monitor its implementation and participate in its evaluation. It became their own experiment.

Step 2: Sustaining ownership through reporting back and learning groups. At the end of every learning workshop, the managers in the participating faculties and top executives, including the Vice Chancellor, were invited to a half-day session where the programme participants explained and demonstrated what they had learned. This provided a mechanism through which the managers could monitor the programme. Learning groups from each faculty also organized feedback sessions for their faculty colleagues, which provided a mechanism for ongoing sharing with other staff and accountability to the organization.

Step 3: Synthesis and self-evaluation. Reflection, in order to draw lessons, was a key feature of the programme. At the end of the first learning cycle of four workshops and field practice, participants reflected on their learning in peer-learning groups and as individuals, and collectively synthesized the lessons learnt.

Step 4: Report back to managers and assessment process. Responsibility for evaluating the programme rested with the Deans and HoD who had agreed to own the programme. After the first learning cycle, they created an 'independent' assessment team, comprising staff and faculties which were not part of the programme.

Step 5: Developing assessment criteria and conducting the assessment. Criteria for assessing the programme were developed during a two-day facilitated workshop with the assessment teams. They sought clear evidence for the following:

- development of personal skills and confidence;
- establishment of a feedback culture with students and among colleagues;
- innovations in teaching, research and consultancy;
- interdisciplinary engagement in research, training and consultancy;
- teamwork and networking;
- enhancement in management qualities;
- being role models in professional conduct; and
- pro-activeness in responding to opportunities and expectations of stakeholders.

Step 6: Planning the scaling up and institutionalization. Following the assessment, options for repackaging the PM/SS programme to involve other categories of staff were suggested. Targeting these groups would require the support of senior management, and therefore a two-day exposure workshop on the programme was organized for the top executive managers. As a result, the senior management group made a verbal commitment to anchor PM/SS in the newly created Human Resource Department, to allow for the institutionalization and targeting of the programme to various categories of staff. The coherent process design as a change process enabled an integrated way to scale up the experiment naturally.

Major outcomes and impacts

Self-awareness and discovery of hidden potentials. Participants had a better understanding of their own potentials, their personality and behaviour and how these influence interaction with other people, and that other people may do things differently. This helped them open up to constructive feedback for self-improvement in personal and professional performance.

Influencing change from within through feedback. Giving and receiving personal feedback created a new pathway for enhancing mutual capacities, so that the group could build on the strengths of each person to achieve a common goal. The independent assessment team observed that programme participants proactively sought the opinions of students and colleagues for the purpose of improving their teaching methods.

Taking initiative, working in teams and promoting peer learning. The programme enhanced teamwork across disciplines and faculties on tasks such as proposal-writing and student supervision. Consequently, the lecturers also encouraged teamwork and peer learning among their students and this widened the students' interaction with other disciplines.

Facilitation skills for interactive learning and collective action processes. The lecturers started to engage with students as co-learners rather than as the sole authority of knowledge. Experience from this type of engagement led to conceptualization of a 'learning wheel' (Hagmann, 2005) for interactive learning/teaching. The 12 'cornerstones' around the wheel represent a checklist of 'success factors' which are used for self-reflection and evaluation as well as for design of interventions and next actions in the process. Examples include 'Incentives that encourage commitment of lecturers' and 'Effective student peer learning groups'.

Overcoming fear to try out new things as reflective practitioners. The concept of life-long learning is based on the ability to reflect and learn from our actions. Fear of failure is a major hindrance to this goal, and this fear is sometimes overwhelming among academics because of their 'expert' mental models. A positive attitude towards learning from experience combined with social support for reflective practice increased the participants' confidence to dare to try out new things.

Enhancing communication for problem-solving. The programme focused on communication skills for conflict management, negotiation and consensus-building. Besides the improved awareness of their own communication patterns, a major impact area has been active listening. Listening is critical in interactive learning and is also a way of providing space for others to participate.

Thinking 'out of the box' to influence development impact through action research and process consultancy. It became clear to the lecturers that influencing change in society, either through research or service-delivery, required a new form of engagement. They developed a second learning wheel, representing an operational framework for action research to increase the relevance and impact of university research. Using this framework, teams across faculties came together and developed proposals. In the process, the division between Agriculture, Veterinary and Forestry/NRM Faculties in the group vanished. The joint vision of a new university and the new personal and professional relationships overcame institutional divisions. Similar learning wheels were developed for process consultancy and for overcoming the culture of jealousy and suspicion in the University – one of the major blockages for performance and growth of individuals in the system.

Developing a culture of commitment and integrity. The programme evaluation showed indications of greater commitment, passion for work and desire to build a legacy of integrity. Two factors seem to have been key in this: 1) the development of empathy with others, leading the participants to 'put themselves in the shoes' of their students and other colleagues; and 2) the challenge to be exemplary, enforced by peer pressure. Unconsciously, these changes also demonstrated leadership qualities which allowed more than 10 of the 26 participants to achieve promotion into leadership positions since the programme began – successes that they strongly associate with personal qualities and skills they gained from the programme. The risk now is that these highly committed people are being overloaded.

Self-assessment of the changes at individual level. During the process, criteria were developed with the group for evaluating the behaviours of someone who was mastering innovation competence. Participants then scored themselves and their peers against each criterion. Figure 4.4 provides an illustration of the impact of the PM/SS programme, based on a composite profile.

Where are we now?

The PM/SS programme started in 2003, the sequence of four learning workshops was completed in 2004 and a workshop to develop the training capacities was held in 2005. Immediately afterwards, the new trainers, with some support, took another group of 35 lecturers through the process. That programme was completed recently.

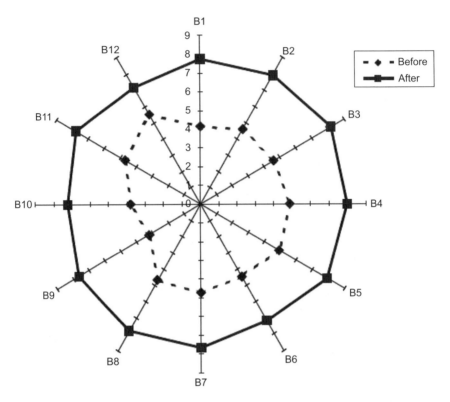

Figure 4.4 Profile ratings before and after the PM/SS programme

Key quality criteria for someone who masters innovation competence

B1 = Uses professional networks and alliances for exchange of information and experiences and to pursue common interest

B2 = Promotes team development and consensus building in teams

B3 = Initiates and facilitates group processes of joint reflection, strategy and vision development and decision making

B4 = Manages and minimizes conflicts

B5 = Actively seeks to develop him/herself professionally and personally

B6 = Tries out new things with courage and without fear of failure

B7 = Deals with unforeseen situations in a positive, pro-active and solution-oriented way

B8 = Shares information in a free, transparent and accountable manner

B9 = Gives and receives feedback as a tool to develop him/herself and others personally

B10 = Develops and pursues clear vision and values in his/her professional environment

B11 = Assumes leadership roles (formal and informal) to enhance individual, team and organizational performance

B12 = Pursues a balanced lifestyle

Sixty staff in Makerere University is quite a critical mass to move with. A concept for scaling up beyond just training new staff has been developed since 2005 and new ideas are emerging continuously. However, funding is still being sought to implement the next 'leap', which is to create a more systemic change process at different levels of Makerere University. The ultimate success of the initiative cannot be sustained by individual competence development alone.

A similar intervention was carried out in a PhD programme at Wageningen University – with similar lessons (Hagmann et al., 2003).

Some key lessons

Designing such a process has to take into account the time needed for engagement and targeting the right triggers for change. One-and-a-half to two years is about the minimum period necessary for substantial personal change.

Without an overall readiness on the part of the university management to engage in change, PM/SS would have been much more difficult. To generate commitment and motivation to learn for change, the management must feel some pressure or discomfort. In this case, there was tremendous pressure from local governments and other employers of Makerere University graduates to reform for relevance, particularly in view of the changed political and economic context. The university was already undertaking several initiatives towards improving relevance, so that the PM/SS programme fitted in well.

Facilitating a learning process aimed at wider organizational change requires high-quality facilitation, rather than teaching pre-conceived modules. The two facilitators' flexibility in designing the programme in an evolutionary way and dealing with emerging issues of concern and making links with the topics that interested the participants helped to motivate them to engage. The neutrality of the facilitators in relation to the disciplinary rivalries that prevail in the university was another major success factor.

Getting the management to own the process is very critical but at the same time not easy. Mechanisms must be designed to allow their continuous involvement and staying informed. To attain this level of involvement, there must be a champion to deal with organizational politics and ensure managers are exposed to the programme in order to appreciate its value.

For wider system change, there has to be a critical mass of people who have adopted the new orientation. This requires more trainers, but those who are interested in becoming trainers need additional training and coaching. In this case, a training-of-trainers was conducted. Quality assurance becomes a critical issue, as the process could otherwise degenerate into a mere training programme rather than a change programme. New trainers need coaching and technical backup as well as a process of continuous reflection and learning as a community of practice.

More and more meetings in the faculties are being facilitated instead of being run by a chairperson. The fact that this capacity now exists inside the organization and has shown to produce better outcomes has made it easy to spread this rather simple change. A participatory approach and joint problem-solving has increased staff engagement and uncovered hidden potential. This single factor created a substantial difference in the way issues are handled in the faculties.

Quality assurance and management during the scaling up process are a key challenge. Without a rigorous system to nurture and coach trainers, the dilution of quality is inevitable. Communities of practice among practitioners and trainers is one way of fulfilling this need, as are regular workshops where new ideas and tools are introduced. However, it will also be important to raise the expectations of students directly so that they can demand a different teaching style and topics around change.

The whole action research experiment was monitored and deeply analysed through an accompanying PhD study on the process (Kibwika, 2006). This provided a deeply analytical dimension to the action research, which could not have been achieved through internal reflection only.

Conclusion

The PM/SS experiment has shown that the starting point on a journey to learning for change is to challenge some entrenched values and beliefs, in order to awaken consciousness and desire for personal change towards a preferred future.

If we are serious in moving towards innovation systems and change in the existing systems, we need to articulate boldly that this is not a task to be mastered with the present mindsets and cultures of hierarchical dominance. These systems, which supposedly aim to develop people's capacities, often actually suppress the potential of younger people, their energy and ideas, and try to make them as bureaucratic and compliant as the system itself.

We need transformation, starting from the personal level, built into peer networks who understand change, who are ready to drive change and have the capacity to strategize for change and influence, rather than waiting for the 'good leader' to come from above. These insights are not only applicable to universities. The same lessons apply to most other public service-provider institutions (e.g. in research and extension, etc.). To succeed, development needs entrepreneurial minds, but unfortunately it is often bureaucratic minds that are supposed to train them.

From marginal to normative: institutionalizing participatory epidemiology

Andy Catley

Introduction

By the mid-1990s participatory approaches and methods were being used by many small-scale community-based livestock projects. Experiences were documented in a special livestock edition of *RRA Notes* in 1994 and included the use of Rapid Rural Appraisal (RRA) and Participatory Rural Appraisal (PRA) methods to prioritize and map livestock diseases. Although community-based and participatory approaches to veterinary care became increasingly popular at this time, veterinary uses of participatory approaches and methods remained localized in the NGO community, and were not widely adopted by research centres, veterinary schools or government veterinary services.

Just over ten years later a new edition of the well-known veterinary textbook *Veterinary Epidemiology* included a section on 'participatory epidemiology' (PE) based on the use of adapted RRA/PRA methods (Thrusfield, 2005). By mid-2007 at least four African veterinary schools were teaching PE at either undergraduate or postgraduate level, and capacity-building in PE was a common feature of programmes intended to strengthen government disease surveillance systems in Africa and beyond, including Europe. Participatory epidemiology was being used in impact assessment of veterinary interventions, disease investigation and epidemiological and economic studies. For some issues, information derived from PE was pivotal for informing policy dialogue and reform. But how did this transformation come about? Here I describe some of the strategies and processes which were used to test and promote the use of PE in veterinary institutions in East Africa. I also present some current challenges facing the application of PE and ensuring benefits to communities.

Strategies for institutionalizing participatory epidemiology

Understand the concerns of the veterinary establishment

In the mid-1990s participatory approaches and methods were normal practice in many disciplines and sectors but were not yet widely used by veterinarians. For example, in 1995 the World Health Organization published guidelines for rapid participatory appraisal to assess human health needs (Annett and Rifkin,

1995) but a year later the equivalent United Nations livestock institution – the Food and Agriculture Organization – was only just becoming aware of the value of community participation in veterinary services (Leyland, 1996). In most government veterinary services and veterinary schools in Africa, awareness of community participation or approaches such as PRA was very limited.

Due to the apparent delays in support to approaches such as PRA by the veterinary establishment, in the late 1990s the International Institute for Environment and Development (IIED) began a project with the Organization of African Unity (now the African Union)/Interafrican Bureau for Animal Resources to examine options for the wider use of PRA-type approaches in veterinary institutions in Africa. Called the 'Participatory Approaches to Veterinary Epidemiology' (PAVE) Project, the first stage of the project was a survey of attitudes and understanding of participatory appraisal among veterinarians working throughout Africa, in various organizations (Catley, 2000). The survey showed that although veterinarians acknowledged that participatory approaches could improve links between professionals and communities, among the main concerns and constraints were the qualitative nature of the data derived from participatory methods, the limited availability of training courses and literature, and negative attitudes towards PRA among colleagues and managers.

To some extent, the concerns of veterinary researchers and epidemiologists about RRA/PRA were justified. For example, in the growing informal literature on veterinary uses of RRA/PRA there was often no mention of triangulation or cross-checking of results. So although veterinarians were using RRA/PRA, rarely did they report clinical examinations of livestock or use basic disease investigation techniques to support their results. This is not to say that conventional and time-consuming disease surveys were needed alongside RRA/PRA work, but that occasionally, some basic veterinary professional diagnosis would have added greatly to the validity of the findings. When RRA/PRA was used by non-veterinarians to understand livestock diseases, in some cases the interpretation of information provided by informants was simply wrong.

Discussion with veterinary researchers and epidemiologists soon after the publication of the initial PAVE survey also indicated that these workers felt that the qualitative nature of RRA/PRA hindered publication in scientific journals. Within their various organizations, career development was partly dependent on research publications in peer-reviewed journals, rather than the impact of the research on communities. These experiences indicated that strategies for introducing RRA/PRA approaches in veterinary institutions needed to include options for adapting some participatory methods into more quantitative tools, and showing how research using RRA/PRA could be published. It was also evident that more profound institutional change was required to change the incentives which governed the ways in which research topics were identified, and the research approaches and methods which were used.

The next stage of the PAVE Project made a deliberate attempt to create a branch of RRA/PRA that veterinarians might call their own. The term 'participatory epidemiology' (PE) was used by PAVE in an attempt to combine the language of participation with a scientifically recognized discipline. In the late 1990s veterinary epidemiology was largely perceived as a quantitative subject, although it had a history of borrowing methods from the social sciences (Schwabe, 1982).

Playing the numbers game: studies on the validity and reliability of participatory epidemiology

In response to some of the concerns outlined above, in 2000 and 2001 the PAVE Project conducted field research in Africa to assess the reliability and validity of PE methods. The general approach was to compare data derived from PE with data produced by conventional livestock disease investigation and epidemiological methods (Table 4.2).

An important aspect of the PAVE studies was to examine when and how to standardize PE methods, to explore the pros and cons of standardization, and to analyse and present the results in different ways for different users. For methods which produced numerical data (e.g. matrix scoring, proportional piling) the approach was to identify the minimum number of repetitions which would allow the analysis and presentation of results using conventional statistics. For these methods, it was also possible to standardize while at the same time, allow flexibility. A matrix scoring method might use some items and indicators which were fixed (standardized) by the researchers, while also allowing informants to add their own items or indicators. The use of informal interviewing as part of a method such as matrix scoring allowed flexible follow-up of interesting results. Some matrix scoring results from PAVE are shown in Figure 4.5

Another key finding from the PAVE studies was that some PE methods were more valid than conventional methods such as questionnaires. A good example was the use of proportional piling to assess livestock disease incidence and mortality with pastoralist communities. The proportional piling methods

Table 4.2 Studies on the reliability and validity of participatory epidemiology

Research summary	Research partners
Diagnosis of a chronic wasting disease in cattle, South Sudan (Catley et al., 2001; 2002b).	Operation Lifeline Sudan (Southern Sector) Livestock Programme; Veterinaires sans frontieres-Suisse; Save the Children UK.
Local characterisation of bovine trypanosomiasis and preferences for disease control, Kenya (Catley et al., 2002a).	Kenya Trypanosomiasis Research Institute; Catholic Relief Services; Diocese of Malindi
Diagnosis of a heat intolerance syndrome in cattle and association with foot-and-mouth disease, Tanzania (Catley et al., 2004).	Faculty of Veterinary Medicine, Sokoine University of Agriculture; Mwanza Veterinary Investigation Centre

Clinical signs	Nuer cattle disease names				
	Liei	*Dat*	*Maguar*	*Doop*	*Macueny*
Chronic weight loss (*W*=0.51***)	10 (6.0-16)	1 (0-2.5)	3 (0-3.0)	1 (0-2.5)	1 (0-2.0)
Animal seeks shade (*W*=0.88***)	0 (0)	20 (17-20)	0 (0)	0 (0-3.0)	0 (0)
Diarrhoea (*W*=0.52***)	4 (0-8.5)	0 (0)	11 (6.0-16)	0 (0)	4 (0-7.5)
Reduced milk yield (*W*=0.51***)	2 (0-4.0)	13 (7.0-20)	3 (0-9.0)	1 (0-2.5)	0 (0-1.0)
Coughing (*W*=0.76***)	0 (0-0.5)	0 (0-0.5)	0 (0-2.0)	19 (16.5-20)	0 (0-0.5)
Reduced appetite (*W*=0.54***)	0 (0)	13 (7.0-20)	0 (0)	5 (0-10)	0 (0)
Loss of tail hair (*W*=0.89***)	20 (16.5-20)	0 (0)	0 (0-3.5)	0 (0)	0 (0)
Tearing (*W*=0.28*)	6 (3.0-13)	2 (0-6.5)	4 (0-8.5)	0 (0-1.5)	3 (0-8.0)
Salivation (*W*=0.50***)	2 (0-3.0)	14 (7.0-20)	3 (0-6.5)	1 (0-2.0)	0 (0-0.5)

Figure 4.5 Matrix scoring of disease signs for diseases of adult cattle in Nyal (a Nuer area in South Sudan, 1999)
Notes: Number of informant groups = 12; *W* = Kendall's Coefficient of Concordance (*p<0.05; **p<0.01; ***p<0.001). The black dots represent the scores (number of seeds) that were used during the matrix scoring. In each cell of the matrix, median scores are presented with 95% confidence limits in parentheses. *Source:* Catley et al., 2001.

tested by PAVE used local disease terminology, local livestock age categories and – as a proportional method – avoided sensitive questions on the absolute number of livestock owned by an informant. An example of results derived from proportional piling is shown in Figure 4.6. Over time, matrix scoring and proportional piling were used not only to measure important epidemiological variables, but also, to explore association between disease and possible causal factors.

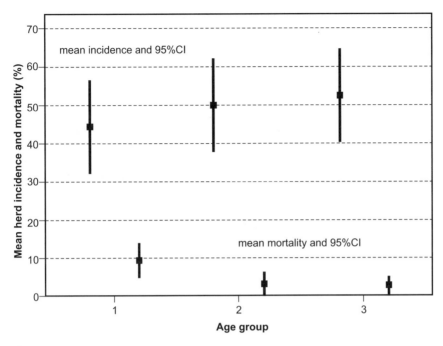

Figure 4.6 Estimates of the incidence and mortality of foot-and-mouth disease in Maasai herds in Tanzania
Notes: Results derived from proportional piling of cattle diseases by age group with 50 individual informants. Local disease names and local definitions of cattle age groups were used. Age group 1 = calves; age group 2 = young stock; age group 3 = adults.

In terms of assessing the validity of PE, the PAVE Project used a variety of conventional veterinary diagnostic methods, from clinical examination of livestock by a veterinarian to the use of laboratory tests. The project also used matrix scoring to compare the characterization and clinical diagnosis of diseases by pastoralists and veterinarians, and used quantitative analytical methods to show the similarity in clinical diagnostic ability between these two groups (Catley, 2006).

Targeted publications and peer-review

A specific strategy of the PAVE project was to publish the results of field studies in respected peer-reviewed journals. In part, this strategy was a response to the very limited use of participatory methods by veterinary researchers and an assumption that once PE studies were published, PE as an approach would become more widely accepted. All three of the field studies in PAVE were published in peer-reviewed journals (Table 4.2), and the initial survey of veterinarians mentioned above was published in the journal of the World Animal Health Organization (Catley, 2000). This series of peer-reviewed publications not only ensured that PAVE studies were subject to expert assessment, but also proved to be invaluable training resources, as described below.

Strategic training and experiential learning

From 2002 to 2004 the Pan African Programme for the Control of Epizootics, through a project funded by DFID called 'Community-based Animal Health and Participatory Epidemiology' (CAPE), supported a series of PE training and mentoring activities in East Africa. Drawing on experiences of institutionalizing participation in government bureaucracies (Thompson, 1995), CAPE aimed high. It assumed that within government veterinary services or veterinary schools, space for testing and discussing PE would not emerge unless senior managers had some understanding of PE approaches and methods. Therefore the first PE training course targeted national government epidemiologists and senior academic staff from veterinary schools from Eritrea, Ethiopia, Kenya, Sudan, Tanzania, Uganda and Somalia. Some specific elements of the training were:

- An initial focus on attitudes and behaviour, and the value of indigenous knowledge on livestock diseases.
- A comparison of the process of triangulation in PE and conventional veterinary diagnosis (which combines different methods and types of information).
- A comparison of optimal ignorance in PE with modern medical or veterinary practise. In the management of many medical or veterinary cases, clinicians rarely identify a specific disease agent – they simply treat the main symptoms.
- Analysis of peer-reviewed PAVE studies (as listed in Table 4.2) leading to a realization that it was possible to combine qualitative and quantitative data derived from PE, and also to publish in scientific journals.
- The role of conventional veterinary diagnostic or epidemiological methods to complement PE, often as one type of triangulation. This attention to the complementary nature of PE helped to remove fears that PE should replace conventional approaches.
- Field testing of PE methods during the training, and placing trainees face-to-face with livestock keepers.
- Attention to forms of PE that were purely qualitative but still very useful. In particular, the use of participatory disease searching during rinderpest eradication programmes was presented and discussed as an inductive, investigative approach.
- Discussion on how PE could be used to add value to the work of the trainees when they returned home.

Follow-up activities after the training included support to postgraduate programmes in veterinary schools in Addis Ababa and Nairobi. Masters students conducted research in pastoralist areas and results were presented in dissertations and, in some cases, in peer-reviewed journals (Mochabo et al. 2004; Rufael et al., 2008). The process of supporting postgraduate students was useful not only due to the experiential learning for the students themselves, but also because their academic supervisors were required to assess PE as an epidemiological approach. Other postgraduate research was later conducted in Kenya (Bedelian, 2004), Nigeria (Idowa, 2005) and Sudan (Elnarsi, 2006), supported by universities in Edinburgh, Ibadan and Khartoum respectively.

Continuous adaptation, wider application and policy influence

By 2007, PE methods had been adapted for a wide variety of uses and had begun to influence policy. In Ethiopia, the assessment of community-based animal health workers (Admassu et al., 2004) was one piece of evidence which led to their legal recognition. Also in Ethiopia, retrospective cohort studies using PE methods showed the limited impact of vaccination on livestock mortality during drought (Catley et al., 2008) and prompted various international and national actors to revise vaccination strategies and best practice. In East Africa, modelling studies on rinderpest (Mariner et al., 2005) helped to raise awareness of issues such as the role of low vaccination coverage in maintaining the disease in pastoralist areas. The cost-benefit analysis of foot and mouth disease in South Sudan (Barasa et al., 2008) produced results which showed that contrary to much professional veterinary opinion, the disease had an important impact on livelihoods and that vaccination made economic sense. Therefore, in areas where it was very difficult to use conventional research methods PE was beginning to fill important information gaps.

The value of PE has also been shown by its use beyond Africa and its promotion by international actors such as the Food and Agriculture Organization and the International Livestock Research Institute (Grace, 2003). The approach has been used in the rinderpest eradication programme in Pakistan, for avian influenza surveillance in south-east Asia, and for foot-and-mouth disease surveillance in eastern Turkey.

Challenges and future directions

The emergence of RRA, PRA and the wider group of participatory learning approaches was intended to improve the relevance and impact of development on poor people. In the area of veterinary medicine, has PE achieved this and if so, how? At one level veterinarians continue to use RRA/PRA methods for the design and evaluation of community-based animal health systems and, in terms of impact, this is perhaps the application of PE in its simplest and most useful form. In the last few years, community-based approaches have become more accepted by the veterinary establishment, and community-based animal health workers are recognized as one type of veterinary paraprofessional by the World Animal Health Organization. If these approaches can be further scaled up, basic PE has a role to play in designing and assessing community-based delivery systems.

At the level of disease control policies and strategies, PE studies have helped to fill gaps in knowledge on the epidemiology and economics of important livestock diseases in marginalized areas, as prioritized by both livestock keepers and veterinarians. Well-designed and focused studies have contributed to policy debate and often provided evidence and insights from areas where conventional epidemiology was very difficult to use. In many cases, PE methods have proved to be far more useful than questionnaires because many epidemiological questions are well-suited to the visualization and scoring methods of PE, and PE uses local language. Research on disease control options seemed to be most valuable when it responded to local priorities and was directly linked to delivery systems, thereby enabling the application of results. Therefore, when used well PE has much in common with participatory research (Conroy, 2004) and can lead to improvements in disease control, with associated benefits to livestock keepers.

As with many other types of participatory learning approaches, PE can be as extractive and data-driven as conventional research and like RRA and PRA, it requires proper training of practitioners and field experience. In common with many other participatory approaches and methods, the issues facing PE are still largely institutional, not methodological. While some research institutions are moving towards incentive arrangements which reward participatory research on animal health (Okuthe et al., 2003), there is still a long way to go to make veterinary research centres more responsive to the needs of poor livestock keepers. There is also the challenge of balancing the concerns of the international community, and local priorities. In international efforts such as the Global Rinderpest Eradication Programme, rinderpest was a disease which was prioritized by livestock keepers, government and international agencies. In the Horn of Africa, participatory approaches were used to good effect in rinderpest eradication in more difficult operational environments, and included community-based delivery systems and participatory disease searching. For other diseases, such as avian influenza, local prioritization of this disease is likely to vary considerably between and within countries and therefore, surveillance and control efforts are likely to become more top-down than bottom-up.

Agricultural innovation for rural development: a Master's programme for professionals working in rural areas in Peru

Maria E. Fernandez and Oscar Ortiz

One of the main challenges of a 'Farmer First' approach is institutionalizing it so that it becomes a permanent component of agricultural research and development. Despite the fact that participatory research and principles were developed at least three decades ago, there are few cases of institutionalization. One of the reasons may be that most of the efforts have been oriented to working with institutions which are in direct contact with farmers while much less attention has been paid to institutions that provide professional and technical training for field workers.

As a result, agronomists and animal science specialists who work directly with farmers and their organizations do not have the knowledge and skills to understand or facilitate participatory processes. One of the main challenges as we move forward then is to complement the often narrow training of agricultural professionals with a more holistic understanding of the social and economic phenomena related to agriculture. The demand for professionals with a more holistic understanding of the importance of participation for innovation, market development, action-oriented research and environmental sustainability is already on the increase.

In 1998, a small group of professors with experience in participatory processes and agricultural development at the National Agrarian University in Lima (UNALM), Peru, was invited to develop a Master's course. Representatives of non-governmental and governmental institutions defined skill needs and priorities and the programme 'Agricultural Innovation for Rural Development' began operation in 2001 (http://www.lamolina.edu.pe/Postgrado/innovacion2005/Default1.htm). Although there was strong support for such an innovative programme at the highest levels of the University – presidency and post-graduate school – organizational bottlenecks were quickly identified. The most challenging of these was the fact that the University was geared mainly to technical fields and had few staff with the experience or qualifications to teach the new topics identified at post-graduate level. As a result, highly qualified professionals from non-governmental institutions, private consultants, other universities or international research organizations, working as visiting professors, were engaged. A link with the Institute for Sustainable Smallholder Production (IPPS), for example, provides the Masters students with opportunities such as involvement in interdisciplinary action-research projects, participation in inter-learning and local planning processes, and institutional networking with their peers nation-wide.

The second challenge was to organize the programme in such a way that fully employed professionals from all over the country could attend. In consultation with prospective candidates, it was found that time for study would not be allowed by the majority of institutions (mainly municipalities, NGOs and government organizations). As a result, the time dedicated to face-to-face courses in a given year could not exceed vacation times. As a result, it was decided to offer the 10 courses as week-long modules over a two-year period. Furthermore, and at the request of participants, the modules were organized in different regions of the country. At the beginning, professors decided where modules might best be organized, but over time the students themselves began offering support to the organization of modules in places where they worked and could provide appropriate practical learning. Readings are provided to the students electronically one month before each module and final papers are due one month after a module has been offered. In some cases, distance learning techniques are utilized including virtual forums and chat sessions.

One of the salient characteristics of the programme is its commitment to building a network of professionals nationally who can provide long-term support to each other. Each class of students (maximum 15) learns to work together and support each other during the two years of their studies. Programming of modules takes into account the occasional doubling up of classes so that different classes of students have an opportunity to get to know each other.

The highest demand has been from agriculture-related professionals, mainly from agronomy and animal sciences, making up 70 per cent of participants between 2003 and 2007. These professionals feel the need to complement their technical education with social science related issues and skills. Candidates have expressed the need to understand rural people's views and aspirations for their families and communities if they are to help design and promote changes that are in line with their expectations.

In October 2006 a group of students doing the module titled 'Agrarian Knowledge and Information Systems' were given the task of assessing the impact of the programme on the national agrarian and information system. Some of their findings are summarized in Table 4.3.

Although students have indicated that course content is directly applicable to their work, and that it has contributed to an increase in capacity for planning and implementing development interventions, including the use of participatory methods, the UNALM has been slow to take ownership. The development of capabilities within the university is very slow and may influence the future sustainability of the Master's programme. To date the UNALM has not taken full responsibility for the programme and some 70 per cent of lecturers are visiting professors who have neither voice nor vote

Table 4.3 Limitations and opportunities of the Agricultural Innovation for Rural Development programme

Limitations of the programme	Opportunities the programme provides
• Limited diffusion of the objectives and innovative activities of the Master's programme within the university • Limited capacity or willingness of the university to include more diverse institutions and professionals to teach in the programme as visiting lecturers • Inflexible university regulations that hinder modular and decentralized activities by not facilitating administrative procedures • Students are not as active as they could be in lobbying for change despite their manifested interest in becoming involved in the programme • The Post-Graduate School and the Department have not bought into the 'project', as evidenced by the high number of visiting professors the programme relies on • Not all visiting professors have the time to advise thesis research projects, which usually study participatory processes	• Students from the provinces have the opportunity to interact with nationally and internationally known professors and lecturers • Students have the opportunity to learn about rural development issues in different parts of a diverse country and access to experiences from different institutions • UNALM and the students can take advantage of alliances and cross-accreditation with universities internationally • IPPS provides support to students and catalyses exchange and networking • Key stakeholders (GOs, NGOs and Farmer Organizations) become aware of the need for better coordination and exchange as a result of exchanges among students • National and regional networks are built among professionals who share development strategies

in matters that affect the decision-making process of either the programme or the Department or the Post-graduate school. Within the UNALM's Faculty of Agriculture there are few opportunities for, or a lack of staff interest in, interdisciplinary degrees, particularly when these involve the Social Sciences. The university will have to become more flexible if it is to accommodate innovation and respond to the demands of decentralization and participatory development.

Despite the difficulties of institutionalization, the programme is an example of a formal Master's course in the most important agrarian university of Peru that is attempting to mainstream participatory principles for rural development. It provides an opportunity for agricultural and other professionals to receive formal training on principles and methods from the perspective of multi-stakeholder involvement in locally managed development for agroecological, community and rural livelihood sustainability.

Mainstreaming participatory rural development studies in China

Li Xiaoyun, Xu Xiuli, Qi Gubo, Lu Min and Ronnie Vernooy

New roles for higher education

The Ministry of Education (MoE) in the People's Republic of China is currently implementing an ambitious and wide-ranging policy reform process to respond to rapidly changing societal demands (Zhou Ji, 2004). Here we reflect on these reforms in the light of some of the main policy directions as set out by the current Minister of Education, Zhou Ji (2005), in his book *Higher Education in China*. Using a recent initiative to institutionalize post-graduate education in Community-Based Natural Resource Management (CBNRM) at China Agricultural University (CAU) in Beijing and Jilin Agricultural University (JLAU) in Changchun as an action-learning case study, we assess the feasibility of implementing the policy reforms.

Expected reform results

On March 3, 2004, the State Council approved the 2003–7 *'Action Plan for Invigorating Education'* by the MoE. This plan is the blueprint for all parties involved in education to implement the strategies of *'Rejuvenating China through Science and Education'* and *'Reinvigorating China through Human Resource Development'* and to speed up educational reform and development in the years to come. The new policy directions set out in the Action Plan are based on the observation that China's society is changing rapidly and that the traditional, rigidly top-down way of organizing and managing the higher education system will no longer provide the country with the necessary human resources 'to achieve modernization' (Zhou Ji, 2005: xiii).

From these fundamental insights, a number of challenges follow. The major ones are described as: 1) training a variety of specialized professionals that meet the demands of socio-economic development; 2) strengthening students' abilities, particularly practical, innovative, creative and entrepreneurial skills; and 3) sharing quality resources (or inputs) more effectively and efficiently, i.e. among the organizations within the system (ibid: 85).

Establishing academic specialities and reforming student training

In order to create new specialities, a number of inputs need to be brought together, according to the ministerial plans: a clear description of the content matter (general level as well as course level), a feasible education plan, a sufficient number of qualified teachers, adequate materials and equipment, and funds. The following guidelines are provided for the adjustment of curricula: increase the general knowledge; increase the number of elective courses; emphasize practical, experimental and social-interaction based courses; employ a cross-disciplinary perspective; use creativity, and stimulate research as part of teaching and training (ibid: 100).

Parallel to the redefinition of specialities, student-training modalities require changes. Narrowly planned and executed training is no longer appropriate. The main directions to follow now are a greater emphasis on basic knowledge and comprehensive abilities, the development of practical skills at the undergraduate level, combining science and arts (this is called 'interdisciplinarity'), the integration of theoretical and practical training, and a greater freedom for students to select courses of their own interest (ibid: 88).

Of special interest are a number of measures proposed to improve graduate education. These include the provision of subsidies to outstanding PhD students, the publication of outstanding degree theses, and the improvement of quality evaluation criteria and information systems to ensure credible graduate evaluations (ibid: 93-94). The development of new specialities, courses and teaching modalities are all part of today's teaching management practices. In addition, the Minister identifies three other elements required for high quality: 1) the adoption of up-to-date textbooks and course materials; 2) the use of modern educational methods based on interaction with students and elicitation of their ideas; and 3) the offering of advice to students (ibid: 90). Teachers, students and senior management staff are all responsible for quality control.

Having outlined some of the main elements of the reform policy, we now turn to the practice.

Introducing participatory curriculum development

In 2005, after many months of preparatory work by a group of teachers, researchers and students, a novel introductory course on CBNRM was delivered at the College of Humanities and Development (COHD), China Agricultural University, Beijing. A group of 24 MSc and PhD students took part in this first post-graduate level CBNRM course in China, with financial and technical support from the International Development Research Centre (IDRC) of Canada. Ten teachers and researchers with backgrounds in both natural and social sciences from a variety of higher education and research organizations, contributed to this pioneering process as course facilitators. The students follow one of the three main programmes at COHD: rural development and management, sociology or regional economics.

The course was developed using a participatory curriculum development methodology and guided by insights from modern adult teaching and learning theory and practice (Taylor, 2003; Qi Gubo et al., 2008). The course is offered as an elective course. Languages used are both Chinese and English, more or less equally. Course materials include a new textbook (in English; we plan to produce a revised textbook in Chinese), so-called Learner's and Facilitator's workbooks (in English), and a binder with additional readings (in English and Chinese).

We use a variety of teaching and research tools. In the courses, these range from case study analysis (and comparison of cases), critical literature review, group proposal writing, group reporting on field research, production of an audio-visual report on the field work, to a puzzle game and role play. In the field research, students themselves, with some guidance from facilitators/ teachers, select a variety of tools, usually including individual and group interviews, participatory mapping (of the natural resource base, and/or of social networks and organizational context), participatory ranking exercises, participant observation, group discussion, photographing and videoing, and role play (as a feedback tool). Participatory monitoring and evaluation tools are used throughout the whole process (Vernooy et al., 2008).

Following delivery of the COHD CBNRM course in 2005 and again in early 2006, a similar course entitled 'Participatory Rural Development: An Introduction' was developed and offered at JLAU in late spring of 2006. Since then, the new courses have been offered yearly at both COHD and JLAU. In 2008, and inspired by colleagues at COHD and JLAU, Hebei Agricultural University followed suit with a new Participatory Rural Development (PRD) course. Several other universities have expressed an interest to continue the innovation process.

To practise active and meaningful participation in teaching and learning is still a novel methodology in China. Introducing, experimenting with, and assessing this methodology in CAU, and later in JLAU, turned out to be a very enriching experience. The course development experiences are part of a larger COHD-led action research and capacity development initiative entitled 'Participatory Learning, Curriculum Development and Mainstreaming of CBNRM in Higher Education in China', which aims to contribute to the development and implementation of CBNRM approaches in rural China (COHD, 2004).

Attuning to reality: training responsive rural development professionals

The general objective of the course was to enable participants to 'use CBNRM concepts, principles and methods for the design of participatory action research proposals relevant to Chinese rural development realities'. A number of interrelated learning objectives are addressed in five linked modules:

- Defining the key elements of a CBNRM approach based on a review of selected international literature and guidance provided by the course facilitators, resulting in a coherent appreciation of interlinked concepts, principles and methodology.
- Trying out a CBNRM research approach in a rural situation in China.
- Differentiating between effective and ineffective joint action learning processes and methodologies, supported by selected literature, a comparative assessment of the field-research assignments, and the guidance of facilitators.
- *For PhD students*: Identifying elements from the international CBNRM literature useful for doing research in the Chinese context, through critical individual reading combined with group discussion of self-selected references.
- Designing a draft CBNRM action research proposal that is clear, coherent, relevant and feasible.

Fellowship support

In 2006, with funding from IDRC, we initiated the Fellowship Support programme to encourage students to carry out thesis fieldwork oriented to CBNRM/PRD, and practise what they have learned in the courses. The objectives of the programme include:

- strengthening participatory action and learning knowledge and skills for CBNRM;
- deepening the understanding of the complexity of Chinese rural realities and of the rural development challenges being faced by local people; and
- contributing to local rural development efforts through joint action research and development.

The Fellowship support allows MSc and PhD students to go to the field for three and six months respectively. This component provides space for students to explore longer-term commitment to a rural development 'project', e.g. by linking to a long-term research or development effort carried out by CAU, JLAU or one of their partners.

During this process, the Fellowship management team (made up of staff and students) organizes regular seminars. These seminars bring interested students and staff together to exchange experiences and insights, support each other, and identify common challenges, questions and interests. Results from the seminars held so far suggest that they contribute significantly to deepening the learning process and forging bonds among students and staff.

Strengthening students' comprehensive abilities

Active student involvement is central in the courses and the Fellowship support programme. They take part in discussion, design, planning, implementation, monitoring and evaluation, and documentation of the efforts. This includes such activities as peer review of proposals, management and administration of funds, reporting, and organization of seminars and exchange events. A golden rule applied throughout the processes is 'no lectures/no lecturing'. We have stuck to this principle in order to encourage learning through active discovery, i.e. 'learning by doing'. In the courses, this has allowed us to combine theoretical insights that support CBNRM (such as from rural development sociology, agro-ecology, political science) with practice.

The course and related fieldwork have made a start in developing the skills for valuing and, more importantly, using a CBNRM approach in today's rural China. This includes elements such as analysing situations and problems from a people's (social actor's) perspective with a holistic and interdisciplinary scientific approach, combining natural and social science knowledge and methods, and keeping a critical eye on the socio-economic and socio-political dimensions of natural resource management and rural development generally. Students and staff have improved their abilities to define CBNRM/PRD oriented research questions, and develop (partially) action-focused CBNRM/PRD research proposals. From a very hard struggle with defining research questions in the first place, students have come a long way (Zhang Li, 2008).

But the exercises in the class and in the field also opened our eyes to the 'darker' side of working for rural development. Many students increased their (theoretical) understanding of participatory action research and CBNRM/PRD, but observed that practising it adequately is still a major challenge.

Creating synergies: sharing quality resources more effectively and efficiently

Our efforts bring together several organizations, reducing professional isolation and building bridges between curricula. This teamwork allows us to bring an inter-disciplinary perspective to the courses, and to the supervision of fieldwork. Our cooperation is instrumental in bringing different *local* perspectives to the forefront, as project leaders from various agroecological sites and socio-economic contexts come together and join forces. This is enriching for students and facilitators/teachers and provides the opportunity to compare and contrast field-study cases, insights and experiences, and to search for commonalities and particularities. Diversity in this way truly brings more life to the course. Another important advantage of this kind of team-effort is the possibility to engage in collective instead of individual content and process reflection. Responsibilities are then carried on multiple shoulders.

Reflecting on the teamwork in a broader innovation perspective, we put forward the suggestion that our positive achievements have much to do with the horizontally oriented, self-organizing nature of our working and learning groups. Assigning tasks and responsibility to the practitioners themselves is another key feature. Collegial relationships are the focus of attention, not reporting relationships. This produces knowledge that is 'close to the ground', with an immediate use.

Conclusions

So far, the CBNRM (PRD) mainstreaming process has been a very enriching experience for all involved. It has also been very labour and time-intensive. But now that the initial steps have been set, we expect that this intensity will be reduced over time. Careful preparations, a strong team, clear intent, good technical and financial support, ongoing and systematic monitoring, involving students as much as possible, and a continuous focus on learning-by-doing have been important to keep things going and on track. The course working groups and the Fellowship support team have been instrumental in the work done to date. Bringing together an interdisciplinary team from various organizations and involving a large number of students are two of the success factors. Insights from theory have served and will serve as guideposts, but it is practice that tells us what works, what does not and where improvement can best be made. We are now ready for further curriculum adjustments.

The new courses and related activities, including our collaborative teaching and research management efforts (including functions such as coordination, facilitation, administration, monitoring and evaluation, documentation and reporting), have opened our eyes, minds and hearts in terms of innovative and inspiring ways to reform Chinese higher education. We have discovered the relevance of CBNRM as a new speciality, in relation to the many potentialities and problems embedded in the complex and rapidly changing rural realities across China. These realities, through our efforts to 'bring' them to the very core of the courses, effectively *create* the curriculum. As a result, we have sharpened our sense of the dynamic (but not easy) roles rural development professionals could play in today's rapidly changing China. Our involvement in the courses and related field-research is guiding us to a new perspective on our studies and work, central to which are the connections with each other and with the people with whom we cooperate in China's rural areas across the country. We are now trying to apply this new perspective in our practice.

Making trans-disciplinary science work for resource-poor farmers

Niels Röling and Janice Jiggins

Strands of experience

Here we address two complementary, but distinct arenas: 1) resource-poor farmers, the outcomes of their farming and the opportunity context within which these outcomes are generated; and 2) agricultural science in interaction with resource-poor agriculture. For each arena, we formulate propositions that are followed by conclusions for action. These particularly need to be taken into consideration by research institutes and universities if they are successfully to meet the needs of resource-poor farmers.

We base our discussion on three strands of experience. The first is a major research programme in Benin and Ghana, 'Convergence of Sciences (CoS)', which started in 2002 and ended with a 'bang' in October 2006 with the simultaneous graduation of eight African and one Dutch PhD students who had carried out research with groups of small-scale African farmers on integrated management of pests and weeds, soil fertility and genetic diversity, and a study of the 'pathways of science' required to develop and execute 'winning ideas'. The second strand comprises our long-standing experience as social scientists in agricultural universities. The final strand derives from our participation in the International Assessment of Agricultural Science and Technology for Development (IAASTD), which assessed agricultural knowledge, science and technology by looking at history, challenges and the options for action, informed by explicit normative goals: nutritional security, livelihoods, human health, and environmental sustainability from a short and longer-term perspective (to 2050). The outcomes of the IAASTD remain contested (cf. Anon, 2008a; Anon, 2008b; Kiers et al., 2008; Stokstad, 2008). The controversies highlight some of the key issues that arise in trans-disciplinary science involving multiple stakeholders.

Resource-poor agriculture

Proposition 1: The principle of Comparative Advantage causes the poverty of resource-poor farmers and degradation of their resources. Resource-poor farmers face unfair competition from farmers in industrial countries and emergent economies. In these conditions, to accept comparative advantage as a design principle for global agricultural trade condemns the 60 per cent of Africans who live by farming to poverty, and their land and other resources to degradation. Pitting resource-poor farmers against farmers who have already captured economies of scale pre-empts the opportunities of the former.

Conclusion: Market protection, accompanied by measures to create access to remunerative markets, credits, inputs and other essentials, is a necessary condition for improving the opportunities of resource-poor farmers. However, protection is anathema to economists, let alone to people who benefit from the current situation.

Proposition 2: African resource-poor farmers are innovative. African agriculture is typically depicted as 'stagnant', but low productivity is not surprising when it is not rational for resource-poor farmers to produce surpluses. That does not mean African agriculture is stagnant. During recent decades, African farmers have adapted to rapid rural population growth notwithstanding the collapse of shifting cultivation, the emergence of pernicious herbaceous weeds, the loss of soil fertility, the reduction of farm sizes and widespread feminization of agriculture, not to speak of the HIV-AIDS pandemic, wars and conflicts and climatic change. Because the opportunities for commercial food production for most remain small, resource-poor farming largely remains (adaptive and innovative) subsistence farming.

Conclusion: The assumption that low productivity is *the* problem of African agriculture, and that therefore intensification must be promoted through a Green Revolution for Africa, is based on a misdiagnosis and means, in effect, more of the same and more wasted years. The question for policy is not: how do I improve farm productivity in Sub-Saharan Africa (SSA), but how can I create opportunities for resource-poor farmers to make some money by farming?

Proposition 3: Institutional development is a necessary precursor to economic growth (North, 2005). A common approach to agricultural development in SSA assumes that agricultural intensification with science-based technology must improve farm-level productivity. Yet the Netherlands, for example reached its position as one of the top three exporters of agricultural products as a result of painstaking attention to and support for institutional development: cooperative banking and input purchasing, land tenure laws, subsidized credit, a huge public apparatus for agricultural research, extension and education, farmers' organizations, and so on. In Africa, Structural Adjustment meant tearing down whatever institutional development had taken place in agriculture.

Conclusion: The current emphasis on science and technology as the entry-point for agricultural development in Africa must shift to an emphasis on institutions that allow resource-poor farming to become more productive and sustainable. Technology availability is not the most constraining factor, opportunity is.

Proposition 4: Brokered Long-term Contractual Arrangements (BLCAs) put money into resource-poor farmers' pockets. A BLCA can be arranged by a farmers' cooperative, a private company, a parastatal or a state trading enterprise that puts together a package of support which allows small farmers to engage in the production of a marketable commodity such as tea, organically grown fruits or other products that farmers cannot easily sell elsewhere. The package typically includes inputs, marketing services, credit and knowledge, and sometimes price stabilization. Small farmers act as out-growers by adopting the package. For instance, the Kenya Tea Development Authority has enabled thousands of small-scale farmers to produce a larger share of Kenya's tea exports than the commercial planters.

Conclusion: BLCAs can create the institutional conditions for expanding market opportunities for some farmers. It is difficult for resource-poor farmers to cater for the demands of supermarkets (Berdegué, 2001), yet supermarkets are capturing an increasing share of the food retail market in developing countries (Reardon, et al., 2003). The BLCA is a tested approach for creating the mix of institutional and technical support that allows resource-poor farmers to access supermarkets.

Agricultural science

Proposition 5: Agricultural research, at best, establishes what is technically possible in a certain agro-ecological zone. However, when scientists make assumptions as to what is useful or desirable, the result is often that the new technologies are not used and remain 'on the shelf' (e.g. NERICA rice varieties). Farmers need to be involved directly in the research.

Conclusion: Zeroing in on the constrained possibilities for technological change faced by resource-poor farmers requires a carefully crafted 'pathway of science' that is kept open-ended by minimizing the 'pre-analytical choices' (Giampietro, 2003; Röling et al., 2004) made before the experimental programme (Nederlof et al., 2007). Pre-analytical decisions, such as selecting certain disciplines to be involved and not others, or defining desirable dependent variables (such as tonnes per hectare), cut off avenues of potentially greater value. To keep all options open, one initially needs a procedure to zero in on what works, is feasible and desirable for the 'ultimate users' who have to live by the results.

Proposition 6: The 'technological treadmill' has obviously failed to reduce rural poverty, especially in Africa. The prevalent model assumes farms to be small firms engaged in the production of the same commodity. Since they are each too small to affect the price, they are all price takers and try to produce as much as possible against the going price. A new technology allows early adopters to capture a windfall profit, but when others follow, this squeezes the price to a point where those who have not yet adopted are forced to adopt or drop out. Their resources are taken up by the 'stayers' and so it goes on, in an endless rat race that creates economies of scale and puts a downward pressure on commodity prices.

Conclusion: An all out effort is required on the part of agricultural economics and policy institutions to develop a better model (Jiggins et al., 1996). Such a model would not look at agriculture as the business of producing only tradable commodities, but would recognize agriculture's place-based multi-functionality in ensuring the continuation of the ecological services on which all life depends as well as its role in local food systems, cultural landscapes and community life. It would look at ways to internalize the high social and environmental costs of agriculture, take food sovereignty seriously and focus on creating fair access to remunerative markets.

Proposition 7: Agricultural research institutes and universities are often dominated by agricultural economists and natural scientists, who typically do not consider the behaviour of real people and social processes as part of their mandate. These institutions have not, as a rule, opened up a discourse about the core of their mandate: how to manage the largely anthropogenic future of ecosystems across all system levels.

Conclusion: The poverty of resource-poor farmers, and especially their lack of prospects and the continual degradation of the resources they depend on, especially in SSA, is part of the anthropogenic predicament. It is the mandate of agricultural research institutes and universities to create fresh perspectives for sustainable futures, and move beyond the mental models that have proven inadequate or downright dangerous. This will require collaboration between natural scientists, agricultural economists and social scientists.

Final reflections

Making trans-disciplinary science work for resource-poor farmers is an issue that requires a global perspective. A key challenge in this regard is to develop curricula that encourage trans-disciplinary science. Taking account of the propositions outlined above would provide a useful starting point for agricultural research and academic institutions in training a new generation of scientists capable of collaborating to tackle the problems of resource-poor farmers in an integrated manner.

The IAASTD is a good sign of the growing recognition by the international community of the need for a more trans-disciplinary approach. This multi-stakeholder process has led to major mutual learning. In the final reports inconsistencies, contradictions and inclusion of both conservative and forward-looking positions remain. But for those who want to find it, there is space for change.

Participation, paternalism and practicality: reconciling sustainability science and indigenous agendas

Robert E. Rhoades

In pursuit of enriching research

What indigenous peoples in the Andes demand is not necessarily a choice of participatory rather than formal research, but a new, mature relationship with outsiders. Indigenous leaders speak of 'equity without paternalism' and 'development with identity'. In this regard, Waters-Bayer (1994) has drawn a useful distinction between 'extractive research', which meets the needs of development agencies and NGOs, and 'enriching research', which is collaborative, addresses local people's values and priorities and helps them to achieve their own goals. Formal, scientific-led research is not necessarily extractive, nor is participatory research necessarily enriching.

Since 1997, I have led an interdisciplinary team of agricultural and natural resource scientists working with UNORCAC (Union of Campesino and Indigenous Organizations of Cotacachi), an indigenous organization, and the cantonal government of Cotacachi, Ecuador, to provide research findings to help make informed decisions about the management of natural resources and agriculture locally. Our project, Sustainable Agriculture and Natural Resource Management (SANREM)-Andes, had a mandate to carry out research and promote reliable information and decision-support tools for sustainable development in mountain regions of the world (see also Turin, this book). The study area is located in the Ecuadorian highland region just north of the equator in the eastern part of Cotacachi canton where approximately 18,000 indigenous people live in 40 communities (*comunas*) distributed around the 'skirt' (*falda*) of Mama Cotacachi, a 4,993 masl volcano.

While our sustainability research was place-based in Ecuador, as scientists we were funded to do research which illuminated scale issues beyond Cotacachi. As academics, we faced pressure from fellow scientists, donors and technical reviewers to meet high standards of rigorous methods and data gathering. However, while scientists see field activities such as collecting soil and water samples, setting up rain simulators or climate monitoring stations, administering long questionnaires or measuring farm sizes as important for providing information for decision making by local communities and decision makers, their immediate relevancy is not so clear to local people.

Our hosts were looking for enriching research. Only in rare cases was there a neat overlap between scientists' and local peoples' interests. For diverse reasons, Cotacacheños were interested in having information they could use to obtain grants, justify projects to the government, create leverage in negotiations and so on. At the same time, we had to do our jobs as scientists, operating in a wider donor and professional arena.

This situation led us to ask: 1) what kind of research did Cotacacheños want, if any? and 2) how could we reconcile local needs with our wider sustainability research? The process of agreeing on an exchange of research for local benefits was not straightforward. A great deal of negotiation between researchers and local people took place on many levels: with the leadership of UNORCAC, individual communities and their leaders, farmers, schools and professors, and water associations. Agreements were often reached through informal conversations or gatherings in which local people would express certain needs which we could fulfil. Specific interests based on real problems were expressed by Cotacacheños in ways that could help them achieve their goal of 'development with identity'. By addressing these requests, SANREM was allowed to stay and continue to do research of interest only to scientists. In the process, trust and confidence grew and friendships were formed. In this regard, our approach was less like 'participation' and more like traditional ethnography (which has been criticized by some advocates of participatory rural appraisal).

By directing resources to research topics identified by local people, a social credit was created for us to pursue research questions not prioritized by them and that otherwise might have been considered extractive (Rhoades and Nazarea, 2006). Three examples of this enriching research are discussed below.

Indigenous children's scholarship fund and biodiversity research

Cotacacheños always stressed the need for education of indigenous children. We therefore agreed to fund selected indigenous children to attend primary or secondary school, and even college, if they would interview their elders on the topic of landraces, using the memory-banking method. The purpose of the project was to document and preserve local knowledge associated with agricultural crops so that neither seeds nor knowledge would be lost (Nazarea, 1998). The children also collected culturally significant plant samples and prepared them for display and storage, as well as planting and maintaining a biodiversity garden. Thus, two goals were accomplished: scientists gained information about changing agrobiodiversity and children were able to learn how to carry out research and attend school.

Farmer-led in situ agrobiodiversity farm

An outgrowth of the memory-banking project was the establishment of a participatory farm in the high zone of Cotacachi called the Ancestral Futures Farm. Its two main objectives were to: 1) create an *in situ* farm whereby culturally significant Andean crops could be grown out and re-distributed to local people; and 2) collaborate with the national genetic resources bank at the Instituto Nacional Autónomo de Investigaciones Agropecurias (INIAP) by obtaining and growing out disappearing Andean crops with local participation. The farm benefited both scientists and local people. Local people received new varieties, exchanged them among themselves, took home some food and received support for their children to go to school. Scientists, in turn, received a great deal of information about local varieties.

The participatory 3-D 'maqueta' model

UNORCAC's leadership needed natural resource information and decision-support tools to help with planning and in negotiations with donors. They also requested information to help them interact with member communities and to help establish planning priorities. One example of how we contributed to UNORCAC's decision support was the construction of a 1:10,000 scale, three-dimensional model of the Cotacachi Andean landscape, called the P3DM (Participatory 3 Dimensional Model) or *maqueta* in Spanish. The use of the *maqueta* in the Andes goes back to Inca times, when physical models were used to plan towns, agricultural fields and irrigation systems. We built and used the model as part of a participatory process whereby spatial information is combined with people's knowledge for advocacy, awareness raising, community planning, conflict resolution and participatory monitoring and evaluation.

The model offered a unique educational opportunity that enabled local people and scientists to visualize and understand issues of human–environment interactions. For the community, it provided a platform for dialogue concerning watershed management and natural resource use. The *maqueta* also enabled researchers to pinpoint local geographical knowledge on the landscape and analyse it in the broader context of the regional economy and ecology.

Conclusion

Our Andean experience shows that local communities want a relationship with researchers that is enriching, not extractive. 'Enriching' does not necessarily mean participatory in a methodological sense. Projects labelled 'participatory' led by NGOs or scientists can be just as extractive as conventional R&D. As indigenous individuals receive education outside their communities and are exposed to global activities, they are becoming increasingly more sophisticated and practical in their understanding of research. Cotacachi indigenous leaders are now writing proposals and running development projects. Researchers who understand and respect self-determination by local communities can negotiate their own scientific programmes by seeking common ground. Working on locally defined problems and doing globally relevant science are not inherent contradictions. In the Andean context the key to reconciling the needs of scientists and of local needs is seeking new forms of equitable collaboration which reach beyond the present and now somewhat tired discourse of 'participation'.

Power, progression and regression in learning for agriculture and development

Jethro Pettit

Introduction

While there have been many successes with alternative learning programmes, there is also a tendency toward 'regression' or 'bouncing back'. Many innovative pedagogical efforts – based on principles of experiential, cyclical and reflective learning – have reverted over time to more conventional, content-driven and top-down forms of education. Learners too often regress to familiar ways of being prior to their educational experience. Rather than focusing on barriers in the external environment – e.g. market forces, institutional conventions or prevailing ideologies – I wonder whether we need to look within progressive pedagogies themselves for gaps which may have left these approaches unable to challenge power differences and have left those involved susceptible to re-conformity. How can learning be facilitated in such a way that it contributes to enduring changes in power relations?

Alternative learning approaches

Enormous innovations in agricultural and development-related education have occurred in the last two to three decades. Even if these changes have been gradual, partial and have faced institutional resistance, there is an awareness among many educators and trainers of the need for alternatives to conventional, content-driven and transfer-of-technology forms of teaching and learning. As a result of this shift, many changes have taken place in the ways in which agricultural scientists, extension workers, rural development workers and farmers are taught or supported to learn what they need to know – be it scientific concepts, process and communication skills, technologies or agricultural methods.

Of course, conventional forms of education and training have also persisted – and have often resisted these alternatives. But it is impossible to deny the impact of numerous efforts to innovate in the way learning and teaching is done, or to ignore the difference these initiatives continue to make in many places. A range of progressive educational traditions have contributed to these changes, and the traditions have themselves evolved as their methodologies have been applied to learning and teaching within agriculture and development. A generalized and incomplete list of these traditions, in no particular order, would have to include:

- adult education;
- popular education;
- learning process approaches;
- reflective learning;
- participatory methodologies;
- action research and action learning;
- experiential learning;
- critical pedagogy;
- transformational learning; and
- systems and complexity thinking.

Within agriculture an abundance of innovations in learning methods can be found. For example, in approaches to participatory technology development, farmer-led research and extension, farmer-to-farmer movements, farmer field schools and experiments in alternative higher education in places like Wageningen, Hawkesbury, Cornell and many others. While there are important differences within and between these traditions and centres of innovation, most share certain key principles that challenge conventional educational norms and which are particularly worth highlighting:

- Experience – recognizing learners' experiences (both past and potential) as a vital form of knowledge that can be integrated with taught content. Within agriculture there is particular interest in building on learners' own experiences and knowledge, especially forms of 'local' or 'indigenous' knowledge which can enhance or challenge 'scientific' knowledge.
- Cycles – facilitating cycles of action, reflection, conceptualization and experimentation. The way these cycles are conceived and practised varies, but many educators share certain basic intentions to make links between practical and theoretical knowledge, usually through some kind of reflection. In the field of agricultural development, many field-based learning programmes have been designed successfully around this principle.
- Reflection – deepening processes of reflection to help learners uncover and interrogate their underlying values, assumptions, ideologies, etc. and to become aware of the foundations of their own and others' perspectives and actions. Reflection and reflective practice are usually connected with an intention to facilitate some degree of personal (or group) consciousness or transformation that is seen as necessary to bring about wider change.

Of course, many additional dimensions can be found within certain traditions. The pedagogical orientation will vary, depending upon which theories of change are adhered to, and whether the key elements of learning are seen as being primarily technical, rational, discursive, ideological, psychological, cultural, systemic, etc. (or some combination of these). The attention given to knowledge and power relations also varies, and informs the choice of learning methods. Nonetheless, it is fair to say that many alternative educators and initiatives have sought to combine these three key principles in one way or another for progressive learning.

Progression or regression?

At the same time, there has been a tendency toward regression or 'bouncing back'. Old habits die hard. One could take time here to point to the ways in which educational norms, historical trends, donor agendas, market and employment pressures, corporate interests, intransigent bureaucracies and various socially embedded relations of power and knowledge contribute to this resistance to progressive educational change. However, I would like to focus here not so much on the 'extra-curricular' institutional and ideological sources of resistance; instead, I wonder whether there are tendencies toward regression within the alternative pedagogies themselves.

What is it about the way that we conceive of and facilitate alternative learning that leaves us with the scope to 'bounce back' to our habitual practices – whether as educators or as learners? Why is it so terribly difficult to shift relations of power and knowledge, even with the very best of pedagogies? Who is really benefiting from the learning, and why do the knowledge, power and interests of some always seem to prevail over others?

One place to look carefully is the three key principles outlined above. In practice, these principles seem to be at their most effective when developing the linguistic and conceptual abilities of learners to recognize and interrogate dominant models of knowledge – both their own and those of others. The principles provide powerful tools for questioning these models, taking them apart, re-constructing them, or trading them in for entirely new ones based on new values and assumptions. Methods of critical analysis, conscientization, reflective practice, systems thinking and many forms of power analysis are used in this process. The commitment to building on experience and practice is also there, importantly, as a way to complete and renew cycles of learning, and in order to connect life experience with abstract concepts. In short, most alternative learning approaches are brilliant at enabling learners to think critically about different ways of seeing and being in the world. But at a certain point they seem to fall short in bringing about more internalized and enduring changes in relations of power and knowledge.

Beyond the linguistic and conceptual

An idea which needs exploring is that many (but not all) of the alternative learning approaches used in agriculture and development, largely with adult learners, are still primarily aimed at facilitating linguistic and conceptual understandings. Many learning cycles, learning loops, transformative learning processes, hierarchies of different kinds of knowledge and intelligences, and other models of reflective and experiential learning, while celebrating diverse ways of learning and knowing, still seem to privilege textual, linguistic and conceptual sense-making as the apex of learning and cognition.

There are some good reasons for this emphasis, but in so doing we pay insufficient attention to other ways of learning and knowing that may be more embodied, intuitive, emotional, imaginal, creative or spiritual in nature. These are aspects of learning and professional development that tend to be played down in both conventional and alternative education. Exceptions can be found in learning approaches such as theatre for development, popular communication, community media, storytelling and the like. Many educators, psychologists, neurologists, creative artists, writers and others have also explored these dimensions, and it is worth looking at what they may have to offer.

Five forms of knowledge

I would characterize five forms of knowledge, intelligence or learning (here used rather too loosely and inter-changeably) that are worth exploring further. I do not see these as replacing the cognitive and conceptual processes developed in alternative learning approaches, but rather balancing and enhancing them so that relations of power and knowledge can be examined and shifted at deeper, more enduring levels:

Embodied knowledge. Life experience and power relations that are internalized, held and expressed at the physiological or somatic level, which can shape our reactions, impulses, sense-making and behaviour, both 'positively' and 'negatively' depending on our socialized norms and expectations. Connected with our emotional and psychological state of being, and often not easily accessed or shifted through the intellect alone.

Intuitive knowledge. The ability to see patterns, solutions, systems and relationships in an intrinsic manner, often without being able to explain in words what processes, formulae or sequences of thinking were used. Often mathematical and logical, and sometimes interfered with or shut down when more linear, procedural models of reasoning are expected of learners.

Emotional knowledge. Our abilities to experience, process and handle emotions, to interpret and respond to the emotions of others, and to relate and communicate with other people. A lot of work has been done in this area, and it is making its way into primary and secondary education, as well as psychotherapy, but is not present in many of the alternative learning models used in agriculture and development.

Creative knowledge. Artistic, creative understanding and expression, that is often not rationalized, conceptualized or verbalized (unless more figuratively). Meanings that are received and communicated visually, through sound, music, movement, touch and other sensory and imaginal experience. Often the temptation is to impose links to conceptual interpretations of this creative knowledge, and its potential to stand alone and to effect changes in knowledge and power is not well recognized.

Spiritual knowledge. The ways in which we experience soul, spirit, divinity or other ways of understanding and connecting with life-forces that are beyond rational or scientific explanation. The role of faith-centred epistemologies and other cultural or indigenous imaginaries – and how they may differ from, enhance or contradict natural and social science epistemologies – are rarely addressed explicitly in alternative learning approaches, but could be.

These five areas are not altogether ignored in alternative learning approaches. Examples which come to mind are 'theatre of the oppressed', forms of participatory communication, storytelling and narrative-based forms of learning, reflective writing, methods of gender and power analysis, citizen and community media, and others. In the larger scheme of things, however, there seems to be a contradiction implicit in the mainstream of alternative pedagogical frameworks themselves. The three key principles that form the basis of most alternative learning schemes do not seem to provide enough scope to engage with these other ways of knowing, learning and being (whether critically or constructively) as much as they could. Instead they privilege conceptual and linguistic sense-making as the apex of knowledge within rather linear cycles, systems and hierarchies of learning and cognition. As a result, change is usually most evident at the level of concepts, consciousness and world view – for which there is much to celebrate – but does not always penetrate to deeper levels of knowing, being and behaving.

This is not an attack on intellectual sense-making or on linguistic and conceptual learning. I agree with the old adage that 'there is nothing so practical as a good theory', especially for challenging relations of power and knowledge. Rather, it is a wish to examine what might be missing from our alternative pedagogies if we want these changes – so critical to an emancipatory Farmer First agenda – really to take root and endure.

So what difference does it make? Assessing the outcomes and impacts of farmer participatory research

Adrienne Martin

Introduction

Early work in participatory research was concerned with both the values of participation and empowerment and a pragmatic emphasis on achieving greater research relevance for resource poor farmers by conducting agricultural research with the active participation of potential end users.

The literature of the 1980s focused on the many examples of approaches and tools which facilitated this participation, primarily in the technology-development process. Evidence was mainly drawn from case studies, identifying common issues and synthesizing lessons. Unsurprisingly, it was noted in the early years of participatory research that 'the effectiveness of participatory methods in terms of time and costs is rarely assessed' and that 'several case studies of projects using innovative methods at the outset ... have not yet produced an evaluation of their experience' (Farrington and Martin, 1988:30). Subsequent work broadened to include consideration of the institutional and policy context for participatory research. Even now, despite the great wealth of participatory experience, there is still a significant degree of controversy on how the impact of participatory research approaches should be assessed.

Here I reflect briefly on what constitutes valid evidence for the efficacy and impact of participatory research, drawing on both the large impact assessment literature and my own experience. The paper suggests that there has been important progress in demonstrating the difference made by participatory approaches to outcomes and impacts, but there remain variations in how the contribution of participatory research is judged, what evidence is considered valid and by whom.

What difference? The construction of comparisons

Assessing the difference made by Farmer Participatory Research (FPR) involves some form of comparison. There are different models of comparison, for example, 'before and after' comparisons, methods which track change over time and – most common in impact assessment of agricultural research – the 'with/without' comparison, which compares the results of the intervention with a comparable situation – real or modelled – without the intervention. The limitations of these methods are discussed extensively in the monitoring and evaluation (M&E) and participatory research literature. In particular, the range and complexity of FPR is such that it is difficult to clearly distinguish what is being compared to what.

Comparisons over time require a description of the starting situation through a situational analysis or baseline study, which can be participatory. However, in many cases where a baseline of the situation at the outset is lacking, the comparison has to be constructed retrospectively. This approach is sometimes dismissed as anecdotal or 'subjective'. It indicates levels of participant's perspectives and levels of satisfaction, but does not provide 'objective' evidence of the magnitude of change. More formal baseline studies measure initial values in relation to specified objectives or indicators in order to provide a basis for monitoring change, but such quantitative baseline studies often fail to examine processes or relationships.

Many projects do not differentiate between testing of their participatory methods and measuring the outcomes. They judge their contribution by the extent to which project objectives are being achieved, e.g. in terms of uptake of technologies or improvements in productivity, and are less concerned to demonstrate systematically how far participatory approaches or other paradigm shifts have contributed to these outcomes.

More process-based approaches generally involve a more detailed 'visioning' of the intended changes, in order to track and monitor whether these changes emerge; examples include outcome mapping, 'impact pathways' or 'theory of change'. These can be compiled as a participatory process involving different stakeholder groups. With the exception of outcome mapping, these approaches have focused mainly on identifying what difference research outputs have made to productivity and income. Using such approaches for participatory research would require a definition of the means and processes, including behavioural change, through which participatory approaches are expected to have certain outcomes.

A more participatory version of this type of method was adopted by the Users' Perspectives With Agricultural Research and Development (UPWARD) network, an Asian network sponsored by the International Potato Centre (CIP), which promotes user participatory approaches in rootcrop research and development (see Campilan et al., this book). In the UPWARD approach, stakeholders participate in planning the impact assessment, and then a theory of impact (technical and socio-economic) is constructed from the empirical findings of participatory assessments at different levels (community, local agency and external R&D institutions), which are discussed in a validation workshop.

'With and without' models

The main critique of the above approaches is that they do not consider what the situation would have been without the intervention. This is relatively straightforward to construct in relation to impacts from adoption of technology, particularly improved germplasm – but much more challenging when complex system changes are involved, or when changes in the ways of doing research are the subject of the enquiry.

Within the international agricultural research community, the counterfactual scenario, or a comparison of the project intervention with a situation (either in reality or as a hypothetical model) in which the intervention did not take place, has become a methodological requirement in impact assessment. The early FPR literature accepted the need for this approach, but the limitations were clearly recognized. Treating 'participatory research' as an experimental variable is problematic because it is a complex of methods, attitudinal changes and underlying values rather than a single methodology. For instance, the UPWARD programme did not take this approach, opting for a case-study method instead, both for ethical reasons and because it was not appropriate to isolate factors in a naturalistic setting.

In order to examine a 'with/without' scenario, the elements for comparison need to be defined in the form of testable hypotheses, which can be generated through a participatory process. More challenging than the development of hypotheses is the specification of what is being compared to what. Nowadays, indeed, finding a comparable area of research with *no* elements of participation is becoming unusual, which makes it difficult to compare participatory research with non-participatory research on the same topic. The principle of randomness is often impossible too, since participants are usually self-selected or purposively selected (Johnson et al., 2004), or subject to inbuilt biases, and so on. Replication of the research in a large number of randomly selected communities is often not feasible; therefore the compromise is to select for diversity and to match control communities as closely as possible to the communities where research is taking place.

Multiple methods

Some of the best evidence of the impact of participatory research is generated by combining different approaches to assessment. For example, a review of the impact of participatory plant breeding (PPB) (Ashby and Lilja, 2004) drew on evidence from a survey of PPB practitioners and expert opinion as well as an economic analysis of barley breeding in Syria, which compared conventional and PPB approaches. Although this was an *ex ante* analysis, it incorporated data from both farmer surveys and data on actual research costs.

The use of multiple assessment methods is particularly relevant in assessing the impact of participatory research in natural resource management (NRM), where there are multiple impacts and complex relationships. In a study by Johnson et al. (2003), conventional adoption studies and econometric analysis were complemented by qualitative data from interviews and focus-group meetings with farmers and other key informants in project and non-project communities.

Some examples

The impact assessment study of the International Center for Tropical Agricultural (CIAT) Cassava Programme in Asia (Dalton et al., 2005) is a detailed assessment of participatory research within a broader NRM context in Thailand and Vietnam. The programme developed and tested technologies (varieties, erosion control, fertilizer and intercropping) with farmers and used participatory extension approaches over a larger number of sites. Researchers were also trained in participatory research methods.

For the impact assessment, in each country, four villages were selected where the project had worked as well as four closely comparable and nearby villages where they had not worked. A range of methods, including survey questionnaires (767 households) and focus group discussions were used with both participants and non-participants. The study found that participatory approaches were particularly important in encouraging the adoption of cassava management technologies.

Differences in adoption rates between participants and non-participants and wealthier compared to poorer farmers were more pronounced for soil conservation practices, including contour ridging and farmyard manure, than for improved varieties and chemical fertilizer. Participation was found to have had an impact on yield gain, independent of technologies. The study suggests that this outcome is related to the enhanced knowledge, experience and managerial capacity gained via participation and experimentation (Dalton et al., 2005:17).

The cassava case also illustrates some of the methodological difficulties in impact assessment of participatory approaches. For instance, there were difficulties in matching participant and non-participant villages and there was no initial baseline or estimation of farmers' knowledge and practices or the institutional practices of research and extension.

Experience from working on the impact assessment in the inception phase of the Sub-Saharan Africa Challenge Programme (SSA CP) (2005–6) also illustrates some of the issues and debates connected with providing evidence for the efficacy of different research approaches. The SSA CP is committed to working within a broader innovation-system context, based on the 'integrated agricultural research for development' paradigm (IAR4D). The IAR4D approach emphasizes integrated approaches across value chains, establishing broader partnerships and 'innovation platforms', strengthening participation, building linkages with policy processes and stimulating institutional change.

The facilitation and mentoring of the programme, including M&E and impact assessment functions, were supported by contracted service providers. Activities included workshops to assist in proposal development, which covered participatory M&E, impact assessment, IAR4D and participatory research and extension. The research teams discussed how indicators would be defined (whose indicators would count and how this process could be more participatory) and developed gender-, poverty- and vulnerability-related indicators. The teams discussed the pathways, processes and institutional relationships through which research outputs might contribute to intended outcomes. The basic principles of comparison were discussed and incorporated into preliminary plans for baseline studies in areas where the programme would work and similar areas where it would not.

The dimension of institutional change and new approaches to partnerships and learning presented particular challenges for M&E and impact assessment. Qualitative but systematic approaches were used to establish the institutional baseline. They included self-assessment by team-members of their individual experiences and understandings of development-oriented research and their expectations regarding IAR4D at the start of the programme, organizational experiences with collaborative research and development and the extent of organizational guidance and support for partnerships. There was an initial introduction to outcome mapping as a method for stakeholders and participants to define the kind of institutional changes required and monitor them over time, allowing for reflection and learning and sharing lessons across different sites.

Important questions were raised about the research focus of the programme and hence the design and implementation of its M&E systems and impact assessment plans. Although most of the research teams monitored institutional change and interaction among partners, for the most part the emphasis in M&E and impact assessment was on understanding how programme activities had brought about changes in value chains, household incomes and policy and institutional environments rather than assessing the impact of the IAR4D methodology *per se*.

The CGIAR Science Council called for the definition of research hypotheses and research designs that would make it possible to identify the effects of the different components of the IAR4D approach in a scientific, statistically based manner. Their concern was to show whether the IAR4D concept works and can generate deliverable international or regional public goods for the end users, whether it delivers more benefits to end users than conventional approaches for the same investment, and whether the approach is sustainable, replicable and scalable.

Clearly M&E and impact assessment are critical to this discussion, but what approaches, processes and tools would be appropriate in these circumstances? Traditional M&E approaches were acknowledged to be inadequate, but the requirement for robust measurement of real outcomes was considered to require something more than participatory feedback and reflection approaches.

But some may doubt whether the required counterfactual can be created that will allow the experimental comparison necessary for a 'proof of concept'. This is particularly so, since the nexus of partnerships and institutional interrelationships within IAR4D cannot be replicated as a 'treatment'.

Notwithstanding these concerns for impact assessment, the SSA CP is supported by a wide range of stakeholders. As emphasized by the IAR4D and innovation systems approach, research is being conducted in partnership with organizations across the research and development. Among these organizations there are different views on what would constitute evidence for the effectiveness of IAR4D and whether there is need for 'proof of concept'. It is ironic that, whereas integrated approaches have developed in response to critiques of reductionism, it appears necessary to reintroduce reductionism in order to examine the specific components of IAR4D.

The programme nevertheless has worked on developing an improved framework to grapple with experimental design, sampling strategy, indicators, outcomes, etc. Comparisons are relatively easier at the level of research sites, but less straightforward at the level of institutional change and innovation platforms. Here, a combination of impact pathway-mapping, individual and group monitoring of institutional and behavioural changes and participatory assessments is likely to be required. The design of these mechanisms represents a current practical challenge.

Conclusions

As participatory research becomes part of wider approaches in research for development and increasingly includes a stronger emphasis on institutional transformation and broader joint learning, the methods for impact assessment will need to develop. How to explore impact among disparate actors, including farmers and strategic researchers, in different contexts? What combination of approaches is appropriate, given different objectives and time frames? What will convince different stakeholders and what recognition is given to their individual requirements? Answers to these questions will be important if impact assessment is to provide a constructive contribution to improving the developmental outcomes of research.

Monitoring for collective learning in rural resource management

Irene Guijt

Introduction

Monitoring systems should provide feedback that can help correct ineffective actions. But practice shows that, when dealing with complex rural development issues that involve collaborative action by a changing configuration of stakeholders, monitoring practice often falls short of its potential. Here I describe how to understand and design monitoring processes that foster learning in concerted action that seeks more equitable and sustainable forms of development.

Institutional transformation, messy partnerships, monitoring and learning

'Institutional transformation' and 'messy partnerships' are two important concepts in rethinking monitoring for collective learning.

'Institutional transformation', in the context of development, seeks systemic reforms of institutions to favour the poor and the environment. Such change processes have implications for monitoring. The non-linearity and unpredictability of change mean that objectives change *en route*, as contexts change, alliances shift and understanding is enhanced. The interconnected efforts on multiple fronts that are needed over a long timeframe in order to achieve such changes cannot be fragmented into actor-specific achievements. Explaining the transformation requires capturing incremental steps rather than the visible result at the end. Adaptive behaviour by the actors involved in the change process is critical.

'Messy partnerships' are one form of coordination through which institutional transformation efforts are channelled. The Brazilian cases discussed below are examples of such partnerships, consisting of local NGOs, small-scale farmers' unions, municipal governments and research institutions. While messy partnerships do projectize activities and form temporary clusters of concerted action, they cannot be assumed to have some stable identity that can be held to account externally for the totality of its actions. These features make mainstream approaches to monitoring less than ideal, as I discuss below.

Learning is essential for societal adaptation and innovative change in rural resource management, in which messy partnerships are common. In the development sector, expectations have grown over recent years about the potential of monitoring to contribute to learning, without understanding how the two relate. Often conflated, they are distinct concepts. In Figure 4.7, the smallest box, 'mainstream', lists activities usually associated with monitoring, while learning requires additional activities (shown in the intermediate box, 'monitoring'). The more these activities are undertaken, the more likely it is that monitoring will enable 'learning', the largest box.

Understanding mainstream monitoring and its limitations

Monitoring has received far less attention conceptually than has evaluation. Though definitions of monitoring vary, several features recur, such as a standardized and systematic (rather than *ad hoc*) effort; regularity, as in a continuous or regular process (rather than one-off or discrete efforts); and data collection.

But much divergence in understanding can be found. For example, the purposes of monitoring vary greatly, with commensurate variation in the type and level of information considered necessary in monitoring systems. A critical point of debate is the extent to which analysis, or the process of 'sense-making', is considered part of monitoring. This leads to variation in whether monitoring includes assessing merit or value, and therefore how it relates to decision making. The variety, ambiguity and generality of definitions of monitoring make it difficult to undertake a detailed critical

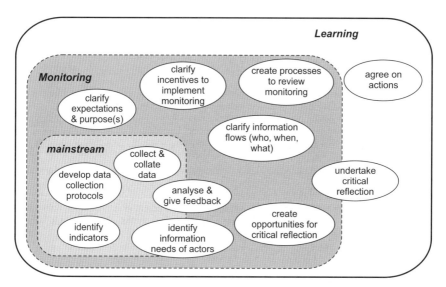

Figure 4.7 The sliding scale from (mainstream) monitoring to learning
Source: Guijt (2008)

review of monitoring for rural resource management, either conceptually or practically.

Given the paucity of understanding about the concept, I analysed three sets of practical guidelines: the classic *Project Monitoring and Evaluation in Agriculture* (Casley and Kumar, 1987), AusAid's guidelines for project cycle management (AusAid, 2000) and the M&E Guide of the International Fund for Agricultural Development (IFAD, 2002). I suggest a set of presuppositions (or implicit assumptions) as an implicit theory of mainstream monitoring (Table 4.4).

Billions of dollars of investment in rural development and resource management rely on these or similar guidelines to enable strategic readjustment and operational improvement. Unfortunately, evidence from rural development projects (Guijt, 2008) indicates that the presuppositions of mainstream M&E guidelines do not necessarily fit well with operational realities. Mainstream monitoring emerged from a theory of change that is based on assumptions

Table 4.4 An implicit theory of mainstream monitoring

Presuppositions of mainstream monitoring

1   That, it is necessary and/or useful to define 'monitoring' as distinct from 'evaluation' and this can be done on the basis of a range of different aspects (e.g. the people involved, the validity of findings, etc.).

2   That, because monitoring is intended principally to serve management, those involved will know how to make monitoring serve management.

3   That strategic analysis and sense-making do not need to be explicitly 'designed for' in monitoring.

4   That a lack of information is the critical issue, requiring most of the investment, rather than developing appropriate processes to make sense of and use the information.

5   That it is possible for stakeholders to anticipate their information needs adequately, at the outset, in terms of a comprehensive and fairly stable set of indicators (with related data collection methods and processes).

6   That certain processes (notably analysis, critical reflection, interpretation, communication), which are needed to transform information into learning, are obvious or simple and/or will occur automatically.

7   That indicators are an appropriate form in which to express and convey all key information, thus enabling learning that supports management decisions.

8   That a balanced picture of information is produced from the chosen set of indicators.

9   That stakeholders have sufficient time, expertise, clarity and willingness to follow the basic steps in sufficient detail for effective results (in quality of information and/or in learning impact).

10 That the steps have a generic validity, irrespective of the context and combinations of stakeholders.

11 That power relations (and the context of these relations) are not noteworthy or do not influence the quality of the design or implementation process, or its outcome, sufficiently to merit special methodological attention – or that power is too difficult to deal with or outside the remit of M&E methodology.

12 That people will know how to deal with and effectively use informal monitoring outside the prescribed formal processes and channels.

13 That it is either not necessary for monitoring processes to learn from, and adapt to, the environment in which they are being implemented – or that this happens automatically.

Source: Guijt, 2008

that are not universally valid. For example, unpredictable change processes and messy partnerships – rather than hierarchical contractual relationships – question the current approach of standardizing monitoring systems and not valuing sense-making as integral to monitoring (see Guijt (2008) for an in-depth discussion on the erroneous basis of mainstream monitoring).

In the mid-1990s, participatory approaches to monitoring and evaluation (PM&E) emerged as an alternative. The guiding principles of PM&E – participation, negotiation, learning and flexibility – suggest in theory that it differs in key respects from mainstream M&E. The main differences relate to the participation of the main audience and active stakeholders in designing and implementing the process, with other issues resulting from this core shift. However, this alternative also does not seem to deliver on the learning promise as I explain below. Many of the problematic presuppositions evident in mainstream monitoring have found their way into PM&E theory and practice.

Putting PM&E to the test in Brazil

Participatory monitoring was the core concern of action research in Brazil with two local NGOs. Neither AS-PTA (*Assessoria e Serviços a Projetos em Agricultura Alternativa*) and its recently started Paraíba project; nor CTA-ZM (*Centro de Tecnologias Alternativas – Zona da Mata*) had systematic monitoring processes and were keen to develop one with their partners. The main drivers throughout the action research process were the local NGOs, working with community-based organizations and individuals. In both cases, rural trade unions (STRs) – local, democratically elected membership organizations of smallholder farmers – were the main partner.

Over the course of about four years, the Paraíba project and CTA-ZM held a series of partner workshops to clarify concepts, design the process, build capacity, and review experiences and data. These workshops were interspersed with periods of group-based work to fill in the details of the monitoring approach(es) identified and undertake data collection. Each site had its own pace and timeline of events. The initial process of establishing a monitoring system involved six basic steps, followed by implementation and review:

1. clarify expectations of the different parties regarding the joint monitoring work;
2. prioritize key activities to be monitored;
3. develop clearer objectives for each activity;
4. prioritize, per activity, which of the many objectives would be monitored;
5. identify indicators for these prioritized objectives; and
6. develop a calendar that outlined the method for collecting and registering information, frequency, place and the roles of different stakeholders.

In total, five experiences of collective monitoring were undertaken in Minas Gerais (agroforesty experiments, local homeopathy, traditional maize variety experiments, mineral salt production for livestock, apiculture) and four in Paraíba (banana weevil control, contour planting, community seed banks, fodder experimentation). A tenth experience involved the Most Significant Change (MSC) method in both locations. Each of these experiences offers insights about participatory monitoring in practice. Five lessons stood out.

Learning from process and from data

Mainstream M&E and PM&E both assume that using data will trigger learning. However, although expressing interest in the data, the STRs did not use it for their own purposes, and other parties made sub-optimal use. It was in developing the monitoring system that many insights were gained. Hence, learning via monitoring happens through the design process as well as the information collected.

Participation and messy partnerships

Messy partnerships demand an interpretation of participation that fosters concerted action, yet respects the uniqueness of partners and their own cultures and rhythms of reflection. Initially, everyone assumed that all stakeholders were equally committed to the partnership. We overvalued consensus as the basis for concerted action, including monitoring. We saw the need to understand organization-specific reflection and learning processes and to strengthen these – and only then consider where overlap exists and concerted monitoring action is potentially beneficial.

Valuing data and dialogue

Dialogue between partners is critically important if data is to be useful. The data alone will not necessarily indicate the direction that improvements need to take. It will require sense-making to reach conclusions on which different actors can act, moving from seeing 'what happens?' to understanding 'why?' and 'so what does this mean for us?' Participatory monitoring requires a better balance between investing in data (indicators, methods, collection) and dialogue (analysis, interpretation, planning).

Differentiated learning events, mechanisms and needs

We assumed that monitoring had to be developed as a single system organized around indicators and an objective hierarchy. Experience showed, however, that it was important to differentiate between technical and organizational monitoring on the one hand, and monitoring the social processes underlying the partnership on the other. Our final analysis treated each development activity as unique, determined by its own organizational mechanisms and dynamics, planning and evaluation cycle and participants.

(Un)sustainability of the process

The process proved unsustainable, with much of the monitoring stopping soon after the action research process ended. Various issues led to this outcome: my role as facilitator fell away, most of the farmers' groups dissolved for various reasons and CTA-ZM changed its working methods. Unless information is useful for the individual partners and embedded in their structures and processes, any form of monitoring is unlikely to be sustained.

Sustaining presuppositions and recognizing new ones

With hindsight, several of the presuppositions of mainstream monitoring were inadvertently sustained in our approach to participatory monitoring. For example, referring to Table 4.4, we still thought in terms of 'monitoring' vs 'evaluation' (presupposition 1) but built in 'analysis' as an evaluative process as part of monitoring. Only later did the focus on learning purposes emerge as a more satisfactory alternative to 'M' vs 'E'. Building in sense-making as integral to monitoring also helped address the problems of presuppositions 3 and 4. However, we did not describe the sense-making process in sufficient detail. We underestimated the importance for farmers and STRs to be supported by the NGOs in carrying out their analysis and did not build analytical stages sufficiently into the existing evaluation and planning processes of the individual partners. We also deviated from mainstreaming monitoring by, for example, recognizing the need for stakeholders to learn how to undertake monitoring and accommodated changing information needs and shifting configuration of stakeholders in the messy partnerships.

During the analysis of the participatory monitoring work in Brazil, what surprised us all was the emergence of a new set of presuppositions which related to participation in monitoring. For instance, that consensus was a solid basis for concerted action; that involving stakeholders in designing the process would ensure their interest in and commitment to it; and that a partnership implies a considerable degree of shared vision and commitment by the partners. We also underestimated the need to sort out logistics – that is, the steps necessary simply to get data collection to happen, in a context where voluntary efforts were all important yet the civil society organizations were operating on a shoestring. We also failed to recognize the importance of understanding and building on the existing governance structures and processes of the individual partners and, from that, identifying where shared monitoring made sense.

Our action research process gave us a more detailed perspective on participatory monitoring than the generic and simplistic set of steps commonly found in guidelines. In particular, the experiences illustrate the tensions between our implicit and explicit expectations and the fluid realities of partners working within their own political contexts and embedded in their own learning pathways. They show the importance of viewing monitoring as a context-specific information, sense-making and communication system that needs to serve diverse learning purposes. These factors, in the context of a messy partnership engaged in concerted action, require considerably more than the simple suggestions for 'using participatory methods' and 'more stakeholder involvement' that mark the PM&E discourse. More thought is needed about existing organizational conditions (Guijt, 2000) and the unique identities of the organizations involved.

The future of monitoring: revising design principles

So where does this leave the development sector? Recognizing that rural resource management is non-linear and dynamic may clarify why mainstream monitoring efforts are limited. If those in rural resource management want to realize the learning potential of monitoring, then processes must be designed based on a new set of principles. A shift is needed to a situation where monitoring is seen as: dialogical (not only a singular rationality), multi-ontological (not only assuming an ordered universe), distributed (not centralized), functioning through relationships and heuristics (not only through data and the hope of omniscience), essential for impact (not just a contractual obligation), sustaining collective cognition (not only the tracking of implementation), and seeking surprise (not only documenting the anticipated).

This final section suggests eight design principles for learning-oriented monitoring of deliberate concerted action undertaken by messy partnerships. They are not a comprehensive set of design principles but derive from my experiences. The first three principles relate to the purpose of monitoring, the next three principles to operational concerns, and the last two to sustaining monitoring practice.

1. Understand *the nature of institutional transformation* being pursued as a social change process (see also principle 3). Four questions need clarifying: What type of institutional transformation is being aimed for? What coordination mechanisms are at work? What ontological basis is present in the type of transformations and coordination mechanisms present (simple, complicated, complex)? What does this tell us about the underlying theory of change that is guiding the concerted action to be monitored?
2. Recognize the effect of particular *actors and partnerships* on monitoring. Analyse the commitment of partners to concerted action, the governance structures and processes of each partner, the allocation of responsibilities

in the partnership, the degree of overlap of information needs, the way in which information is shared, and monitoring capacities.

3. Specify distinct monitoring processes in terms of *learning purposes*, in order to enable a more precise definition of tasks, protocols and responsibilities. Nine learning purposes are likely to be relevant, though not necessarily simultaneously or equally. Five pertain to management of the development intervention: financial accountability, operational improvement, strategic adjustment, contextual understanding and capacity strengthening. Four are also part of the development interventions themselves: research, self-auditing, advocacy and sensitization.

4. Plan for *sense-making as* well as information. The sense-making process must be appropriate (i.e. multi-ontological). Seek to understand how sense-making can take place by and between partners, how insights are best communicated, which capacities are needed to make this possible and allocate appropriate resources to this end.

5. Balance *formal* protocols and *informal* processes, incorporating everyday interactions of sharing and debate into the monitoring system, and linking the informal sphere to formal processes and channels. Informal processes are not only crucial for ongoing sense-making but also a source of information-sharing.

6. Value and seek diverse types of *information*, related specifically to the nature of development (principle 1) and the learning function (principle 3) that has to be met. Understand which processes exist and/or are needed to ensure that information is shared and debated and informs decisions.

7. Ensure the *institutionalization* of learning-oriented monitoring. Concerted efforts are needed to ensure that policies, practices, methodologies, responsibilities and incentives are aligned to make monitoring, as discussed here, possible. This requires explicit investment.

8. Approach monitoring as an *evolving practice*, thus allowing it to become a dynamic knowledge-production process, which, when subjected to regular critical reviews and adaptations, remains relevant and useful.

The notion of development-as-project is being replaced by the recognition that shifting institutionalized injustice requires the adoption of a more diverse understanding of societal transformation. The idea of development as delivered contractually by organizations is being replaced by the understanding that messy partnerships and other types of alliances are the new configurations within which institutional transformation unfolds.

Monitoring, when conceived as a socially negotiated, evolving methodology for structuring information flows and use, offers an approach to help construct 'pathways to sustainability' (Leach et al., 2007). It is not resolved by a tweaking of methods, or different tools. It requires a considered reassessment of the epistemic and ontological perspectives and principles that underpin monitoring, and determine its feasibility, relevance and usefulness.

Participatory Impact Pathways Analysis

Boru Douthwaite, Sophie Alvarez, Graham Thiele and Ronald Mackay

Introduction

Participatory Impact Pathways Analysis (PIPA) allows participants in a workshop to make explicit their assumptions and hypotheses about how their projects will achieve impact (see also http://impactpathways.pbwiki.com). These hypotheses can be used as the basis for *ex ante* impact assessment, monitoring and evaluation of the project's progress along its impact pathways, and the identification of impact hypotheses required for *ex post* impact assessment. People act on the basis of their understanding of how the world works – their 'theories of action' (Argyris and Schön, 1974): we do X because we believe, based on past experience or what we've read, that Y will happen. This applies to projects and programmes as well. So it follows that if you can improve a project's theories of action you can improve how people implement it.

This has long been recognized by a particular branch of evaluation, called programme theory evaluation, which describes projects' theories of action in a 'logic model' and then evaluates the project using the model as a framework (Chen, 2005). Logic models describe how project outputs are developed with, and used by, others to achieve chains of outcomes that contribute to eventual impact on social, environmental or economic conditions.

Impact assessment workshops

PIPA was first used in a workshop in January 2006 in Ghana, with seven projects funded by the CGIAR Challenge Programme on Water and Food. To date, 19 PIPA workshops have been held with 400 participants. PIPA centres on a three-day workshop bringing together project implementers, participating 'next users' (people and organizations who will use what the project will produce), end users (people served by the next users) and politically important actors. The workshop process is designed to help participants surface, discuss and describe their hypotheses for how project strategies and outputs could eventually contribute to desired goals such as poverty reduction. The description of these hypotheses is a description of the project's impact pathways. PIPA therefore helps:

- clarify, reach mutual understanding and communicate the project's intervention logic and its potential for achieving impact;

- understand other projects working in the same programme and identify areas for collaboration;
- generate a feeling of common purpose and better programmatic integration (when more than one project is represented in the workshop);
- produce a narrative describing the project's intervention logic and possible future impacts (thus a form of *ex ante* impact assessment); and
- produce a framework for subsequent monitoring and evaluation.

The workshop begins with participants developing a problem tree (see Figure 4.8, Box 1) that links the problems the project is directly addressing with the social, environmental and/or economic conditions it wishes to

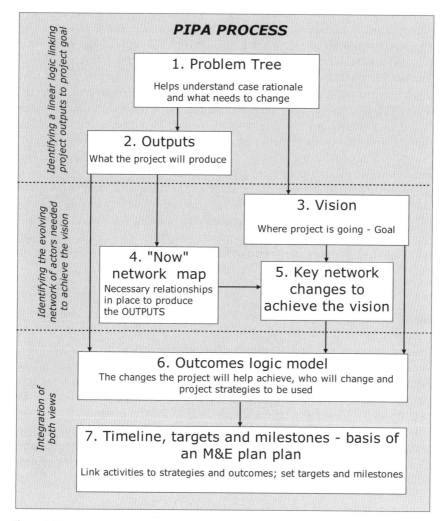

Figure 4.8 The PIPA process

improve. The branches of a problem tree end when it has identified a problem that the project will directly address (cf. Renger and Titcomb, 2002). Once identified, these 'determinant' problems help define the outputs the project needs to develop to help solve them (2). Outputs are defined as things the project produces that others use.

Participants then carry out a visioning exercise (3), which borrows from appreciative inquiry (Acosta and Douthwaite, 2005), to describe project success in the future. We have found that having a relatively short time horizon helps keep the vision concrete. However, it is sometimes useful to construct visions for after the end of a project to stretch participants to think about who will be using and promoting project outputs once the project has finished, and so who they really need to be working with.

The second part of the workshop involves participants drawing networks of people and organizations (the actors) already working in the area in which the project wishes to intervene, or is already intervening (4). They then build influence towers (cf. Schiffer, 2007) to indicate the relative influence of each actor in the respective networks they have drawn. Next to the towers they indicate if the actor's attitude is negative, neutral or positive to what the project is trying to do. They then redraw the maps showing how the actors should be linked to achieve the project's vision. They then record the most important changes in the networks and actors' attitudes, explain why the changes are important and who needs to do what to make them happen. This forms the basis of a project's scaling strategy (5).

The final part of the workshop involves distilling and integrating what has been produced into the outcome logic model (6), filling in one table for each of the four main stakeholder groups – next users, end users, politically important actors and project implementers. This table describes what changes in knowledge, attitudes, skills and practice will result from the development and use of project outputs.

Use of workshop outputs

The outputs from a PIPA workshop and afterwards can be used for a number of purposes. Our work has focused on using the information for *ex ante* impact assessment – that is, predicting likely project outcomes and impacts, and the opportunities and threats to their achievement. More recently we have worked to develop a practical approach to impact pathways evaluation – the monitoring and evaluation of projects' progress along their impact pathways (7). Outputs can also be used to set the foundation for *ex post* impact assessment, and for producing programme-level network maps that can help guide and monitor programmatic integration.

Conclusions

Testing the impact hypotheses contained within the framework through regular reflection workshops, as described here, constitutes action research on how to foster developmental impact based on the use of research outputs. Our hope is that PIPA will change researchers' perceptions of monitoring and evaluation to something they want to do to help them do a better job, rather than something they feel they have to do to satisfy the donor.

Tracking the impact of policy task forces in Uganda

Pascal C. Sanginga, Annet Abenakyo, Rick Kamugisha, Adrienne M. Martin and Robert Muzira

Policy task forces and natural resource management

Drawing from the body of work and experience that show the importance of participatory processes and institutional innovations in natural resources management (NRM), we facilitated a five year (2000–4) participatory learning and action research (PLAR) project that aimed at strengthening social capital for improved policies and decision making in NRM (Sanginga et al., 2005a, 2005b). The PLAR project was premised on the grounds that social capital is an important asset which people draw on in pursuit of their livelihood objectives, and particularly for improving management of their natural resources, accelerating adoption of NRM technologies and improving policy formulation and implementation in rural communities (Bridger and Luloff, 2001; Collier, 1998; Grootaert and Narayan, 2004; Ostrom 2000a, 2000b; Rudd, 2000).

The PLAR project conducted research in Kabale district in the south-western highlands of Uganda. It developed and tested mechanisms and approaches for strengthening social capital and facilitating participatory processes for the formulation and implementation of local by-laws to improve NRM (Sanginga et al., 2005a). The project involved the formation and facilitation of village-level Policy Task Forces (PTFs). The PTFs championed the review, formulation and implementation of a set of community by-laws for controlling soil erosion, planting trees, controlling animal grazing, managing wetlands and regulating alcohol drinking (for details see Sanginga et al., 2007). The PTFs created a platform for dialogue between communities, local government councils and R&D organizations on the analysis of NRM.

One year after the by-law project ended, we conducted a study to investigate and document its specific outcomes, potential impacts and sustainability. The tracking study combined iterative participatory approaches and tools with more conventional household and community survey methods and semi-structured, key informant interviews. A framework called an After Action Review (AAR) was used to help structure collective reflection, analysis and learning (CIDA, 2003; Sanginga et al. 2008), using the following six questions:

1. What was supposed to happen? Why?
2. What actually happened? Why?
3. What is the difference? Why?
4. What went well? Why?
5. What could have gone better? Why? and
6. What lessons can we learn?

Because AAR tends to focus more on positive feedback, other reflexive practices were used to unravel some of the negative consequences of the PLAR. This involved discussions on how the by-laws affect people's livelihood options; the categories of people that are likely to benefit or lose out because of the by-laws; what categories of the community will have difficulty in complying, the reasons why and what arrangements can be introduced for those who fail to comply or have difficulty in complying; and how to encourage community participation in implementation and monitoring of the by-laws. Feedback sessions were organized to validate findings, and to identify strategies for dealing with challenges and obstacles to successful implementation, sustainability and uptake of the by-laws, community action plans and policy task forces. Quantitative and individual insights were obtained from semi-structured interviews with a sub-sample of 46 households and 29 key informants. Table 4.5 outlines the three groups of community-defined indicators used to track social capital outcomes.

Adaptive management and social capital formation

A major finding of this study is that the key outcome of the participatory by-law formulation and implementation is the creation of more social capital. There was significant improvement in both the cognitive, structural, bridging and linking dimensions of social capital. These include increased awareness and knowledge of by-laws, changes in behaviour and attitudes, and compliance with collective norms that place community interests above those of individuals. The different PTFs increased the ability of farmers' groups to engage with external agencies, either to draw on useful resources or to influence policies. These findings are in line with studies that provide evidence on the effects of institutions in boosting social capital levels (Stolle and Hooghe, 2003). They also lend credence to studies that point to the role

Table 4.5 Community-based indicators for tracking social capital outcomes

Performance area	Outcomes and indicators
Participation	• Continuous attendance at meetings and community activities • Number of farmers participating in various policy meetings, task forces and community NRM activities • Number of women participating in meetings • Number of farmers involved in implementing by-laws • Change in motivation and expectations from participation • Extent of women's participation in making decisions
Performance	• Number of meetings of task forces and policy meetings at community level • Number of meetings conducted by the task forces • Level of compliance with the by-laws • Perception of effectiveness of by-laws and task forces by community members • New skills and knowledge level • Extent of collective action in NRM • Trees and grasses planted along the trenches • Increased number of trenches • Reduced conflicts • Resource mobilization and allocation for collective action • Neighbouring communities seeking information and visiting • Demand of NRM technologies • Number of nursery beds • Evidence of positive change in NRM
Sustainability	• New action plans developed • Ability to take independent actions and decisions • Ability to analyse and explain issues and problems • Community willingness to plant trees and get seeds on their own • New activities initiated • Increased community savings to invest in NRM activities • Number of meetings of task forces and policy meetings • Linking with other development organizations

of diverse forms of social capital in enhancing human capital (Uphoff and Mijayaratna, 2000; Coleman, 1988).

In addition to gains in human and social capital, enforcement of by-laws has also been an important driver of adoption of agroforestry technologies and important mechanisms for conflict management. The by-law formulation and implementation processes have proved to be robust over time, and growing in confidence. They have continued operating well after the end of the PLAR project. Although it is still too early to draw clear conclusions, these results suggest that social capital can be not only productive, but also persistent. However, because participatory processes usually focus on group consensus, they often fail to deal with power, politics and inequality in community processes. Enforcement of by-laws, for example, did not always ensure fairness, especially to women and the elderly. We need alternative ways to reach such farmers and build their capacities to exploit these new opportunities.

Conclusions

Much effective innovation in the policy and institutional arenas is location and context specific. As in the case of the PLAR project, it is also often limited to community or micro-level interventions as effective participation is possible at this scale. It is not known how such social and institutional innovations at the micro-level influence the meso- and macro levels. In their recent analysis of adaptive management experiences, Stringer et al. (2006) recognize the challenges of scaling up participatory processes, particularly to influence national-level policies. The challenge has always been comparability, transferability and replicability beyond local communities, to generate quality benefits to more people, in wider geographic areas.

Limited experience with participatory processes suggests that the 'hard-to-reach' can be reached, and that they can be empowered to exploit emerging opportunities. The practical issue is how to learn from and multiply these fragmented successes. As illustrated by the PLAR project, AARs can provide a useful framework to improve our tracking of the impact of different initiatives. Action research should examine what strategies and approaches can work in different contexts to reach the hard-to-reach, and the best ways for maximizing social learning across different scales.

Using Participatory Impact Assessment (PIA) to inform policy: lessons from Ethiopia

Dawit Abebe, Andy Catley, Berhanu Admassu and Gezu Bekele

Introduction

Participatory approaches and methods are emerging as an alternative to conventional approaches to studies and research in remote pastoral communities. Participatory approaches and methods are often viewed as purely qualitative, but some standardization and repetition of participatory approaches and methods allows numerical data to be collected and analysed using conventional statistical tests. When used well, participatory approaches and methods can generate both qualitative insights and usually more accurate quantitative data than more conventional approaches and methods (Chambers and Mayoux, 2003).

Participatory impact assessment (PIA) uses tools originating from other forms of participatory methods such as participatory rural appraisal (PRA) and participatory learning and action (PLA) with some adaptation to measure indicators of changes over time (Guijt, 1998). Participatory approaches and methods have been widely applied by veterinary epidemiologists in marginalized areas (Catley, 2005; Thrusfield, 2005) as well as to assess animal health projects in Nepal (Young et al., 1994), Somaliland/north Somalia (Catley, 1999), Afghanistan (Blakeway, 1998), southern Sudan (Catley, 1999) and Tanzania (Nalitolela and Allport, 2002).

Assessing the impact of community animal health workers in Ethiopia

We report here on how participatory methods were used to assess the impact of a three-year community-based animal health worker (CAHW) project implemented in Dollo Ado and Dollo Bay districts, Ethiopia. The step-by-step approach followed is shown in Box 4.1.

A PIA methodology specific to the CAHW project was designed. Participatory tools such as semi-structured interviews (SSI), before-and-after proportional piling, disease scoring and ranking, and matrix scoring were used to collect information required (Table 4.6). Simple drawings on cards and locally available materials (stones, sticks, leaves, etc.) were used to represent indicators and as a counter to measure changes. Data derived from before-and-after disease impact scoring, and from matrix scoring of service providers were analysed using SPSS Version 11.0. For matrix scoring data, the median and range were calculated and agreement between informant groups was assessed using the Kendall coefficient of concordance (W). Disease scoring data were summarized using the median. Changes in disease impact were compared for diseases that were treated or prevented by CAHWs versus diseases that were not treated or prevented by CAHWs, using the Wilcoxon Signed Ranks test.

Evaluating impacts

The CAHW project impact assessment showed significant reduction in disease impact for diseases handled by CAHWs compared with diseases not handled by CAHWs. In camels, there was significant reduction (p<0.001) in the impact of the mange, trypanosomiasis, helminthiasis, anthrax and non-specific respiratory disease. In cattle there was a significant reduction (p<0.001) in the impact of blackleg, anthrax and helminthiasis. In sheep and goats there was a significant reduction (p<0.001) in the impact of mange, helminthiasis, contagious caprine pleuropneumonia, orf and non-specific diarrhoea.

The relative strengths and weakness of the different animal health service providers was assessed using a matrix scoring method adapted from Catley et al. (2001). For each indicator, there was evidence of strong agreement between

---

Box 4.1 Key steps for participatory impact assessment in Ethiopia

Step 1. Define and prioritize the key questions to be answered through the assessment. These may include questions related to policy and legislation, project design, implementation, monitoring and evaluation, etc. However, the number of questions to be answered through the PIA should be limited to only 3–4 to keep the assessment focused.

Step 2. Define the geographical and time limits of the project as perceived by the community.

Step 3. Identify and prioritize a maximum of five locally defined impact indicators. This can be facilitated by simply asking the beneficiaries the ways in which they benefit from having the project. The indicators should be very specific and not general, for example 'we drink more milk' instead of 'we get milk from our livestock'.

Step 4. Decide which methods to use to measure the indicators, and test the methods. Participatory tools suitable to measure each of the identified indicators need to be selected and tested in the field.

Step 5. Determine sampling and sample size. Selection of a sampling method depends on various factors such as accessibility, social and wealth differences, etc. Sample size is also decided based on resources and time available. However, where the sampling unit is a group of people the minimum sample size used is 10 informant groups, and where the sampling unit is a household the minimum sample size used is 50 household informants.

Step 6. Measure changes in the impact indicators during the project and undertake statistical analysis. Although many impact indicators have a qualitative nature, it is possible to measure them systematically and express them numerically. A wide range of PRA tools such as ranking, scoring and diagramming are available to measure qualitative impact indicators. Data generated using participatory tools can be analysed using standard statistical packages such as SPSS.

Step 7. Assess project attribution to the changes observed in the impact indicators. Non-project factors may have contributed to the changes observed during the project, and therefore, the importance of the project inputs and activities relative to other factors need to be assessed. Semi-structured interviews are used to identify factors that contributed to the observed change, and simple ranking methods can be used to rank the factors in order of importance.

Step 8. Triangulate the changes in the impact indicators using process indicators. The findings of the impact assessment can be cross-checked with monitoring information.

Step 9. Feed back and verify the results with the community and other stakeholders.

---

the informant groups. The project inputs and activities such as increased use of modern veterinary services provided by CAHWs and vaccination campaigns involving CAHWs were rated as the most important factors to which the reductions in disease impact could be attributed. CAHWs were considered to be highly accessible, available, affordable and trustworthy relative to other service providers. They were also perceived to be suppliers of a good quality service. Specific types of positive impact attributed to CAHW activities were increases in milk, meat, income and draught power. The findings of the PIA were used to inform and influence policy changes supporting CAHWs in pastoral areas (Catley and Leyland, 2002; Hopkins and Short, 2002).

Table 4.6 Summary of methods used for PIA of CAHW project

Information required	Methods	Type of informant	Number of repetitions
Defining the project in terms of its geographical coverage and period of operation	Available map at the project level	Project staff	1
Information on major historical events of the project area	Timeline	Individual, old person in community	10
Compare livestock incidence before the project with incidence after the project for different livestock species; general livestock diseases incidence and mortality; specific diseases incidence and mortality	Before and after proportional piling	Average of 25 people per site of 2 groups	10
Factors influencing livestock health during the project	Disease ranking	Average of 25 people per site of 2 groups	10
Change in animal health service provision	Matrix scoring of service providers	Average of 25 people per site of 2 groups	10
Major sources of livelihood benefits derived from livestock and overall change before and after the project	Before and after proportional piling	Average of 25 people per site of 2 groups	10
Overall change in livelihood before and after the project (How have peoples' livelihoods changed during the project?)	Before and after livelihood scoring and ranking of key factors	Average of 25 people per site of 2 groups	10
General information as part of other methods	SSI to probe for more information	Ad hoc	N/a

The relative importance of livestock as a source of livelihood, and local perceptions of specific benefits derived from improved animal health were assessed. Perceptions of the main benefits derived from livestock (all species) before and after the project are shown in Figure 4.9.

From impact assessment to policy change

The participatory impact assessment of the CAHW project was very successful in influencing policy supporting CAHWs in pastoral areas. The key policy and legislative changes resulting from this process included a proclamation by the Ethiopian Government in 2003 which legalized privatized CAHW systems in pastoral areas of the country, and the publication in 2004 of the 'National Minimum Standards and Guidelines for the Design and Establishment of CAHW systems in Ethiopia' by the Federal Ministry of Agriculture and Rural Development.

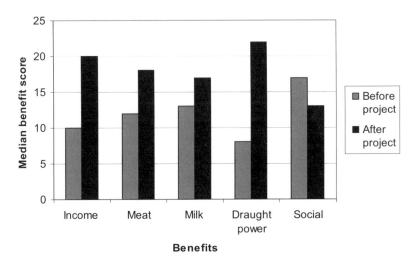

Figure 4.9 Benefits derived from improved animal health during the CAHW project

The use of participatory impact assessment approaches to inform policy processes is based on three fundamental assumptions. First, scientific data will always be interpreted differently by different stakeholders, and this problem can be overcome if stakeholders work collectively to define problems and conduct research to propose solutions. Second, research has a role to play in the policy process but only if it responds to the key questions of stakeholders and is conducted using methods and researchers who are known and trusted. Third, many policy makers have limited direct experience of pastoralist areas and misperceptions about pastoralism are partly due to this lack of exposure. Research and learning approaches such as PIA can be used to put policy makers face-to-face with pastoralists, while also collecting information in a participatory and systematic way.

PART V

Looking forward

The future of the Farmer First movement: towards an innovation alliance

Ian Scoones and John Thompson

Where do we go from here?

The twentieth anniversary of the original Farmer First workshop (1987) and fifteenth anniversary of the Beyond Farmer First workshop (1992) have provided an opportunity to examine both accomplishments and disappointments with farmer-centred innovation.

The preceding sections of this book are the distillation of the December 2007 workshop deliberations and the wide-ranging, stimulating and at times impassioned debates they inspired. In this concluding paper, we shift attention from a reflection on past achievements and missed opportunities to a focus on future prospects and challenges.

Lessons from Farmer First Revisited

Recently, major policy pronouncements and publications have placed agriculture at the heart of the international development agenda. Getting agricultural science and technology research, extension and education working better for poor farmers, herders and resource managers is seen as vital – to improving productivity, to reducing poverty and to managing resources sustainably and equitably. This requires renewed efforts to revitalize agricultural research and development (R&D) systems globally.

Of the range of issues raised in this book, several stand out as priority concerns.

Upstream vs. downstream

The move 'upstream' of much agricultural R&D has, in the view of many contributors, created an unhealthy separation of 'pure' or 'basic' science, often dominated by laboratory-based molecular biological approaches, from the more applied agricultural sciences. This has resulted in users (notably farmers) becoming increasingly distant from research activities, with less input into priority setting, testing and adaptation. Better science, with greater uptake, often results from user engagement upstream, as well as downstream, but the agricultural R&D community seems increasingly poor at facilitating upstream engagement. Much of the downstream work has been taken up by NGOs and farmers' organizations, but these are often not well integrated with key upstream science actors. Linking farmers to labs – and not just research station fields – requires some major thought, both in terms of new practices and protocols, but also in the wider governance of science and technology at all levels (below). Interesting experiences exist within and beyond the national and international agricultural research centres which could be usefully drawn upon to create new innovation networks which connect farmers and lab scientists.

Software vs. hardware

Today, the institutional setting for technological innovation in agriculture is changing rapidly. It has grown much more complex over the past 20 years, involving plural systems and multiple sources of innovation. Yet, despite their many achievements, the global institutions, created for agricultural R&D in the 20th century, with their narrow sectoral focus are inadequately prepared to address today's interrelated and multi-sectoral Farmer First agendas. Institutional reforms and innovations are needed to facilitate greater coordination across international agencies and with the new actors in the global arena, including civil society, the business sector and philanthropy. The assumption that the international agricultural R&D community only deals with 'global public goods' presumes that universal, spill-over results are all that matter. Contributors to this book repeatedly emphasize the point that, while these are essential, many of the most significant impacts on poverty reduction and improved livelihoods result from highly context-specific engagements over extended periods. This means dealing with the 'software' of institutions and social processes, as well as the technology 'hardware'.

Public and private

Several authors point to signs that new thinking is beginning to refashion the ways that the currently archaic and ineffective public agricultural systems might work in future, but a significant challenge will be to think hard about the policy measures and incentives that might influence the governance of private sector R&D systems. This will have to go beyond rhetorical claims and public relations concessions which have characterized many 'public–private' engagements to date. Instead, measures will need to go to the heart of corporate strategy and financing, if some private sector resources – both intellectual and financial – can be unleashed for the public good in the more complex, diverse, risk-prone agricultural regions. New initiatives such as the African Agricultural Technology Foundation (AATF) perhaps provide the basis for such new organizational innovations, but the real interests and politics of such arrangements must become more of a focus, interrogating bland assumptions about corporate social responsibility and public–private partnerships.

Capacity of the national agricultural research and extension systems (NARES)

The assumption that the NARES must deal with local-level adaptation of generic results and technological 'magic bullets' produced by the international centres assumes a very linear approach to innovation and technology transfer, which the Farmer First movement has challenged for two decades. Yet the model still remains resistant to change. This approach, modelled on the successes of the Asian Green Revolution of the 1960s and 70s, has been shown to work in relatively few situations. The lack of capacity of many NARES, particularly in Africa following structural adjustment, has to be acknowledged, with the international centres, universities and independent research organizations and networks taking on a more active role in facilitating processes of innovation. This has important implications for the future role of the international agricultural research system in supporting a new African Green Revolution, in association with new partners such as AGRA, the Alliance for a Green Revolution in Africa, and its major philanthropic sponsors, the Bill and Melinda Gates Foundation and the Rockefeller Foundation.

Innovation in innovation systems

The dynamic new world of agriculture is opening space for a wider range of actors in innovation, including civil society organizations and the private sector, as well as farmers. Linking technological progress with institutional innovations and markets to engage this diverse set of actors is at the heart of a future Farmer First agenda. Many authors in this book have noted that these changes focus attention on wider innovation systems. With the development of new domestic and international value chains, innovation becomes less driven by science (supply side) and more by markets (demand side). New demand-driven approaches stress the power of users – women and men farmers, consumers and interests outside of agriculture – in setting the research agenda and the importance of research in a value chain from 'plough to plate'. Innovation in this setting requires feedback, learning and collective action among this much broader set of actors. It also requires capacity, not just in terms of scientific and technical expertise, but also the ability to meaningfully and equitably participate in the joint learning processes that characterize innovation. This, in turn, implies the need for institutional change and empowerment amongst a broadened set of stakeholders. Thus, a more nuanced approach to Farmer First innovation systems is required that sees agricultural R&D as part of context-specific innovation systems, where particular economic, social, cultural and political processes influence how research is done and how research influences innovation. This has been accepted, for instance, by the CGIAR as part of the Sub-Saharan Africa Challenge Programme (SSA CP), coordinated by the Forum for Agricultural Research in Africa (FARA), which offers the potential for testing and exploring a new set of relationships and processes. A future challenge for the Farmer

First movement is creating and defending institutional and political space for innovative experiments like the SSA CP to manoeuvre, while preventing them from being constrained by institutional inertia and existing biases within the international system and those of other partners.

Social science capacity

That a broader innovation systems approach which puts farmers – alongside other technology beneficiaries – first requires a wider set of skills, has been recognized as a key priority by many contributors to this book. The decline in social science capacity (beyond economics) in agricultural R&D systems has been tangible, and there remain *very* few political scientists, psychologists, social anthropologists and sociologists, for example, on full-time, core-funded posts in CGIAR centres. Much social science work – some of it of very high quality – often occurs in an *ad hoc* way through short-duration project funds and outside core commitments. This results in a lack of professional advancement and inadequate institutionalization. This has been one of the major failings of the CGIAR over the past two decades as it attempted to embrace participatory, farmer-oriented approaches. Increasing investments in social science capacity and making cross-sectoral collaboration and problem-focused research a strategic priority will help prevent Farmer First R&D from being relegated to mere interaction with farmers at the late stages of delivery of near-finished research products.

Institutional learning and change

Time and again, contributors to this book emphasize how learning about agricultural innovation is (or should be) a collaborative process, often involving stakeholders from distinct communities with diverse and sometimes conflicting priorities, interests and capacities. The creative tensions that arise through these collaborations and the vital role that communication plays in joint learning are key ingredients in the innovation process. In addition, a number of authors demonstrate how the impacts and outcomes of many agricultural innovation activities are often very narrowly defined when based on conventional impact assessment methodologies. While such approaches have an important role, they may distract from wider lesson learning and reflexivity if used as the sole metric for assessment. A broadening of impact assessment is required to encompass participatory learning approaches. Such approaches have been advocated by the ILAC (Institutional Learning and Change) group of the CGIAR, as well as an increasing number of independent networks and alliances. A range of examples discussed in this book combine learning approaches with both qualitative and quantitative participatory impact assessment. Embedding such approaches in scientific organizations at all levels involves a number of practical and organizational challenges, but the demonstrable results – on improved research focus and outcomes, on policy change and on wider poverty reduction and sustainability goals – are tangible and exciting.

The political economy of innovation

Various authors highlight how agricultural R&D and innovation policy emerge together and how certain ideas and approaches get embedded in institutional and organizational arrangements, linked to particular professional, bureaucratic and sometimes commercial interests. Challenging mainstream science and policy is therefore not only about garnering new 'evidence', but about creating new alliances, networks and political configurations. When ideas are deeply entrenched in bureaucratic structures, educational systems, media representations and political processes, shifting them can be an uphill battle. This becomes a particular challenge when such framings are linked to powerful global R&D institutions and public–private partnerships, with large financial and political clout. Today, when global agricultural knowledge networks are increasingly powerful, getting alternative voices heard – particularly those of poor farmers, farm workers and consumers – is especially challenging. Of course, science does not emerge independently of the economic, social, and political settings in which it is created. As various authors in this volume observe, normative values and political imperatives are implicated in the elaboration of scientific questions and technical recommendations in agriculture, even though these may be 'hidden' by their presentation as objective, 'technical' issues. Unpacking the origins of and reasons for the persistence of certain ideas and approaches is an important Farmer First research agenda which potentially opens up new opportunities for alternative perspectives on seemingly intractable problems.

Governance of agricultural science and technology

The argument that the governance of the international agricultural research system needs to move beyond out-dated, expert-driven, elitist structures and processes to ones that are more representative and responsive to the users of its products is a common thread linking all three Farmer First books. While an old debate, many authors urged specific attention and urgent action, rather than continued obfuscation and delay. Several contributors forcefully argue that a focus on the governance of science and technology raises specific questions about the very nature of agricultural innovation systems: questions of participation and inclusion; access and control; justice and rights and accountability and responsibility. With so much of the current policy debate about agricultural innovation systems couched in rational technical and economic terms, there has been little scope to assess critically the wider social and political implications of new ways of organizing, funding and governing agricultural R&D. Clearly, changes must include giving farmers' organizations and their representatives a much more concrete role within the governance systems of national, regional and international agricultural organizations, and a central role in core decision-making and strategic bodies, such as the CGIAR's Science Council. The current membership of the Science Council means that the legitimacy of its priority setting and strategic direction can be challenged. This undermines the capacity of the system to deliver genuinely global public goods. But governance of the public international agricultural system is only one part of a broader challenge. In an era where private sector R&D is premised on closed access intellectual property arrangements, commercial confidentiality and a need to recoup large sunk costs, models of learning, participation and partnership can seem rather quaint and outdated. While there are signs that new thinking is beginning to refashion the ways that the currently archaic and ineffective public agricultural systems work, a significant future challenge will be to think hard about the policy measures and incentives that might influence the governance of private sector R&D systems.

Personal and professional rewards and incentives

Fundamental issues of personal and professional behaviour lie at the heart of many of the issues mentioned above, preventing the wider success and impact of Farmer First-oriented agricultural R&D. Encouraging greater reflexivity and learning in research and development, admitting mistakes and learning from them, and accepting that not all innovations will always work out are all important. But to encourage such behaviours will require some major shifts in the way professional incentive structures, organizational hierarchies and reward systems operate within the agricultural science community. As various contributors to this book show, much interesting, exciting and innovative work in national and international agricultural research systems occurs at the margins, very often hidden – operating through informal, below-the-radar arrangements, such as the way Participatory Plant Breeding emerged. Such activities need to be acknowledged, appreciated and brought centre stage much earlier and given the organizational support and recognition they demand.

Towards an innovation alliance

Over the past two decades, those promoting the Farmer First agenda have moved from being a diverse and somewhat diffuse group of dissident researchers and practitioners to a highly potent and influential force that has challenged the dominant transfer of technology paradigm and shifted the focus of agricultural research and development to recognize and work to strengthen farmers' own capacity to innovate. Contributors to this book have identified concrete ways to build on these achievements and chart a course for the future. There appears to be broad agreement that there is an urgent need to reinforce and expand the 'Farmer First movement' and create a more united and coherent front. However, it is equally clear that this should not be through a singular approach or methodology, but instead through a set of commonly agreed guiding principles that enhance local capacities to innovate, involve farmers, particularly poorer and marginalized people, in the innovation process, and result in improved productivity, enhanced social justice and reduced poverty. In turn, such principles need to be clear and widely applicable, and not obscured by academic jargon, pet methodologies or institutional turf wars.

The strength of the Farmer First movement over the past 20 years has been its diversity and breadth, and some have argued that any attempt to organize, formalize and institutionalize it may only serve to stifle creativity and innovation. Yet collaboration and coherence are required to have wider impacts at this critical juncture. Thus the idea of a Farmer First 'Innovation Alliance' emerged at the workshop. This is envisaged as a loose but active 'community of practice', dubbed a 'dissident network' at the workshop. It must include not just long-standing Farmer First proponents, but a much wider network of actors, including, critically, private sector players and other major stakeholders in agricultural innovation systems.

Below we set out actions needed, including those identified by workshop participants and others made by contributors to this book. Taken together, they present key elements of an emerging agenda for an Innovation Alliance. This would:

- Explore the principles and practices of a Farmer First approach to innovation systems, involving through action research, documentation and reflection;
- Experiment with institutional learning and change in agricultural R&D organizations, and supporting 'dissenting networks' for change;
- Mentor and support across a Farmer First 'community of practice', especially giving support to junior people (to publish, to present, to share in different settings) and to those who are in organizational cultures and contexts which are not supportive of them;
- Work on clear and accessible impact assessment approaches and tools appropriate for a Farmer First context, and test them in different innovation system contexts;
- Facilitate and support South–South exchanges and networking for farmers' organizations, and explore how to generate the politics of demand in different settings;
- Support curriculum design and development processes for agricultural education (from schools to skill-based training to professional and tertiary education) and conduct tracing and tracking studies of students involved in participatory agricultural education to identify how personal and professional change happens, and with what longer term results; and

- Link people and networks (and websites and information sources) using Web 2.0 technologies and virtual social networking approaches, and provide support for independent clearinghouses for information on technology options and alternatives to reduce transactions costs for farmers in searching for options, including mapping, cataloguing and documenting Farmer First experiences and contacts geographically through web-based formats.

In sum, approaches to farmer participatory research have played a crucial role in improving agricultural R&D over the past 20 years, particularly in complex, diverse, risk-prone regions. Despite these achievements, however, agricultural R&D systems are currently constrained from meeting their wider goals by a combination of professional intransigence, organizational inertia and the quixotic search for silver bullets and quick fixes. Action is needed to overcome these obstacles and redirect energies towards supporting the emergence of agricultural R&D systems that capitalize on local skills and knowledge in order to promote innovation, enhance productivity and reduce poverty. This will require a broad coalition of research and education organizations, private companies, development agencies, farmers' federations and others – an Innovation Alliance. Such an alliance could help reinvigorate and expand the Farmer First movement, bringing much-needed clarity, commitment and creativity to its still vital agenda. Furthermore, it could shift the debate on farmer involvement in agricultural R&D beyond a focus on participatory methods to one that addresses fundamental issues – of personal and professional behaviour, of power and politics, of governance and organizational style. The good news is that much of the knowledge, experience and capacity to do this already exist in the organizations, networks and partnerships represented in this book – and in many others. Thus, there is a good chance these ambitious aims can be realized, if the will and impetus are there to build a truly dynamic Farmer First movement, one capable of radically transforming agricultural research and development policy and practice in the twenty-first century.

Appendix 1: List of participants and contributors

(Participants at the Farmer First Revisited workshop are indicated with an asterisk*)

Abebe, Dawit*
Research and Policy Specialist, Feinstein International Center, Friedman School of Nutrition and Policy, Tufts University, Addis Ababa. dawit.abebe@fic-et.org

Abenakyo, Annet
CIAT, Kampala. a.abenakyo@cgiar.org

Adekunle, Adewale*
Sub-Saharan African Challenge Program, FARA. aadekunle@fara-africa.org

Adwera, Andrew*
African Centre for Technology Studies (ACTS), Nairobi. a.adwera@ids.ac.uk

Admassu, Berhanu
Pastoralist Livelihoods Program Coordinator, Feinstein International Center, Friedman School of Nutrition and Policy, Tufts University, Addis Ababa. berhanu.admassu@fic-et.org

Albright, Kerry*
Research into Use programme, NR International, UK. k.albright@nrint.co.uk

Alvarez, Sophie
Evaluation specialist, CIAT, Colombia. b.s.alvarez@cgiar.org

Arce Moreira, Maria*
Policy Adviser, Practical Action. maria.arce@practicalaction.org.uk

Ashby, Jacqueline A.
Development sociologist, CIP. j.ashby@cgiar.org & jacashby@gmail.com

Assefa, Amanuel*
Agri Service Ethiopia, Addis Ababa. kidus_aman@yahoo.com

Ba, Awa Faly*
Programme coordinator, IED (*Innovations Environnement Développement*) Afrique. awafba@sentoo.sn

Banda, Khamarunga
Head of the policy and research directorate of the National African Farmers' Union of South Africa. khamarunga@hotmail.com / khamarunga@nafu.co.za

Bekele, Gezu
Research Assistant, Feinstein International Center, Friedman School of Nutrition and Policy, Tufts University, Addis Ababa. gezu.bekele@fic-et.org

Best, Rupert
Independent consultant on rural enterprise development. rupertbest@gmail.com

Boadi, Richard
Legal Counsel, African Agricultural Technology Foundation (AATF), Nairobi. r.boadi@aatf-africa.org

Bokanga, Mpoko
Executive Director, African Agricultural Technology Foundation (AATF), Nairobi. m.bokanga@aatf-africa.org

Burgoa, William
Field facilitator, K´ANCHAY, North-Potosi, Bolivia. aguilawill@hotmail.com

Campilan, Dindo
Social scientist, Impact Enhancement Division, and leader/coordinator of the UPWARD Partnership Program, CIP. d.campilan@cgiar.org

Castillo, Renee
Former coordinator, Rural Development Projects, CARE Regional Office, Cajamarca, Peru. castillr90@hotmail.com

Catley, Andy
Research Director for Policy Process, Feinstein International Center, Tufts University, Ethiopia. andrew.catley@tufts.edu

Chitsike, Colletah
Regional Coordinator Southern Africa, International Centre for development oriented Research in Agriculture (ICRA). colletahc@yahoo.com

Chuma, Edward*
University of Zimbabwe. chuma@africaonline.co.zw

Colfer, Carol J. Pierce
Anthropologist, Center for International Forestry Research (CIFOR), Bogor, Indonesia. c.colfer@cgiar.org

Crane, Todd A.*
Lecturer, Technology and Agrarian Development group, Wageningen University. todd.crane@wur.nl

Damene, Belew
Project coordinator, Self Help Development International (SHDI). belewdg2005@yahoo.co.uk

del Rosario, Beatriz P.*
IFAP Asian Regional Coordinator, Paris. beatriz.delrosario@ifap.org

Delve, Robert
Senior Scientist, Tropical Soil Biology and Fertility Institute, CIAT, Nairobi. r.delve@cgiar.org

Dennig, Anne*
Linking Local Learners. dennig@btinternet.com

Devkota, Krishna Prasad
Programme Officer, Local Initiatives for Biodiversity, Research and Development (LI-BIRD), Nepal, and currently PhD Student at the Center for Development Research (ZEF), University of Bonn. kdevkota@zef.uzpak.uz

Diaw, Chimere
Leader, African Model Forests organization, Cameroon.
c.diaw@africanmodel forests.org

Dixon, John*
Director, Impacts Targeting and Assessment Program, CIMMYT. j.dixon@cgiar.org

Doering, Don*
Gates Foundation. don.doering@gatesfoundation.org

Douthwaite, Boru*
Technology policy analyst, CIAT, Colombia. bdouthwaite@gmail.com

Ekwamu, Adipala
Regional Universities Forum for Capacity Building in Agriculture (RUFORUM), Kampala.
eadipala@ruforum.org

Ely, Adrian*
Science and Technology Policy Research Unit, University of Sussex.
a.v.ely@sussex.ac.uk

Ewbank, Richard
Impact Assessment Advisor, FARM-Africa. richarde@farmafrica.org.uk

Faure, Guy
Innovation and Development Research Unit, CIRAD, Montpellier. guy.faure@cirad.fr

Fernandez, Maria E.*
International consultant on gender, smallholder agriculture and community participation. mefernandezme@gmail.com

Fisher, Robert
Senior researcher, Australian Mekong Resource Centre, University of Sydney.
rjfisher@ozemail.com.au

Gabriel, Julio
Leader, Potato Genetic Improvement, PROINPA, Bolivia. jgabriel@proinpa.org

Gildemacher, Peter
Former Junior Professional Officer, Nairobi Regional Office, CIP. p.gildemacher@kit.nl

Glover, Dominic*
Post-doctoral fellow, Technology and Agrarian Development Group, Wageningen University. dominic.glover@wur.nl

Gonsalves, Julian
Senior program adviser, CIP UPWARD Partnership Program, the Philippines.
juliangonsalves@yahoo.com

Guijt, Irene
Independent advisor on learning processes and systems in (rural) development and natural resource management. iguijt@learningbydesign.org

*Gummert, Martin**
Postharvest development specialist, IRRI, the Philippines. m.gummert@cgiar.org

*Gupta, Anil K.**
Professor, Indian Institute of Management, Ahmedabad, and founder of the Honey Bee network. anilg@iimahd.ernet.in / anilg@sristi.org

*Hagmann, Jürgen**
Institute for People, Innovation and Change in Organisations (PICOTEAM), PICO Southern Africa, Pretoria. jurgen.hagmann@picoteam.org

*Hall, Andy**
Coordinator, UNU-MERIT's Learning Innovation and Knowledge initiative–LINK. hall@merit.unu.edu

Hartwich, Frank
Senior lecturer, Department of International Agriculture, Swiss College of Agriculture. frank.hartwich@shl.bfh.ch

Hocdé, Henri
Collective Action, Policies and Markets Research Unit, CIRAD, Montpellier. henri.hocdé@cirad.fr

Horton, Douglas
Independent Consultant. d.horton@mac.com

*Howlett, David**
Department for International Development, UK. d-howlett@dfid.gov.uk

Jiggins, Janice
Wageningen University, The Netherlands. janice.jiggins@inter.nl.net

Jones, Monty P.
Executive Director, Forum for Agricultural Research in Africa (FARA), Accra. m.jones@fara-africa.org

Joshi, Krishna Dev
Research Fellow, CAZS-Natural Resources, Bangor University, c/o CIMMYT, Kathmandu. kdjoshi@mos.com.np

*Kaaria, Susan**
Program Officer for Environment and Economic Development, Ford Foundation, Office for Eastern Africa. s.kaaria@fordfound.org

Kaganzi, Elly
Economic Opportunities Advisor, Community HIV/AIDS Mobilization Program (CHAMP), Kigali, Rwanda. ekaganzi@champ.org.rw

Kahiu, Ignatius
Project Manager, Uganda Food Security Initiative, AFRICARE-Uganda. igkahiu@africaonline.co.ug

Kakuhenzire, Rogers
Plant pathologist, National Agricultural Research Organization (NARO-Uganda), Uganda. rmkakuhenzire@hotmail.com

Kamugisha, Rick
Africa Highlands Initiative, CIAT-Kabale. rnkamugisha@yahoo.com

Kanouté, Assétou*
Director, *Association pour le Développement des Activités de Production et de Formation* (ADAF/Gallè), Mali. adafgalle@afribonemali.net

Kanté, Salif
Coordinator, *Projet de Renforcement des Capacités pour une Agriculture Durable* (PRECAD), Mali. precad@afribonemali.net

Kariuki, Leonard Nduati
Chairman, Kenya National Federation of Agricultural Producers, Kenya. producers@kenfap.org

Kashaija, Imelda
Head, Kachwekano Zonal Agricultural Research and Development Institute, National Agricultural Research Organization (NARO-Uganda). ikashaija@yahoo.co.uk

Kasindei, Aloyce
Project Officer, Babati Agricultural Development Project, FARM-Africa. farmafrica@farmafrica.org.uk

Kibue, Michael*
Sustainable Agriculture and Rural Development (SARD) Initiative on livestock, Kenya. sardlivestock06@yahoo.com

Kibwika, Paul
Institute for People, Innovation and Change in Organisations (PICOTEAM), PICO Uganda, Kampala. paul.kibwika@picoteam.org

Killough, Scott*
Associate Vice President for Sustainable Agriculture and Rural Livelihoods, World Neighbors. skillough@wn.org

Kimaro, Faithrest
Senior Officer, Babati Agricultural Development Project, FARM-Africa. farmafrica@farmafrica.org.uk

Kumar, Vikas
Research Associate, Gramin Vikas Trust, Jharkhand, India. kumar_vika@rediffmail.com

Leach, Melissa*
Team Leader, Knowledge, Technology and Society Team, Institute of Development Studies. University of Sussex. m.leach@ids.ac.uk

Li, Xiaoyun*
Professor and Dean, College of Humanities and Development, China Agricultural University, Beijing. xiaoyun@cau.edu.cn

Lightfoot, Clive*
Director, Rural African Ventures Investments company, UK.
clive.lightfoot@linkinglearners.net

Lu, Min
Associate professor, College of Agronomy, Jilin Agricultural University, Changchun.
lumin99cn@126.com

Mackay, Ronald
Evaluation specialist and Professor Emeritus, Concordia University, Canada.
mackay.ronald@gmail.com

Magombo, Tennyson
Former Research Associate, CIAT. tennysonmagombo@yahoo.co.uk

Magor, Noel P.
Head, Training Centre, IRRI, Los Banos, the Philippines. n.magor@cgiar.org

Mao, Miankui
PhD student, College of Humanities and Development (COHD), China Agricultural
University (CAU). miankui@gmail.com

Martin, Adrienne*
Leader, Livelihoods and Institutions Group, Natural Resources Institute, University of
Greenwich, Chatham, UK. a.m.martin@gre.ac.uk

McDougall, Cynthia
Team leader of the CIFOR's adaptive collaborative management research in Nepal (1999-
2002 and 2004-2007). c.mcdougall@cgiar.org

Meinzen-Dick, Ruth
Coordinator of the CGIAR Systemwide Program on Collective Action and Property
Rights (CAPRi), IFPRI, Washington, D.C. r.meinzen-dick@cgiar.org

Mignouna, Hodeba
Technical Operations Manager, African Agricultural Technology Foundation (AATF),
Nairobi. h.mignouna@aatf-africa.org

Millstone, Erik*
Science and Technology Policy Research Unit, University of Sussex.
e.p.millstone@sussex.ac.uk

Moberly, Richard*
Department for International Development, UK. r-moberly@dfid.gov.uk

Muchiri, Nancy
Communications and Partnership Manager, African Agricultural Technology Foundation
(AATF), Nairobi. n.muchiri@aatf-africa.org

Mulvany, Patrick
Senior Policy Adviser, Practical Action. patrick.mulvany@practicalaction.org.uk

Muzira, Robert
CIAT, Kampala. rmuzira@yahoo.com

Mwangi, Lucy Wangari*
Kenya National Federation of Agricultural Producers (KENFAP).
lucymwangi@kenfap.org

Nang'ayo, Francis
Regulatory Affairs Manager, African Agricultural Technology Foundation (AATF),
Nairobi. f.nangayo@aatf-africa.org

Nazarea, Virginia*
University of Georgia, USA. vnazarea@uga.edu

Ngwenya, Hlamalani J.*
Institute for People, Innovation and Change in Organisations (PICOTEAM), PICO
Southern Africa, Pretoria. hlami.ngwenya@picoteam.org

Niangado, Oumar
Representative, Syngenta Foundation in West Africa, Bamako.
oniangado@afribonemali.net

Njuki, Jemimah*
Senior scientist, CIAT, Harare. j.njuki@cgiar.org

Nyimbo, Vincon*
Director, Agriculture Business Development Company. vnyimbo@yahoo.co.uk

Oliveros, Oliver
DURAS Project Coordinator, Global Forum on Agricultural Research (GFAR) c/o
Agropolis International, Montpellier. oliveros@agropolis.fr

Omanya, Gospel Oluoch*
Seed Systems manager, African Agricultural Technology Foundation (AATF), Nairobi.
g.omanya@aatf-africa.org

Orrego, Ricardo
Research assistant, Integrated Crop Management Division, CIP. r.orrego@cgiar.org

Ortiz, Oscar*
Leader, Integrated Crop Management Division, CIP. o.ortiz@cgiar.org

Otiniano, Ronal
Former field facilitator, Cajabamba office, CARE-Peru. otiniano@yahoo.com

Peacock, Christie*
FARM Africa, christiep@farmafrica.org.uk

Peters, Andrew R.*
Chief Scientific Advisor, Global Alliance for Livestock Veterinary Medicines (GALVmed).
andy.peters@GALVmed.org

Pettit, Jethro*
Research Fellow, Institute of Development Studies, University of Sussex.
j.pettit@ids.ac.uk

Pinto, Yvonne*
Gates Foundation. yvonne.pinto@gatesfoundation.org

Prabhu, Ravi*
Alliance of the CGIAR Centers. r.prabhu@cgiar.org

Pradel, Willy
Research assistant, Integrated Crop Management Division, CIP. w.pradel@cgiar.org

Prasad, Satish Chander
Consultant Plant Breeder, Gramin Vikas Trust, Jharkhand, India.
satishprasad@sancharnet.in

Qi, Gubo*
Professor and Director, Rural Development and Management program, College of Humanities and Development, China Agricultural University, Beijing.
qigupo@cau.edu.cn

Rawal, Krishna Bahadur
Programme Coordinator, SUPPORT Foundation, Kanchanpur, Nepal.
supportmn@ntc.net.np

Rhoades, Robert E.*
Distinguished Research Professor, University of Georgia, USA. rrhoades@uga.edu

Richards, Paul*
Technology and Agrarian Development Group, Wageningen University.
paul.richards@wur.nl

Roa, Julieta R.*
Socio-economist, Philippine Rootcrops Research and Training Center (PhilRootcrops).
j.r.roa@cgiar.org

Röling, Niels*
Wageningen University, The Netherlands. n.roling@inter.nl.net

Romney, Dannie*
CABI Africa. d.romney@cabi.org

Rubyogo, Jean Claude*
Seed system specialist, CIAT/Pan-Africa Bean Research Alliance (PABRA), Lilongwe, Malawi. j.c.rubyogo@cgiar.org

Salahuddin, Ahmad*
Consultant sociologist, IRRI, Bangladesh, conducting PhD research on the PETRRA project at Adelaide University, Australia. salahuddin@irribd.org

Sanginga, Pascal C.
Senior programme specialist, International Development Research Centre, Nairobi.
psanginga@idrc.or.ke

Sanyang, Sidi
Senior Professional, Forum for Agricultural Research in Africa (FARA), Accra.
s.sinyang@fara-africa.org

Sarch, Terri*
Department for International Development, UK. t-sarch@dfid.gov.uk

Sasu, Lydia*
Development Action Association (DAA) Ghana. daa@africaonline.com.gh

Scoones, Ian*
Professorial Fellow, Knowledge, Technology and Society Team, Institute of Development Studies, University of Sussex. i.scoones@ids.ac.uk

Shambu Prasad, C.*
Associate Professor, Xavier Institute of Management, Bhubaneswar, India. shambu@ximb.ac.in

Slaa, Salutary
Research and Policy Officer, FARM-Africa. farmafrica@farmafrica.org.uk

Sperling, Louise
Senior Scientist, CIAT, Rome. l.sperling@cgiar.org

Spielman, David J.
Research Fellow, International Food Policy Research Institute (IFPRI), Addis Ababa. d.spielman@cgiar.org

Sulaiman, V. Rasheed
Director, Centre for Research on Innovation and Science Policy (CRISP), Hyderabad. rasheed.sulaiman@gmail.com

Témé, Bino
Director, Institute of Rural Economy, Bamako, Mali. bino.teme@ier.ml

Thiele, Graham
Leader, Impact Enhancement Division, CIP, Peru. g.thiele@cgiar.org

Thompson, John*
Research Fellow, Knowledge, Technology and Society Team, Institute of Development Studies, University of Sussex. j.thompson@ids.ac.uk

Thorp, Susanna*
WREN media. s.thorp@wrenmedia.co.uk

Torrez, Omar
Field facilitator, Asociación de Servicios Artesanales y Rurales (ASAR), Bolivia. otorrez05@yahoo.es

Traoré, Samba*
Director, Cinzana Agronomic Research Station at Ségou, Mali. samba.traore@ier.ml

Triomphe, Bernard*
Innovation and Development Research Unit, CIRAD, Montpellier France. bernard.triomphe@cirad.fr

Tripp, Rob*
Research Associate, Overseas Development Institute, London. rtrobtripp@gmail.com

Turín, Cecilia*
PhD Candidate, Rural Sociology Department, University of Missouri, Columbia. ceciliaturincanchaya@mizzou.edu

Uphoff, Marguerite*
Paediatrician, Ithaca, NY.

Uphoff, Norman*
Head, Program on Sustainable Rice Systems, Cornell International Institute for Food, Agriculture and Development. ntu1@cornell.edu

Vallejos, Juan
Project Coordinator, PROINPA Foundation, Bolivia. j.vallejos@proinpa.org

Van Mele, Paul*
Program leader, Learning and Innovation Systems at the Africa Rice Center (WARDA), Cotonou, Benin. p.vanmele@cgiar.org

van Veldhuizen, Laurens
ETC Foundation, The Netherlands, and coordinating member of the Prolinnova International Support Team. l.van.veldhuizen@etcnl.nl

van Walsum, Edith*
Director, Centre for Information on Low External Input and Sustainable Agriculture (ILEIA), Amersfoort, The Netherlands. e.van.walsum@ileia.nl

Vargas, Elizabeth*
Social agronomist, CIPCA, La Paz. elivargass@yahoo.com

Vernooy, Ronnie
Senior program specialist, IDRC, Ottawa, and adjunct professor, College of Humanities and Development, China Agricultural University, Beijing. rvernooy@idrc.ca

Virk, Daljit Singh
Senior Research Fellow, CAZS-Natural Resources, Bangor University, UK. d.s.virk@bangor.ac.uk

von Grebmer, Klaus
Director, Communications Division, IFPRI, Washington, D.C. k.vongrebmer@cgiar.org

Waters-Bayer, Ann*
Agricultural sociologist, ETC Foundation, The Netherlands, and member, Prolinnova International Support Team. ann.waters-bayer@etcnl.nl

Watts, Jamie*
Project Coordinator, ILAC Initiative, c/o Bioversity International, Rome. j.watts@cgiar.org

Wettasinha, Chesha
Tropical agriculturist, ETC Foundation, The Netherlands, and member, Prolinnova International Support Team. c.wettasinha@etcnl.nl

Winarto, Yunita T.*
Senior lecturer, Department of Anthropology, Faculty of Social and Political Sciences, University of Indonesia, Depok. winyun@indo.net.id

Witcombe, John R.*
Professor, CAZS-Natural Resources, Bangor University, UK. j.r.witcombe@bangor.ac.uk

Woldegiorgis, Gebremedhin
Coordinator, Root and Tuber Crops Research Program, Ethiopian Institute of Agricultural Research (EIAR). gebregiorgis2003@yahoo.com

Xu, Xiuli
Associate professor, College of Humanities and Development, China Agricultural University, Beijing. xxl@cau.edu.cn

Yan, Zhao-Li*
Rangelands Specialist, International Centre for Integrated Mountain Development (ICIMOD) and Assistant Professor, Chengdu Institute of Biology, Chinese Academy of Sciences. yanzhaoli@hotmail.com

References

Acosta, A. and Douthwaite, B. (2005) 'Appreciative inquiry: an approach for learning and change based on our own best practices', *ILAC Brief* 6, IPGRI, Rome.

Adato, M. and Meinzen-Dick, R. (eds) (2007) *Agricultural Research, Livelihoods and Poverty: Studies of Economic and Social Impacts in Six Countries*, IFPRI, Washington, D.C.

Admassu, B., Nega, S., Haile, T., Abera, B., Hussein, A. and Catley, A. (2004) 'Impact assessment of a community-based animal health project in Dollo Ado and Dollo Bay districts, southern Ethiopia', *Tropical Animal Health and Production* 37: 33–48.

AIPE (2007) *Proceedings of the International Seminar on Mainstreaming the Human Right to Food in the National Constitution*. AIPE, Sucre.

Alders, C., Haverkort, B. and Veldhuizen, L. van (1993) *Linking with Farmers. Networking for Low External Input Sustainable Agriculture. ILEIA Readings in Sustainable Agriculture*, Intermediate Technology Publications, London.

Almekinders, C.J.M., Thiele, G. and Danial, D.L. (2007) 'Can cultivars from participatory plant breeding improve seed provision to small scale farmers?' *Euphytica* 153: 363–372.

Annett, H. and Rifkin, S.B. (1995) *Guidelines to Rapid Participatory Appraisal to Assess Community Health Needs*, Division of Strengthening of Health Services, World Health Organization, Geneva.

Anon. (2008a) 'Off the rails?', Editorial, *Nature Biotechnology* 26: 247.

Anon. (2008b) 'Deserting the hungry?', Editorial, *Nature* 451: 223–4.

Argyris, C. and Schön, D.A. (1974) *Theory in Practice: Increasing Professional Effectiveness*, Jossey-Bass, San Francisco, CA.

Arnold, E. and Bell, M. (2001) 'Some new ideas about research for development' in *Partnership at the Leading Edge: A Danish Vision for Knowledge, Research and Development*, pp. 279–316, Danish Ministry of Foreign Affairs, Copenhagen.

Ashby, J.A. and Lilja, N. (2004) 'Participatory research: does it work? Evidence from participatory breeding', in *New Directions for a Diverse Planet, Proceedings of the 4th International Crop Science Congress, 26 Sep – 1 Oct 2004, Brisbane, Australia*, Published on CDROM. Available from: www.cropscience.org.au/icsc2004

AusAid (2000) *AusGuide: Managing Projects through the Activity Cycle*, AusAid, Canberra.

Barasa, M., Catley, A., Machuchu, D., Laqua, H., Puot, E., Tap Kot, D. and Ikiror, D. (2008). 'Foot-and-mouth disease vaccination in South Sudan: benefit-cost analysis and livelihoods impact', *Transboundary and Emerging Diseases*, in press.

BARC (2007) 'Development Project Proposal for National Agricultural Technology Project (NATP)', Bangladesh Agricultural Research Council, Dhaka.

Bedelian, C. (2004) 'The impact of malignant catarrhal fever on Maasai pastoral communities in Kitengela Wildlife Dispersal Area, Kenya', MSc. dissertation, University of Edinburgh.

Bell, M. (2006) 'Background paper for the L20 workshop on Furthering Science and Technology, March 2006', UNU-MERIT, Maastricht. Available from: http://www.l20. org/publications/21_sY_Sci_background_Bell.pdf

Benjaminsen, T.A. (1997) 'Natural resource management, paradigm shifts, and the decentralization reform in Mali', *Human Ecology* 25:121–143.

Bentley, J. and Van Mele, P. (2005) 'Creative learning methods', in Van Mele, P., Salahuddin, A. and Magor, N.P. (eds) *Innovations in Rural Extension: Case Studies from Bangladesh*, pp. 63–76, CABI Publishing, Wallingford, UK.

Bentley, J., Boa, E., Van Mele, P., Almanza, J., Vasques, D. and Eguino, S. (2003) 'Going Public: a new extension method', *International Journal of Agricultural Sustainability* 1: 108–123.

Berdegué, J. (2001) *Co-operating to Compete: Associative Peasant Business Firms in Chile*, Published doctoral dissertation, Wageningen University, Wageningen, The Netherlands.

Berg, I.K. (1994) *Family based services: A solution-focused approach*, Norton, New York.

Best, R. (2002) 'Farmer participation in market research to identify income generating opportunities', CIAT Working Document, CIAT Africa, Uganda.

Best, R. and Kaganzi, E. (2003) 'Farmer participation in market research to identify income-generating opportunities', CIAT Africa Highlight No. 9, CIAT, Uganda.

Biggs, S (2008) 'The lost 1990s? Personal reflections on a history of participatory technology development', *Development in Practice* 18: 489–505.

Biggs, S.D. and Smith, S. (2003) 'A paradox of learning in project cycle management and the role of organizational culture', *World Development* 31: 1743–1757.

Blakeway, S. (1998) 'Report of participatory monitoring and evaluation consultancy visit to DCA-Heart, A report prepared for the Dutch Committee for Afghanistan', Vetwork UK, Musselburgh, Scotland.

Braun, A., Thiele, G. and Fernandez, M. (2000) 'Farmer field schools and local agricultural research committees: complementary platforms for integrated decision making in sustainable agriculture', *AgREN Paper* 105, ODI, London.

Bridger, J.C. and Luloff, A.E. (2001) 'Building the sustainable community: is social capital the answer?' *Sociological Inquiry* 71:458–472.

Campilan, D. (1995) 'Enhancing the user-oriented diagnostic framework through knowledge systems thinking', in UPWARD, *Taking Root: Proceedings of the Third UPWARD Review and Planning Workshop*, pp. 131–145, UPWARD, Los Baños, Philippines.

Campilan, D. (1997) 'User participation in agricultural R & D: turning the principle into practice', in UPWARD, *Local R & D. Institutionalizing Innovations in Rootcrop Agriculture*, pp. 13–25, UPWARD, Los Baños, Philippines.

Campilan, D. (2002) 'The importance of local knowledge in conserving crop diversity', SciDevNet Indigenous Knowledge Policy Brief, Available from: www.scidev.net/ dossiers/indigenous_knowledge.

Campilan, D. (2005) 'A livelihood systems framework for participatory agricultural research', in Gonsalves, J., Becker, T., Braun, A., Campilan, D., de Chavez, H., Fajber, E., Kapiriri, M., Rivaca-Caminade, J. and Vernooy, R. (eds) *Participatory Research and Development for Sustainable Agriculture and Natural Resource Management: A Sourcebook, Volume 1: Understanding Participatory Research and Development*, pp. 212–219, CIP-UPWARD, Los Baños, Philippines and IDRC, Ottawa, Canada.

Casley, D.J. and Kumar, K. (1987) *Project Monitoring and Evaluation in Agriculture*, The World Bank, Washington, D.C.

Castillo, G. (1995) 'Secondary crops in primary functions: the search for systems, synergy and sustainability', Working Paper Series 2, CIP-UPWARD, Los Baños, Philippines.

Catley, A. (1999) 'Monitoring and impact assessment of community-based animal health projects in Southern Sudan: Towards participatory approaches and methods', Vetwork UK, Musselburgh, Scotland.

Catley, A. (2000) 'The use of participatory appraisal by veterinarians in Africa', *Office international des epizooties revue scientifique et technique* 19: 702–714.

Catley, A. (2005) *Participatory Epidemiology: A Guide for Trainers*, African Union and Interafrican Bureau for Animal Resources, Nairobi.

Catley, A. (2006) 'The use of participatory epidemiology to compare the clinical veterinary knowledge of pastoralists and veterinarians in East Africa', *Tropical Animal Health and Production* 38: 171–184.

Catley, A. and Leyland, T. (2002) 'Overview: community-based animal health workers, policies, and institutions', *PLA Notes* 45: 4–7.

Catley, A., Abebe, D., Admassu, B., Bekele, G., Abera, B., Eshete, G., Rufael, T. and Haile, T. (2008) 'Impact of drought-related vaccination on livestock mortality in pastoralist areas of Ethiopia', *Disasters*, in press.

Catley, A., Chibunda, R.T., Ranga, E., Makungu, S., Magayane, F.T., Magoma, G., Madege, M.J. and Vosloo, W. (2004) 'Participatory diagnosis of a heat-intolerance syndrome in cattle in Tanzania and association with foot-and-mouth disease', *Preventive Veterinary Medicine* 65: 17–30.

Catley, A., Irungu, P., Simiyu, K., Dadye, J., Mwakio, W., Kiragu J. and Nyamwaro, S.O. (2002a) 'Participatory investigations of bovine trypanosomiasis in Tana River District, Kenya', *Medical and Veterinary Entomology* 16: 1–12.

Catley, A., Okoth, S., Osman, J., Fison, T., Njiru, Z., Mwangi, J., Jones, B.A. and Leyland, T.J. (2001) 'Participatory diagnosis of a chronic wasting disease in cattle in southern Sudan', *Preventive Veterinary Medicine* 51: 161–181.

Catley, A., Osman, J., Mawien, C., Jones, B.A. and Leyland, T.J. (2002b) 'Participatory analysis of seasonal incidences of diseases of cattle, disease vectors and rainfall in southern Sudan', *Preventive Veterinary Medicine* 53: 275–284.

Ceesay, M., Reid, W.S., Fernandes, E.C.M. and Uphoff N. (2006) 'The effects of repeated soil wetting and drying on lowland rice yield with System of Rice Intensification (SRI) methods,' *International Journal of Agricultural Sustainability* 4: 5–14.

Chaiklin, S. and Lave, J. (eds) (1993) *Understanding practice: perspectives on activity and context*, CUP, Cambridge.

Chambers, R. (1983) *Rural Development: Putting the Last First*, Harlow, London.

Chambers, R. (2002) 'Professional error, critical awareness and good science', Unpublished paper for the International conference on Why Has Impact Assessment Research Not Made More of a Difference? San Jose, Costa Rice. Available from: http://tumi.lamolina.edu.pe/ipps/Nuevas%20Perspectivas%20DR/npdr10.pdf [accessed 26 October, 2007].

Chambers, R. and Mayoux, L. (2003) 'Reversing the paradigm: quantification and participatory methods', Available from: http://www.enterprise-impact.org.uk/pdf/Chambers-MayouxUpdate.pdf [accessed 26 October 2007].

Chambers, R., Pacey, A. and Thrupp, L-A. (eds) (1989) *Farmer First: Farmer Innovation and Agricultural Research*, IT Publications, London.

Chen, H.T. (2005) *Practical Program Evaluation: Assessing and Improving Planning, Implementation, and Effectiveness*, Sage Publications, California.

China Agricultural Technology Extension System Reform Research Taskforce (2004) 'China agricultural technology extension: Status quo, problems and solutions', *Management World* 5: 49–75 (in Chinese).

CIDA (2003) *Knowledge Sharing. Methods, Meetings and Tools*, Canadian International Development Agency, Ottawa.

CIP (1989) *Annual Report. Worldwide Potato and Sweetpotato Improvement*, CIP, Lima, Peru.

Clark, R. (2002) 'Participatory research and development processes and techniques. A training manual', Visayas State College of Agriculture, Baybay, Leyte, Philippines.

COHD (2004) 'Participatory learning, curriculum development, and mainstreaming of CBNRM in higher education in China', Research proposal, College of Humanities and Development, CAU, Beijing.

Coleman, J.S. (1988) 'Social capital in the creation of human capital', *American Journal of Sociology* 94: 95–120.

Collier, P. (1998) 'Social capital and poverty', *World Bank Social Capital Initiative Working Paper* no 4. World Bank, Washington, D.C.

Conroy, C. (2004) *Participatory Livestock Research: A Guide*, ITDG Publishing, Rugby.

Coupe, S. and Lewins, R. (2007) *Negotiating the Seed Treaty*, Practical Action Publishing, Rugby.

Dalton, T., Lilja, N., Johnson, N. and Howeler, R. (2005) 'Impact of participatory natural resource management research in cassava-based cropping systems in Vietnam and Thailand', Working Document 23, CGIAR Systemwide Programme on Participatory Research and Gender Analysis for Technology Development and Institutional Innovation, Cali, Colombia. Available from: http://www.prgaprogram.org/modules/ DownloadsPlus/uploads/PRGA_ Publications/General/WD23_CIAT-PRGA.pdf

Daniel, I.O. and Adetumbi, J.A. (2004) 'Seed supply for vegetable production at small holder farms in south western Nigeria', *Euphytica* 140: 189–196.

David, S. and Sperling, L. (1999) 'Improving the technology delivery mechanisms: lessons from bean seed systems research in east and central Africa', *Agriculture and Human Values* 16: 381–388.

DeDatta, S.K. (1981) *Principles and Practices of Rice Production*, John Wiley & Sons, New York.

Deng, N. and Wan, B. (eds) (2001) *The 21st Century China's Agricultural Science and Technology Development Strategy*, China Agriculture Press, Beijing.

Derrien, F. (2005) 'The IFAP Committee on Agricultural Research. Report on the Meeting 5–6 September, 2005', IFAP, Paris.

Desclaux and Chiffoleau (2006) 'Participatory plant breeding: the best way to breed for sustainable agriculture?' *International Journal of Agricultural Sustainability* 4: 119–130.

Development Fund (2007) 'Report of conference Can Africa Feed Itself? Oslo, Norway, June 6–8th 2007', Development Fund, Norway. Available from: www.agropub.no/ asset/2636/1/2636_1.pdf

Diao, X. and Hazell, P. (2004) 'Exploring market opportunities for African smallholders', paper prepared for the Conference 'Assuring food security in Africa by 2020: Prioritizing actions, strengthening actors, and facilitating partnerships', April 1-3, 2004, Kampala, Uganda.

Digal, L. (2007) 'Regoverning markets: Best practices and lessons learned', Paper presented at the IFAP Asian Committee Meeting, November 7–8, 2007, Hanoi, Vietnam.

Dobermann, A. (2004) 'A critical assessment of the system of rice intensification', *Agricultural Systems* 79: 261–281.

Dorward, A., Poole, N., Morrison, J.A., Kydd, J. and Urey, I. (2003) 'Markets, institutions and technology: missing links in livelihoods analysis', *Development Policy Review* 21: 319–32.

Douthwaite, B. (2002) *Enabling Innovation: A Practical Guide to Understanding and Fostering Technological Change*, Zed Books, London.

Earl, J. and Kodio, A. (2005) 'Participatory landscape/lifescape appraisal', in K. Moore (ed.), *Conflict, Social Capital and Managing Natural Resources: A West African Case Study*, pp. 77–88, CABI Publishing, Wallingford, UK.

Ejigu, J. and Waters-Bayer, A. (2005) *Unlocking Farmers' Potential: Institutionalising Farmer Participatory Research and Extension in Southern Ethiopia*, Project Experiences Series 2, FARM-Africa, London.

Ekboir, J. (2003) 'Why impact analysis should not be used for research evaluation and what the alternatives are', *Agricultural Systems* 78: 166–184.

Elnarsi, H.O. (2006) 'Prevalence and ranking of bovine trypanosomiasis in Unity State, Sudan, by participatory epidemiological, clinical and laboratory testing', MVSc. thesis, University of Khartoum.

ETC Group (2007) *The World's Top 10 Seed Companies in 2006*, ETC Group, Ottawa. Available from: www.etcgroup.org/upload/publication/pdf_file/615

Ewbank, R., Kasindei, A., Kimaro, F. and Slaa, S. (2007) 'Farmer participatory research in northern Tanzania', *FARM-Africa Working Paper* 11, FARM-Africa, London.

FARA (2005) 'Promoting inclusiveness of civil society organizations (CSOs) in African agricultural research agenda: A FARA/GFAR collaborative initiative', Meeting Report, FARA, Accra, Ghana.

Farelli, F. and Brandsma, J.M. (1974) *Provocative therapy*, Meta Publications, Cupertin, California.

Farrington, J. and Martin, A. (1988) 'Farmer participation in agricultural research: a review of concepts and practices', *Occasional Paper* No. 9, ODI, London.

Fernández-Baca, E.C. (2004) 'Building social capital through advocacy coalitions in natural resource management in the rural Andes: Who forms alliances?' Masters dissertation, Iowa State University.

Ferris, S., Kaganzi, E., Best, R., Ostertag, C., Lundy, M. and Wandschneider, T. (2006) *A Market Facilitator's Guide to Participatory Agroenterprise Development*, CIAT, Cali, Colombia.

Flora, C., Campana, F., Garcia Bravo, M., and Fernández-Baca, E. (2006) 'Social capital and advocacy coalitions: examples of environmental issues from Ecuador', in Rhodes, R. (Ed.), *Development with Identity. Community, Culture and Sustainability in the Andes*, pp 267–297, CABI Publishing, Cambridge, MA.

Frazen, H., Begenmann, A.P.F., Wadsack, J.A. and Rudat, H. (1996) 'Variety improvement in the informal sector: aspect of new strategies', in Eyzaguirre, P. and Iwanaga, M. (eds), *Participatory Plant Breeding. Proceedings of a Workshop, 26–29 July 1995, Wageningen, The Netherlands*, pp. 19–30. International Agricultural Research Centre, Wageningen, The Netherlands and International Plant Genetic Resource Institute, Rome, Italy.

Fuller, D. (2005) 'Crop cultivation: the evidence', 'Farming: stone age farmers of the savanna' and 'Farming: tropical forest zones', in Shillington, K. (ed.) *Encyclopedia of African History*, Fitzroy Dearborn, NY.

Gayao, B. (1995) 'Case 1. From diagnosis to action research: the case of sweetpotato homegardens in Northern Philippines', in UPWARD, *Taking Root. Proceedings of the Third UPWARD Review and Planning Workshop, pp. 36–40*, UPWARD, Los Baños, Philippines.

Giampietro, M. (2003) *Multi-Scale Integrated Analysis of Agro-Ecosystems*, CRC Press, Boca Raton.

Gomez, K.A. and DeDatta, S.K. (1971) 'Border effects in rice experimental plots', *Experimental Agriculture* 7: 87–97.

Gonsalves, J., Becker, T., Braun, A., Campilan, D., de Chavez, H., Fajber, E., Kapiriri, M., Rivaca-Caminade, J. and Vernooy, R. (eds) (2005) *Participatory Research and Development for Sustainable Agriculture and Natural Resource Management: A Sourcebook*, CIP-UPWARD, Los Baños, Philippines and IDRC, Ottawa, Canada.

Government of Uganda. (2000) 'Master Document of the NAADS Task force and Joint Donor Groups', National Agricultural Advisory Development Services (NAADS), Ministry of Agriculture, Animal Industry and Fisheries, Kampala.

Grace, D. (2003) 'Participative trypanosomiasis control in Burkina Faso: Lessons Learned, Ways Forward', Working Paper 2, International Livestock Research Institute, Nairobi.

GRAIN (2005) 'Food sovereignty. Turning the world's food system upside down', Seedling. Barcelona, Spain. Available from: www.grain.org/seedling_files/seed-05-04-01.pdf

Grootaert, C. and Narayan, D. (2004) 'Local institutions, poverty and households in Bolivia', *World Development* 32: 1179–1198.

Guerra, L.C., Bhuiyan, S.I., Thuong, T.P. and Barker, R. (1998) *Producing More Rice with Less Water in Irrigated Systems*. SWIM Paper 5, International Water Management Institute, Colombo.

Guijt, I. (1998) 'Participatory monitoring and impact assessment of sustainable agriculture initiatives', Available from: http://www.iied.org/pubs/display.php?o=61 39IIED&n=10&l=24&a=I%20Guijt&x=Y [accessed 3 November 2007].

Guijt, I. (2000) 'RNRKS Project Completion Summary Sheet for 'Participatory monitoring and output assessment of rural regeneration and sustainable agriculture in Brazil', IIED, London.

Guijt, I. (2008) 'Seeking surprise: rethinking monitoring for collective learning in rural resource management', PhD thesis, Wageningen University, Wageningen.

Gupta, A.K. (2006) 'From sink to source: The Honey Bee Network documents indigenous knowledge and innovations in India', *Innovations: Technology, Governance, Globalization* 1: 49–66.

Gura, S. (2007) *Livestock Genetics Companies: Concentration and Proprietary Strategies of an Emerging Power in the Global Food Economy*, League for Pastoral Peoples and Endogenous Livestock Development, Germany. Available from: www.pastoralpeoples.org/gura_livestock_genetics.htm

Hagedoorn, J., Link, A.N. and Vonortas, N.S. (2000) 'Research partnerships', *Research Policy* 29: 567–586.

Hagmann, J. (2002) 'Competence development in Soft Skills/Personal Mastery', Report on a consultancy mission to design a learning programme at Makerere University, Uganda.

Hagmann, J. (2005) 'Learning wheel – creating common frameworks for joint learning, action and knowledge management', *AgREN Paper* 52, ODI, London.

Hagmann, J., Almekinders, C., with Bukenya, C., Guevara, F., Hailemichael, A., Isubikalu, P., Kamau, G., Kamanga, B., Kibwika, P., Limnarankul, B., Matiri, F., Mutimukuru, T.,

Ngwenya, H., Opondo, C., Zhang, L., Breitschuh, U. (2003) 'Developing 'Soft Skill' in higher education', *PLA Notes* 48: 21–25.

Hagmann, J., Chuma, E., Murwira, K. Connolly, M. (1999) 'Putting process into practice: operationalising participatory extension', *AgREN Paper* 94, ODI, London.

Hall, A. (2006) 'Public private sector partnerships in an agricultural system of innovation: concepts and challenges', *UNU-MERIT Working Paper* 2006–002, United Nations University/Maastricht Economic and Social Research and Training Centre on Innovation and Technology, Maastricht, The Netherlands.

Hall, A. (2007) 'The origins and implications of using innovation systems perspectives in the design and implementation of agricultural research projects: Some personal observations' *UNU-MERIT Working Paper* 2007–013, United Nations University/Maastricht Economic and Social Research and Training Centre on Innovation and Technology, Maastricht, The Netherlands.

Hall, A., Sulaiman, R., Clark, N. and Yoganand, B. (2003) 'From measuring impact to learning institutional lessons: an innovation systems perspective on improving the management of international agricultural research', *Agricultural Systems* 78: 213–241.

Hall, A., Sulaiman, R., Clark, N., Sivamohan, M.V.K. and Yoganand, B. (2002) 'Public–private sector interaction in the Indian agricultural research system: an innovation systems perspective on institutional reform', in Byerlee, D. and Echeverría, R. (eds), *Agricultural Research Policy in an Era of Privatization*, CABI Publishing, Wallingford, UK.

Hall, A.J. (2005) 'Capacity development for agricultural biotechnology in developing countries: an innovation systems view of what it is and how to develop it', *Journal of International Development* 19: 611–630.

Hall, A.J., Clark, N.G., Sulaiman, V.R., Sivamohan, M.V.K. and Yoganand, B. (2000) 'New agendas for agricultural research in developing countries: policy analysis and institutional implications', *Knowledge, Policy and Technology* 13: 70–91.

Hall, A.J., Sivamohan, M.V.K., Clark, N., Taylor, S. and Bockett, G. (2001) 'Why research partnerships really matter: innovation theory, institutional arrangements and implications for developing new technology for the poor', *World Development* 29: 783–797.

Hall, A.J., Sulaiman, V.R., Clark, N., Sivamohan, M.V.K. and Yoganand, B. (2002) 'Public-private sector interaction in the Indian Agricultural Research System: an innovation systems perspective on institutional reform', in Byerlee, D. and Echeverria, R.G. (eds) *Agricultural Research Policy in an Era of Privatization*, pp. 155–176, CABI Publishing, Wallingford, UK.

Hall, A.J., Yoganand, B., Sulaiman, V.R., Raina, R., Prasad, S., Naik, G. and Clark, N.G. (eds) (2004) *Innovations in Innovation: Reflections on Partnership and Learning*, ICRISAT, Patancheru, India and NCAP, New Delhi, India.

Hardon-Baars, A. (1997) 'Users' perspectives. Literature review on the development of a concept', Working Paper No. 4, UPWARD and Department of Household and Consumer Studies, Wageningen Agricultural University, Wageningen.

Harwood, R., Place, F., Kassam, A. and Gregerson, H. (2006) 'International public goods through integrated natural resources management research', *Experimental Agriculture* 42: 375–397.

Haverkort, B., Van der Kamp, J. and Waters-Bayer, A. (1991) *Joining Farmers' Experiments. Experiences in Participatory Technology Development. ILEIA Readings in Sustainable Agriculture*, IT Publications, London.

Hidayat, R. and Adinata, K.S. (2001) 'Farmers in Indonesia: escaping the trap of injustice', Paper presented to the Programme Advisory Committee (PAC) Meeting, FAO Programme for Community IPM in Asia, 26–28 November, 2001, Ayutthaya, Thailand.

Hiemstra, W., Reijntjes, C. and van der Werf, E. (1992) *Let Farmers Judge. Experiences in Assessing the Sustainability of Agriculture. ILEIA Readings in Sustainable Agriculture,* IT Publications, London.

Hocdé, H., Triomphe, B., Faure, G. and Dulcire, M. (2008) 'From participation to partnership, a different way for researchers to accompany innovation processes: challenges and difficulties', in Sanginga, P., Waters-Bayer, A., Kaaria, S., Njuki, J. and Wettasinha, C. (eds) *Innovation Africa: Enriching Farmers' Livelihoods,* pp. 135–150, Earthscan, London.

Hope, A. and Timmel, S. (1984) *Training for Transformation: A Handbook for Community Workers, Book I,* Mambo press, Zimbabwe.

Hopfield, J. (1982) 'Neural networks and physical systems with emergent collective computational abilities', *Proceedings of the National Academy of Sciences, USA, Biophysics* 79: 2554–2558.

Hopkins, C. and Short, A. (2002) 'Participatory impact assessment in Ethiopia: linking policy reform to field experiences', *PLA Notes* 45: 23–28. Available from: http://www.africa.upenn.edu/eue_web/pastoral.htm [accessed 5 November 2007].

Horie, T., Shiraiwa, T., Homma, K., Katsura, K., Maeda, S. and Yoshida, H. (2005) 'Can yields of lowland rice resume the increases that they showed in the 1980s?' *Plant Production Sciences* 8: 257–272.

Horton, D., Alexaki, A., Bennett-Lartey, S., Brice, K.N., Campilan, D., Carden, F., de Souza Silva, I., Duong, L.T., Khadar, I., Maestrey Boza, A., Kaeys Muniruzzaman, I., Perez, I., Somarriba Chang, M., Vernooy, R. and Watts, J. (2003) *Evaluating Capacity Development: Experiences from Research and Development Organizations Around the World,* International Service for National Agricultural Research (ISNAR), Netherlands; IDRC, Canada; ACP-EU Technical Centre for Agricultural (CTA), Netherlands.

Hurst, G. and Brown, C. (eds) (2006) 'A good place to start. The IDS Knowledge Services guide to finding development information on-line'. Available from: http://www.ids.ac.uk/index.cfm?objectId=25867CA5-0C86-CEA8-B366F50BE0E71705

Hutchins, E. (1995) *Cognition in the Wild,* MIT Press, Cambridge, MA.

Idowa, S.O. (2005) 'Participatory epizootiological research of animal health development in Oluhunde village, Lanlate, Oyo State, Nigeria', MPVM thesis, Faculty of Veterinary Medicine, University of Ibadan.

IFAD (2002) *Managing for Impact in Rural Development: A Guide for Project M&E,* IFAD, Rome.

IFAP (2006) 'Negotiating linkages: farmer organizations, agricultural research and extension', Updated briefing in 2006 based on the original of 1995, IFAP, Paris.

IFAP (2007a) 'How to improve farmers' influence on agricultural research', IFAP, Paris. Available from: http://www.ifap.org/en/issues/documents/Backgroundpaper ResearchEAR3-06.pdf

IFAP (2007b) 'IFAP and GFAR collaboration during 2006 and 2007', IFAP, Paris.

IIED (2006) 'Citizens space for democratic deliberation on GMOs and the future of farming in Mali'. Available from: www.iied.org/NR/agbioliv/ag_liv_projects/verdict.html

ILEIA, Greenpeace and Oxfam (2007) see www.farmingsolutions.org

ISNAR (1985) 'The user's perspective in international agricultural and national agricultural research: a background document', ISNAR, The Hague.

Isubikalu, P. (2007) *Stepping Stones to Improve Upon the Functioning of Participatory Agricultural Extension Programmes: Farmer Field Schools in Uganda*, PhD Thesis, Wageningen University.

Iturralde, P. (2007) 'Incidencia política desde los actores sociales', Workshop organized by AGRECOL Andes, 3–5 October, 2007, Cochabamba, Bolivia.

Jiggins, J., Lightfoot, C. and Reintjes, C. (1996) 'Mobilising science and technology to get agriculture moving in Africa: A response to Borlaug and Dowswell', *Development Policy Review* 13: 89–103.

Johnson, N., Lilja, N., Ashby, J.A. and Garcia, J.A. (2004) 'The practice of participatory research and gender analysis in natural resource management', *Natural Resources Forum* 28: 189–200.

Johnson, N.L., Lilja, N. and Ashby, J.A. (2003) 'Measuring the impact of user participation in agricultural and natural resource management research', *Agricultural Systems* 78: 287–306

Jones, R.B., Audi, P.A. and Tripp, R. (2001) 'The role of informal seed systems in disseminating modern varieties: the example of pigeon pea from a semi-arid area of Kenya', *Experimental Agriculture* 37: 539–548.

Joshi, K.D., Sthapit, B.R., Subedi, M. and Witcombe, J.R. (2002) 'Participatory plant breeding in rice in Nepal', in Cleveland, D.A. and Soleri, D. (eds), *Farmers, Scientists and Plant Breeding: Integrating Knowledge and Practice*, pp. 239–267, CABI Publishing, Wallingford, UK

Kabir, H. and Uphoff, N. (2007) 'Results of disseminating the System of Rice Intensification with Farmer Field School methods in Northern Myanmar', *Experimental Agriculture* 43: 463–476.

Kemmis, S. and McTaggart, R. (1988) 'Introduction: the nature of action research', in Kemmis, S. and McTaggart, R. (eds), *The Action Research Planner*, 3rd edn, Deakin University Press, Australia.

Kibwika, P. (2006) *Learning to Make Change. Developing Innovation Competence for Recreating the African University of the 21st Century*, Wageningen Academic Publishers, Wageningen.

Kiers, E.T, Leaky, R.R.B., Izac, A.M., Heinemann, J.A., Rosenthal, E., Nathan, D. and Jiggins, J. (2008) 'Agriculture at the cross-roads', *Science* 320: 320–321.

Killough, S. (2003) 'Farmer-led extension: A comparative analysis of characteristics and outcomes of three programmes in Latin America', Unpublished Ph.D. dissertation, University of Reading, Reading, U.K.

Killough, S. (2005) 'Farmer participation in agricultural research and extension', in Gonsalves, J., Becker, T., Braun, A., Campilan, D., de Chavez, H., Fajber, E., Kapiriri, M., Rivaca-Caminade, J. and Vernooy, R. (eds). (2005) *Participatory Research and Development for Sustainable Agriculture and Natural Resource Management: a Sourcebook. Volume 1: Understanding Participatory Research and Development*, pp. 23–31, UPWARD, Philippines and IDRC, Canada.

Knox, A., Meinzen-Dick, R. and Hazell, P. (2002) 'Property rights, collective action, and technologies for natural resource management: a conceptual framework', in Meinzen-Dick, R., Knox, A., Place, F. and Swallow, B. (eds) *Innovation in Natural Resource Management: The Role of Property Rights and Collective Action in Developing Countries*, pp. 12–44, Johns Hopkins University Press, Baltimore and IFPRI, Washington, D.C.

Kuhn, T. (1962) *The Structure of Scientific Revolutions*, University of Chicago Press, Chicago.

Lama, T.L. and Hidalgo, O. (2003) 'Enhancing production and on-farm maintenance of quality potato seed in Nepal', in UPWARD, *From Cultivators to Consumers: Participatory Research with Various User Groups*, pp. 30–36, CIP-UPWARD, Los Baños, Philippines.

Lanham, R. (2006) *The Economics of Attention. Style and Substance in the Age of Information*, University of Chicago Press, Chicago.

Laranang, L.B. and Basilio, C.S. (2003) 'Community-based production of healthy sweetpotato planting materials in Central Luzon, Philippines', in UPWARD, *From Cultivators to Consumers: Participatory Research with Various User Groups*, pp. 19–29, CIP-UPWARD, Los Baños, Philippines.

Laulanié, H. (1993) 'Le système de riziculture intensive malgache', *Tropicultura* 11: 110–114.

Laulanié, H. (2003) *Le Riz à Madagascar: un Développement en Dialogue avec les Paysans*, Editions Karthala, Paris.

Leach, M., Scoones, I. and Sterling, A. (2007) 'Pathways to sustainability: an overview of the STEPS Centre approach', STEPS Approach Paper, STEPS Centre, Brighton.

Lele, U. and Goldsmith, O. (1989) 'The development of national agricultural research capacity: India's experience with the Rockefeller Foundation and its significance for Africa', *Economic Development and Cultural Change* 37: 305–343.

Lesser, E.L. and Stork, J. (2001) 'Community of practice and organizational performance', *IBM Systems Journal* 40: 831–841. Available from: http://www.research.ibm.com/journal/sj/404/lesser.html [accessed 2007-10-02]

Leyland, T. (1996) 'The case for a community-based approach with reference to southern Sudan', in FAO, *The World Without Rinderpest*, pp. 109–120, FAO Animal Health and Production Paper 129, FAO, Rome.

Li, X., Zuo, T. and Qi, G. (2006) 'Partial assessment of application of participatory research approaches in China', Paper for Workshop on Mainstreaming and Institutionalizing Participatory Research Approaches in China, 7–8, March, 2006, Beijing.

Lizares-Bodegon, S., Gonsalves, J., Killough, S., Waters-Bayer, A., van Veldhuizen, L. and Espineli, M. (2002) *Participatory Technology Development for Agricultural Development: Challenges for Institutional Integration*, IIRR, Philippines and ETC-Ecoculture, Netherlands.

Lockeretz, W. (1991) 'Information requirements of reduced-chemical production methods', *American Journal of Alternative Agriculture* 6: 97–103.

Lundy, M. and Gottret, M.V. (2005) 'Learning alliances: an approach for building multi-stakeholder innovation systems'. Available from: www.idrc.ca/uploads/user-S/11605726301Anexo_1-IRC_LA_book_chapter.pdf [accessed 26 October, 2007].

Lundy, M., Gottret, M.V. and Ashby, J. (2005) 'Learning alliances: an approach for building multi-stakeholder innovation systems', *ILAC Brief* 8, The Institutional Learning and Change (ILAC) Initiative, Bioversity International, Rome.

Lundy, M., Gottret, M.V., Cifuentes, W., Ostertag, C.F. and Best, R. (2003) *Design of Strategies to Increase the Competitiveness of Smallholder Production Chains. Field Manual*, CIAT, Cali, Colombia.

Lyon, F. and Afikorah-Danquah, S. (1998) 'Small-scale seed provision in Ghana: social relations, contracts and institutions for micro-enterprise development', *AgREN Paper* 84, ODI, London.

Maredia, M., Howard, J., Boughton, D., Naseen, A., Wanzala, M. and Kajisa, K. (1999) 'Increasing seed system efficiency in Africa: concepts, strategies and issues',

Michigan State University International Development Working Paper. Department of Agricultural Economics, MSU, East Lansing, Michigan.

Mariner, J., McDermott, J., Heesterbeek, J.A.P., Catley, A. and Roeder, P. (2005) 'A model of lineage-1 and lineage-2 rinderpest virus transmission in pastoral areas of East Africa', *Preventive Veterinary Medicine* 69: 245–262.

Marti, N. and Pimbert, M. (2006) 'Barter markets: sustaining people and nature in the Andes', IIED, London. Available from: www.iied.org/pubs/pdfs/14518IIED.pdf

Matlon, P.J. (2003) 'Foreword', *Agricultural Systems* 78:123–125.

Mauss, M. (1972) [Mauss & Hubert, 1902], *A general theory of magic* (trans. Robert Brain), Routledge, London.

McDonald, A.J., Hobbs, P.R. and Riha, S.J. (2006) 'Does the system of rice intensification outperform conventional best management? A synopsis of the empirical record,' *Field Crops Research* 96: 31–36.

Meinzen-Dick, R.S. and Di Gregorio, M. (eds) (2004) 'Collective action and property rights for sustainable development', *2020 Focus 11*, IFPRI, Washington, D.C. Available from: http://www.ifpri.org/2020/focus/focus11.htm

Minantyorini, C., Widyastuti, A., Djazuli, M. and Widowati, S. (1996) 'Local knowledge of sweetpotato in Flores, Indonesia: what next?', in UPWARD, *Into Action Research, Partnerships in Asian Rootcrop Research and Development*, pp. 11-26, CIP-UPWARD, Los Baños, Philippines.

Ministry of Agriculture of China (2007) *China Agricultural Statistics Yearbook 2006*, China Statistics Press, Beijing.

Mishra, A and Salokhe, V.M. (2008) 'Seedling characteristics and the early growth of transplanted rice under different water regimes', *Experimental Agriculture* 44: 1–19.

Mishra, A., Whitten, M., Ketelaar, J.W. and Salokhe, V.M. (2006) 'The System of Rice Intensification (SRI): A challenge for science, and an opportunity for farmer empowerment towards sustainable agriculture', *International Journal of Agricultural Sustainability* 4: 193–212.

Mochabo, K.O.M., Kitala, P.M., Gathura, P.B., Ogara, W.O., Catley, A., Eregae, E.M. and Kaitho, T.D. (2004) 'Community perceptions of important camel diseases in Lapur Division of Turkana District, Kenya', *Tropical Animal Health and Production* 37: 187–204.

Moore, K. (ed.) (2005) *Conflict, Social Capital and Managing Natural Resources: A West African Case Study*, CABI Publishing, Wallingford, UK.

Moser, C.M. and Barrett, C.B. (2003) 'The disappointing adoption dynamics of a yield-increasing, low external-input technology: The case of SRI in Madagascar', *Agricultural Systems* 76: 1085–1100.

Mulvany, P.M. (2005) 'Corporate control over seeds: limiting access and farmers' rights', *IDS Bulletin* 36: 68–73.

Murwira, K., Wedgwood, H., Watson, C., Win, E.J. and Tawney, C. (2001) *Beating Hunger, The Chivi Experience: A Community-based Approach to Food Security*, IT Publications, London.

Nalitolela, S. and Allport, R. (2002) 'A participatory approach to assessing the impact of a community-based animal health project with Maasai communities in Tanzania', *PLA Notes* 45: 17–22.

Namara, R.E., Hussain, I., Bossio, D. and Verma, S. (2007) 'Innovative land and water management approaches in Asia: productivity impacts, adoption prospects and poverty outreach', *Irrigation and Drainage* 56: 335–348.

Nasirumbi, L., Rubyogo, J.C., Ugen, M., Namayanja, A. and Luyima, G. (2008) 'Participatory variety selection to speed up bean variety dissemination: lessons from Uganda', in Thijssen, M.H., Bishaw, Z., Bashir, A., de Boef. W.S. (eds), *Farmers' Seeds and Varieties: Supporting Informal Seed Supply in Ethiopia*, pp. 113–118, Wageningen International, Wageningen.

National Bureau of Statistics of China (2006) *China Statistical Yearbook 2005*, China Statistics Press, Beijing.

National Committee on Science and Technology (1997) *China's Agricultural Science and Technology Policies*, China Agriculture Press, Beijing.

Nazarea, V. (1998) *Cultural Memory and Biodiversity*. University of Arizona Press, Tucson.

Nederlof, E.S., Röling, N. and van Huis, A. (2007) 'Pathway for agricultural science impact in West Africa: Lessons from the Convergence of Sciences programme', *International Journal of Agricultural Sustainability* 5: 247–264.

North, D. (2005) *Understanding the Process of Economic Change*, Princeton University Press, Princeton.

O'Hara, P. (2005) *Linking People to Policy: From Participation to Deliberation in the Context of Philippine Community Forestry*, IIRR, Philippines; IDRC, Canada; Department of Environment and Natural Resources (DENR), Philippines.

Okuthe, O.S., Kuloba, K., Emongor, R.A., Ngotho R.N., Bukachi, S., Nyamwaro, S.O., Murila, G. and Wamwayi, H.M. (2003) 'National Agricultural Research Systems experiences in the use of participatory approaches to animal health research in Kenya', in Sones, K. and Catley, A. (eds) *Primary Animal Health Care in the 21st Century: Shaping the Rules, Policies and Institutions*, Proceedings of an international conference, 15–18 October 2002, Mombasa. African Union/Interafrican Bureau for Animal Resources, Nairobi.

Orr, A. and Magor, N.P. (2002) 'PETRRA Project Strategy', PETRRA-IRRI, Dhaka.

Ortiz, O., Frias, G., Ho, R., Cisneros, H., Nelson, R., Castillo, R., Orrego, R., Pradel, W., Alcazar, J. and Bazán, M. (2008) 'Organizational learning through participatory research: CIP and CARE in Peru', *Agriculture and Human Values* 25: 419–431.

Ostertag, C.F. (1999) 'Identifying and assessing market opportunities for small rural producers. Tools for decision-making in NRM', CIAT, Cali, Colombia.

Ostrom, E. (2000a) 'Social capital: a fad or a fundamental concept?' in Dasgupta, P. and Seralgedin, I. (eds), *Social Capital a Multifaceted Perspective*, pp. 172–214, World Bank, Washington, D.C.

Ostrom, E. (2000b) 'Collective action and the evolution of social norms', *Journal of Economic Perspectives* 14: 137–158.

Padre, S., Sudarshana and Tripp, R. (2003) 'Reforming farm journalism. The experience of *Adike Pathrike* in India', *AgREN Paper* 128, ODI, London.

Painter, T., Sumberg, J. and Price, T. (1994) 'Your *terroir* and my 'action space': implications of differentiation, mobility and diversification for the *approche terroir* in Sahelian West Africa', *Africa* 64: 447–463.

Pal, S. and Jha, D. (2007) 'Public-private partnerships in agricultural R&D: challenges and prospects', in Ballabh, V. (ed.) *Institutional Alternatives and Governance of Agriculture*, pp. 151–171, Academic Foundation, New Delhi.

Patel, K.B., Maina, M., Hagmann, J., Woomer, P.L. (2001) 'Curriculum development and transformation in rural development and natural resource management', Documentation of a Strategy Workshop Conducted at the Rockefeller Foundation's

Bellagio Center in Italy, 12–16 November, 2001, RUFORUM publication, Kampala, Uganda.

Peavey, F. (1994) *Strategic Questioning*, New Society Publishers, Philadelphia.

Peters, D., Tinh, N.T., Thai, T.M., Phan, H.T., Nguyen, T.Y. and Hoanh, M.T. (2001) *'Pig Feed Improvement through Enhanced Use of Sweet Potato Roots and Vines in Northern and Central Vietnam'*, CIP-UPWARD, Los Baños, Philippines.

Picton, P. (2000) *Neural Networks*, 2nd edn, Palgrave, Basingstoke.

Pimbert, M. (2007) 'Transforming knowledge and ways of knowing for food sovereignty', Paper for Conference on Endogenous Development and Bio-Cultural Diversity, the Interplay of Worldviews, Globalisation and Locality, 3–5th October 2006, Geneva, Switzerland. Available from: www.iied.org/NR/agbioliv/documents/ FoodSovereigntyBio-CulturalDiversity.pdf

Pimbert, M. and Wakeford, T. (2002) 'Prajateerpu: a citizens jury/workshop on food and farming issues', IIED, London.

Place, F. and Swallow, B. (2000) 'Assessing the relationships between property rights and technology adoption in smallholder agriculture: a review of issues and empirical methods', CAPRi Working Paper 2, IFPRI, Washington, D.C. Available from: http:// www.capri.cgiar.org/pdf/capriwp2.pdf

Planning Commission (2006) 'Towards faster and more inclusive growth – An approach to the 11th Five Year Plan', Draft Approach Paper to the XI Plan, Government of India, New Delhi.

Prain, G. (1995) 'Sweetpotato in Asian production systems: An overview of UPWARD's first phase research', in UPWARD, *Taking Root. Proceedings of the Third UPWARD Review and Planning Workshop, pp. 1–35*, UPWARD, Los Baños, Philippines.

Prain, G. and Bagalanon, C.P. (1998) *Conservation and Change: Farmer Management of Agricultural Biodiversity in the Context of Development*, UPWARD, Los Baños, Laguna.

Pretty, J (2005) *The Earthscan Reader in Sustainable Agriculture*, Earthscan, London.

Qi, G., Xu, X., Zuo, T., Li, X., Chen, K., Gao, X., Ji, M., Lin, L., Mao, M., Li, J., Song, Y., Long, Z., Lu, M., Yuan, J. and Vernooy, R. (2008) 'Introducing participatory curriculum development in China's higher education: the case of Community-Based Natural Resource Management', *Journal of Agricultural Education and Extension* 14: 7–20.

Quizon, J., Feder, G. and Murgai, R. (2001) 'Fiscal sustainability of agricultural extension: the case of the farmer field school approach', *Journal of International Agricultural and Extension Education* 8: 13–22.

Raina, R. (2003) 'Institutions and organisations; enabling reforms in Indian agricultural research and policy', *International Journal of Technology Management and Sustainable Development* 2: 97–116.

Raina, R., Sangar, S., Rasheed Sulaiman, V. and Hall, A.J. (2006) 'The soil sciences in India: policy lessons for agricultural innovation', *Research Policy* 35: 691–714.

Ramanjaneyulu, G.V., Rajitha, N. and Ravindra, A. (2007) 'Taking roots: experiences with System of Rice Intensification in Andhra Pradesh', Centre for Sustainable Agriculture, WASSAN and WWF-Dialogue Project, Secunderabad.

Ramasamy, S., ten Berge, H.F.M. and Purushothaman, S. (1997) 'Yield formation in rice in response to drainage and nitrogen application', *Field Crops Research* 51: 65–82.

Randriamiharisoa, R., Barison, J. and Uphoff, N. (2006) 'Soil biological contributions to the System of Rice Production', in Uphoff, N., Ball, A., Fernandes, E.C.M., Herren, H., Husson, O., Laing, M., Palm, C., Pretty, J., Sanchez, P., Sanginga, N. and Thies, J.

(eds), *Biological Approaches to Sustainable Soil Systems*, pp. 409–424, CRC Press, Boca Raton, FL.

Reardon, T., Timmer, C.P., Barrett, C.B. and Berdegué, J. (2003) 'The rise of supermarkets in Africa, Asia and Latin America', *American Journal of Agricultural Economics* 85: 1140–1146.

Reijntjes, C., Haverkort, B. and Waters-Bayer, A. (1992) *Farming for the Future*, Macmillan Education, UK.

Renger, R. and Titcomb, A. (2002) 'A three-step approach to teaching logic models', *American Journal of Evaluation* 23: 493-503.

Rhoades, R. and Nazarea, V. (2006) 'Reconciling local and global agendas in sustainable development: participatory research with indigenous communities', *Journal of Mountain Science* 3: 334–346.

Rhoades, R.E. (1990) 'The birth of UPWARD', in UPWARD, *Proceedings of the Inaugural Planning Workshop on the User's Perspective with Agricultural Research and Development*, pp. 6–8, UPWARD, Los Baños, Philippines.

Rhoades, R.E. and Booth, R.H. (1982) 'Farmer back to farmer: a model for generating acceptable agricultural technology', *Agricultural Administration* 11: 127–137.

Richards, P. (1986) *Coping with Hunger: Hazard and Experiment in an African Rice-farming System*, Allen & Unwin, London.

Riesman, P. (1974) *Freedom in Fulani Social Life: An Introspective Ethnography*, M. Fuller, transl. University of Chicago Press, Chicago.

Rohrbach, D., Minde, I. and Howard, J. (2004) 'Looking beyond national policies: regional harmonization of seed market', in Rohrbach, D. and Howard, J. (eds), *Seed Trade Liberalization in Sub-Saharan Africa. Workshop Proceedings, Dec. 5–6th, 2002, Matopos Research Station, Bulawayo, Zimbabwe*, pp. 14–35, ICRISAT- Bulawayo, Zimbabwe.

Röling, N., Hounkonnou, D., Kwame Offei, S., Tossou, R. and Van Huis, A. (2004) 'Diagnostic studies linking science to farmers' innovative capacity: Case studies from Benin and Ghana', *Netherlands Journal of Life Sciences* 53: 211–235.

Röling, N.G. and Jiggins, J. (1998) 'The ecological knowledge system', in Röling, N.G. and Wagemakers, M.A.E. (eds), *Facilitating Sustainable Agriculture: Participatory Learning and Adaptive Management in Times of Environmental Uncertainty*, pp 283–311, Cambridge University Press, Cambridge.

Rubyogo, J.C., Sperling, L. and Assefa, T. (2007) 'A new approach for facilitating farmers' access to bean seed', *LEISA Magazine* 23: 27–29.

Rudd, M.A. (2000) 'Live long and prosper: collective action, social capital and social vision', *Ecological Economics* 34: 131–144.

Rufael, T., Catley, A., Bogale, A., Sahle, M. and Shiferaw, Y. (2008) 'Foot and mouth disease in the Borana pastoral system, southern Ethiopia and implications for livelihoods and international trade', *Tropical Animal Health and Production* 40: 29–38.

Ryan, J. (2006) 'International public goods and the CGIAR niche in the R for D continuum: operationalizing concepts'. Available from: http://www.sciencecouncil. cgiar.org/meetings/meeting/SC5/Item_13_IPGs_&_R-D_Continuum.pdf [accessed on 6 November 2007].

Salahuddin, A., Van Mele, P. and Magor, N.P. (2008) 'Pro-poor values in agricultural research management: PETRRA experiences in practice', *Development in Practice*, 18: 619–626.

Sanginga, P., Abenakyo, A., Kamugisha, R., Martin, A. and Muzira, R. (2008) 'Tracking outcomes of social and institutional innovations in natural resource management', in Sanginga, P., Waters-Bayer, A., Kaaria, S., Njuki, J. and Wettasinha,

C. (eds) *Innovation Africa: Enriching Farmers' Livelihoods*, pp. 220–235, Earthscan, London.

Sanginga, P., Best, R., Chitsike, C., Delve, R., Kaaria, S. and Kirkby, R. (2004) 'Enabling rural innovation in Africa: An approach for integrating farmer participatory research and market orientation for building the assets of rural poor', *Uganda Journal of Agricultural Sciences*, 9: 942–957.

Sanginga, P., Kamugisha, R. and Martin, A. (2007) 'The dynamics of social capital and conflict management in multiple resource regimes: a case of the Southwestern Highlands of Uganda', *Ecology and Society* 12: 6 [Online] http://www.ecologyandsociety.org/vol12/iss1/art6/

Sanginga, P.C., Chitsike, C.A., Njuki, J., Kaaria, S. and Kanzikwera, R. (2007) 'Enhanced learning from multi-stakeholder partnerships: lessons from the Enabling Rural Innovation in Africa programme', *Natural Resources Forum* 31: 273–285.

Sato, S. and Uphoff, N. (2007) 'A review of on-farm evaluations of system of rice intensification methods in Eastern Indonesia', *CAB Reviews: Perspectives in Agriculture, Veterinary Science, Nutrition and Natural Resources* 2: 54.

Satyanarayana, A., Thiyagarajan, T.M. and Uphoff, N. (2006) 'Opportunities for water saving with higher yield from the System of Rice Intensification', *Irrigation Science* 25: 99–115.

Scarborough, V., Killough, S., Johnson, D. and Farrington, J. (1997) *Farmer-led Extension: Concepts and Practice*, IT Publications, London.

Schein, E. (1992) *Organizational Culture and Leadership*, Jossey-Bass, San Francisco.

Schiffer, E. (2007) 'The power mapping tool: A method for the empirical research of power relations', *IFPRI Discussion Paper* 00703, IFPRI, Washington, D.C.

Schwabe, C. (1982) 'The current epidemiological revolution in veterinary medicine. Part I', *Preventive Veterinary Medicine* 1: 1–15.

Scoones, I. and Thompson, J. (1994) *Beyond Farmer First: Rural People's Knowledge, Agricultural Research and Extension Practice*, IT Publications, London.

Scoones, I., Leach, M., Smith, A., Stagl, S. Stirling, A. and Thompson, J. (2007) 'Dynamics: dynamic systems and the challenge of sustainability', *STEPS Working Paper 1*, STEPS Centre, Brighton.

Seboka, B. and Deressa, A. (2000) 'Validating farmers' social network for local seed supply in Central Rift Valley of Ethiopia', *Journal of Agri. Educ. Ext.* 6: 245–254.

Seely Brown, J. and Duguid, P. (1991) 'Organizational learning and communities of practice', *Organization Science* 2: 40–57.

Selener, D. (1997) *Participatory Action Research and Social Change*, Cornell University, Ithaca, New York.

Selener, D., Chenier, J., Zelaya, R., with Endara, N., Fadherbe, J. and Jacques, A. (1996) *Farmer to Farmer Extension: Experiences from the Field*, IIRR, Ecuador.

Senge, P.M. (1990) *The Fifth Discipline: The Art and Practice of the Learning Organization*, Doubleday Dell Publishing Inc., Bantam New York.

Shambu Prasad, C., Basu, P. and Hall, A. (2005) 'Assessing System of Rice Intensification as a process: evidence from India', Paper presented at the 4th Annual IWMI Tata Partners (ITP) Meet, February 24–26 on 'Bracing up for the future', Institute of Rural Management Anand (IRMA), Anand, India.

Shambu Prasad, C., Beumer, K. and Mohanty, D. (2007) 'Towards a Learning Alliance: SRI in Orissa', Xavier Institute of Management, Bhubaneswar and WWF-Dialogue project, Patancheru, India.

Sheehy, J.E., Peng, S., Dobermann, A., Mitchell, P.L., Ferrer, A., Yang, J.C., Zou, Y.B., Zhong, X.H. and Huang, J.L. (2004) 'Fantastic yields in the system of rice intensification: fact or fallacy?' *Field Crops Research* 88: 1–8.

Simon, H. (1971) 'Designing organizations for an information-rich world' in Greenberger, M. (ed.) *Computers, Communications and the Public Interest*, pp. 37–72, Johns Hopkins University Press, Baltimore, MD.

Sinclair, T.R. (2004) 'Agronomic UFOs waste valuable scientific resources', *Rice Today* 3: 43.

Sinclair, T.R. and Cassman, K.G. (2004) 'Agronomic UFOs,' *Field Crops Research* 88: 9–10.

Sinha, S.K. and Talati, J. (2007) 'Productivity impacts of the system of rice intensification (SRI): A case study in West Bengal, India', *Agricultural Water Management* 87: 55–60.

Sinung-Basuki, R., Kusmana, and Ahman, D. (2003) 'Producer-consumer chain in the potato chips industry of Indonesia', in UPWARD, *From Cultivators to Consumers: Participatory Research with Various User Groups*, pp. 131–146, UPWARD, Los Baños, Philippines.

Sperling, L. (ed.) (1992) 'Actes de la conference sur le lancement des variétés, la production, et la distribution des semences de haricot dans la région des Grands Lacs. Goma, Zaire, 2–4 Novembre 1989', CIAT African Workshop Series No. 18, CIAT, Kampala, Uganda.

Sperling, L. and Cooper, H.D. (2003) 'Understanding seed systems in seed security', in *Improving the Effectiveness and Sustainability of Seed Relief. Proceedings of a Stakeholders' Workshop in Rome, 26–28 May, 2003*. FAO, Rome.

Stokstad, E. (2008) 'Dueling visions of a hungry world', *Science* 391: 1474–1476.

Stolle, D. and Hooghe, M. (2003) 'Conflict approaches to the study of social capital. Competing explanations for causes and effects of social capital', *Ethical Perspectives* 10: 22–45.

Stoop, W., Uphoff, N. and Kassam, A. (2002) 'A review of agricultural research issues raised by the System of Rice Intensification (SRI) from Madagascar: opportunities for improving farming systems for resource-poor farmers', *Agricultural Systems* 71: 249–274.

Stringer, L.C., Dougill, A.J., Fraser, E., Hubacek, K., Prell, C. and Reed, M.S. (2006) 'Unpacking "participation" in the adaptive management of social–ecological systems: a critical review', *Ecology and Society* 11: 39. Available from: http://www.ecologyandsociety.org/vol11/iss2/art39/.

Sulaiman V.R (2006) 'New insights into promoting pro-poor rural innovation: lessons from civil society', Paper presented at the 4th Globelics International Conference, 4–7 October 2006, Trivandrum.

Sulaiman, V.R and Hall, A.J (2004) 'Towards Extension-Plus: opportunities and challenges', *Policy Brief* 17, National Centre for Agricultural Economics and Policy Research, New Delhi.

Sulaiman, V.R. and Hall, A.J. (2002) 'Beyond technology dissemination: reinventing agricultural extension', *Outlook on Agriculture* 31: 225–233.

Sumberg, J. (2005) 'Systems of innovation theory and the changing architecture of agricultural research in Africa', *Food Policy* 30: 21–41.

TAC (2000) 'Stripe Review of Plant Breeding in the CGIAR', Report of the Technical Assistance Committee, CGIAR, Washington, D.C.

Tansey, G. and Tasmin, R. (2008) *The Future Control of Food. A Guide to International Negotiations and Rules on Intellectual Property, Biodiversity and Food Security*. Earthscan,

London and IDRC, Canada. Available from: www.idrc.ca/en/ev-118094-201-1-DO_ TOPIC.html

Taylor, P. (2003) *How to Design a Training Course: Participatory Curriculum Development.* Voluntary Services Overseas, London.

Thompson, J. (1995) 'Participatory approaches in government bureaucracies: facilitating the process of institutional change', *World Development* 23: 1521–1554.

Thompson, J., Millstone, E., Ely, A., Marshall, F., Shah, E. and Stagl, S. (2007) 'Agrifood system dynamics: pathways to sustainability in an era of uncertainty', *STEPS Working Paper* 4, STEPS Centre, Brighton.

Thrusfield, M. (2005) *Veterinary Epidemiology*, 3rd edn, Blackwell Science, Oxford.

Timms, J. and Clark, R. (2004) 'Improvement and innovation', Quick Start Workshop Workbook, Queensland University, Australia.

Tripp, R. (1997) *New Seed and Old Laws – Regulatory Reform and the Diversification of National Seed Systems.* IT Publications on behalf of the Overseas Development Institute, London.

Tripp, R. (2003) 'How to cultivate a commercial seed sector?' paper prepared for the Symposium on Sustainable Agriculture in the Sahel, 1–5 December, 2003, Bamako, Mali.

Tripp, R. (2006) *Self-Sufficient Agriculture. Labour and Knowledge in Small-Scale Farming,* Earthscan, London.

Tripp, R. and Rohrbach, D. (2001) 'Policies for African seed enterprise', *Food Policy* 26: 147–161.

Uphoff, N. (2003) 'Higher yields with fewer external inputs? The System of Rice Intensification and potential contributions to agricultural sustainability', *International Journal of Agricultural Sustainability* 1: 38–50.

Uphoff, N. (2005) 'The development of the System of Rice Intensification', Gonsalves, J., Becker, T., Braun, A., Campilan, D., de Chavez, H., Fajber, E., Kapiriri, M., Rivaca-Caminade, J. and Vernooy, R. (eds) *Participatory Research and Development for Sustainable Agriculture and Natural Resource Management: A Sourcebook, Volume 3: Doing Participatory Research and Development,* pp. 119–125, CIP-UPWARD, Los Baños, Philippines and IDRC, Ottawa, Canada.

Uphoff, N. (2007) 'Reducing the vulnerability of rural households through agroecological practice: considering the System of Rice Intensification (SRI)', *Mondes en Développement* 35: 4.

Uphoff, N. and Mijayaratna, C.M. (2000) 'Demonstrated benefits of social capital: the productivity of farmers' organisations in Gal Oya, Sri Lanka', *World Development* 28: 1875–1840.

Uphoff, N., Ball, A., Fernandes, E.C.M., Herren, H., Husson, O., Laing, M., Palm, C., Pretty, J., Sanchez, P., Sanginga, N. and Thies, J. (eds) (2006) *Biological Approaches to Sustainable Soil Systems,* CRC Press, Boca Raton, FL.

UPWARD (2003) *From Cultivators to Consumers: Participatory Research with Various User Groups,* International Potato Center and UPWARD, Los Baños, Philippines.

Uy, J.C. (2007) 'The case of NORMIN Veggies of Northern Mindanao in the Philippines', Paper presented at the IFAP Asian Committee Meeting, November 7–8, 2007, Hanoi, Vietnam.

Valdivia, C., Gilles, J.L., Motavalli, P., Seth, A., Garrett, K., Marks, L., Vargas, S., Turin, C., Cusicanqui, J., Garcia, M., Jimenez, E., Aguilera, J. (2006) 'Adapting to change in vulnerable Andean ecosystems: practices and strategies to address market and climate change', Long Term Research Project No.4, Sustainable Agriculture and

Natural Resource Management Collaborative Research Support Program (SANREM CRSP), USAID Title II, University of Missouri, Columbia, USA.

Van de Fliert, E., Braun, A.R., Asmunati, R., Wiyanto and Widodo, Y. (1997) 'One step back, two steps forward: sweetpotato ICM development in Indonesia', in UPWARD, *Local R & D. Institutionalizing Innovations in Rootcrop Agriculture*, pp. 153–168, UPWARD, Los Baños, Philippines.

Van der Ploeg, J.D. (1993) 'Rural sociology and the new agrarian question. A perspective from the Netherlands', *Sociologia Ruralis* 33: 240–260.

Van der Veen, R. (2000) 'Learning natural resource management' in Guijt, I., Berdegue, J. and Loevinsohn, M. (eds) *Deepening the Basis of Rural Resource Management. Proceedings of a Workshop*, pp. 15–22, ISNAR, The Hague.

Van Mele, P. (2006) 'Zooming-in, zooming-out: a novel method to scale up local innovations and sustainable technologies', *International Journal of Agricultural Sustainability* 4: 131–142.

Van Mele, P. and Zakaria, A.K.M. (2005) 'From concept to impact: developing and communicating multipurpose seed drying tables in Bangladesh', in Gonsalves, J., Becker, T., Braun, A., Campilan, D., de Chavez, H., Fajber, E., Kapiriri, M., Rivaca-Caminade, J. and Vernooy, R. (eds), *Participatory Research and Development for Sustainable Agriculture and Natural Resource Management, Volume 3: Doing Participatory Research and Development*, pp. 91–105, CIP-UPWARD/IDRC, Los Banos.

Van Mele, P., Salahuddin, A. and Magor, N.P. (2005a) *Innovations in Rural Extension: Case Studies from Bangladesh*. CABI Publishing, Wallingford, UK.

Van Mele, P., Salahuddin, A. and Magor, N. (2005b) 'People and pro-poor innovation systems', in Van Mele, P., Salahuddin, A. and Magor, N. (eds), *Innovations in Rural Extension: Case Studies from Bangladesh*, pp. 257–296, CABI Publishing, Wallingford, UK.

Van Mele, P., Zakaria, A.K.M., Hosne-Ara-Begum, Harun-Ar-Rashid and Magor, N.P. (2008) 'Videos that strengthen rural women's capability to innovate', *Development in Practice*, submitted.

Van Mele, P., Zakaria, A.K.M., Nasrin, R., Chakroborty, B., Haque, M.M. and Rodgers, J. (2005c) 'Bringing science to life: video development for women-to-women extension', in Van Mele, P., Salahuddin, A. and Magor, N.P. (eds), *Innovations in Rural Extension: Case Studies from Bangladesh*, pp. 49–60, CABI Publishing, Wallingford, UK.

Vanclay, J., Prabhu, R. and Sinclair, F. (2006) *Realizing Community Futures*, Earthscan, London.

Veldhuizen, L. van, Wongtschowski, M. and Waters-Bayer, A. (2006) 'Farmer Access to Innovation Resources (FAIR): an international review of experiences to provide practical guidelines', Paper presented at Innovation Africa Symposium, 20–23 November 2006, Kampala, Uganda.

Vernooy, R., Li, X., Xu, X., Lu, M. and Qi, G. (eds) (2008) *Learning from the Field: Innovating China's Higher Education System*. Cambridge University Press, New Delhi and IDRC, Ottawa. Available from: http://www.idrc.ca/en/ev-122332-201-1-DO_TOPIC.html

Via Campesina (1996) *Tlaxcala Declaration of Vía Campesina*. Available from: www.viacampesina.org/main_en/index.php?option=com_content&task=view&id=445&Itemid=28

Virk, D.S. and Witcombe, J.R. (2007) 'Trade-offs between on-farm varietal diversity and highly client-oriented breeding – a case study of upland rice in India', *Genetic Resources and Crop Evolution* 54: 823–835.

Warnaars, M. and Pradel, W. (2007) 'A comparative study of the perceptions of urban and rural Farmer Field School participants in Peru', Urban Harvest Working Paper Series 4, May 2007, CIP, Peru.

Waters-Bayer, A. (1994) 'The ethics of documenting rural people's knowledge: investigating milk marketing among Fulani women in Nigeria', in Scoones, I. and Thompson, J. (eds) *Beyond Farmer First: Rural People's Knowledge, Agricultural Research, and Extension Practice*, pp. 144–150, IT Publications, London.

Waters-Bayer, A., van Veldhuizen, L., Wongtschowski, M. and Killough, S. (2005) 'Innovation Support Funds for farmer-led research and development', *IK Notes* No. 85, World Bank, Washington D.C.

Wenger, E. and Lave, J. (1991) *Situated Learning: Legitimate Peripheral Participation*, Cambridge University Press, Cambridge.

Wettasinha, C., Wongtschowski, M. and Waters-Bayer, A. (2006) *Recognising Local Innovation: Experiences of Prolinnova partners*, IIRR, Philippines and Prolinnova, Netherlands.

Whitby, B. (1997) 'Why the Turing Test is AI's biggest blind alley', Available from: http://www.informatics.sussex.ac.uk/users/balyw/tt.html [accessed 17 September 2007].

Winarto, Y.T. (2002) 'From farmers to farmers, the seeds of empowerment: the farmers' self governance in Central Lampung,' in Sakai, M. (ed.) *Beyond Jakarta: Regional Autonomy and Local Societies in Indonesia*, pp. 270–89, Crawford House Publishing, Adelaide.

Winarto, Y.T. (2005) 'Striving for self-governance and democracy: the continuing struggle of the integrated pest management farmers,' in Erb, M., Sulistyanto, P. and Faucher, C. (eds) *Regionalism in Post-Suharto Indonesia*, pp. 193–210, Routledge-Curzon, London and New York.

Winarto, Y.T., Choesin, E.M., Fadli, Ningsih, A.S.H. and Dormono, S. (2000) 'Satu dasa warsa pengendalian hama terpadu: Berjuang menggapai kemandirian dan kesejahteraan', Unpublished research report, Indonesian FAO-Inter Country Program, Jakarta.

Windfuhr, M. and Jonsén, J. (2005) *Food Sovereignty: Towards Democracy in Localised Food Systems*, IT Publications, London.

Witcombe, J.R., Joshi, K.D., Gyawali, S., Musa, A.M., Johansen, C., Virk, D.S. and Sthapit, B.R. (2005) 'Participatory plant breeding is better described as highly client-oriented plant breeding. I. Four indicators of client-orientation in plant breeding', *Experimental Agriculture* 41: 299–319.

World Bank (2006) 'Enhancing agricultural innovation: How to go beyond the strengthening of research systems', Economic Sector Work Report, The World Bank: Washington, DC.

World Bank (2007) *World Development Report 2008: Agriculture for Development*, World Bank, Washington, DC.

Xu, X. (2004) 'The poor-oriented agricultural science and technology policies', doctoral dissertation, China Agricultural University, Beijing.

Young, J., Dijkema, H-P., Stoufer, K., Ojha, G. and Thapa, L. (1994) 'Evaluation of an animal health improvement programme in Nepal', *RRA Notes* 20: 58–65.

Yuan L.P. (2002) 'A scientist's perspective on experience with SRI in China for raising the yields of super-hybrid rice', in Uphoff, N., Fernandes, E., Yuan, L., Peng, J., Rafaralahy, S. and Rabenandrasana, J. (eds), *Assessments of the System of Rice Intensification: Proceedings of an International Conference, Sanya, China, April 1–4, 2002*, pp. 23–25. CIIFAD, Ithaca, NY Available from: http://ciifad.cornell.edu/sri/proc1/sri_06.pdf

Zerbe, N. (2001) 'Seeds of hope, seeds of despair: towards a political economy of the seed industry in southern African', *Third World Quarterly* 22: 657–673.

Zhang, L. (2008) *Into a New Orbit: Changing China's Higher Education System – in Person.* China Agricultural University Press, Beijing.

Zhou, J. (2004) 'The 2003-2007 Action Plan for invigorating education', Beijing. Available from: http://www.cvae.com.cn/allfile/20040324/new1_005.html

Zhou, J. (2005) *Higher Education in China,* Thomson Learning Asia, Singapore.

Index